D0163426

Trust and Mistrust in International Relations

Trust and Mistrust
in International Relations

Andrew H. Kydd

PRINCETON UNIVERSITY PRESS

PRINCETON AND OXFORD

Copyright © 2005 by Princeton University Press

Published by Princeton University Press, 41 William Street, Princeton,
New Jersey 08540
In the United Kingdom: Princeton University Press, 3 Market Place, Woodstock,
Oxfordshire OX20 1SY

All Rights Reserved

Library of Congress Cataloging-in-Publication Data

Kydd, Andrew H., 1963–
    Trust and mistrust in international relations / Andrew Kydd.
        p. cm.
    Includes bibliographical references and index.
    ISBN-13: 978-0-691-12170-3 (alk. paper)
    ISBN-10: 0-691-12170-2 (alk. paper)
    1. International relations. 2. Trust.   I. Title.

    JZ1305.K93 2005
    327.1'01—dc22

                                        2004022495

British Library Cataloging-in-Publication Data is available

This book has been composed in Galliard

Printed on acid-free paper. ∞

pup.princeton.edu

Printed in the United States of America

10 9 8 7 6 5 4 3 2

To Paul and Priscilla Kydd

Contents

Figures

Tables

Acknowledgments

IN 1984 I TOOK a year off from Princeton and worked at a small cabinet-making shop in Brooklyn making Shaker style furniture. Each weekend I would scour the bookstores and then during the week, on my lunch break, I would read what I had found. One day I happened upon Robert Axelrod's *The Evolution of Cooperation* and it was a life altering experience. I had previously majored in physics but was becoming more interested in international relations, and Axelrod's book pointed the way to a more rigorous approach to analyzing politics. Back at Princeton, I wrote a thesis with Richard Falk who spurred my interest in international cooperation and institutions.

At the University of Chicago in the late 1980s and early 1990s, I was very fortunate in my teachers and fellow students. My dissertation committee: Duncan Snidal, James Fearon, and Stephen Walt, were helpful and patient with me during a long process. Charles Glaser was a very insightful and supportive shadow member of the committee. My friends and fellow students were extremely important to my education and general well being. I would especially like to thank Dale Copeland, Angela Doll, Martha Few, Hein Goemans, Atsushi Ishida, Barbara Koremenos, Alicia Levine, Walter Mattli, Sharon Morris, Monica and Ivan Toft, and Barbara Walter. The PIPES workshop led by Duncan Snidal and Charles Lipson was a wonderful and stimulating environment. Kevin Esterling, Steve Laymon, Thurston Nabe, and Jim Fearon were musically essential.

The origins of this book lie in my dissertation, but the first recognizable draft was begun during my first job at UC Riverside. UCR provided a great environment to work and I would like to thank my colleagues there, especially Juliann Allison and Shaun Bowler, for their help and support.

I continued work on the book during a sabbatical at Harvard as a visiting scholar at the John M. Olin Institute for Strategic Studies and I thank Monica Toft and Stephen Rosen for inviting me. The project was finally completed after I returned to Harvard as an assistant professor the following year. At Harvard, I must especially thank the participants at a conference on the manuscript: Bear Braumoeller, Stephen Brooks, Jeffry Frieden, Yoshiko Herrera, Lisa Martin, Gregory Mitrovitch, Robert Powell, and Monica Toft, for their insightful and helpful comments which greatly improved the manuscript. I thank the Weatherhead Center for International Affairs for sponsoring the conference. I would also like to thank my other colleagues in the Government Department, especially Jorge Dominguez, Devesh Kapur, Rod MacFarquhar, and Dennis Thompson.

Several research assistants and other students were very helpful: Chris Angel, Shahid Dad, Quoc-Anh Do, Eric Lesser, Darya Nachinkina, Satoru Takahashi, Yuan Wang, and Carlos Zepeda.

Many of the chapters benefited from comments received at presentations. Elements of chapters 2 and 3 were presented at the CUIPS workshop at Columbia University, the Institute of Social Science at Tokyo University, and the 2003 International Studies Association conference and I thank Tanisha Fazal, Page Fortna, Erik Gartzke, Brianna Avery, Atsushi Ishida, Motoki Watabe, and Ned Lebow. Chapter 5 was presented at the PIPES workshop at the University of Chicago, and at the Positive Political Theory seminar at Berkeley and I thank Duncan Snidal, Charles Lipson, Milan Svolik, Daniel Drezner, Lloyd Gruber, Robert Powell, and Patrick Egan. Chapters 7 and 8 were presented at the Davis Center at Harvard and I thank Mark Kramer for inviting me to present as well as for pointing me towards sources on the Cold War. I especially thank Marc Trachtenberg, Kenneth Schultz, Randall Schweller, and Yoshiko Herrera for detailed and helpful comments on the manuscript.

Yoi and Katya provided lots of love and support. Our life together has been more than I could have hoped for. Finally, thanks to my parents, Paul and Priscilla Kydd, for supporting me in all my endeavors.

PART I

Trust and International Relations

CHAPTER 1

Introduction

WHEN MIKHAIL GORBACHEV came to Washington D.C. in December 1987 for a summit meeting with Ronald Reagan, the U.S. President took the opportunity to repeat for the cameras one of his favorite Russian proverbs. The phrase, *doveryai no proveryai* (trust but verify), became indelibly associated with the two men and the end of the Cold War.[1] The phrase nicely captured the mistrust that plagued the superpower relationship while at the same time suggesting that trust could be rebuilt if words were accompanied by deeds that could be verified. As if inspired by the proverb, the Intermediate-range Nuclear Forces (INF) treaty signed at the summit contained verification provisions that were unprecedented in U.S.-Soviet arms control.

This book is about the role of trust and mistrust in international relations and the Cold War. I define trust as a belief that the other side is trustworthy, that is, willing to reciprocate cooperation, and mistrust as a belief that the other side is untrustworthy, or prefers to exploit one's cooperation. The topic is important because trust and mistrust can make the difference between peace and war. States that trust each other sufficiently can cooperate; states that do not may end up in conflict. As a result, states constantly make inferences about each other's motivations. In the Cold War, for instance, from George Kennan's famous 1947 article on the sources of Soviet conduct to the debates over Gorbachev's policies of *glasnost* and *perestroika*, the United States was obsessed with the question of whether the Soviet Union was innately expansionist and whether and over what it could be trusted (Kennan 1947; Allison 1988).

Indeed, trust is central to our understanding of the Cold War. Two of the most important questions asked about the Cold War are why it began and why it ended when it did. Another key question is how the European states managed to cooperate with each other and eventually with Germany so soon after a devastating war that sowed deep fears and hatreds. These three questions are all related to international trust. With respect to the origins of the Cold War, many authors in the "post-revisionist" school of Cold War historiography have traced the origins of the Cold War to mistrust (Gaddis 1983; Leffler 1992). These authors argue that

---

[1] David K. Shipler, "The Summit: Reagan and Gorbachev Sign Missile Treaty and Vow to Work For Greater Reductions" *New York Times,* December 8, 1987, A1.

the Soviet Union and the United States were both animated by a search for security—a defensive goal—but that their desire for security propelled them into conflict. Thus, the Cold War takes on a tragic cast, because if only the two sides could have trusted each other, the conflict could have been avoided (Collins 1997). For instance, Deborah Larson argues that there were "missed opportunities" to end the conflict when both sides' interests supported a cooperative deal but mistrust prevented them from realizing it (Larson 1997: 5). Some argue that the United States should have pursued a policy of reassurance, to overcome this mistrust (Lebow and Stein 1994: 375–76).

Ranged against this interpretation are both "traditionalist" and "revisionist" accounts. Traditionalists in the United States believe that the Cold War was driven by the expansionist goals of the Soviet Union. The Soviets are seen as genuinely aggressive, not reacting to the West in a defensive manner. Hence, the West had to firmly oppose the Soviet Union through the policy of containment (Feis 1970). The West mistrusted the Soviets, it is true, but this mistrust was fully justified because the Soviets were untrustworthy. The mirror-image revisionist thesis argues that the Soviet Union was primarily defensively motivated while the capitalist West was the imperialistic and aggressive party. The Soviet Union, devastated by the war and fearing that Germany would eventually rise again from the ashes, had legitimate security interests in controlling its periphery. The United States, driven by the quest for markets for goods and investment, sought to roll back the advance of socialism and make the world safe for international capital (Kolko and Kolko 1972). For the revisionists, the United States is the untrustworthy actor, and Soviet mistrust is justified.

The question of European cooperation and German rehabilitation is also a matter of trust. During the 1930s, the European states had moved from cooperation to conflict. Germany had proven itself extremely untrustworthy and attacked its neighbors with genocidal fury. The task of overcoming this mistrust was formidable. Yet the European nations gradually raised their level of cooperation to heights never before achieved. From the alliance Britain and France signed at Dunkirk in 1947 through the founding of NATO to the rearmament of Germany, the Europeans and Americans cooperated and built institutions to cement their cooperative relationships. U.S. hegemony is often credited with fostering this cooperation, but the mechanism by which hegemony can foster cooperation in the face of mistrust is poorly understood.

Trust also plays a prominent role in debates about the end of the Cold War. Some argue that the key factor in the end of the Cold War is Soviet economic decline. Because the Soviet economy was stagnant while the West continued to grow, the Soviets were simply forced to concede defeat in the forty-year struggle (Brooks and Wohlforth 2000/01; Wohlforth 1994/95). For these analysts, the end of the Cold War is characterized by capitulation, not reassurance. Others argue that trust building was central to the end of the Cold War. They claim that the Soviet Union changed fundamentally with Gorbachev's accession to power. The Soviets became less expansionist and more defensive in their international orientation (Risse-Kappen 1994; Checkel 1993; Evangelista 1999; Mendelson 1993, 1998; English 2000). This change led the Soviets to favor a more cooperative relationship with the West; in effect, it made them trustworthy. However, because preferences are not directly observable, the Soviets needed to take significant visible steps to reassure the West. Most important among Gorbachev's trust building initiatives were the INF treaty of 1987, the withdrawal from Afghanistan, and the eventual noninterference in the Eastern European revolutions of 1989 (Larson 1997: 221–34; Kydd 2000b: 340–51).

Thus, trust plays an important role in the debates about the beginning and end of the Cold War, and about European cooperation. The fact that many of these debates remain unresolved highlights the need for a better theoretical understanding of trust and cooperation in international relations. Toward this end, this book develops a theory of how trust affects cooperation between two actors as well as in larger groups, how it is eroded through aggressive behavior, and how it is enhanced through cooperative gestures designed to reassure.

There are four main implications of the theory of trust developed here. First, cooperation requires a certain degree of trust between states. The threshold of trust required for cooperation depends on a set of variables including a state's relative power and costs of conflict. Second, though conflict between trustworthy states is possible, when we see conflict it is a sign that one or both of the states are likely to be untrustworthy. Thus, we, as external observers, should become less trusting of the parties involved in a conflict, just as they themselves do. Third, in multilateral settings, hegemony—the presence of a very powerful state—can promote cooperation, but only if the hegemon is relatively trustworthy. Untrustworthy hegemons will actually make cooperation less likely. Fourth, if two parties are genuinely trustworthy, they will usually be able to reassure each other of this fact and eventually cooperate with each other. The key mechanism that makes reassurance possible is "costly signaling," that is, making small but significant gestures that serve to prove that one is trustworthy.

With respect to the Cold War, these implications support three arguments. First, the Cold War was most likely a product of expansionist drives on the part of the Soviet Union, not a mutual desire for security accompanied by mistrust.[2] Soviet expansionist behavior increased the suspicions

[2]I merely state the claims here; evidence for and against will be considered in the historical chapters that follow.

of contemporaries, and it should also increase our own, given the lack of contrary evidence that the Soviets were benignly motivated. Second, the European states were able to cooperate with each other, the United States, and Germany after World War II because the United States, as a trustworthy hegemon, enabled them to overcome serious mistrust problems. Contrary to prevalent explanations, the United States neither provided a free ride to the Europeans nor coerced them into accepting an American-preferred order. Finally, the Cold War was ended through a process of costly signaling. Gorbachev made a number of dramatic gestures that increased Western trust and dispelled the suspicions that underlay the forty-year conflict. Soviet economic decline, while important, does not by itself explain this process.

In this chapter I will first define what I mean by trust and distinguish this meaning from related ones. Second, I will discuss the role of trust in existing theories of international relations and lay out the essentials of my alternative approach. Finally, I will briefly discuss the methodological approach of the book.

DEFINING TRUST

Trust can be understood in many different ways.[3] The definition that I will adhere to is that trust is a belief that the other side prefers mutual cooperation to exploiting one's own cooperation, while mistrust is a belief that the other side prefers exploiting one's cooperation to returning it. In other words, to be trustworthy, with respect to a certain person in a certain context, is to prefer to return their cooperation rather than exploit them. To be untrustworthy is to have the opposite preference ordering. Cooperation between two actors will be possible if the level of trust each has for the other exceeds some threshold specific to the situation and the actors.

Some concepts from game theory will help make this understanding of trust more precise. In the single play Prisoner's Dilemma, illustrated in Figure 1.1, each side has a dominant strategy to defect, that is, it is in their interest to defect no matter what they think the other side will do. Even if one side thinks the other will cooperate, it will want to defect. This means that *actors with Prisoner's Dilemma preferences are untrustworthy* as defined above because they prefer to meet cooperation with defection.

---

[3]See Hardin 2002: 54, for a discussion and critique of different conceptions of trust; Coleman 1990: 91–116, for an influential discussion of trust from a rational choice perspective; and Hoffman 2002, for a discussion of the concept in international relations. See also Luhmann 1979; Seligman 1997; Bigley and Pearce 1998; Braithwaite and Levi 1998; and Ostrom and Walker 2003.

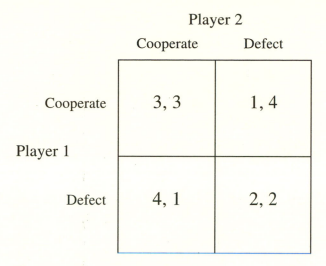

Figure 1.1 The Prisoner's Dilemma

As a result, in the Prisoner's Dilemma, mutual defection is usually thought to be unavoidable and it is the only Nash equilibrium in the game.[4] Each player believes that the other side would prefer to exploit cooperation rather than reciprocate it, and they are right. Two untrustworthy actors facing each other will not cooperate.

In the Assurance Game, illustrated in Figure 1.2, the player's preferences are different. As in the Prisoner's Dilemma, each side prefers to defect if it thinks the other side will defect. However, if one side thinks the other will cooperate, it prefers to cooperate as well. This means that *players with Assurance Game preferences are trustworthy.* They prefer to reciprocate cooperation rather than exploit it.[5] The fact that in the Assurance Game it makes sense to reciprocate whatever you expect the other side to do means there is a Nash equilibrium in which both sides cooperate. Cooperation is possible between trustworthy types who know each other to be trustworthy. There is also a Nash equilibrium in which the players do not cooperate, because each side prefers to meet defection with defection. However, in the Assurance Game as so far stated, this equilibrium seems unlikely given that both players prefer the equilibrium involving mutual cooperation and

---

[4]A Nash equilibrium is a set of strategies that are best responses to each other (Osborne 2004: 21).

[5]Trust is not equivalent to reciprocity, however. Reciprocity is a behavioral pattern, returning good for good and ill for ill (Keohane 1986: 8). Trust is a belief that the other side is willing to engage in reciprocity.

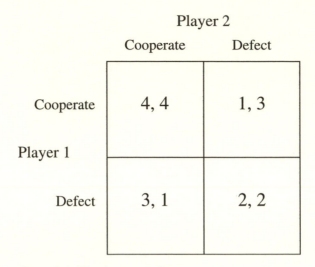

Figure 1.2 The Assurance Game

nothing is preventing them from coordinating on that one rather than the less desirable mutual defection equilibrium.

Players with Assurance Game preferences might fail to cooperate, however, if they were not *sure* that the other side had Assurance Game preferences. For instance, if one side thought the other might have Prisoner's Dilemma preferences, it would be natural to hesitate before cooperating, because the other side would then have a dominant strategy to defect. If the other side had Prisoner's Dilemma preferences, persuading them that you plan to cooperate would not induce them to cooperate in return, because they would prefer to exploit cooperation rather than reciprocate it. The Assurance Game player might then decide to defect, not because it prefers mutual defection, but because it fears that the other side has a dominant strategy to defect and therefore cannot be persuaded to cooperate. This is the problem of mistrust. Trustworthy Assurance Game actors may fear that they face an untrustworthy Prisoner's Dilemma player, and hence decide to not cooperate.[6]

Along these lines, we can think of the *level of trust* one actor has for another as the *probability it assesses that the other actor is trustworthy* (Hardin 2002: 28). For instance, if player 1 thinks there is a t_2 chance that player 2 has Assurance Game preferences, we can think of t_2 as player 1's level of

---

[6]For similar analyses of trust in international relations, see Snyder 1971; Bennett and Dando 1982, 1983; Wagner 1983; Plous 1985, 1987, 1988, 1993; and Glaser 1997: 184.

trust for player 2. Similarly, player 2 will think there is a t_1 chance that player 1 is trustworthy, and has Assurance Game payoffs, and a $1 - t_1$ chance that player 1 is untrustworthy and has Prisoner's Dilemma payoffs. The greater t_1 and t_2, the more likely the other side is to be trustworthy, and the higher the level of trust.

Finally, cooperation is possible when the level of trust for the other exceeds a *minimum trust threshold* for each party (Luhmann 1979: 73). The minimum trust threshold will depend on the party's own tolerance for the risk of exploitation by the other side. In the example above based on the Prisoner's Dilemma and the Assurance Game, if each side anticipates that the other side will cooperate if they are an Assurance Game type and defect if they are a Prisoner's Dilemma type, cooperation gives player 1 (if it is an Assurance Game type) a payoff of $t_2 \times 4 + (1 - t_2) \times 1$, while defection yields $t_2 \times 3 + (1 - t_2) \times 2$; so cooperation will make player 1 better off than defection if the level of trust, t_2, exceeds 0.5 (the same calculation holds for player 2). Thus if the other side is at least 50 percent likely to be trustworthy, it is worthwhile cooperating with them, but if the level of trust falls below 50 percent, trustworthy actors will defect because of mistrust. The minimum trust threshold for the actors in this case is therefore equal to 50 percent, and cooperation is possible if the level of trust exceeds the minimum trust threshold.

To trust someone, then, as I will use the concept, is to believe it relatively likely that they would prefer to reciprocate cooperation. To mistrust someone is to think it is relatively likely that they prefer to defect even if they think one will cooperate. This conception of trust is related to but distinct from others in the literature. Two in particular are especially prevalent in the study of international relations: trust as belief that the other will cooperate in a Prisoner's Dilemma and trust as a belief about anticipated behavior rather than about preferences.[7]

The Prisoner's Dilemma and similar extensive form games are the most common models used to analyze trust (Deutsch 1958; Dasgupta 1988; Kreps 1990: 65–72; Gibbons 2001; Camerer 2003: 83–92). However, these models fail to provide an adequate framework for understanding trust. In the single shot Prisoner's Dilemma and related extensive form games there is a dominant strategy to exploit the other side, and, hence,

---

[7]Three others are more tangentially related. Trust can be thought of as an equilibrium selection device in games with multiple equilibria like the Assurance Game. Trustworthiness can be thought of as a propensity to tell the truth, as in cheap talk models (Farrell and Rabin 1996; Sartori 2002). Finally, trust can be thought of as a form of social capital (Fukuyama 1995, 1999).

no reason to trust anyone.[8] This makes trust irrational by definitional fiat, and forces those using such models to conceive of trust as a form of naiveté and trustworthiness as a species of irrationality (Camerer 2003: 85). It presupposes that no rational self-interested actor could possibly prefer mutual cooperation to exploiting the other side's cooperation. Yet examples of such a preference ordering are easy to come by, for instance a state that just wishes to be secure might rationally prefer not to develop an expensive new weapons system if it were assured that its neighbors would show similar restraint. That is, rational self-interest can support cooperation even in single shot games.

The Prisoner's Dilemma framework also makes it difficult to investigate the uncertainty which is at the heart of trust problems. In these games, strictly speaking, there is no uncertainty about motivations or behavior since everyone has a dominant strategy to defect. As a result, to attain any degree of realism, analysts must smuggle uncertainty in through the back door. Coleman, in his influential discussion of this type of trust game essentially adds incomplete information without drawing the game tree (Coleman 1990: 91–116) and many other treatments add uncertainty about what the other side will do without treating it formally. Since trust is fundamentally concerned with this kind of uncertainty, uncertainty needs to be at the center of the model, not left as an informal addendum to a complete information game.

These problems also dog the repeated Prisoner's Dilemma. In the indefinitely repeated Prisoner's Dilemma, cooperation can be sustainable if the players care enough about future payoffs because they will fear that attempts to exploit the other side will be met with retaliation (Axelrod 1984). This framework has been used to analyze trust in experimental settings (e.g., Deutsch 1958; Swinth 1967; Kollock 1994; Parks, Henager, and Scamahorn 1996), as well as in more philosophical discussions. Russell Hardin argues that "I trust you because your interest encapsulates mine, which is to say that you have an interest in fulfilling my trust" where the source of this interest is the desire to keep mutually beneficial relationships going over time (Hardin 2002: 3). However, the repeated Prisoner's Dilemma model suffers from the same problem as the one shot game. There is no uncertainty in the game about whether the other side prefers to sustain the relationship. Either future payoffs are valued highly enough to make sustained cooperation worthwhile, or they are not and the parties will rationally defect. Trust is therefore perfect or nonexistent. To adequately model trust in the context of the repeated

---

[8] The unsuitability of the Prisoner's Dilemma as a model of trust was first pointed out, to my knowledge, by Gordon Tullock in a brief comment (Tullock 1967). See also Held 1968 and Birmingham 1969.

Prisoner's Dilemma one must introduce some uncertainty, either about preferences or about how much the parties value future interactions, so that the players can be rationally uncertain about whether the other side does prefer to reciprocate cooperation. The resulting game is essentially a repeated version of the mixed Assurance/Prisoner's Dilemma game just discussed.[9]

A second alternative conception of trust is to think of it as a belief about the probability that the other side will cooperate. That is, a belief about the likely behavior of the other side, not about their preferences. Diego Gambetta defines trust in this way, "When we say we trust someone or that someone is trustworthy, we implicitly mean that the probability that he will perform an action that is beneficial or at least not detrimental to us is high enough for us to consider engaging in cooperation with him" (Gambetta 1988: 217). Partha Dasgupta seconds this definition, "I am using the word 'trust' in the sense of correct expectations about the *actions* of other people" (Dasgupta 1988: 51)[10] as does Deborah Larson in her analysis of trust in the Cold War (Larson 1997: 12). Some scholars focus their inquiry on the *intentions* of other states, intentions to cooperate or defect (Edelstein 2000, 2002). One reason for defining trust as a expectations about behavior rather than beliefs about preferences is that behavior may seem more important than preferences. Behavior after all, is directly observable and clearly matters to others, while preferences are difficult to observe and do not directly affect others.

The problem with this conception of trust, however, is that trusted individuals sometimes fail to cooperate. In particular, if I am untrustworthy, I can anticipate that others who know this about me will fail to cooperate with me, even if they themselves are trustworthy. In international relations, a state like Hitler's Germany that has invaded its neighbors and committed atrocities in the past can expect that other states will not cooperate with it in the future. The reason is not that the other states are untrustworthy, the problem is that they think that Hitler is untrustworthy. Hitler might think Britain the most trustworthy state in the world, and yet realize that the likelihood that Churchill will cooperate with him is zero. As this example demonstrates, the motivations behind anticipated actions are crucial if one wishes to understand them. Therefore it is necessary to conceive of trust

---

[9]See Kydd 2000c: 412 for a version in which both players have identical Prisoner's Dilemma stage game preferences but there is uncertainty about how much they care about the future. Long-term thinkers are worried about being taken advantage of by fly-by-night operators. In terms of the definition discussed above, the long-haul types are trustworthy because they prefer to reciprocate cooperation while the fly-by-nighters are untrustworthy. See Hwang and Burgers 1999 for a similar but non-Bayesian analysis.

[10]Despite this Dasgupta actually focuses on motivations and presents one of the earliest incomplete-information games along the lines developed here (Dasgupta 1988: 52, 62).

in terms of underlying motivations, not just expected behavior.[11] With trust defined, we can turn to the place of trust in international relations theory.

TRUST AND INTERNATIONAL RELATIONS

The most obvious difference between international relations and domestic politics is that international relations take place in anarchy, whereas politics within states is conditioned by hierarchy. There has been considerable debate, however, about what, if anything, this distinction means in terms of the behavior that should be expected in each realm (Waltz 1979: 110; Milner 1991; Powell 1993). Much of this debate has its origins in conflicting ideas about the role of trust in a Hobbesian anarchy. I will first discuss trust under anarchy and the realist theories that are directly concerned with this problem, including the approach of this book. Then I will briefly discuss alternative liberal and constructivist perspectives on trust in international relations.

Anarchy and Trust

Thomas Hobbes was one of the first to theorize about the pernicious effects of anarchy. In the famous thirteenth chapter of *Leviathan*, he writes of the dreadful circumstances that prevail among men when, "there is no power able to over-awe them all."

> And from this diffidence of one another, there is no way for any man to secure himselfe, so reasonable, as Anticipation; that is, by force, or wiles, to master the persons of all men he can, so long, till he see no other power great enough to endanger him: And this is no more than his own conservation requireth, and is generally allowed. Also because there be some, that taking pleasure in contemplating their own power in the acts of conquest, which they pursue farther than their security requires; if others, that otherwise would be glad to be at ease within modest bounds, should not by invasion increase their power, they would not be able, long time, by standing on their defense, to subsist.
>
> (Hobbes 1968 [1651]: 184–45)

Here Hobbes argues that the best way to achieve security under anarchy is to destroy the power of others who might pose a threat. Preemptive or preventive attack is the best path to survival; one needs to attack

---

[11] The two conceptions could be reconciled if the behavioral definition was recast as an expectation that the other side will cooperate conditional on their having a high enough level of trust of one's self, or where they bear no risk from the transaction. But then we might as well talk about motivations rather than behavior.

others before they attack.[12] Hobbes understands that this might seem a bit extreme and that the reader may be wondering if it is really necessary to lash out at all potential threats. Why not simply maintain a strong defense, and only fight if attacked? Standing on the defense is inadvisable, Hobbes argues, because not everyone is motivated by security alone; some pursue conquest "farther than their security requires." The world is not composed solely of security seekers who would be happy to live and let live. In a world where other actors may be more aggressively motivated, the security seeker must attack preemptively and destroy the power of others because otherwise, eventually, he will be ground down by recurrent attacks (Kavka 1986: 97).

Applied to international relations, the Hobbesian argument says that given anarchy and mistrust, security seeking states will pursue aggressive policies up to and including war. This conflict will sometimes be tragic, because, in some cases, both sides will be motivated by security, a defensive consideration, not aggression. Hence, there is said to be a "security dilemma," a term coined by John Herz at the dawn of the Cold War (Herz 1950; Jervis 1978). Insecure states will pursue power to make themselves more secure; this renders other states less secure, and their efforts to catch up in turn render the first state less secure in a vicious circle. International conflict is a tragic clash between states with fundamentally benign desires to survive. In the latter years of the Cold War, Kenneth Waltz founded his influential structural realist theory of international relations on the security dilemma, and used it to argue for the virtues of bipolar systems and the irrelevance of economic interdependence (Waltz 1979).

A key component of the Hobbesian explanation of conflict is mistrust, the belief that other states may be aggressively motivated. Scholars disagree, however, on the precise role that trust plays in the security dilemma. Two existing schools of thought, offensive and defensive realism, both descended from Waltz's structural realism, contribute important insights about trust and international relations, but have serious limitations. To address these problems, I develop a new approach that I call *Bayesian realism* because it starts from the core realist assumption of the state as a unitary rational actor and relies on a game theoretic analysis of beliefs and behavior based on the Bayesian theory of belief change.[13] The three schools of thought and their key assumptions are shown in Table 1.1.

---

[12] Preemptive attack is motivated by the expectation of an imminent attack by the other. Preventive war is motivated by a longer term fear that one's enemy is gaining ground which will leave one open to coercion or attack in the future. See Levy 1988.

[13] In terms of the intrarealist debate, the approach is essentially a marriage of the neoclassical realist focus on states with different motivations (Schweller 1994, 1996, 1998; Kydd 1997b; Rose 1998) and the defensive realist concern with signaling motivations.

TABLE 1.1
Views on Anarchy and Trust

	State Motivations	Level of Trust
Offensive Realism	Security	Low
Defensive Realism	Security	Variable
Bayesian Realism	Mixed	Variable

OFFENSIVE REALISM

The most loyal Hobbesians argue that there is an irreducible level of mistrust between states that prevents cooperation. Adherents to this view include John Mearsheimer and other offensive realists.[14] Offensive realists assume that "survival is the primary goal of great powers" (Mearsheimer 2001: 31). Since motivations are hard to discern, however, there is always uncertainty about the intentions of other states, a permanent state of distrust (Waltz 1979: 91–92, 118, 1988: 40; Mearsheimer 2001: 31–32; Copeland 2000: 15).[15] In effect, offensive realists treat uncertainty and distrust as a permanent background feature of the international system—an element of the structure. Mistrust is a constant, like anarchy, not a variable, like relative power. As Mearsheimer puts it, "There is little room for trust among states. Although the level of fear varies across time and space, it can never be reduced to a trivial level" (Mearsheimer 1994/5: 11, 1990: 12, 2001: 32). In effect, states make worst case assumptions about other states' motivations (Keohane and Martin 1995: 43–44; Brooks 1997: 447–50). Other states may be expansionist, and one cannot tell for sure, so there is no point attempting to differentiate between states based on their underlying motivations. From an offensive realist standpoint, there is little use in studying international trust, because the level of trust is never high enough to affect behavior.

[14]There are currently many strands of realist thought operating under a variety of labels. Waltz's (1979) theory was called "neo-realism" or "structural" realism. Snyder (1991: 12) introduced the term "aggressive" realism which has been transmuted to "offensive" realism, which was embraced by Mearsheimer for his refinement of Waltz. In my view, offensive realism is closest in spirit to Waltz's theory because Waltz argues that states of differing motivations behave the same, a key offensive realist claim. Others consider Waltz closer to defensive realism because he claims that states maximize security, not power. However, Waltz provides no compelling argument as to why power maximization is not behaviorally equivalent to security maximization under his theory.

[15]Waltz's famous dictum that states "at a minimum, seek their own preservation and, at a maximum, seek universal domination" suggests that the diversity of state goals is important, but his analysis focuses exclusively on security seeking states.

Offensive realists also argue that mistrust in the international system never gets cleared up because security seekers behave the same as more aggressive states. Offensive realists claim that the violent nature of the international system—the constant competition and war—is not a result of the individual natures of states. As Waltz puts it, "in an anarchic domain, a state of war exists if all parties lust for power. But so too will a state of war exist if all states seek only to ensure their own safety" (Waltz 1988: 44). Expansionist states will invade for gain; security seekers to protect themselves; both will extend their power as far as they can. According to Mearsheimer, "states seek to survive under anarchy by maximizing their power relative to other states, in order to maintain the means for self defense" (Mearsheimer 1990: 12, 2001: 30–40; Labs 1997). A key implication of this argument is that since security seekers and aggressive states behave the same, they cannot be distinguished by their behavior, and, hence, the mistrust that causes conflict cannot be overcome. Mistrust and conflict form a self-reinforcing cycle in which the mistrust causes conflict that reinforces the mistrust.

A final implication of offensive realism is that to explain international events, attention should be focused not on the elements of the structure that are constant, anarchy and mistrust, but on those that vary, most importantly, relative power and the number of great powers (Mearsheimer 2001: 43). Wars are caused by shifts in relative power, miscalculations about power due to multipolarity, unbalanced power, the ease of conquest, etc. Long rivalries such as the Cold War are a simple result of the fact that the United States and the Soviet Union were the two strongest powers—the only ones that could hurt each other. While the Cold War was a product of mistrust, in the same way that it was a product of anarchy, it was not because the United States and Soviet Union mistrusted each other for some special reason, or more than they distrusted anyone else. Pick any two states, make them the most powerful states in the world, and they will mistrust each other enough to fight a cold war, if not a hot one.

The offensive realist approach is consistent with a static theory of international relations given pessimistic assumptions about initial levels of trust. As I show in chapter 2 in a static model of trust and cooperation, if the level of trust is too low, states will not cooperate regardless of their own motivations, and conflict will result between security seekers. However, once the game is made dynamic, so that states can make reassuring gestures to build trust over time, offensive realism is undermined. In a dynamic version of the security dilemma, modeled in chapter 7, rational security seeking states can reassure each other and cooperate regardless of how low the initial level of trust is. As a result, the level of trust can be raised sufficiently to support cooperation. This poses a serious problem for offensive realism, suggesting that powerful states need not end up in conflict if they are rational security seekers.

DEFENSIVE REALISM

In contrast to offensive realism, other scholars argue that mistrust does not always prevent cooperation, although it does occur frequently and is responsible for much international conflict. This perspective is often identified with Robert Jervis who coined the term "spiral model" (Jervis 1976: 62) and it is also associated with defensive realism, particularly the work of Charles Glaser (1992, 1994/95, 2002).[16]

Defensive realism shares the basic Hobbesian framework focusing on unitary actors operating in an anarchic environment. Like the offensive realists, defensive realists assume that states are security seekers. Glaser asserts, "states are motivated only by the desire for security" (Glaser 2002: 4). Adherents of the spiral model believed that the Soviets were security seekers like the Americans (Jervis 1976: 64,102). Charles Osgood, an early spiral modeler, called those who believe the Soviets were aggressive "neanderthals," while making it plain that, in his opinion, both sides in the Cold War sought security (Osgood 1962: 29). Stephen Van Evera argues that his version of realism assumes, "that states seek security as a prime goal, for reasons rooted in the anarchic nature of the international system" (Van Evera 1999: 11). Conflict between states is therefore genuinely tragic rather than a clash between good and evil (Spirtas 1996).

Defensive realism diverges from offensive realism in its analysis of how pervasive the mistrust is, and whether it is possible to do anything about it. Where offensive realists see mistrust as pervasive and constant, defensive realists see it as variable and amenable to change. Some states trust each other enough to cooperate. These states can have normal relations, enjoying mutual security. Other states, unfortunately, develop deep levels of mutual distrust for each other. To these states, the security dilemma logic applies, and conflict results.

Defensive realists and spiral modelers differ in their analysis of what produces the breakdown in trust and what can be done about it. Defensive realists adhere to the rational actor assumption and focus on signaling (Glaser 1994/95: 67). States sometimes engage in competitive arms racing behavior which can lower their mutual level of trust. To address the problem, they can signal their true motivations to each other by engaging in cooperative gestures that reassure. Factors affecting their ability to signal include the nature of military technology, or the "offense-defense balance" (Jervis 1978; Van Evera 1999: 117). When offensive weapons predominate, security seekers will have to develop offensive capabilities like more aggressive states; when defensive technologies are strong,

---

[16]For an overview of defensive realism, also derived from Waltz and coined by Snyder, see Taliaferro (2000/01).

security seekers can invest in defense and signal their nonaggressive goals.

Spiral modelers abandon the rational actor assumption and focus their analysis on psychological biases (Jervis 1976: 67; Larson 1997: 19). One such bias is the tendency of actors with benign self-images to believe, without justification, that others share this benign image, so that if others engage in hostile behavior it must be a result of malevolence on their part. Spiral modelers also have a psychological theory of reassurance, often known as Graduated Reciprocation in Tension-reduction (GRIT) for the version proposed by Osgood (Osgood 1962). GRIT argues that unilateral cooperative gestures can build trust and establishes a set of conditions that will maximize their effectiveness. While both of these theories are presented as nonrational or psychological, we will see in chapters 3 and 7 that they contain rational cores that can easily be modeled game theoretically.

Defensive realism, like offensive realism, makes some important contributions but has certain shortcomings. The main improvement over offensive realism is the openness to the possibility that the level of trust varies in important ways; it may sometimes be high enough to sustain cooperation and may sometimes be low enough to prevent it. However, the focus on security seeking states is problematic for three reasons. First, it prevents defensive realism from developing a complete strategic theory of international relations. For instance, Stephen Walt's theory of alliances argues that states balance against the threat presented by "other" states that may be aggressive in order to improve their security (Walt 1987: 18). But if the other states may be aggressive, it is not clear why the state under advisement is not, and it would seem that a complete theory of international relations must give full consideration to the incentives and constraints facing both security seeking and aggressive states (Schweller 1994). Otherwise it is impossible to capture the strategic dynamics facing states which are uncertain about each other's motivations.[17]

Second, the assumption of security seeking states biases the analysis in favor of explanations involving psychological bias. States are assumed to be uncertain about each other's motivations. For the theorist to also assume that states are security seekers is to imply that a state that thinks some other state is expansionist is making a mistake. The subject of inquiry then becomes how to explain such mistakes, and this makes psychological theories associated with the spiral model quite attractive. If instead we assume that states may be expansionist as well as security seeking, then mistrust is not necessarily a mistake and the bias towards psychological theories is eliminated.

[17]For this reason, defensive realism is perhaps best thought of as a theory of the foreign policy of security seeking states, rather than a theory of international relations.

Third, to build into the theory the assumption that states are security seekers is to treat as an assumption something that should be the subject of empirical inquiry. States are uncertain about each other's motivations. As analysts, we wish to investigate these beliefs and understand their origins. We therefore need to make our own judgments about state motivations, in order to determine whether a state's beliefs are correct or not. We will doubtless find cases where states are mistaken and others in which they are substantially correct. To arrive at these judgments requires empirical inquiry; an examination of the record of events and any documents that are available. We cannot simply assume the answer to such a question before we begin.

BAYESIAN REALISM

The approach I develop here shares certain assumptions with offensive and defensive realism, but departs from them in important ways. I start from the same Hobbesian framework and assume that states in anarchy may face threats to their survival so that security becomes an important goal. However, I also assume that states have many other goals and some may be willing to pursue conquest "farther than their security requires" as Hobbes puts it. Thus, some states may be interested primarily in security, others may be more aggressively motivated. I further assume that because there has been enough variation in state motivations historically, and because motivations are difficult enough to discern, states may be rationally uncertain about the motivations of other states. That is, despite whatever shared culture they may have, states can reasonably wonder what the motivations of other states are.

With this foundation, I then apply Bayesian theory to the question of how states form beliefs about each other's motivations, and how they behave in response to these beliefs. Instead of assuming certain motivations and then characterizing beliefs that fail to reflect them as mistakes, I simply ask how states of various motivations behave in situations with varied beliefs about each other. Bayesian theory provides a framework for answering such questions assuming the decisionmakers behave rationally given their beliefs and change their beliefs rationally in response to new information.

The Bayesian framework supports the defensive realist claim that states with benign motivations that believe each other to be benign can get along. Well justified trust can sustain cooperation. Conversely, states that have malevolent motivations and know this about each other will not get along. Well justified mistrust will lead to conflict and possibly war.

Contrary to defensive realism, however, Bayesian analysis does not reveal an inherent tendency towards unjustified mistrust in international relations. Rather, it indicates that *convergence on correct beliefs is more likely than convergence on incorrect beliefs.* That is, although the learning process is noisy and prone to errors of all kinds, beliefs over time and on average are more likely to converge towards reality than to diverge from it. This implies that if a state is a security seeker, other states are more likely to eventually discover this rather than to remain convinced that it is aggressive. If a state is interested in power or expansion for its own sake, other states are more likely to come to believe this than to think that it is a defensively motivated security seeker. Mistaken beliefs may arise, whether unjustified trust or unjustified mistrust, but over time they are more likely to be corrected than to remain or be further exaggerated.

This claim about beliefs, combined with the fact that state motivations are assumed to vary freely, implies that of the conflicts we observe, a relatively small percentage will be driven by mistaken mistrust. If we see a conflict, it is more likely to have arisen because one or more of the parties has genuine non-security-related motivations for expansion, or is untrustworthy. Therefore we should become more confident that one or both sides was aggressive, and less confident that both sides were motivated primarily by security.

However, Bayesian realism does not assume that states know each other's motivations perfectly, or find them out easily. Nor, as will be discussed in chapter 7, can one simply ask if a state is aggressive or not. A Hitler has every bit as much incentive to pretend to be modest in his ambitions as someone who is genuinely uninterested in world conquest. There are many obstacles in the way of rational learning about the motivations of other states. However, there are also tremendous incentives to get it right. Misplaced trust can lead to exploitation; misplaced distrust can lead to needless and costly conflict.

The mechanism that enables states to learn about each other's motivations is cooperation. Because of the importance of avoiding unnecessary conflict, states are often willing to take a chance by cooperating with another country, in hopes of establishing mutual trust. These gestures provide the occasion for rational learning because they help to distinguish trustworthy states from non-trustworthy ones—security seekers from the more aggressive. In circumstances where security seekers and more aggressive states behave differently, trust can be built by observing what states do.

Preferences, Identity, and Trust

Bayesian realism posits that state preferences vary, some states are basically security seekers and others are more expansionist. In the next chapter, in the context of a model of the security dilemma, I will show how a set of underlying structural variables including relative power and the costs of conflict help account for this variation. However, other, less "realist," factors have an important influence on state preferences as well, and are therefore important in understanding trust in international relations. This underlines the necessity of integrating realist theories with other theories of preference and identity formation (Legro 1996; Moravcsik 1997). While that task will not be central to this book, I will briefly discuss how two prominent schools of thought, liberalism and constructivism, contribute to such an analysis in ways that are particularly important in the case of the Cold War.

LIBERALISM

Liberal theories of international politics focus on how the domestic political system aggregates social preferences to generate national policy (Moravcsik 1997: 518). Such theories take as inputs the preferences and political power of important social actors, and the political institutions through which they interact. Variations in the interests and power of the different groups, or in the institutional environment, produce changes in policy that affect international behavior.

The most prominent liberal theory relating to trust is the well-known idea of the democratic peace. Pairs of states that are both democratic hardly if ever fight, while the same obviously cannot be said for pairs in which only one state is a democracy or in which neither is democratic (Rummel 1983; Doyle 1983a, b; Russett 1993; Chan 1997; Ray et al. 1998). Several explanations have been advanced to account for this finding, some of which relate to international trust. Kant made the argument that ordinary citizens are averse to war because they suffer the costs especially acutely (Kant 1991: 100). Democracy empowers the average citizen, at least in comparison to more restrictive regimes, so democracies may have a higher cost of fighting (Bueno de Mesquita and Lalman 1992: 153). Jack Snyder argues that cartelized political systems favor expansionist interests while democracy dilutes their influence and weakens their ability to promulgate expansionist myths (Snyder 1991: 39). Bruce Bueno de Mesquita and his colleagues argue that narrowly based regimes are more aggressive because they focus on doling out private goods to their retainers, while more broadly based regimes must focus on providing public goods to mass audiences (Bueno de Mesquita et al. 1999). Nondemocracies, therefore, may have a higher evaluation of the gains from conquest.

Putting these ideas together, liberal theory can be said to support two basic points related to international trust. First, because democracies find war costly and of little intrinsic benefit, democracies are more likely to be security seeking states. Conversely, nondemocratic states are sometimes more aggressive, less constrained by their citizens, more volatile. They may be security seekers, or they may not be; there is more variation in the preferences of nondemocratic states. Second, given that democracy is a readily visible characteristic of a regime, other states will have relatively high confidence that a democracy is a security seeker (Bueno de Mesquita and Lalman 1992: 155). A pair of democratic states should have well-founded trust for each other because they are security seekers themselves and think the other side likely to be one too. Hence, there can be said to be a democratic security community, in which states correctly trust that disputes will be resolved short of force (Deutsch et al. 1957; Adler and Barnett 1998). Nondemocracies, having closed regimes, will not automatically be perceived as security seekers. Hence if they are to build trust, they must rely on other mechanisms, such as the type of signaling described in chapter 7.

Thus, liberal theory suggests that democracies are more likely to be security seekers than nondemocracies, and will have a higher degree of trust for each other than they do for nondemocracies. Both preferences and prior beliefs will be influenced by regime type. In the context of the Cold War, this suggests that U.S. trust for the Soviets should have been low, given their regime type, and that in the late 1980s the United States should have been sensitive to signs of democratization, such as the elections to the Congress of People's Deputies in 1988.

CONSTRUCTIVISM

The key concept in constructivist approaches is state identity. Identity has many definitions in the political science literature.[18] Two related conceptualizations focus on a set of norms that identify appropriate behavior and a type of state one aspires to be or group of states one aspires to belong to (Ruggie 1998; Wendt 1999; English 2000). Some constructivists focus on the domestic sources of state identity, looking at the culture and identities of groups within society (Hopf 2002). Others argue that state identities are affected by international factors. Aggressive behavior on the part of another causes fear and leads one to view it as an enemy, causing one to adopt the enemy role and in turn wish to do the other harm. Self-restraint and cooperation fosters trust and feelings of solidarity and, in turn, generates moderate preferences (Wendt 1999: 357). No pattern of identity is given in the nature of anarchy; anything can happen.[19]

Many constructivists would stress the incompatibility of their project with realism. However, there is little doubt that state identity affects state preferences, and, hence, the extent to which a state is trustworthy or not. A particularly important source of identity and prior beliefs in the context of the Cold War is ideology. Both sides had well articulated ideologies

---

[18] For an overview of definitions and conceptualizations of identity, see Abdelal et al. 2004.

[19] For a constructivist critique that reaffirms the primacy of Hobbesian enemy roles, see Mercer 1995.

that provided answers to questions about their own state's identity and the trustworthiness of other states on the international scene. As I will discuss in chapter 4, communist ideology, founded on class conflict, posited a relationship of general enmity between the socialist states and the capitalist world. Capitalist states were believed to be hostile both to the Soviet Union and to each other. Intracapitalist conflict could provide opportunities for tactical cooperation with capitalists, but the overall relationship would be hostile. Ideology, therefore, gave the Soviets a high level of gains from conflict, and a low level of trust. American anticommunism ultimately provided a similar set of ideological lenses, but, as we will see, this view was not dominant at the outset of the Cold War.

Constructivists also argue that identity change was important at the end of the Cold War (Koslowski and Kratochwil 1994). Much of the debate about Soviet motivations in the 1980s was over whether they were being conciliatory because they were simply recognizing a temporary weakness, or because they had experienced a genuine transformation of identity into a state that no longer sought to expand its influence and subvert others. For instance, Robert English argues that the Soviets experienced a change in identity and became convinced that the Soviet Union should be a part of the community of Western democratic states (English 2000). Constructivist analyses have therefore been prominent in debates over the end of the Cold War and I will return to them in chapter 8.

Liberalism and constructivism offer insights into the preferences and prior beliefs that underly the strategic models of trust explored in subsequent chapters. A complete understanding of trust in international relations must integrate realist analysis of international strategic interaction with other theories of preference and identity formation offered by nonrealist theories.

METHODOLOGY

This book makes extensive use of game theoretic models of international relations. These are abstract, stylized representations of certain aspects of the world, expressed in the language of mathematics.[20] There are at least two important benefits of formal theorizing. First, it forces one to specify all the assumptions that one is making and verify that the logical connections

---

[20]See Powell 1990, 1999; Downs and Rocke 1990; Niou, Ordeshook, and Rose 1989; and Bueno de Mesquita and Lalman 1992. For methodological reflections on rational choice in international relations, see Lake and Powell 1999 and Sprinz and Wolinsky 2004. For a critique of the approach in IR, see Walt 1999 and the responses, subsequently collected in Brown et al. 2000. For discussion of rational choice in the study of American politics, see Green and Shapiro 1994 and Friedman 1996.

between these assumptions and the subsequent claims is ironclad. Second, it provides a common and rigorous theoretical language that enables others to check the soundness of one's results, making the theoretical enterprise more cumulative. The chief criticisms that have been leveled against it are that it tells us nothing that we did not already know and that its practitioners have failed to do adequate empirical work to validate it (Walt 1999).

I develop a set of closely related game theoretic models about trust, mistrust and reassurance. These models constitute the core of a rational choice theory of trust and conflict. In each chapter I derive general implications from the models about how the preferences, beliefs, and other attributes of the players influence their ability to cooperate under various conditions. In the historical chapters I describe the important actors, their preferences and beliefs, to the extent that they can be reconstructed, and how their beliefs and behavior correspond to the implications of the theory. For my data, I rely on published documents and secondary historical sources. The goal is to improve our understanding of the fundamental role that trust plays in international relations theory and of the role it played in the Cold War by making use of game theory's ability to clarify arguments and rigorously derive implications from assumptions.

How can the models be used to elucidate historical questions? This question is part of the broader issue of how political science, international relations, and the study of history intersect and interact. The connection between nonformal political science and history has been extensively debated (Elman and Elman 2001) and both sides have been enriched. The intersection of formal theory and statistical empirical work is also a focus of methodological research (Signorino 1999) with many applications (e.g., Bueno de Mesquita et al. 1999). However, formal theory and history have remained unfortunately estranged (Braumoeller 2003: 388; for exceptions see Bates et al. 1998 and Schultz 2001).

There are two ways models can contribute to historical analysis. First, models may make predictions about relations between observable indicators which can be verified by examining the historical data in a particular case, or set of cases, just as nonformal theories do (Levy 2001:48). This is the standard process of scientific inference where observable data are used to make inferences about unobservable causal relations posited by the theory (Hempel 1966: 6; King, Keohane, and Verba 1994: 75). For instance, in chapter 6, I compare the implications of three different theories of hegemony in the context of the post-World War II period. The theory I advance predicts active willing cooperation on the part of the European states, while the other two predict passivity or cooperation in response to U.S. coercion. The historical record provides many instances in which the Europeans willingly initiated cooperation, supporting the first theory.

A second way in which models can shed light on history is by helping us make inferences about other sometimes difficult to observe phenomena, namely state preferences and beliefs.[21] Some states are relatively transparent and data on their preferences can be gathered from foreign office records, interviews, and other public records. Others are more closed and give few direct visible clues about their motivations. In such cases, the state's behavior and the structure of the situation it finds itself in can be used to make inferences about its beliefs and motivations.

The effort to find such "revealed preferences" is widely argued to be inherently circular (e.g., observed cooperation suggests a state prefers to cooperate which explains why it cooperated) or bound to be frustrated by strategic considerations. Jeffry Frieden argues that, "where actors are strategic, we cannot infer the cause of their behavior directly from their behavior" (Frieden 1999: 48; see also Snidal 1986: 40–41). He gives an example in which a firm demands a tariff instead of the quota it really wants because it knows the government, which most prefers free trade, will reluctantly grant a tariff, but would reject a quota. In this case, the firm is not asking for what it most wants and the government is not implementing its favorite policy either. The inference is that the strategic setting prevents actors from revealing their true preferences through their behavior.

While it is true that the strategic setting certainly influences how we should interpret behavior, it is not the case that strategic considerations always prevent inferences about preferences. Models provide a set of variables, including the unobserved beliefs and preferences and other observable variables, and a theory of how the variables relate to each other. This structure may enable one to reason backwards from observed events to unobserved beliefs and motivations (Lewis and Schultz 2003; Signorino 2003).[22]

When can this process succeed in shedding light on state preferences and beliefs? In the kind of incomplete-information game theoretic models that are appropriate for such situations, there are broadly speaking two kinds of equilibria, *pooling* and *separating*. In pooling equilibria, actors with

---

[21]At a high enough level of generality, these tasks are the same. The general problem of inference involves creating a model based on certain assumptions and seeing which values of certain variable parameters maximize the relative likelihood of the realized data (King 1989: 22). Whether the parameters represent causal coefficients or preferences affects the structure of the model but not the nature of inference.

[22]For a pioneering example in the context of the Cold War, see Gamson and Modigliani 1971. Unfortunately Gamson and Modigliani's decision model does not rigorously deduce connections between behavior and underlying preferences and beliefs, which in turn undermines confidence in the resulting inferences from observed behavior. For a related literature on inferring preferences from voting behavior, see Poole and Rosenthal 1997; Voeten 2000; and Martin and Quinn 2001.

different motivations behave similarly, so no light is shed on their under-lying preferences. This corresponds to the offensive realist world in which security seeking and expansionist states behave the same, so no inferences can be made about state motivations. In separating equilibria, in contrast, actors with different preferences and beliefs behave differently. In this case, one can reason backwards from actions to preferences. The information provided by the actor's behavior may not be conclusive, and there will often still be room for doubt. However, in separating equilibria one ends up with beliefs that are, on average, more likely to be correct than the prior beliefs one had before observing the behavior. Consider a historical question such as what we can learn about Stalin's motivations from his behavior in the Berlin crisis. To claim that we can learn anything is to claim that Stalin faced a separating equilibrium in a game of incomplete-information in which, if he had more moderate motivations, say, he would have not initiated the crisis or would have ended it sooner. Should we infer from Gorbachev's 1985 test moratorium that Soviet preferences with respect to the arms race had shifted? If we believe that he was playing his part in a separating equilibrium in which a hard line Gorbachev would have rejected the moratorium idea, such an inference is supported. By better understanding how separating equilibria work in incomplete-information games we may be able to better ground our answers to these questions of historical interpretation. In this way, game theory may directly enhance our historical understanding.

Note that in making inferences about preferences and beliefs, we as scholars are doing exactly what the subjects we study were doing. The participants in any historical episode have some advantages over us and some disadvantages. Their advantages are their better understanding of their own motivations and perceptions, things which we must make infer-ences about from the writings they leave behind and from their actions. Their disadvantages may include a lesser degree of knowledge of the other side's motivations and beliefs, if documents have become available from the other side. But even if some documentary evidence is available, we are still in a position of making inferences about the beliefs of each side, just as the participants were.

A ROAD MAP

This chapter and the next constitute the introduction to the book. The next chapter presents a model of trust in the context of the security dilemma, one of the foundational structures of international relations.

The main body of the book consists of three pairs of chapters. Chapter 3 focuses on the spiral model, a key component of defensive realism, and analyzes how trust can be eroded by competitive behavior. A common explanation of conflict is that interstate competitions, such as arms races, worsen mutual mistrust by convincing states that their rivals are out to get them. The chapter addresses how this worsening of mistrust can happen and how likely it is that it will occur between states that are actually trustworthy. Chapter 4 looks at the beginning of the Cold War and the increasing distrust between the United States and the Soviet Union as an instance of this phenomenon. As mentioned earlier, the central argument is that this growing mistrust was probably justified and not a misperception. The origins of the Cold War are probably not a tragedy of misperceptions or uncertainty induced failures to cooperate. Rather, a more likely hypothesis is that each side, but particularly the Soviet Union, harbored non-security-related motivations for expansion that would have led them to exploit, not reciprocate the cooperation of their rival.

The next pair of chapters examine trust and cooperation under hegemony. Chapter 5 presents a trust game involving multiple actors, which provides the tools to analyze how trust impacts cooperation when there are many actors with different interests, geographical situations, and relative capabilities. Chapter 6 applies the model to post-World War II European cooperation between the United States, Germany, and the rest of Europe. While many have argued that hegemony facilitated cooperation in the post-war era, the role of trust in hegemonic theory is understudied. I show that for hegemony to promote cooperation, the hegemon must be relatively trustworthy, in comparison to other states.

The final pair of chapters focuses on reassurance, looking at how states starting from a position of mistrust can reassure each other about their motivations and promote cooperation. Chapter 7 presents a model of reassurance via costly signals that shows how states can reassure each other by running risks of exploitation by the other side. Chapter 8 analyzes the end of the Cold War in these terms, focusing on the process of reassurance that took place between East and West. Here I argue that the Soviet Union changed from an expansionist state to a security seeker, but that this change was not transparent. Therefore, Gorbachev implemented a policy of costly signaling to reassure the West.

Conclusion

Trust is a central issue in international relations, and that centrality is exemplified in the most important struggle of the second half of the twentieth century, the Cold War. When states can trust each other, they can live at peace, provided that they are security seekers, uninterested in expansion for its own sake. States that are security seekers therefore pay close attention to the motivations of others, attempting to determine who is a fellow security seeker and who is more inherently aggressive. In the Cold War, the United States attempted to determine if the Soviets were security seekers who could be reconciled with the status quo if sufficiently reassured about U.S. intentions, or were more aggressive. The end of the Cold War was marked by reassuring gestures on the part of the Soviets designed to alter Western perceptions of their motivations. How these processes work is the subject of this book.

CHAPTER 2

Trust and the Security Dilemma

TRUST PROBLEMS abound in international relations. A country that is in an exposed position next to a common enemy trusts that its more distant ally is steadfast and will prefer to come to its aid if it is attacked, rather than sit on the sidelines. Its ally, in turn, trusts that the more exposed state has not made the alliance in order to launch provocations against the enemy with the aim of entangling its ally in an unnecessary war. Two countries signing an arms control agreement trust that the other side is not so strongly motivated to harm them that they will engage in systematic efforts to fool the verification procedures and violate the agreement. A group of countries that impose sanctions on another country trust each other not to take advantage of the other countries' abstention to sell the target country what it wants at an inflated price. Given the ubiquity and importance of trust, a well-grounded theoretical understanding of it is essential to the study of international relations.

This chapter will begin to analyze the fundamental question of how trust affects the ability of states to cooperate in anarchy. As discussed in the last chapter, the idea that anarchy produces incentives for aggression even among defensively motivated actors goes back to Hobbes. The logic was refined during the Cold War under the rubric of the security dilemma. John Herz introduced the term and argued, "Since none can ever feel entirely secure in such a world of competing units, power competition ensues, and the vicious circle of security and power accumulation is on" (Herz 1950). Herbert Butterfield argued that the Cold War was a result of "Hobbesian fear," and that both sides might have benign motivations but their uncertainty about the other side's motivations led to a tragic conflict (Butterfield 1951: 21). Later, Robert Jervis analyzed the security dilemma with the aid of the Prisoner's Dilemma and the Assurance Game, and argued that the security dilemma was especially intense when offensive postures were superior to and indistinguishable from defensive postures (Jervis 1978). These ideas led to further work on how military technology and other aspects of the structure of the system could exacerbate or ameliorate the security dilemma (Snyder, G. 1984; Glaser 1994/95, 1997; Van Evera 1999).

However, the role of trust in the security dilemma has been poorly understood. I will show how trust determines whether cooperation under anarchy is possible, and how trust interacts with other variables, such as relative power and the costs of conflict, to facilitate or hinder cooperation. The result refines and challenges previous understandings of the security dilemma. For instance, one of the implications of the chapter is that even when first strike advantages are strong (sometimes known as offense dominance), high levels of trust can produce cooperation. Thus, the level of trust is a crucial variable in anarchic situations. When there is high trust there can be cooperation despite unfavorable structural conditions.

The chapter will also make two broad points with respect to the offensive and defensive realist perspectives on trust in international relations. The offensive realist position that all states behave the same because the level of trust is too low is at least theoretically coherent in the sense that this is indeed what happens in one equilibrium of the model of the security dilemma developed below. However, the claim is empirically contingent because there is another equilibrium with higher levels of trust in which security seeking states cooperate and reinforce their mutual trust. The model therefore reinforces the basic point that *a world of security seekers, who are known to be security seekers, would be peaceful.* Thus, to assume that the level of trust is so low as to eliminate any possibility of this second cooperative equilibrium is to needlessly limit the scope of the theory.

The existence of this second equilibrium also begins to challenge the defensive realist analysis of trust. This approach assumes that states are security seekers, but that this is not common knowledge, and so that mistrust often leads to conflict. However, as the model shows, if states are really security seekers and trust each other enough to cooperate, uncertainty will be lessened, if not removed, as trust is built. Thus, beliefs should tend towards mutual trust rather than the reverse. These issues will be more fully explored in subsequent chapters.

THE SECURITY DILEMMA GAME

There have been a wide variety of game theoretic representations of the security dilemma, from Jervis's simple Prisoner's Dilemma and Stag Hunt games (Jervis 1978) to Robert Axelrod's repeated Prisoner's Dilemma (Axelrod 1984) to Robert Powell's Guns vs. Butter model (Powell 1999, chap. 2) to the crisis bargaining literature in general (e.g., Fearon 1994). However existing models are inadequate to analyze the role that trust plays in the security dilemma because they either assume complete information about the preferences of the actors involved or model the wrong type of uncertainty about preferences. As I argued in the previous chapter, trust should be conceived of in terms of the beliefs one side has about the likelihood that the other prefers to reciprocate cooperation rather than exploit it. As a belief about underlying motivations, trust must be modeled in an

Player 2

	Cooperate	Defect
Cooperate	$0, 0$	$(\pi_1-\phi_2)g_1 - (1-\pi_1+\phi_2)l_1 - c_1,$ $(\pi_2+\phi_2)g_2 - (1-\pi_2-\phi_2)l_2 - c_2$
Defect	$(\pi_1+\phi_1)g_1 - (1-\pi_1-\phi_1)l_1 - c_1,$ $(\pi_2-\phi_1)g_2 - (1-\pi_2+\phi_1)l_2 - c_2$	$\pi_1g_1 - (1-\pi_1)l_1 - c_1,$ $\pi_2g_2 - (1-\pi_2)l_2 - c_2$

Player 1

Figure 2.1 The Security Dilemma Game

incomplete-information setting, which means that complete information games such as the Prisoner's Dilemma are inadequate to understand trust. The crisis bargaining literature does use incomplete-information models but it focuses on uncertainty about the bargaining leverage of the two sides, and, hence, on distributional questions about who gets what. Trust is more a matter of whether each side will honor whatever bargain has been reached, rather than on what bargain is reached in the first place (Fearon 1998). This chapter will present a model of the security dilemma that builds on a simple representation of anarchy by adding uncertainty about the motivations of other states. Equilibria in the model will allow us to analyze the role that trust plays in fostering or hindering cooperation.

Consider the model of the security dilemma illustrated in Figure 2.1. Posit two states that face a potential conflict of interest over some issue, perhaps territory or alliance partners or some other issue of interest. Each state receives a payoff normalized to zero from holding its own, either maintaining control over its own territory or keeping the international status quo as it is. In addition, state i would receive a gain of g_i from altering the status quo in its favor at state j's expense. This payoff represents how much player i covets what player j has, how much i would like to take from j if i could get away with it. As I will define more precisely below, security seekers have low values of g_i, expansionist states have higher values. Each state also would suffer a loss l_i if the other side succeeded in making a gain at its expense.

Each state has two options: to take no action to alter the status quo, labeled cooperate, or to try to alter the status quo in its favor, labeled defect. The specific meaning attached to these options will vary depending on the context. Two important contexts in the Cold War are arms racing and the struggle for influence around the world. In an arms race context cooperation could mean refraining from building a new weapons system, such as the hydrogen bomb or an antiballistic missile system. Defection would mean going ahead with the program in hopes of winning the ensuing arms race and attaining some military advantage. In the struggle for influence context, cooperation could mean honoring an agreement to respect a third country's neutrality, or some agreed-upon division of spheres of influence, while defecting could be attempting to subvert members of the adversary's camp. For instance, the Soviets can be considered to have defected when they authorized North Korea's invasion of South Korea in 1950, since it was an attempt to wrest an area from the U.S. sphere.

If both sides cooperate, the status quo remains in place and each side gets a payoff of zero. If one side attempts to alter the status quo, a conflict of some kind takes place. This need not be all out war, it could be a diplomatic crisis or some lesser conflict. If both players defect simultaneously, player i's chance of prevailing in the dispute is π_i and player j's chance is $\pi_j = 1 - \pi_i$. Thus, π_i is player i's relative power or bargaining leverage in the dispute. The higher π_i the more likely player i is to get what it wants in a conflict. Also, assume there is an advantage to initiating the conflict while the other player is unprepared, an advantage to striking first or catching them off guard. If player i defects while player j does not, player i's probability of prevailing is $\pi_i + \phi_i$ while player j's is $\pi_j - \phi_i$ where ϕ_i represents the advantage to initiating the conflict and $0 < \pi_i - \phi_i < \pi_i + \phi_i < 1$. Thus ϕ_i is an increment to the relative power or bargaining leverage of whichever player initiates the dispute. If there is a conflict, the winner takes all and both sides pay a cost, $c_i > 0$. Notation in the game is summarized in Table 2.1.

TABLE 2.1
Notation in the Security Dilemma Game

g_i	Player i's value for gaining at the expense of j.
l_i	Player i's potential loss if j gains at i's expense.
π_i	The likelihood that player i wins if both defect.
ϕ_i	Player i's advantage of initiating a conflict.
c_i	Player i's cost of conflict.
t_i	The prior likelihood that player i is trustworthy (a security seeker).
m_i	Player i's minimum trust threshold.

How should the players play this game? If player i thinks j will defect, it wants to defect as well because of the disadvantage of being unprepared for a conflict.[1] Therefore mutual defection is a Nash equilibrium of the game and no off diagonal outcome can be.

Mutual cooperation can be an equilibrium if each side prefers to cooperate when they think the other side will. This will be the case if $0 > (\pi_i + \phi_i)g_i - (1 - \pi_i - \phi_i)l_i - c_i$, for both players, which can be solved for the following condition:

$$g_i < g_i^* \equiv \frac{c_i + l_i}{\pi_i + \phi_i} - l_i. \tag{2.1}$$

The critical value g_i^* forms a boundary between types who wish to defect while others cooperate and those who prefer mutual cooperation. If one player's potential gains from expansion exceeds this threshold, the only equilibrium in the game is mutual defection. If not, then mutual cooperation is an equilibrium as well.

Thus, the value each side places on expansion serves to distinguish between trustworthy types, who prefer to reciprocate cooperation (have Assurance Game payoffs), and untrustworthy types who prefer to exploit it (have Prisoner's Dilemma payoffs). If $g_i \leq g_i^*$, then player i is trustworthy, otherwise player i is untrustworthy. In the context of the security dilemma, I will also use the terms "security seeking" and "expansionist" where security seekers are trustworthy and expansionists are not.

- *Security seekers* have limited expansionist goals ($g_i \leq g_i^*$) and are trustworthy.
- *Expansionists* have more extreme goals ($g_i > g_i^*$) and are untrustworthy.[2]

Note, whether a state is a trustworthy security seeker or an untrustworthy expansionist type depends on both its goals and on its strategic situation. An examination of equation 2.1 makes this clear. A state's goals are represented by the gains from successfully initiating a conflict, g_i. This parameter could represent hoped for territorial gains, improved terms of trade, imperial control, prestige, or any material or ideational goal which could be attained through a successful conflict. If a state has very little to gain from conflict, a low value for g_i, this makes it more likely to be a security seeker. In the extreme case, if $g_i = 0$, the state will be a security seeker regardless of the context because it simply has nothing to gain and only wishes to protect

---

[1] If the other side defects, defection nets $\pi_i g_i - (1 - \pi_i)l_i - c_i$ and cooperation $(\pi_i - \phi_j)g_i - (1 - \pi_i + \phi_j)l_i - c_i$ and the former beats the latter because $\phi_j > 0$.

[2] These and related terms are often used in a variety of ways in the field. A distinction is usually made between security seekers (or maximizers), status quo powers or satisfied states on the one hand, and expansionists, revisionists, greedy states or power maximizers on the other (Wolfers 1962: 18, 67; Schweller 1996).

itself. However, most states have some international ambitions, however modest, even if it is only to gain prestige or economic well-being. For all states with $g_i > 0$, the strategic situation will help determine whether they are security seekers.

The strategic situation enters the inequality in the form of the likelihood of success in a conflict, π_i, the advantage of initiating a conflict as opposed to being surprised, ϕ_i, and the costs of conflict c_i. The likelihood of success, π_i, can be thought of as a function of a state's power. The more power, the greater π_i, and lower g_i^*, $\left(\frac{\partial g_i^*}{\partial \pi_i} < 0 \right)$ making state i more likely to be expansionist. More powerful states, being more likely to succeed in a conflict, will initiate disputes over issues that weaker states would be willing to let alone. For instance, in the early twentieth century, Germany fortified its border with France but not with Holland. The Netherlands was viewed as a security seeker because a war between Germany and Holland would likely end in defeat for Holland. France might be expansionist, in part, because a war between France and Germany could lead to a German defeat. This logic extends to a range of issues besides all out war. In general, the greater a state's chance of success in breaking an agreement, the more likely it is to be untrustworthy.

This also provides a theoretical underpinning for the common observation that we can infer more about someone's true motivations from how they behave towards those weaker than themselves, than from how they behave towards those who are more powerful. Where one side is much more powerful than the other, it will be free to use that power to impose its will, so if it has even small expansionist goals, these will be revealed. In international relations, this provides a rationale for judging the intentions of states by how they behave towards weaker states. Soviet coercion in Eastern Europe was therefore a disturbing signal to Western Europeans, while American interventions in the third world were worrisome to other states.

Increasing the first strike advantage, ϕ_i, will also lower g_i^*, $\left(\frac{\partial g_i^*}{\partial \phi_i} < 0 \right)$ making state i more likely to be expansionist. If taking another state by surprise pays big dividends in a conflict, states will be tempted to try *fait acomplis* in an effort to secure their hoped for gains before the other side can effectively respond (Van Evera 1999: 35). This can turn security seekers into expansionists because their gains become more readily realizable if surprise can be achieved.

Lowering the costs of conflict, c_i, will lower g_i^*, $\left(\frac{\partial g_i^*}{\partial c_i} > 0 \right)$ turning some borderline security seekers into untrustworthy expansionists. Conversely, if the costs of war go up this will raise g_i^*, converting expansionists into trustworthy security seekers. The most dramatic recent elevation in the costs of war was, of course, the advent of nuclear weapons. When each side has many nuclear weapons that can survive a first strike (ϕ_i is low enough) even states with substantial revisionist goals will be effectively security seekers when it comes to all out war. Of course, this may not prevent them from being expansionists on lesser issues where nuclear weapons are not relevant. Nonetheless, it will make the deliberate surprise initiation of major war for gain much less likely than in the past.

Finally, increasing the potential loss from conflict, l_i, raises the threshold, $\left(\frac{\partial g_i^*}{\partial l_i} > 0\right)$ making a state more likely to be a trustworthy security seeker. For instance, two great powers competing for influence in a peripheral country could face a loss of economic investments if one side succeeds in edging out the other. The greater such potential losses, the more likely a state is to be a security seeker and prefer an agreement to a conflict in which each tried to eliminate the other's influence, other things being equal.

To recap, the distinction between security seeking and expansionist states depends both on their intrinsic goals and on their strategic context. Security seekers are trustworthy because they are willing to cooperate if they think that the other side is a security seeker as well. If both players are security seekers, they can both do well by not attacking, leaving both sides secure. In contrast, expansionist states are untrustworthy because even if they believe that the other side is a security seeker, and hence is willing to reciprocate cooperation, they will still want to defect. If one or both players are expansionist, then the only equilibrium is mutual defection. In the presence of an expansionist state, security seekers also act aggressively by defecting. Thus, the Security Dilemma Game above contains in a single framework both the Prisoner's Dilemma and the Assurance Game that have been used to analyze trust in international relations, but improves on them by grounding them in a simple model of conflict with associated variables for the potential gains, losses, chance of winning, and costs suffered. The model shows that trustworthiness, which is a function of state motivations as well as the strategic situation, is crucial for determining when states can cooperate.

Introducing Uncertainty

So far, however, the Security Dilemma Game does not fully capture the definition of trust in the previous chapter, because it does not model the uncertainty actors face over the preferences of other actors. As I argued in the previous chapter, trust should be conceived of in terms of beliefs about preferences, with greater trust corresponding to greater certainty that the other side is trustworthy, or prefers to reciprocate cooperation.

To represent this kind of uncertainty in the model, posit that each player's value for gain at the expense of the other side can take on one of two values, g_i^s and g_i^e where $g_i^s < g_i^* < g_i^e$.[3] Security seekers place a low value on increasing their holdings at the other side's expense, g_i^s, while expansionist types place a higher value, g_i^e. Nature starts the game by choosing whether each side is a security seeker or is expansionist.[4] The likelihood that player j is a trustworthy security seeker is t_j. There is a t_j chance that player j is a security seeker with a value for expansion equal to g_j^s and a $1 - t_j$ chance that player j is an expansionist with a higher value for expansion of g_j^e. The greater the likelihood that player j is an untrustworthy expansionist, the lower the level of trust.

Where do these prior levels of trust, t_1 and t_2, come from? Past experience is one answer. While any game must start somewhere, history is continuous, so the prior beliefs in any game are the product of previous, unmodeled interactions. For instance, for the Soviets in 1945 recent history included extreme conflict with the West, starting with the intervention on behalf of the White forces in the civil war, and finishing with the Nazi invasion in 1941. However, it also included a period of war time cooperation with the Allies, including generous lend-lease supplies from the United States. All these experiences influenced the Soviet Union's prior beliefs going into the Cold War.

The two decisions by Nature determining the players' types imply that there are four possible combinations of types in the game: both players may be security seekers, player 1 may be a security seeker while player 2 is an expansionist, player 1 may be an expansionist while player 2 a security seeker, and both players may be expansionists. These four possible states of the world are illustrated in Table 2.2 and the prior probability of each combination of types occurring is given in the cells.

The players are informed of their own type, but not that of the other player. The players therefore know their own payoffs with certainty, but they remain uncertain about what the other side's payoffs are. The player's preferences are private information, something that each side knows but that the other side does not know. After each player's type is determined and the players are informed of their types, the players must choose to cooperate or defect. As in the complete information case just discussed, they choose in ignorance of what the other side has chosen, so that the moves are effectively simultaneous. The game then ends.

---

[3] An alternative assumption would be to have g_i distributed continuously over the positive real numbers. The results are basically similar to the two type framework, so I have chosen the simpler setup. I employ a continuous type framework in chapter 5.

[4] Nature is a game theoretic convention for factors outside the control of the players, about which they may be uncertain.

TABLE 2.2
The Four Possible States of the World

		Player 2	
		Security Seeking (Trustworthy)	Expansionist (Untrustworthy)
Player 1	Security Seeking (Trustworthy)	$t_1 t_2$	$t_1(1 - t_2)$
	Expansionist (Untrustworthy)	$(1 - t_1)t_2$	$(1 - t_1)(1 - t_2)$

EQUILIBRIA WITH UNCERTAINTY

How should the players play the game under uncertainty? Expansionist types have a dominant strategy to defect. Being untrustworthy, they prefer to exploit the other side rather than reciprocate cooperation. The only question, therefore, is what the security seeking types should do. There are two pure strategy Nash equilibria of the game, as illustrated in Figure 2.2.[5] The horizontal axis is the likelihood that player 1 is a security seeker, t_1, while the vertical axis is player 2's likelihood of being a security seeker, t_2. Thus, points towards the origin correspond to low levels of mutual trust and points towards the upper right hand corner represent high mutual trust.

The Noncooperative Equilibrium

In the noncooperative equilibrium, the security seeking types, like the expansionist types, defect regardless of their beliefs. If the other side is expected to defect for sure, regardless of its value for expansion, defection is the best strategy for security seeking types.

The noncooperative equilibrium is possible for any level of trust and for all possible payoff values. For low levels of mutual trust, near the origin of Figure 2.2, this equilibrium makes a lot of sense. There, the two sides are convinced that the other side is likely to be an untrustworthy expansionist, and, hence, have a dominant strategy to defect. In this zone, mistrust decisively prevents cooperation. If one side is relatively trusting but the

[5] In a pure strategy equilibrium each player chooses a definite strategy to play, as opposed to a mixed strategy equilibrium in which they randomly select their strategy according to a certain probability distribution. There is also a mixed strategy equilibrium in the game which is discussed in the Appendix. The parameter values used in the illustration are $g_i^s = 0$, $g_i^e = 0.5$, $l_i = 1$, $c_i = 0$, $\pi_i = 0.5$, and $\phi_i = 0.25$.

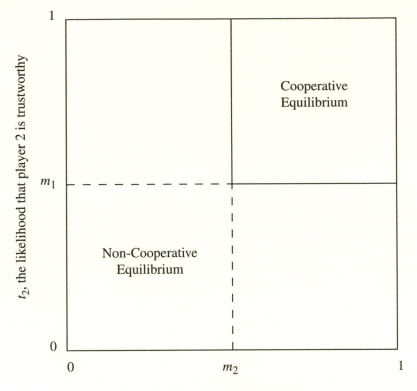

Figure 2.2 Equilibria in the Security Dilemma Game

other side is not, in the upper left and lower right corners of Figure 2.2, the equilibrium also is sensible, though somewhat more tragic. If player 1 trusts player 2 but not the other way around, player 1 might want to cooperate but because it knows that player 2 does not trust it, it will be prevented from doing so. Thus, even asymmetric mistrust can inhibit cooperation.

The noncooperative equilibrium is also possible in the upper right corner, where the two sides are relatively trusting. This is because the other side is expected to defect for sure, whether they are security seeking or expansionist, so the best response is to defect, even for security seekers. Here, however, the equilibrium is less intuitively compelling because security seekers are coordinating on defecting when they could just as easily coordinate on cooperation, as in the complete information game between security seekers. Thus, while the noncooperative equilibrium is possible here, it is unlikely in comparison to the cooperative equilibrium discussed next.

The Cooperative Equilibrium

In the cooperative equilibrium, the security seeking types of both players cooperate while expansionist types defect. Security seekers are willing to cooperate because they have a high enough estimate that the other side is a trustworthy security seeker, and will also cooperate to overcome their worry that the other side might be expansionist and plan to defect. That is, security seekers are willing to cooperate because they trust each other enough. This equilibrium is therefore found in the upper right corner of Figure 2.2, where both players have high enough levels of trust.

Since the cooperative equilibrium is only possible for high enough levels of mutual trust, there must be lower bounds on the level of trust for each player, below which the equilibrium is impossible. These are the minimum trust thresholds for the equilibrium, denoted m_i. They can be derived by comparing the payoff for cooperation, $t_j(0) + (1 - t_j)[(\pi_i - \phi_j)g_i^s - (1 - \pi_i + \phi_j)l_i - c_i]$ with the payoff for defection, $t_j[(\pi_i + \phi_i)g_i^s - (1 - \pi_i - \phi_i)l_i - c_i] + (1 - t_j)[\pi_i g_i^s - (1 - \pi_i)l_i - c_i]$ and noting that cooperation beats defection if the following condition holds:

$$t_j \geq m_i \equiv \frac{\phi_j}{\frac{c_i + l_i}{g_i^s + l_i} - \pi_i - \phi_i + \phi_j}. \tag{2.2}$$

For the cooperative equilibrium to be possible, this condition must be satisfied for both players. If the two sides trust each other sufficiently, they can cooperate in the Security Dilemma Game, provided that they are actually trustworthy. In the upper right-hand corner, t_2 and t_1 are both greater than the cut-off value; therefore, in this zone the cooperative equilibrium is possible. Outside this zone, one or both of the actors is too mistrustful to cooperate.

What does the model say about the link between trust and cooperation? I discuss several implications of the model, four that pertain to when cooperation is achievable, and two on how behavior in the Security Dilemma Game affects subsequent beliefs, after the game has been played.

ACHIEVING COOPERATION

For cooperation to take place, the level of trust each player has for the other side, t_j, must exceed a minimum trust threshold m_i, which is a function of the player's payoffs ($t_j \geq m_i$). This ties together in a concise mathematical framework the intuition that trust is a matter of beliefs about the motivations of the other, and, hence, can vary in strength, and must exceed a certain threshold for cooperation to be possible (Hardin 2002: 12). Here, trust is a variable t_j ranging from zero to one, representing the likelihood that the other side prefers to reciprocate cooperation rather than exploit it. For trust to lead to cooperative behavior, it must exceed a certain threshold, and this threshold itself may vary depending on a state's motivations and strategic circumstances. Thus, a failure to cooperate can be explained in two ways. First, two actors can fail to cooperate if there is a low level of mutual trust, if t_j is at the low end of its range, towards zero. Second, two actors can fail to cooperate even with a relatively high level of mutual trust, with t_j at the top of its range near 1, if the minimum trust threshold, m_i is still higher.

Mutual trust is necessary for cooperation. Of course, the model was set up in a symmetrical fashion, to focus on mutual trust. One could look at a one-sided version in which one player moves first and, hence, bears all the risk of potential betrayal (Kydd 2000b: 331). Indeed, much of the trust literature has focused on these sorts of situations (for instance, Coleman 1990). In most contexts in international relations, however, there is potential for betrayal on both sides. In an arms control treaty, both sides can exploit the other by hiding weapons. In an alliance context, each side can betray the other, one by failing to come to the other's aid, the other by provoking a needless conflict once the alliance is signed. Reassurance may be easier if one side is trusting of the other, but in order to achieve full mutual cooperation, mutual trust is usually necessary.

More specific implications relating to the possibility of cooperation include the following. Again, both a state's intrinsic motivations and its strategic situation matter.

Implication 2.1 *The greater the potential gains from conflict, g_i, the more trusting a state must be to cooperate, $\left(\frac{\partial m_i}{\partial g_i} > 0 \right)$.*

The closer the security seeker is to being expansionist—the greater the potential gains it perceives from conflict—the more trusting it will have to be to be willing to cooperate. Thus, it will not take much mistrust to convince states that have irredentist goals to fail to cooperate. Since they are on the border of being untrustworthy to begin with, it will not take much distrust of others to convince them to defect.

Implication 2.2 *The greater a state's relative power, π_i, the more trusting it has to be to be willing to cooperate $\left(\frac{\partial m_i}{\partial \pi_i} > 0 \right)$.*

Making a state more powerful—increasing the chance that it will prevail in a dispute—makes conflict comparatively more attractive, so the state will be less concerned about avoiding it. Strong states therefore are willing to engage in conflict at levels of trust that a weaker state would consider high enough to merit taking a chance on cooperation. This may help explain historical divergences between United States and European attitudes towards confronting various security threats, from the Soviet Union during the Cold War to more recent cases such as Iraq. The United States, being more powerful, prefers to act in a a noncooperative way and initiate conflicts at levels of trust that the Europeans feel justifies cooperation.

Implication 2.3 *The greater the advantage from initiating a conflict, ϕ_i and ϕ_j, the more trusting the states need to be to cooperate $\left(\frac{\partial m_i}{\partial \phi_i} > 0 \right)$ and $\left(\frac{\partial m_i}{\partial \phi_j} > 0 \right)$.*

If there is little difference between responding belatedly to a conflict initiated by the other side and defecting simultaneously, then cooperation will be easy to achieve because the minimum trust threshold, m_i will be low. In the limit case, if $\phi_j = 0$, so the other side cannot reap any benefit from taking advantage of one's cooperation, then a security seeker will be willing to cooperate no matter how low the level of trust. On the other hand, if ϕ_j and ϕ_i are high, then being caught off guard is very bad and attacking while the other side cooperates, while still not optimal for a security seeker, is less bad than it might be.

This result speaks to the literature on the offense-defense balance and the security dilemma. Starting with Quester (1977) and Jervis (1978), and continuing on through Glaser and Kaufmann (1998) and Van Evera (1999), an important strand of literature on the security dilemma concerns how military technology and other factors influence the stability of the system by exacerbating or ameliorating the security dilemma. The result supports this literature by indicating that increasing what may be thought of as the first strike advantage, ϕ_i, can prevent cooperation between security seekers, holding the level of trust constant. However, the model also supports the inference that increasing both the level of trust and the first strike advantage at the same time may have no effect on stability or even improve it. This sheds light on the stability of post-Cold War Europe. Conventional military technology is arguably as offense dominant today as it has ever been in recorded history, given the speeds with which forces move, the accuracy of long range weapons, and the ability of modern transportation to sustain forces across great distances. This offense dominance is offset, however, by greatly increased levels of trust, at least among European democracies, resulting in greater stability rather than less. In the model's terms, if m_i increases but t_j increases more, security seekers can still cooperate in equilibrium.

Implication 2.4 *The greater the costs of conflict, c_i, the less trusting the players need to be to cooperate $\left(\frac{\partial m_i}{\partial c_i} < 0 \right)$.*

Increasing the costs of conflict lowers the minimum trust threshold, m_i, so that more fearful actors will be willing to cooperate. Making conflict more costly makes players willing to undergo greater risks in an effort to avoid it.

Thus, increasing the costs of conflict has two effects. First, it makes states more likely to be security seekers rather than expansionists, as was discussed previously. Second, it increases a state's willingness to risk cooperation even with remaining uncertainty about the other side's motivations. Thus, raising the cost of conflict increases the likelihood of cooperation through two paths. Nuclear weapons again provide the most extreme example. With relatively secure second strike forces, the level of trust needed to prevent all out war is relatively low because of the devastation that would automatically ensue regardless of which side started it.

The final variable to discuss is the potential losses from conflict, l_i. The effect of increasing the potential losses turns out to depend on the relative size of the costs of fighting and the gains from potential conflict. If $c_i > g_i^s$, then $\frac{\partial m_i}{\partial l_i} > 0$, so that the greater the potential losses, the more trusting they need to be to cooperate. If the costs of fighting are less than the potential gains, $\frac{\partial m_i}{\partial l_i} < 0$, and increasing the potential loss will make cooperation possible for lower levels of trust. This indicates that for states that are pure security seekers, or nearly so, increasing the potential downside of a war makes cooperation harder, by raising the necessary level of trust. For more greedy states, states near the threshold of being expansionist for whom the costs of conflict are not so great, increasing the potential downside of a war may exercise a restraining influence, and make cooperation easier for lower levels of trust.

Summing up these implications, cooperation is possible if both sides' level of trust exceeds a minimum trust threshold that is determined by their motivations and the structure of the situation. In situations where the costs of conflict are high and the advantage of striking first is low, the minimum trust threshold is low and cooperation is easier to establish. Conversely, the lower the costs of conflict, the higher the minimum trust threshold will be, and the harder it will be to get cooperation going. More powerful states will require a greater level of trust to cooperate, as will states with greater expansionist desires.

THE EFFECTS OF COOPERATION AND NONCOOPERATION

The next two implications have to do with learning in the Security Dilemma Game. Before the actors play the game, they start off with their prior beliefs about how likely the other side is to be security seeking, or trustworthy. These prior beliefs are the probability estimates t_1 and t_2. After the actors play, they may learn something about the other side, so their beliefs may change. Whether beliefs change or not depends on which equilibrium takes place.

Implication 2.5   *In the noncooperative equilibrium, the players do not learn about the other player's type, so their level of trust does not change. If security seeking types are too mistrustful to cooperate, they will fail to learn if the other side is security seeking or not, so they will remain distrustful. Thus, distrust can be self-perpetuating.*

The reason that beliefs do not change in the noncooperative equilibrium is because security seeking types and expansionist types do the same thing—they defect. This type of equilibrium is known as a pooling equilibrium because both types pool on doing the same thing. Because they behave in the same way, there is no way to tell them apart by looking at their behavior. Thus, at the end of the game the players are no wiser than they were at the beginning and their beliefs remain the same. Since the noncooperative equilibrium is the only possible equilibrium for low levels of trust, and in the noncooperative equilibrium the players do not learn anything from observing the other player play the game, it follows that if the players start out too mistrustful to cooperate, they will remain so after the game. This is a somber finding, much in the spirit of offensive realist pessimism about the impact of mistrust on cooperation in international relations, as I will discuss in a moment.[6] It also accords with learning models in repeated situations in which once the expected value of a new option declines below a certain level, it will not be tried anymore so that one will cease to learn about its true value (Schultz 2004). This means that the old option could be chosen permanently over the new even if the new is better because a few bad experiences with the new option prevents any future learning.

Implication 2.6   *In the cooperative equilibrium, the players learn about each other's type after observing their behavior. If the other side cooperates, it is identified as security seeking and if it does not, it is identified as expansionist. When players are more trusting, they will learn more about each other's trustworthiness, because they are willing to take a chance on cooperating with each other.*

Things are different in the cooperative equilibrium. In the cooperative equilibrium security seeking types cooperate and expansionist types defect, this kind of equilibrium is known as a separating equilibrium because the two types separate by pursuing different strategies. Because of this, the players learn who is who. If you see the other player cooperate, you know he must be security seeking. If you see him defect, you know he must be expansionist. Thus, at the end of the game, the players have resolved their uncertainty. Their trust has either been confirmed or disconfirmed.

---

[6]This implication also accords with some of the literature on social capital which argues that cultures of mistrust can perpetuate themselves over time, though this literature may be conflating trust and trustworthiness (Gambetta 1988; Hardin 2002: 103).

Thus, those who start out with optimistic beliefs about the trustworthiness of others will either have them reinforced, leading to mutually beneficial cooperative relationships, or have them dashed, leading to a short-term loss followed by no cooperation with that particular person. Thus, the more trusting one starts out, the more fluid one's beliefs will be, because one will be willing to experiment. Trust can lead to greater trust, and security seeking types will continue to cooperate with each other.

These two implications begin to shed light on the offensive and defensive realist arguments about trust in international relations. The noncooperative equilibrium is the offensive realist argument in a nutshell. Security seeking and expansionist states behave alike by defecting because of a lack of trust, so there is no point worrying about motivations. This situation perpetuates itself because since they behave the same, there is no way to learn which type you are facing. Mistrust leads to noncooperation, which leaves the mistrust untouched, which leads to more noncooperation. However, in the cooperative equilibrium security seeking states experiment with cooperation, discover other security seekers who reciprocate the cooperation, and establish mutually trusting, cooperative relationships. Sometimes another state defects and is identified as an expansionist, but then that state has revealed its nature and others can subsequently not cooperate with it. Thus, the Security Dilemma Game shows how contingent the offensive realist analysis is on the level of trust and the other parameters that determine the minimum trust threshold. Offensive realists can argue that the extent of the cooperative equilibrium is quite small because of the low level of trust and high benefit from initiating a conflict. However, if the level of trust and the costs of conflict are high enough, then the level of trust may exceed the minimum trust threshold, leading to cooperation. Thus, the question of which equilibrium holds is an empirical one as well as a theoretical one. The cooperative equilibrium in the Security Dilemma Game cannot be ruled out a priori.

With respect to the defensive realist arguments, the cooperative equilibrium demonstrates that if we posit rational security seekers with high enough levels of mutual trust we should get cooperation and reassurance, rather than convergence on mistaken mistrust. Thus, the model highlights a mechanism for building well-founded trust between security seekers, and conversely, indicates that conflict may be more often the result of the presence of genuinely expansionist powers. In the cooperative equilibrium, if conflict erupts it is because one or both states is actually expansionist, so that the conflict is not tragic and the resulting mistrust is not a mistake. This does not decisively refute defensive realist claims, however, because the defensive realist argument is more sophisticated than can be captured in this model, as I will show in the next chapter.

A final question worth considering is how external observers should react to observed cooperation and defection. External observers, like the participants, may wish to use the behavior of the parties to make inferences about their motivations. In the Security Dilemma Game, this task is particularly simple. There are two cases. In the noncooperative equilibrium, since the players pool on defection, there is no way for the external observer to learn about their preferences. Thus, the observer's prior beliefs remain in place, just as those of the players do. In the cooperative equilibrium, however, the players separate and trustworthy players cooperate while untrustworthy players defect. Here the external observer can make inferences about preferences from behavior. If a player cooperates, the observer can identify it as a security seeker; if it defects, the observer knows it is expansionist. The observer's beliefs, in the Security Dilemma Game, react identically to those of the parties. This will not quite be the case in the game explored in the next chapter, where I will return to this issue in greater depth. For now, it suffices to note that separating equilibria convey information to external parties about the players' motivations, just as they do to the players themselves.

Conclusion

The Security Dilemma Game lets us formulate the problem of mistrust in a rigorous way, and generates implications about how the interaction between levels of trust and the goals and structural situation of the actors affect the possibility of cooperation. The game confirms the common idea that conflict can be a product of mistrust. Conflict arises when trust falls too low because there is a minimum trust threshold, above which the rational thing to do is cooperate, and below which the rational thing to do is defect. Thus, the Security Dilemma Game provides a solid grounding for our intuitions about the role of trust in the genesis of conflict and cooperation.

The Security Dilemma Game is fairly simple, however, and leaves many question unanswered. The game posits only two players, when some issues involve more than two actors. It is a single shot game, and therefore tells us less than it might about how trust can be built over time. And, it does not capture the possibility that trust can be eroded through competition, even though the actors themselves are actually trustworthy, an argument that is widespread in the international relations literature and a cornerstone of the defensive realist position. These limitations will be addressed in subsequent chapters, starting in the next chapter with an analysis of the last issue, the genesis of potentially unjustified fear.

APPENDIX

The Security Dilemma Game also has a mixed strategy equilibrium in which the expansionist types defect and the security seekers cooperate with likelihood x_i and defect with likelihood $1 - x_i$, where x_i is derived by equating the payoff for cooperation, $t_j x_j(0) + (1 - t_j x_j)[(\pi_i - \phi_j)g_i^s - (1 - \pi_i + \phi_j)l_i - c_i]$ with the payoff for defection, $t_j x_j[(\pi_i + \phi_i)g_i^s - (1 - \pi_i - \phi_i)l_i - c_i] + (1 - t_j x_j)[\pi_i g_i^s - (1 - \pi_i)l_i - c_i]$ and solving for x_j which yields

$$x_j = \frac{m_i}{t_j}.$$

These mixing probabilities are calculated to make the other side indifferent between cooperating and defecting, so that they, in turn, will be willing to randomize over their strategies. The equilibrium is possible wherever the cooperative equilibrium is possible, and is strictly Pareto inferior to it. One of its peculiar features is that the more likely the players are to be security seekers, that is, the more trusting they are, the more likely they are to defect. This must be so because the more trusting the players are, the greater incentives the security seekers have to cooperate, so to keep them indifferent between cooperating and defecting, they must defect with greater likelihood. In my view this equilibrium is even less plausible than the noncooperative equilibrium where the cooperative equilibrium is possible. It would involve not only coordinating on a equilibrium Pareto inferior to the focal cooperative equilibrium, it would mean coordinating on a complicated randomization that makes the players indifferent between cooperating and defecting. Given the existence of obviously focal pure strategy equilibria, mixed strategy equilibria make little sense in the Security Dilemma Game, or the games in the subsequent chapters. In future I will restrict attention to pure strategy equilibria.

PART II

Fear and the Origins of the Cold War

CHAPTER 3

The Spiral of Fear

IN HIS COMPREHENSIVE history of the Truman administration and the origins of the Cold War, Melvyn Leffler blames the conflict on a spiral of mutual fear between the United States and the Soviet Union, caused by the fact that, "each side, in pursuit of its security interests, took steps that aroused the other's apprehensions" (Leffler 1992: 99). Leffler's understanding of the Cold War echoes British Foreign Secretary Edward Grey's account of the onset of World War I written nearly seventy years previously (Grey 1925: 89). Grey argued that the arms increases of each side were taken as evidence of hostile intent by the other side. Thus, arms increases not only provoke matching buildups by the other side, they make the other side more fearful of one's basic intentions, persuading them that one is aggressive and untrustworthy. This argument is usually called the spiral model following Jervis (1976: 58) and it is a primary component of defensive realism, as described in chapter 1.[1]

This chapter will further develop the model from the last chapter to investigate the arguments underlying the spiral model. The spiral model is usually thought of as a psychological theory. However, the basic arguments are quite compatible with a game theoretic framework in which states are uncertain about how the other side perceives their own motivations. Such a rationalist approach to the spiral model enables it to fit more appropriately within the rational unitary actor approach underlying most realist theory. The game generates hypotheses about the likelihood that security seekers will end up in conflict with each other, and about how we as external observers should update our beliefs when we see the parties engage in conflictual behavior.

There are two primary implications of the model. The first is that the spirals of unjustified mistrust identified by Grey and Leffler are indeed possible in a world of rational actors. This supports defensive realism and highlights the fact that the spiral model does not depend on psychological bias to drive it. The second implication, however, is that such spirals are rare in comparison with conflicts between actors who are genuinely untrustworthy. Thus, as outside observers who may not have access to privileged information about the motivations of the parties, when we see

[1] For earlier formulations and later developments, see Butterfield 1951; Glaser 1992; and Kydd 1997a.

conflict we should become more suspicious, more convinced that the parties are untrustworthy. This is one of the central Bayesian realist arguments, the occurrence of conflict should lead the observer to be more suspicious of the parties' motivations, just as the parties themselves become more suspicious. Absent strong, countervailing direct evidence that the parties are trustworthy, the observer's level of trust for the parties should fall.

The Spiral Model

The foundations of the spiral model are in the security dilemma. States in an anarchic world mistrust each other's intentions and fail to cooperate. The spiral model develops on this foundation to argue that the steps that states take to increase their security not only make others less secure directly by making them relatively weaker, they also make others more fearful or mistrustful. That is, as Grey argued, arms increases are regarded as evidence of hostile intent. A failure to cooperate, therefore, can weaken trust between two states.

A key point to note about this argument is that the failure to cooperate increases mistrust between security seekers, that is, between states that are fundamentally trustworthy. This is the punch of the spiral model argument: trustworthy states become fearful of each other, so the resulting conflict between them is a tragic product of misperceptions. The generation of mistrust between untrustworthy actors is not surprising or enlightening as an explanation of conflict. If two rival drug dealers have a shoot-out, it is not especially interesting to explain this with reference to mistrust. They are perfectly correct to mistrust each other because they are untrustworthy. The spiral model, much more intriguingly, argues that security seekers—trustworthy states—can come to mistrust each other through a pattern of mutual interaction that both sides pursue solely to increase their security. Security seekers persuade each other that they are aggressive by attempting to increase their own security. Thus, the spiral model argues that anarchy is even more tragic than the security dilemma would indicate.

The question then arises, why do security seekers perceive the arms increases of others as evidence of aggressive motivations, when they themselves are increasing their arms out of a desire to be secure? Herbert Butterfield provides the key mechanism in a simple argument. Because states know their own motivations well, they believe that other states also know them. Therefore, security seeking states think that everyone else knows that they are security seekers. When a security seeker encounters hostility from another state, therefore, it can only be explained as a consequence of the other state's innate aggression. Since one's own benign motivations are clear, hostility cannot be explained as a result of fear of oneself, it must result from aggression on the part of the other (Butterfield 1951: 21).[2] In reality, of course, others are not fully aware of one's own benign nature; they may have all kinds of different beliefs about one's motivations. The consequence of this psychological blunder can be severe. Two security seekers laboring under these delusions will react fearfully and reinforce each other's fear.

As so far expressed, this is a model of cognitive limitation, or nonrational behavior. The departure from rationality involves a contradiction between two assumptions. First, Butterfield assumes that security seeking states do not envision the possibility that others might fear them. Second, he assumes that other states do, in fact, fear them; others are uncertain about their motivations. Because states are not envisioning something that is possible, they are cognitively limited. This limitation drives the spiral with a vengeance. States escalate out of fear and interpret other's escalations as signs of hostile intentions because the other cannot possibly be motivated by fear.

Because of its reliance on cognitive limitation, Butterfield's understanding of the spiral model raises an important question. What would happen if security seekers were not *certain* that others trusted them, but were merely uncertain about what others' beliefs about them were? That is, what if we alter Butterfield's first assumption to be consistent with his second? This involves positing that states are uncertain about each other's beliefs about their own motivations, and know this about each other, know that they know it, etc. As we will see in the next chapter, this assumption is far more realistic. The United States, at least, was deeply uncertain of how it was perceived by the Soviets and made many attempts to discern and influence these beliefs. It might be the case that altering this assumption eliminates the possibility of spirals. Jervis hints that awareness of the other side's possible fear can eliminate the spiral effect (Jervis 1976: 82, 112–13). However it might be that spirals remain possible, even with fully rational, self-aware actors. Spiral theorists do not squarely address this question. Another way of posing this question is to ask what a rational choice version of the spiral model would look like. This question is particularly acute for defensive realism, which adheres to the basic rational actor approach common to realism.

The Security Dilemma Game of the previous chapter provides a starting point for such an analysis but does not fully capture the spiral logic. In the Security Dilemma Game each side can be one of two types, security seeking or expansionist. I posited beliefs about how likely each player is to be trustworthy, t_1 for player 1, t_2 for player 2, and, crucially, I have assumed

---

[2]For later expositions of this idea, see Osgood 1962: 29; Gamson and Modigliani 1971: 42; and Jervis 1976:68.

that these beliefs are *common knowledge*. That is, each side knows how likely the other side thinks they are to be trustworthy. Player 1 knows t_1, so player 1 knows how trusting player 2 is of player 1. Thus, I have assumed away the uncertainty that spiral theorists focus on. In the Security Dilemma Game, each player *does* know how the other side regards it, and is not making any mistakes about this. While this assumption is a useful starting point, in reality states may be uncertain about how the other side perceives them. Does the other side think I am relatively likely to be trustworthy, or is the other side more fearful of me? This is uncertainty about the beliefs of the other side, a matter of beliefs about beliefs. To incorporate this kind of uncertainty, we need to add more types to the framework. This will enable us to determine if spirals can develop between fully rational actors, or if they are necessarily a product of cognitive limitation.

In what follows I will present a game theoretic version of the spiral model, that clarifies the conditions under which a spiral can arise and how it works. In particular, I focus on the key role of beliefs about beliefs; each side's beliefs about how the other side views them.

THE SPIRAL GAME

Consider a modified version of the Security Dilemma Game from Figure 2.1 called the Spiral Game.[3] The payoffs and structure of the game are the same as before. As before, there are two types, security seekers, for whom $g_i \leq g_i^*$, and expansionists for whom $g_i > g_i^*$. The prior likelihood that the other state j is a security seeker, denoted event JS, is t_j, that is $p(JS) = t_j$. Conversely, the likelihood the player j is an expansionist, event JE, is $p(JE) = 1 - t_j$.

To introduce uncertainty about the other side's beliefs, posit that the two parties then receive some additional information about the other side's motivations. This information could come from many different sources. As a stylized example, imagine that each country has a secret agent high in the other side's foreign service. These spies gather information for a year and then send a secret report back to their home country. The intelligence report may suggest that the other side is expansionist and likely to invade, or it may say that their military preparations are defensively motivated and are nothing to worry about.

This information will have two effects. First, each country, after receiving the report, will modify its beliefs. If it receives a positive report, it will become more trusting; if it gets a negative report, it will become less

---

[3]I call my game theoretic representation of the spiral model the Spiral Game, to distinguish it from the broader set of arguments that fall under the spiral model heading, some of which are psychological. See the end of this chapter for a glossary of my uses of the word "spiral."

trusting. Second, each side knows that it too is being spied on. Therefore, each state will be uncertain what the other side believes about its own motivations. If the other side got a good report, they will be more trusting; if they got a bad one, they will be more suspicious. Of course, each state will have some idea of the likelihood of various reports being sent. In particular, if a state is a security seeker, it will think that the other side is more likely to have received a report attesting to this rather than one saying it is expansionist. Thus, after the reports are sent, each side will form beliefs about the other side's beliefs about its own motivations, and these beliefs will depend on its own type.

To model this type of belief structure, posit that Nature reveals some information to each player about the type of the other player. Nature sends player i a message about player j, $\mu_j \in \{js, je\}$, either js for security seeking or je for expansionist.[4] These messages convey some information to the player about the other side's type, that is, if a player receives the js signal, it is evidence that the the the other side is likely to be security seeking. However, these signals are not perfectly accurate. You cannot be sure what type you face after receiving the signal because it is possible to get the wrong signal. The likelihood that the message that state i receives about state j is correct is denoted $1 - \varepsilon_j$ while the likelihood that the message is in error is ε_j where $1 - \varepsilon_j$ is assumed to be bigger than ε_j. Thus, I assume that the information is more likely to be right than wrong. (Otherwise the signal could simply be taken at the reverse of its face value, js would signify expansionist while je would stand for security seeking.) Each side sees the signal addressed to it, but not the one addressed to the other side. The likelihoods that the signals are in error, ε_1 and ε_2, are common knowledge. Notation in the Spiral Game is summarized in Table 3.1.

To sum up, Nature first distinguishes types based on their preferences, making each player security seeking or expansionist. Then by sending signals about the players types, Nature determines whether the players are trusting or fearful. After the signals from Nature, each player can update its beliefs about whether the other side is security seeking or expansionist. If player i gets the js signal, it will become more trusting of player j, whereas if it gets the je signal, it will become more fearful. Thus, after the signals are sent, each player will be either security seeking and trusting, security seeking and fearful, expansionist and trusting, or expansionist and fearful.

The four possible types for each player are illustrated in Table 3.2, which is the analog for the Spiral Game of Table 2.2 of the previous chapter.

---

[4] I adopt the convention that capital letters stand for events and lower case for messages about those events. Thus, JS is the event that player j is a security seeker, while js is the message that j is a security seeker. See Kydd 1997a and Morrow 1994a for uses of this modeling device.

TABLE 3.1
Notation in the Spiral Game

g_i	Player i's value for gain.
l_i	Player i's potential loss from conflict.
π_i	The likelihood that player i wins if both defect.
ϕ_i	Player i's advantage of initiating a conflict.
c_i	Player i's cost of conflict.
t_i	The prior likelihood that player i is a security seeker.
m_i	Player i's minimum trust threshold.
$\mu_j \in \{js, je\}$	The messages from Nature about j's type.
ε_j	The likelihood the message is in error.

Player 1's type is represented by the rows of the table, while player 2's type is represented by the columns. With two players and four possible types for each, there are sixteen possible pairs of types of players that could play the game, as represented by the cells of the table. In the upper left cell, both players are security seeking and trusting. In the next cell to the right, player 1 is security seeking and trusting but player 2 is security seeking and fearful, etc. The likelihood of each of these possibilities actually happening will depend on the probabilities that govern the initial moves by Nature, the likelihoods that the players are security seeking, t_1, and t_2, and the likelihoods that the signals are in error, ε_1 and ε_2. These likelihoods are given in the cells of Table 3.2.

For instance, in the upper left corner, the likelihood that both players are security seekers and trusting is $t_1 t_2 (1 - \varepsilon_1)(1 - \varepsilon_2)$. This corresponds to the likelihood that both players are security seeking, $t_1 \times t_2$, multiplied by the likelihood that both players got the (correct) js message and so became trusting, which is $(1 - \varepsilon_1) \times (1 - \varepsilon_2)$. In the next cell over, the likelihood that player 1 is a security seeking trusting type while player 2 is a security seeking but fearful type is $t_1 t_2 \varepsilon_1 (1 - \varepsilon_2)$. This is the product of the likelihood that both players are security seeking, $t_1 \times t_2$, and the likelihood that player 1 got the right signal but player 2 got the wrong signal and so became fearful, $\varepsilon_1 \times (1 - \varepsilon_2)$. The entries in the other cells are similarly derived.

Given that the signals from Nature are more likely to be right than wrong, a state's beliefs should shift when it receives them. If a country receives the report saying the other side is a security seeker, it should become more trusting, if it receives a report saying the other side is

TABLE 3.2
The Sixteen Possible States of the World

Player 1's Type	Player 2's Type			
	Security seeking/ Trusting	Security seeking/ Fearful	Expansionist/ Trusting	Expansionist/ Fearful
Security seeking/ Trusting	$t_1 t_2$ $\times (1-\varepsilon_1)(1-\varepsilon_2)$	$t_1 t_2 \times \varepsilon_1(1-\varepsilon_2)$	$t_1(1-t_2)$ $\times (1-\varepsilon_1)\varepsilon_2$	$t_1(1-t_2) \times \varepsilon_1\varepsilon_2$
Security seeking/ Fearful	$t_1 t_2 \times (1-\varepsilon_1)\varepsilon_2$	$t_1 t_2 \times \varepsilon_1\varepsilon_2$	$t_1(1-t_2)$ $\times (1-\varepsilon_1)(1-\varepsilon_2)$	$t_1(1-t_2)$ $\times \varepsilon_1(1-\varepsilon_2)$
Expansionist/ Trusting	$(1-t_1)t_2$ $\times \varepsilon_1(1-\varepsilon_2)$	$(1-t_1)t_2$ $\times (1-\varepsilon_1)(1-\varepsilon_1)$	$(1-t_1)(1-t_2)$ $\times \varepsilon_1\varepsilon_2$	$(1-t_1)(1-t_2)$ $\times (1-\varepsilon_1)\varepsilon_2$
Expansionist/ Fearful	$(1-t_1)t_2 \times \varepsilon_1\varepsilon_2$	$(1-t_1)t_2$ $\times (1-\varepsilon_1)\varepsilon_2$	$(1-t_1)(1-t_2)$ $\times \varepsilon_1(1-\varepsilon_2)$	$(1-t_1)(1-t_2)$ $\times (1-\varepsilon_1)(1-\varepsilon_2)$

expansionist, it should become more fearful. The question remains, how much more trusting, how much more fearful? Bayes' rule allows us to calculate the posterior beliefs.[5] For example, let us consider a security seeking player i's beliefs about player j after receiving the js signal that player j is security seeking. This can be expressed $p(JS|js)$, the likelihood that player j is security seeking given that player i received the js signal, and is as follows.

$$p(JS|js) = \frac{t_j(1 - \varepsilon_j)}{t_j(1 - \varepsilon_j) + (1 - t_j)\varepsilon_j}$$

With a little algebra, it is possible to show two things about player i's posterior level of trust after receiving the js signal. First, it is higher than the prior, that is, $p(JS|js) \geq t_j$. This means that, as we expected, after receiving the js signal player i becomes more trusting than it was before. Second, the greater the possibility that the signal is in error, ε_j, the less trusting player i will be, that is, the lower $p(JS|js)$ will be. In the limit, if ε_j is equal to one half, so that the signal is just as likely to be wrong as right, then player 1's beliefs will not change at all, and $p(JS|js) = t_j$. Conversely, the more accurate the signal is, the lower ε_j, the more trusting player i will be after getting it, the higher $p(JS|js)$. This is intuitive because the more likely the signal is to be accurate, the more weight player i should put on it and the more player i's beliefs should change.

What if player i receives the je message? The posterior belief is the following.

$$p(JS|je) = \frac{t_j\varepsilon_j}{t_j\varepsilon_j + (1 - t_j)(1 - \varepsilon_j)}$$

If we examine player i's level of trust after receiving the je message, we can see that player i becomes less trusting, $p(JS|je) \leq t_j$. Once again, the message is functioning as it ought to. The greater the likelihood that the signal is in error, the less effect the je message will have on player i's beliefs, so the more trusting player i will be. As before, if the signal is pure noise, then the posterior belief will be unchanged—$p(JS|je)$ will equal the prior t_j. The more accurate the signal, the smaller ε_j is, the more effect the je signal will have, and the lower will be player i's level of trust.

The effect of the reports from the spies on beliefs about the other's motivations is illustrated in Figure 3.1. The vertical axis is player i's trust for player j, so low values of trust are at the bottom and trust grows as one moves up. For the sake of the numerical example, assume the initial level of trust is 0.5, so player i thinks it equally likely that player j is security seeking and expansionist. The horizontal axis represents time, and shows how the

[5] See Bayes 1958 for a reprint of the original eighteenth-century paper, and Osborne 2004: 502–05 for a modern textbook presentation in a game theoretic context.

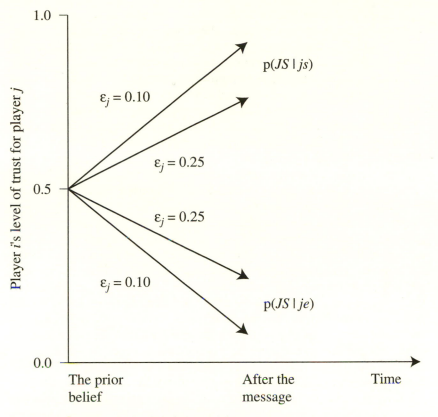

Figure 3.1 Learning in the Spiral Game (1)

beliefs change after player i receives the message from Nature. The top two lines represent the increase in trust that happens from getting a good report about the other player. The downward sloping lines represent the decrease in trust that occurs when player i gets a bad report about player j. The more steeply sloping lines, the top and bottom line, are when the the likelihood of the message being correct is 90 percent, so that the likelihood of error, ε_j, is 0.1. Here if player i receives the js report and so becomes trusting, its trust for player j goes up to 0.9. If player i receives the je report, its trust for player j declines to 0.1, or 10 percent. The inner lines represent the case when the message's chance of being wrong is higher, at 25 percent. Here the increase in trust after a good signal is less strong, only to 75 percent, and the decrease in trust after a bad signal is also less severe, to 25 percent. This illustrates the fact that the more accurate the reports, the closer to certainty are the beliefs after receiving them.

In addition to their effects on the players' beliefs about the other side's preferences, however, the messages have another effect on the players' beliefs. Each side knows that a message is going to the other side telling them about the state's motivations. If the report says the state is security seeking, the other side will become more trusting; if the report says the state is expansionist, the other side will become more fearful. Thus, each state (and type) can form a belief about how likely the other side is to be trusting, and how likely they are to be fearful. They must form beliefs about beliefs. Spiral theorists assume that security seekers believe that the other side trusts them completely. The information structure here is more general, allowing us to examine the implications of many possible beliefs.

Let us first consider player i's beliefs about whether player j is trusting or fearful. If state i is security seeking, its belief that state j is trusting is simply its belief that the message received by player j was correct, which is $1 - \varepsilon_i$. A correct report would indicate that player i is security seeking, because that is the truth. Its belief that player j is fearful is equivalent to the possibilty that player j got the ie signal, which is ε_i. Thus, the security seeking trusting type of state i thinks that the likelihood that the other side is trusting is high, $1 - \varepsilon_i$, and the likelihood that the other side is fearful is low, ε_i. Now consider the expansionist version of state i. If state i is expansionist, its belief that player j is trusting is equal to its belief that the other side got the wrong message, is, which is ε_i. Its belief that player j is fearful is equal to its belief that the message was correct, $1 - \varepsilon_i$. Thus the expansionist type of player i thinks it more likely that player j is fearful than the security seeking type does. Player i's beliefs about whether player j is trusting or fearful depend on player i's own type. The security seeking type of player i will be more convinced that player j is trusting, while the expansionist type will be more convinced that player j is fearful.

If the reports are perfectly accurate ($\varepsilon_j = 0$) these beliefs converge to certainty. Security seeking types become certain that other states perceive them as such, and expansionist types are also aware that their cover is blown and the other side knows they are expansionist. The greater the likelihood of error in the messages (higher values of ε_j) the greater the likelihood that the other side is guessing wrong about one's type. Security seeking types must consider the possibility that the other side is fearful of them, expansionist types rejoice in the possibility that the other side is trusting of them. Thus, each side's beliefs about the other side's beliefs depends on their own type and on the likelihood of error in the reports.

By expanding the set of types in this way we can examine a richer set of beliefs sufficient to address the concerns raised in the theory of the spiral model. States are uncertain about the motivations of the other side; they may be security seeking and trustworthy or expansionist and untrustworthy. In addition, states are uncertain about how the other side views them. The other side may think they are likely to be security seeking, or the other side may think that they are likely to be expansionist. Both security seeking and expansionist types share this uncertainty, though naturally security seeking types think the other side is more likely to be trusting than the expansionist types do. Thus, in deciding how to behave in an interdependent situation, as I will analyze in the next section, states have to consider a more complicated set of possibilities than they did in the Security Dilemma Game.

EQUILIBRIA IN THE SPIRAL GAME

The structure of play in the Spiral Game is just as in the Security Dilemma Game of the previous chapter. Each player has a single decision to make, cooperate or defect, and they must choose in ignorance of what the other side has chosen. Hence, they make their decisions based on their beliefs after they receive their messages from Nature.

There are three symmetric equilibria in the Spiral Game, a noncooperative equilibrium, and a cooperative equilibrium, which are the same as in the Security Dilemma Game, and the spiral equilibrium, which is unique to the Spiral Game.[6] The equilibria are illustrated in Figure 3.2. The figure is analogous to Figure 2.2, the horizontal axis is player 2's prior level of trust for player 1, t_1, while the vertical axis is player 1's prior trust for player 2, t_2. The payoffs are the same as before and the error rates of the signals are set equal to 25 percent ($\varepsilon_j = 0.25$).[7] In all equilibria, expansionist types, whether trusting or fearful, will defect regardless of beliefs or expectations about the other side because they have a dominant strategy to defect. Security seeking types may or may not cooperate, depending on the equilibrium.

The Noncooperative Equilibrium

First, there is a noncooperative equilibrium, as in the Security Dilemma Game, in which both players and all four types defect. Security seeking types, even ones who are trusting of the other side, prefer to reciprocate defection, so if they think the other side will defect for sure, then they will prefer to defect as well. As in the Security Dilemma Game, this equilibrium is possible for all levels of beliefs, as long as all four types are expected to defect. Thus in Figure 3.2, the noncooperative equilibrium is possible everywhere. For low levels of trust, it is the only equilibrium in the game.

---

[6]There are also two asymmetric equilibria which combine elements of the spiral and cooperative equilibria which are discussed in the Appendix.

[7]Namely: $g_i^s = 0, g_i^e = 0.5, l_i = 1, c_i = 0, \pi_i = 0.5$, and $\phi_i = 0.25$.

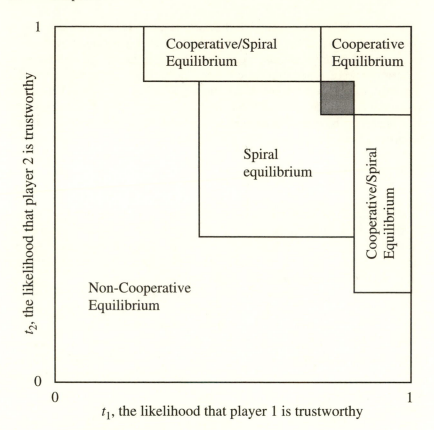

Figure 3.2 Equilibria in the Spiral Game

However, for higher levels of mutual trust, more cooperative equilibria are also possible.

The Cooperative Equilibrium

Second, there is a cooperative equilibrium in which security seeking types cooperate and expansionist types defect. In Figure 3.2, the cooperative equilibrium is the upper right hand corner, where mutual trust is high (t_1 and t_2 are both greater than 0.75).

In this equilibrium, both trusting and fearful security seekers must trust the other side sufficiently to be willing to cooperate. The binding constraint is that the fearful type of each player must have a level of trust for the other that exceeds the minimum trust threshold required for cooperation. The minimum trust threshold can be derived by comparing the payoff for cooperation, $p(JS|je)(0)+(1-p(JS|je))[(\pi_i-\phi_j)g_i^s-(1-\pi_i+\phi_j)l_i-c_i]$ with the payoff for defection, $p(JS|je)[(\pi_i+\phi_i)g_i^s-(1-\pi_i-\phi_i)l_i-c_i]+$ $(1-p(JS|je))[\pi_i g_i^s-(1-\pi_i)l_i-c_i]$ and solving for when the former beats the latter which gives the following:

$$p(JS|je) \geq m_i \equiv \frac{\phi_j}{\frac{c_i+l_i}{g_i^s+l_i}-\pi_i-\phi_i+\phi_j}.$$

This minimum trust threshold is the same as in the Security Dilemma Game, the difference here is that the fearful security seeker has a lower level of trust because of the negative message received about the other side.[8] The cooperative equilibrium is possible in the Spiral Game if the fearful security seeker's level of trust exceeds the minimum trust threshold. Note in Figure 3.2, the cooperative equlibrium is possible over a smaller range of the initial priors than was the case in the Security Dilemma Game analyzed in chapter 2. In the Security Dilemma Game, the cooperative equilibrium was possible if the prior levels of trust were greater than 0.5; now they must exceed 0.75. The prior level of trust has to be higher here because the signal which makes the security seeking fearful types more fearful makes them less willing to cooperate. To still be willing to cooperate, they must have had a greater level of trust to start with.

The Spiral Equilibrium

Next, there is a spiral equilibrium which is unique to the Spiral Game. In this equilibrium only the security seeking and trusting types cooperate, whereas the security seeking and fearful types defect, as shown in Table 3.3. The spiral equilibrium is possible in the central box of Figure 3.2. Here the level of trust is not high enough to get the fearful types to cooperate, so the cooperative equilibrium is not possible.[9]

To sustain this equilibrium, two sets of conditions must hold. First, the trusting types must be willing to cooperate even though only the trusting type on the other side is expected to cooperate as well. Second, the fearful type must be too fearful to cooperate, given that only the trusting type on the other side is expected to cooperate. It is important to realize that

---

[8] We can substitute in the expression for $p(JS|je)$ given above and solve for the prior beliefs as follows

$$t_j \geq \frac{\phi_j(1-\varepsilon_j)}{\phi_j(1-\varepsilon_j)+\left[\frac{c_i+l_i}{g_i^s+l_i}-\pi_i-\phi_i\right]\varepsilon_j}.$$

This gives the lower bounds of the cooperative equilibrium depicted in Figure 3.2.

[9] It is perhaps worth emphasizing that the trusting types do cooperate in the spiral equilibrium. Thus, it is possible in a spiral equilibrium for both sides to cooperate, if they happen to both be trusting. The result will be mutual reassurance.

TABLE 3.3
Strategies for Each Type in the Spiral Equilibrium

Type	Strategy
Security Seeking and Trusting	Cooperate
Security Seeking and Fearful	Defect
Expansionist and Trusting	Defect
Expansionist and Fearful	Defect

these two conditions are somewhat different from those that underly the cooperative equilibrium. There, both security seeking types cooperated, so the important question was, how likely is the other side to be security seeking? Here the crucial question is how likely is the other side to be both security seeking *and trusting* since both conditions must hold if a state is to cooperate. Thus, we need to consider a new set of beliefs, how likely the trusting security seeker thinks the other side is to be a trusting security seeker, denoted $p(JS, is|IS, js)$, and how likely the fearful security seeker thinks the other is to be to be a trusting security seeker, denoted $p(JS, is|IS, je)$. The security seeking and trusting player i's posterior belief that player j is security seeking and trusting is the product of the likelihood that j is security seeking times the likelihood that j got the correct message about player i:

$$p(JS, is|IS, js) = p(JS|js)(1 - \varepsilon_i).$$

Since player i is security seeking, improving player j's information should make player j more likely to be trusting. Therefore, the more accurate the information, the more confident a trusting security seeker is that the other side is a trusting security seeker.

The fearful security seeker's belief that the other side is a trusting security seeker is the product of the likelihood that they are a security seeker times the likelihood that they got the correct message:

$$p(JS, is|IS, je) = p(JS|je)(1 - \varepsilon_i).$$

Again, increasing the accuracy of the message player j receives about player i (lowering ε_i) will raise player i's confidence that player j got a correct signal about its motivations, and, hence, is trusting.

With these beliefs in hand, the conditions that make the spiral equilibrium possible are simply stated. The security seeking trusting type must be trusting enough to cooperate,

$$p(JS, is|IS, js) \geq m_i, \tag{3.1}$$

while the security seeking fearful type must be too fearful,

$$p(JS, is \mid IS, je) < m_i. \tag{3.2}$$

If these conditions hold for both players, the spiral equilibrium is possible.[10] In Figure 3.2, if the level of trust falls below the lower or left-hand boundaries of the spiral equilibrium, the trusting types will become too fearful to cooperate. Note that the spiral equilibrium is possible for levels of trust lower than the cooperative equilibrium of the Security Dilemma Game from the previous chapter. This is because the *js* message, which the trusting types receive, reassures them and increases mutual trust, making cooperation possible for lower levels of prior trust. In contrast, if the level of trust exceeds the upper and right-hand boundaries of the spiral equilibrium, the fearful types will become so trusting that they will be willing to cooperate rather than defect.

The spiral equilibrium and the cooperative equilibrium overlap in the upper right corner of Figure 3.2 in the shaded region. This is because in the spiral equilibrium, fearful types are expected not to cooperate, which reduces the incentive to cooperate for the other side. In the shaded region, the fearful types would be willing to cooperate if they thought their counterparts would cooperate on the other side (hence, the cooperative equilibrium is possible), but if they think the fearful type on the other side will not cooperate, they prefer not to as well (hence, the Spiral equilibrium is also possible). It would be Pareto improving for them to coordinate on cooperating in this circumstance so I would argue that the cooperative equilbrium is more likely than the spiral equilibrium in the region in which they are both possible.

Defection and Fear

The reason for developing the Spiral Game was to examine the argument that security seeking types can grow more fearful of each other as a result of mutual defection. To do this we need to look at beliefs after the players play, and these will depend on the equilibrium.

[10] Solving for the priors, for the trusting type,

$$t_j \geq \frac{\phi_j \varepsilon_j}{(1 - \varepsilon_j)(1 - \varepsilon_i)\left[\frac{c_i + l_i}{\sigma_i^s + l_i} - \pi_i - \phi_i + \phi_j\right] - \phi_j(1 - 2\varepsilon_j)}$$

while for the fearful types

$$t_j \leq \frac{\phi_j(1 - \varepsilon_j)}{\varepsilon_j(1 - \varepsilon_i)\left[\frac{c_i + l_i}{\sigma_i^s + l_i} - \pi_i - \phi_i + \phi_j\right] + \phi_j(1 - 2\varepsilon_j)}.$$

In the noncooperative equilibrium, as in the coresponding equilibrium in the Security Dilemma Game, beliefs do not change in response to behavior. Because all types are pursuing the same strategy, defecting, they cannot be differentiated based upon their behavior.

In the cooperative equilibrium, learning is very straightforward. If the other player defects, they are identified as expansionist for sure. If the other side cooperates, they are identified as security seeking for sure. This is identical to the situation in the Security Dilemma Game. Here again there is no mistaken spiral, because if the parties grow more fearful of each other, it is with good reason because they are, in fact, untrustworthy. There is no possibility for mistaken fear to arise in the cooperative equilibrium.

In the spiral equilibrium, however, things are different. Here, if the other side cooperates, they are identified as security seeking and trusting for sure. The posterior level of trust goes to one. This is the same as in the cooperative equilibrium; cooperative behavior reassures the other side completely.

If the other side defects, however, the observing state is still uncertain about what type it faces. The other side could be expansionist, or it could be security seeking but fearful of the other player. This makes the spiral possible. What we would like to know is, if player j defects (event JD), what should one's beliefs be about the likelihood that it is security seeking? These beliefs differ for each type, and they are shown in Table 3.4. It is worth pausing a moment to point out that these expressions are the core of the Spiral Game, the bit of math towards which this chapter has been leading. The whole thrust of the spiral model argument is that security seeking states become more fearful of each other because they observe the other side defect. These expressions tells us what a player will believe after observing a defection by the other side. If the spiral model logic works in the case of perfectly rational actors, then this posterior level of trust will

TABLE 3.4
The Likelihood that Player j Is Trustworthy Given that He Defected

If player i is a trusting security seeker	$p(JS\|IS, js, JD) = \dfrac{t_j(1-\varepsilon_j)\varepsilon_i}{t_j(1-\varepsilon_j)\varepsilon_i + (1-t_j)\varepsilon_j}$
If player i is a fearful security seeker	$p(JS\|IS, je, JD) = \dfrac{t_j\varepsilon_j\varepsilon_i}{t_j\varepsilon_j\varepsilon_i + (1-t_j)(1-\varepsilon_j)}$
If player i is a trusting expansionist	$p(JS\|IE, js, JD) = \dfrac{t_j(1-\varepsilon_j)(1-\varepsilon_i)}{t_j(1-\varepsilon_j)(1-\varepsilon_i) + (1-t_j)\varepsilon_j}$
If player i is a fearful expansionist	$p(JS\|IE, je, JD) = \dfrac{t_j\varepsilon_j(1-\varepsilon_i)}{t_j\varepsilon_j(1-\varepsilon_i) + (1-t_j)(1-\varepsilon_j)}$

have declined, and it will be of interest to see how much and what affects the degree of decline.

Without further ado, it is easy to show that this posterior level of trust, after seeing a defection, *is* lower than the prior level of trust, as it should be. Defection lowers the level of trust. Unlike in the cooperative equilibrium, though, it has not reduced trust to zero, there is still uncertainty about whether the other player is security seeking or expansionist. An important implication of this is that, though the level of trust has been lowered, this increasing suspicion may be a "mistake" in the sense that the other side may actually be trustworthy. Mutual defection can lower mutual trust between security seeking types. The defecting state may have been a fearful type. Security seekers can grow more fearful of each other as a result of actions that they take to make themselves more secure.

To see how these beliefs work, consider the example illustrated in Figure 3.3. This is a continuation of the story from Figure 3.1. We now have player i's beliefs about player j at three stages. First, the initial prior, t_j, before any new information has come in. Second, the belief after the message about player j has come in, which separates the trusting from the fearful types. Finally, the beliefs after observing a defection, where each type of player i has a separate belief. As before, at the start of the learning process, player i thinks player j has a 50 percent chance of being security seeking ($t_j = 0.5$) and, hence, an equal likelihood of being expansionist.

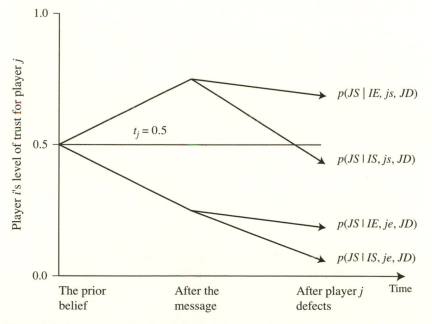

Figure 3.3 Learning in the Spiral Game (2)

The message has a 75 percent chance of being correct ($\varepsilon_j = 0.25$).[11] This means that if player i receives the js signal it will become more trusting and its belief that player j is security seeking will increase to 0.75, as shown in the upward slanting line. If player 1 receives the je signal, in contrast, its level of trust will decline to 0.25, as indicated by the downward sloping line. At this point, where the trusting type thinks player j is 75 percent likely to be security seeking but the fearful type thinks this is only 25 percent likely to be the case, they observe a defection in the spiral equilibrium.

In response to the observed defection, the level of trust of all four types declines. The greatest decline in trust is for the trusting security seeker, the second from the top. If player i is security seeking and trusting its belief that player j is trustworthy will decline from 0.75 to only 0.43, below the prior belief of $t_j = 0.5$ indicated by the horizontal line. The defection, in other words, has more than wiped out the reassuring effect of the initial positive signal from Nature. Note that in this case, player i thinks there is a 25 percent chance that player j got the ie signal and is therefore fearful, so player i is not by any means sure that its benign motivations are well known. Butterfield and Jervis argued that spirals happen because security seekers think the other side knows they are defensively motivated, and so interpret any hostility as a sign of aggression. In this case, the state thinks there is a 25 percent chance that the other side thinks it is an expansionist. Yet, its level of trust still declines sharply as a result of the other state's defection. Thus, where the spiral equilbrium holds, escalations will be provocative even though the players are not certain that the other side trusts them.

Let us consider the implications of these beliefs for the Spiral Game.

Implication 3.1   *In the spiral equilibrium, if both sides are security seeking and fearful, they will defect. So long as there is any chance at all that the other side is trusting, their defection will cause a decline in trust.*

This is the most basic implication of the spiral equilibrium. It is possible for states to rationally grow more fearful after seeing the other side defect. If we define a "spiral" to be a process in which states grow more suspicious of each other's motivations because of mutual defection, spirals are possible in the spiral equilibrium. Earlier arguments about the spiral model need to be qualified, however. Spirals can develop between perfectly rational actors; they do not depend on psychological bias or extreme beliefs. In the spiral equilbrium it is not necessary for the security seeker to be sure that the other regards it as a security seeker for the spiral logic to work. Spirals are possible as long is there is any chance at all that the other side thinks you are a security seeker. This may seem like a strong boost for defensive realism and the spiral model argument that there is something inherent in

---

[11] To keep the figure clear, I drop the case where $\varepsilon_j = 0.10$.

the structure of international relations that drives states to mistrust each other unnecessarily. However, the next section qualifies this by exploring how likely spirals are to develop between genuine security seekers.

Looking at Figure 3.3, we can deduce another implication.

Implication 3.2 *Defection will be more damaging to trust if the observer is security seeking than if it is expansionist.*

If player j defects, the security seeking type of player i will become more suspicious as a result of this act than the expansionist type of player i. This is illustrated in Figure 3.3 by the contrast between the upper and lower lines in each pair. The lower lines in each pair are the security seeking types of player i, and their trust declines dramatically in response to the defection. The upper lines are the expansionist types of player i, and their trust does not decline nearly as much. If player i is expansionist and trusting, its level of trust will only decline from 0.75 to 0.69, while the expansionist fearful type's level of trust only declines from 0.25 to 0.2. The reason that the expansionist types do not find defection as provocative is that the expansionist type, knowing it is expansionist, thinks it is relatively more likely that the other side is fearful of them, and is defecting out of fear. The security seeking type, knowing itself to be security seeking, thinks it less likely that the other side is fearful, and, hence, finds the escalation more provocative. In the case of the Cold War, David Lake argues that the West was more strongly provoked by the Soviet informal empire than the Soviets were by the Western "anarchic alliance" (Lake 2001). The model implies that we can infer from this that the West was more likely to be security seeking than the Soviet Union.

This speaks to a problem that spiral theorists have long wrestled with, namely how to deal with the expansionist and fearful state. Glaser (1992) argues that the logic of the spiral model indicates that one should reassure a fearful state but resolutely oppose an expansionist state. These recommendations come into conflict when one thinks it likely that one faces an expansionist and fearful state. If one attempts to reassure it, it will simply take advantage of all conciliatory gestures because it is driven by its aggressive motivations. On the other hand, if one resolutely opposes it, one may aggravate its fear and push it over the brink into some form of overt conflict. This problem has been thought to be difficult to solve, though the distinction between offense and defense is often invoked, along with a recommendation to build up defensive forces while avoiding offensive ones.

What the model shows, however, is that this problem is not as severe as one might think. As indicated in Figure 3.3, expansionist types are much less likely to be provoked than security seeking types. Expansionist types, knowing that they are expansionist, do not become as mistrustful in the wake of defections by the other side. They have a higher estimate of the likelihood that the other side is fearful of them, and, hence, think it quite possible that the other is defecting out of fear. Thus, the problem of how to treat the fearful expansionist type is not as much of a problem as has been thought. Resolute policies can be used with less fear of provocation than would be warranted if the likelihood that the state is security seeking were higher.

The model also sheds some light on when the problem of the expansionist and fearful state will be more or less severe. As the information environment improves, ε_1 and ε_2 decease, this problem will diminish because expansionist types will become quite sure that the other side is on to them and, hence, is defecting out of fear. If the information environment is poor, however, ε_1 and ε_2 are near 0.5, then the problem will be more severe because the security seeking and expansionist types will have similar beliefs and expansionist types will be less sure that the other side is fearful of them. The greater the likelihood that the expansionist type thinks the other side might trust them, the more provocative a defection will be and the worse the problem of this type of state will become.

Another implication concerns how these posterior levels of trust respond to changes in the accuracy of the information states have about each other, ε_1 and ε_2. It is easy to show that $\frac{\partial p(JS|IS, js, JD)}{\partial \varepsilon_i} > 0$ and $\frac{\partial p(JS|IE, js, JD)}{\partial \varepsilon_i} < 0$ and similarly for the fearful types, leading to the following implication.

Implication 3.3 *Increasing the accuracy of information about a player will make the decline in trust for another player who defects more severe if the first player is a security seeker and less severe if it is expansionist.*

The reasoning here is, if the other side is trustworthy, they will only defect if they are also fearful. From the perspective of a security seeking type, this is increasingly unlikely as the signal about their own type becomes more accurate. A defection therefore comes as more of a surprise and sharply deepens the level of mistrust. From the perspective of an expansionist type, however, the other side's posterior level of trust falls as the signal accuracy improves. If player 1 is expansionist and ε_1 is smaller, then player 2 becomes more likely to be fearful. Player 1, knowing this, is less surprised by a defection; a trustworthy player 2 could very well have defected out of fear.

THE EXTERNAL OBSERVER'S PERSPECTIVE

A final set of implications have to do with the external observer's perspective. So far we have considered how the participants' beliefs react to each other's defections. But what should we as social scientists and historians think when we observe defection? We can analyze this problem by considering the perspective of someone who knows how accurate the information is, ε_1 and ε_2, but not the content of the messages. As observers, therefore, we have prior beliefs about how likely the states are to be security seekers and expansionists, and we also have beliefs about how likely they are to be trusting or fearful of each other. However, we are not certain in any of these beliefs and wish to use the parties' behavior to update our beliefs rationally, just as the players do.

For the external observer, as for the parties, the posterior level of trust will depend on what equilibrium is being played. The cases of the noncooperative and the cooperative equilibria are the same in the Spiral Game as they were in the Security Dilemma Game of the last chapter. In the noncooperative equilibrium, a pooling equilibrium, since all types behave the same by defecting, external observers will learn nothing about the players' preferences. The posterior beliefs will be the same as the priors. In the cooperative equilibrium, the types separate cleanly so that if a player cooperates, the observer knows it is a security seeker and if it defects, the observer knows it is expansionist. Thus, cooperative equilibria are quite informative to external observers, while noncooperative equilibria are completely uninformative.

The case of the spiral equilibrium is less clean cut, but still informative. In a spiral equilibrium, if a player cooperates, the observer can deduce that it is a trusting security seeker, and, hence, is definitely trustworthy. This much is the same as in the cooperative equilibrium. If the player defects, however, the situation is more complicated. I will consider four questions. First, how should the external observer's beliefs change in response to one side defecting, leaving aside what the other side might have done? Second, if one side cooperates but the other defects, how should our level of trust for the uncooperative player change? Third, if both sides defect, what affects how much our level of trust for each player falls? Fourth, if we see mutual defection, how likely is it that both sides are security seekers, and that the conflict is therefore tragic?

If an observer sees player 2 defect, but does not observe what player 1 does, its posterior level of trust for player 2 will be the following:[12]

$$p(2S|2D) = \frac{t_2[t_1\varepsilon_1 + (1 - t_1)(1 - \varepsilon_1)]}{t_2[t_1\varepsilon_1 + (1 - t_1)(1 - \varepsilon_1)] + 1 - t_2}.$$

The first implication we can draw from this is that the external observer should become less trusting of a party after observing it defect; the posterior

---

[12] I switch to the players' proper names (1 and 2) to signify that as external observers we are interested in the motivations of specific actors.

level of trust is lower than the prior level, $p(2S|2D) < t_2$. This result is similar to that in the cooperative equilibrium but not as extreme; the observer's trust is weakened but not destroyed.

Implication 3.4 *In the spiral equilibrium, defection lowers an external observer's level of trust for a noncooperative actor.*

This may seem rather obvious, but it is surprisingly at variance with typical spiral model arguments. As discussed in chapter 1, defensive realists and spiral theorists proceed from the assumption that states primarily seek security, and attempt to explain their defection through a combination of fear and security concerns. The ability to come up with such an explanation is taken as evidence for the acceptability of maintaining the original assumption of security seeking states. This style of argumentation, however, is inconsistent with Bayesian updating on the part of the observer, or social scientist. The observer, like the parties, is not certain of the motivations of the states concerned. The observer, like the parties, must make inferences about these motivations from the observable indicators, including the parties' behavior. The fact that it is possible that a noncooperative party is a fearful security seeker does not mean that this possibility is the most likely one, nor that the observer's level of trust should be constant, much less fixed at certainty that the parties are security seekers. Rational social scientists need to update their beliefs in accordance with Baysian theory, not maintain fixed beliefs in the face of contrary evidence.

Next, consider the case where the observer sees one side cooperate and the other side defect. If player 1 cooperates and player 2 defects, the observer's posterior level of trust for player 2 is as follows:

$$p(2S|1C, 2D) = \frac{t_2 \varepsilon_1 (1 - \varepsilon_2)}{t_2 \varepsilon_1 (1 - \varepsilon_2) + (1 - t_2)\varepsilon_2}. \tag{3.3}$$

This posterior level of trust may be lower than the prior, as in the case just discussed, because player 2's defection sends a bad signal about its own motivations. However, the observer now sees player 1 cooperate. This has the direct effect of reassuring the observer about player 1; the observer is now convinced that player 1 is a trusting security seeker. Intriguingly, however, player 1's cooperation also has the indirect effect of reassuring the observer about player 2. Player 1 received the message that player 2 is a security seeker, and therefore became trusting and cooperated. Player 1's cooperation has the effect of conveying the benign message about player 2 to the external observer, which goes some ways towards counteracting the negative signal conveyed by player 2's own defection. Which effect will dominate depends on the accuracy of the messages, ε_1, and ε_2.

As the information improves about player 1, ε_1 gets smaller, the external observer becomes more suspicious of player 2 $\frac{\partial p(2S|1C,2D)}{\partial \varepsilon_1} > 0$. The external observer has seen player 1 cooperate. Therefore, player 1 has shown itself to be a security seeker, because only trusting security seekers cooperate. The better the information about player 1, the more likely it is that player 2 knew that player 1 was a security seeker before it had to move. Since better information about player 1 makes player 2 more likely to be trusting, it becomes less likely that player 2 is a fearful security seeker, and more likely that it defected out of expansionist motivations. Therefore, the external observer becomes less trusting of player 2, the better the information about player 1 is.

As the information about player 2 becomes less accurate, ε_2 increases, the observer's posterior level of trust declines, $\frac{\partial p(2S|1C,2D)}{\partial \varepsilon_2} < 0$. Since player 1 cooperated, we know that it is a trusting security seeker. Since it is trusting, it must have received the benign message about player 2's motivations. The less likely this message is to be correct, the less likely player 2 is to really be trustworthy, and so the less the external observer will trust player 2. Thus, the less accurate the information about player 2, the less influence player 1's cooperation will have on the observer's level of trust for player 2.

The observer's level of trust for player 2 in the case that player 1 cooperates and player 2 defects is illustrated in Figure 3.4. The vertical axis is the observer's level of trust for player 2, higher values indicate greater

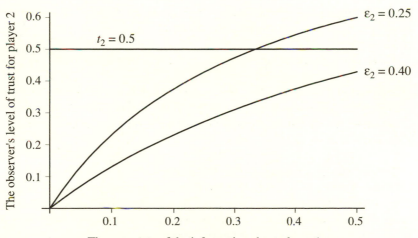

Figure 3.4 The External Observer's Beliefs about Player 2 if Player 1 Cooperates and Player 2 Defects

trust. The prior level of trust for player 2 is set at $t_2 = 0.5$, so player 2 is equally likely to be security seeking or expansionist. The horizontal axis is the accuracy of the information about player 1, ε_1. Towards the origin we have accurate information about player 1; farther away the information becomes increasingly less accurate. The top curve represents the case where $\varepsilon_2 = 0.25$, a middling level of accuracy of information about player 2. In this case, if the information about player 1 is not very accurate, to the right, the observer may end up more trusting of player 2 than it started (note the curve goes above the horizontal line representing the prior belief, 0.5). This is because player 1's cooperation signals the observer that it got a good message about player 2, and since the information about player 1 is not accurate, it is quite possible that player 2 got a mistaken message about player 1 and ended up fearful. As the accuracy of the information about player 1 improves, however, to the left, the observer's level of trust for player 2 declines to zero, because player 1's cooperation shows it to be a security seeker, and if the information about a security seeker is good, the other side should cooperate if it is a security seeker as well.

The bottom curve represents the case where the information about player 2 is less accurate, $\varepsilon_2 = 0.40$. In this case, the external observer's level of trust for player 2 will decline from the prior belief regardless of the accuracy of the information about player 1 (note the curve is below 0.5 throughout). The information about player 2 is so inaccurate that the signal sent by player 1's cooperation is swamped by player 2's defection. The observer realizes that player 1 is trusting, but also knows that this may very well be a mistake, and player 2's defection is taken as stronger evidence about player 2's motivations. Once again, the better the information about player 1, the less trusting the external observer will grow to be of player 2.

These considerations are summed up in the following implication.

Implication 3.5 *If one side cooperates and the other defects, an external observer's level of trust for the defecting party will fall further the more accurate the information about the side that cooperates is, and the less accurate the information about the side that defects is.*

This implication has bearing on the analysis of the Cold War. In several instances, a case can be made that the United States cooperated in the early Cold War while the Soviets defected. Because U.S. society was relatively open and the Soviet Union relatively closed, it seems safe to argue that Russian information about the United States was more accurate than U.S. information about Russia. This exacerbates the negative impact of Soviet noncooperation. Better information about the United States should have led the Soviets to be more trusting, hence, more likely to cooperate in the spiral equilibrium if they were security seeking. The fact that they defected raises the likelihood that they were expansionists.

Next, consider the case in which both parties defect. If both players defect, the external observer's posterior level of trust for player 1 is

$$p(1S|1D, 2D)$$
$$= \frac{t_1 t_2 \varepsilon_1 \varepsilon_2 + t_1(1 - t_2)(1 - \varepsilon_2)}{t_1 t_2 \varepsilon_1 \varepsilon_2 + t_1(1 - t_2)(1 - \varepsilon_2) + (1 - t_1)t_2(1 - \varepsilon_1) + (1 - t_1)(1 - t_2)}.$$

It can easily be shown that as an external observer we should become less trusting of a player after witnessing mutual defection, $p(1S|1D, 2D) < t_1$. More interesting, but also intuitive, is the fact that the posterior level of trust for a state will be lower the more likely the observer thinks the *other* state is to be a security seeker, $\frac{\partial p(1S|1D,2D)}{t_2} < 0$. If the observer thinks the other state is likely to be a security seeker, it sees less excuse for the defection of the first state, and therefore its level of trust for it falls strongly. Conversely, if the other state is likely to be an expansionist, the first state is likely to be fearful, and the observer's level of trust for it will not fall as much after seeing it defect.

> **Implication 3.6** *If both sides defect, the observer's level of trust for each will decline. The decline in the observer's level of trust for one side will be smaller the more likely the other side is to be expansionist.*

This implication also has direct relevance for the Cold War. Instances of mutual defection should make us as observers more suspicious of both the United States and the Soviet Union. However, as a result of previous behavior or other factors, we may believe that one side is more trustworthy than the other going into the interaction. If, with the traditionalists, we believe that the Soviet Union is not very trustworthy, our level of trust for the United States will not fall very much even if the United States defects, because we think the United States was motivated by fear. Revisionists, who think the United States likely to be expansionist, will not become too much more suspicious of the Soviet Union following Soviet defections.

Finally, we can ask how likely the external observer should believe it to be, having seen mutual defection, that *both* players are security seekers. In the spiral equilibrium, the fearful security seekers defect, and if two of them face each other, then both will become increasingly suspicious of each other even though both have security seeking preferences and have defected out of fear of the other. This is the scenario envisioned by Jervis, Butterfield, and Sir Edward Grey, the spiral of fear between security seekers. I call this type of spiral a "tragic spiral" because the fears on both sides are mistaken, since both sides are really security seeking. In contrast, a "nontragic" spiral is a spiral in which at least one side is expansionist, so that the fears that build up are at least partly justified, and conflict would have been inevitable in any case.

While the Spiral Game shows that tragic spirals are possible, it is worth considering how likely they are. Should we expect tragic spirals to be rare or common? Another way of asking this is, in what fraction of cases of mutual defection are both parties really trustworthy security seekers? Bayes rule and Table 3.2 yield the following.

$$p(1S, 2S|1D, 2D)$$
$$= \frac{t_1 t_2 \varepsilon_1 \varepsilon_2}{t_1 t_2 \varepsilon_1 \varepsilon_2 + (1 - t_1)t_2(1 - \varepsilon_1) + t_1(1 - t_2)(1 - \varepsilon_2) + (1 - t_1)(1 - t_2)}$$

As expected, after the defection the observer is less trusting of the two players; the posterior likelihood that they are both security seekers is less than the prior, $p(1S, 2S|1D, 2D) < t_1 t_2$. If you increase the accuracy of the signals, (lower ε_i), the function decreases. That is, the more likely the parties are to have accurate information, the less likely it is that an observed conflict will actually be a tragic spiral. The more accurate the information, the less likely the security seekers will be fearful. Since it takes a mistaken fearful security seeker to generate a tragic spiral, tragic spirals become less likely as mistakes become rarer.

The likelihood of tragic spirals is illustrated in Figure 3.5. The vertical axis is the percentage of conflicts that are tragic spirals, in which both players are security seeking but defect out of fear. The horizontal axis is the likelihood that the message is incorrect, ε_i, so near the origin, the

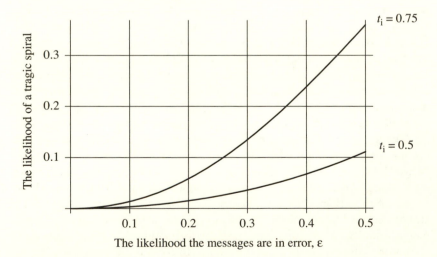

Figure 3.5 The Likelihood of a Tragic Spiral

message is accurate and, to the right, the information gets less and less accurate. Here I illustrate the symmetric case, where ε_1 equals ε_2. The curves indicate the proportion of conflicts that are tragic spirals. The top curve is the case where the prior levels of trust, t_1 and t_2, are equal to 0.75; the bottom curve is the case where the prior level of trust is 0.5. In the top case where the players are more likely to be security seeking, the likelihood of a conflict being a tragic spiral is higher. For instance, for relatively inaccurate information, $\varepsilon_i = 0.4$, there is a 24 percent chance that an observed conflict is a tragic spiral. Even with these optimistic priors, however, the likelihood of a conflict being a tragic spiral is relatively small. As information improves, the likelihood of facing a tragic spiral declines, approaching zero as the error rate of the message declines to zero.

In the bottom curve where the players have a 50 percent chance of being security seekers, the likelihood of a conflict being a tragic spiral even when $\varepsilon_i = 0.4$ is only 7 percent and declines quickly with more accurate information. If we use the numbers from the example illustrated in Figure 3.3, the likelihood of a tragic spiral explaining a conflict is only 2 percent. In other words, if the players are equally likely to be security seeking or expansionist, and the information they get about the other side has a 25 percent chance of being wrong, only 2 percent of observed mutual conflicts will be tragic spirals. The other 98 percent will involve expansionist states so conflict will be inevitable and not tragic.

This suggests the following implication of the model.

Implication 3.7 *Tragic spirals between security seekers are likely to be a small proportion of observed conflicts, especially as information improves.*

This reminds us that we should not jump to conclusions about the nature of observed conflicts, thinking that they must be tragic occurrences between basically security seeking individuals. It is far more likely that they are not tragic and involve genuinely expansionist individuals who are not interested in cooperation (Oye 1986: 7).

A final implication of the model for external observers has to do with the question of which equilibrium is being played. As we have just seen, what the observer should believe about a player after observing its behavior depends on what equilibrium the players enact. Unfortunately, the observer may be as uncertain about what equilibrium is being played as it is about whether the players are trustworthy or not. One reason for this is the possibility of multiple equilibria discussed earlier. The noncooperative equilibrium is technically possible throughout the parameter space, and, hence, is possible wherever the spiral and cooperative equilibria are. The spiral and cooperative equilibria also overlap in the shaded area of Figure 3.2.

Fortunately, the Spiral Game does suggest what evidence would be useful in drawing inferences about what equilibrium is being played: direct evidence about the parties' beliefs. If the players engage in noncooperative behavior but the available data suggests that they do not grow more suspicious of each other, this is strong evidence that the noncooperative equilibrium is being played. In turn, we as analysts should not grow more suspicious of them, and the offensive realist worldview will be appropriate. Conversely, if the parties do grow more fearful of each other in the wake of defections, anticipate that this will happen, and discuss the pros and cons of various strategies with reference to the effects on others' perceptions of their motivations, it is strong evidence that either the spiral or the cooperative equilibrium is in place. In both of these equilibria, beliefs change in response to behavior and the parties are aware of this. As to the distinction between the spiral and cooperative equilibrium, the spiral equilibrium will be supported if evidence suggests that players grow less trusting of each other in response to noncooperation but not totally convinced that the other side is untrustworthy. The cooperative equilibrium will be supported if the players' beliefs swing radically in reaction to observed defections, such that they become totally convinced the adversary is expansionist.

These considerations can be summed up in the following implication.

Implication 3.8 *If beliefs do not change in response to behavior, the noncooperative equilibrium is supported. If beliefs change radically in response to behavior, the cooperative equilibrium is supported. If beliefs change gradually in response to behavior, the spiral equilibrium is supported.*

One possible objection to this whole line of analysis is to argue that we as external observers should try to uncover direct evidence about the motivations and beliefs of the actors, and not allow ourselves to be swayed by obvious public events. After time has passed, we often gain access to documents that contain such direct evidence. Should not these be the focus of analysis, and should we not be explaining events with reference to such evidence, rather than letting events color our understanding of the preferences and beliefs discussed by the documents?

Historical documents are very important. However, sometimes, for some countries, they continue to be elusive and incomplete. A major case in the context of the Cold War is, of course, the Soviet Union. While we now have access to Soviet documents undreamed of during the Cold War, the overall record is still sporadic. More generally, documents provide one source of information about state preferences and beliefs; state behavior provides another. To form a full picture, both sources should be used; in fact a more complete model of historical learning would explicitly model other sources of information and how they are produced by states, recorded in archives, and uncovered and used by historians. Given that events are always available for analysis and documents only sometimes, there is an obvious priority in developing statistical tools for the analysis of the implications of the events themselves (Signorino 2003; Lewis and Schultz 2003). The task is no less pressing for qualitative researchers. Many of the most crucial interactions internationally are with states with the least degree of openness, such as North Korea. The content of documents can modify our beliefs if they contain evidence that counteracts the impact of state actions, but even in the best cases they do not render the events irrelevant to our beliefs. In the historical chapters that follow, I will attempt to informally combine evidence from historical materials along with analysis of the impact of events on beliefs.

Conclusion

The spiral model can be understood as a rational response to uncertainty about how others perceive one's own motivations. When security seeking types are not sure how much others trust them, they will grow more suspicious of each other if they fail to cooperate. This does not mean that tragic spirals are likely, however, or that when we see conflict we should interpret it as a tragic spiral. Conflict between genuinely expansionist types is more likely. However, to determine whether a tragic spiral has occurred, of course, requires historical investigation. The next chapter turns to the question of the origins of the Cold War. Conflict certainly occurred, and a good case can be made that beliefs became more suspicious, at least on the American side. Thus, the early Cold War would seem to qualify as a spiral. Whether the conflict was a tragic spiral or a nontragic one will be the key question.

Appendix

Glossary of the Term "Spiral"

I use the word "spiral" in several related phrases:

Spiral Model: The general set of arguments, some rational, some psychological, developed by historians and political scientists to the effect that security competition between security seeking states can exacerbate mistrust.

Spiral Game: My game theoretic representation of a subset of these arguments.

Spiral Equilibrium: One equilibrium in this game, in which spirals may happen.

Spiral: One possible outcome in a spiral equilibrium, in which both sides defect and hence grow more fearful of each other.

Tragic Spiral: One kind of spiral, in which both sides are security seeking.

Nontragic Spiral: The other and more prevalent kind of spiral, in which at least one side is expansionist.

The Spiral/Cooperative Equilibria

In addition to the equilibria discussed above, there are two asymmetric equilbria. In one, the security seeking types of player 1 both cooperate, as in the cooperative equilibrium, while for player 2, the security seeking trusting type cooperates while the security seeking fearful type defects, as in the spiral equilibrium. In the other one, these roles are reversed, player 1 plays as in a spiral equilibrium while player 2 plays as in a cooperative equilibrium. Let player i be the one who cooperates when fearful and player j be the one who only cooperates when trusting.

For the fearful type of player i to cooperate, it must be that it is willing to cooperate given that only the security seeking and trusting type of player j is expected to cooperate. Therefore, the condition required for this to happen is the reverse of that in the spiral equilibrium, $p(JS, is|IS, je) \geq m_i$. Given that this is the case, the security seeking and trusting type of player i will definitely be willing to cooperate, since it is more trusting than the security seeking fearful player i.

For player j, the security seeking trusting type must be willing to cooperate, given that both trusting and fearful security seeking types of player i will cooperate. The condition here is $p(IS|is) \geq m_j$ which, solving for the priors, gives

$$t_i \geq \frac{\phi_i \varepsilon_i}{(1 - \varepsilon_i)[\frac{c_j + l_j}{g_j^i + l_j} - \pi_j - \phi_j + \phi_i] - \phi_i(1 - 2\varepsilon_i)}.$$

Note this is lower than the constraint in the spiral equilibrium because both security seeking types of player i are cooperating. For the security seeking and fearful type of player j, he must not be willing to cooperate even though both security seeking types of player i are expected to cooperate, so the condition here is the reverse of that in the cooperative equilibrium, $p(IS|ie) \leq m_j$.

CHAPTER 4

The Origins of Mistrust: 1945–50

> My task as minister of foreign affairs was to expand the borders of
> our Fatherland. And it seems that Stalin and I coped with this task
> quite well.
>
> —V. M. Molotov

IN THE SPRING of 1945 American, British, and Soviet armies converged on
Germany, destroyed its military forces, and occupied the country. American
and Soviet soldiers shook hands over their defeated enemy and many hoped
that, with Fascism overthrown, the world could return to peace. Over
the next five years, however, relations between the wartime allies deteriorated and by 1950 two armed camps faced each other across the boundary
separating the Eastern and Western blocs.

In this chapter I will use historical evidence in conjunction with the
implications of the Spiral Game to make inferences about the most likely
explanation of the Cold War. I will focus on the motivations, beliefs and
actions of the United States and Soviet Union from 1945–50. I argue that
there is a fair amount of direct evidence that the United States was a security
seeker, and at least some direct evidence that the Soviets were expansionist. The United States was also relatively trusting of the Soviet Union in
early 1945, and grew progressively more fearful by 1950, whereas the
Soviets appear to have been fearful throughout. Finally, the United States
cooperated in important ways in the early Cold War, reflecting its more
trusting beliefs, while the Soviet Union defected in a series of important
cases. The efforts of the Soviet Union to dominate the weak states on its
periphery in Eastern Europe, the Near East, and the Far East increased
Western fears of Soviet motivations. Furthermore, these actions should
also increase the suspicions of external observers and historians, given the
absence of strong evidence that these fears were misplaced and a limited
amount of documentary evidence that they were well-founded. These find-
ings have relevance for the debate over the origins of the Cold War. In
particular they correspond with the traditionalist view that explains the
Cold War with reference to Soviet expansionist motives and undermine
the postrevisionist view based on offensive and defensive realism. The historical record supports the inference that the Cold War is most likely to

have been a nontragic spiral in which the United States started out as a trusting security seeker and was converted by Soviet defections into a fearful one.

In the next section I will discuss several views of the Cold War, drawn from the international relations theory and historiographical literature. Then, I review the early history of the Cold War and Soviet efforts to control its periphery, and trace the effects of these efforts on Western perceptions, and in light of the implications of the Spiral Game, on our own.

EXPLAINING THE ORIGINS OF THE COLD WAR

The origins of the Cold War are the subject of a vast and growing literature (Kort 1998). There are a host of competing explanations that can be organized in many ways. I will focus on explanations concerned with the motivations and beliefs of the two sides.

The literature on the origins of the Cold War is commonly structured around four schools of thought based on the motivations attributed to the two parties, depicted in Table 4.1, which is adapted from Table 2.2.[1] Postrevisionists argue that both sides were security seekers. Traditionalists code the United States as a security seeker and the Soviets as expansionist. Revisionists code the Soviets as security seeking and the United States as expansionist. Orwellians code both states as expansionists.

Postrevisionism (Offensive and Defensive Realism)

The postrevisionist perspective holds that both sides were security seekers. John Lewis Gaddis, the father of the postrevisionist approach,[2] argues, "Both Washington and Moscow wanted peace, but strong internal influences caused each to conceive of it in contradictory ways. These clashing perceptions of a common goal wrecked the Grand Alliance at the moment of victory, creating an ironic situation in which simultaneous searches for peace led to the Cold War." (Gaddis 1972: 3). The strongest recent argument on behalf of this perspective in the historiographic literature is Melvyn Leffler's *A Preponderance of Power.* According to Leffler, as quoted in the previous chapter, "Neither the Americans nor the Soviets sought to harm the other in 1945. But each side, in pursuit of its security interests,

---

[1]See Gamson and Modigliani 1971: 26 for a similar taxonomy of Cold War theories. The perspective I am calling "Orwellianism" is usually omitted from discussions of the U.S. literature, though it is included by Gamson and Modigliani and is represented by a few prominent authors. Some fail to distinguish it from revisionism.

[2]Gaddis has subsequently shifted to the traditionalist camp, see chapter 8.

TABLE 4.1
Perspectives on the Cold War

		U.S.S.R.	
		Security Seeking	*Expansionist*
U.S.	*Security Seeking*	Postrevisionism (Offensive and Defensive Realism)	Traditionalism
	Expansionist	Revisionism	Orwellianism

took steps that aroused the other's apprehensions." (Leffler 1992: 99). The Cold War is not anyone's fault; it was a product of anarchy and security fears.

The postrevisionist assumption that the United States and Soviets were both security seekers is shared by both offensive and defensive realism. Given that the two theories have quite divergent implications, two very distinct versions of postrevisionism must be kept in mind.[3] The offensive realist explanation of the Cold War treats the level of mistrust as a background variable and focuses on power. States seek security, but cannot trust each other, so are forced to compete for power. The United States and the Soviet Union were the most powerful states in the system after the Second World War, and, as such, were destined to confront each other. This is not because they distrusted each other's motivations any more than they distrusted anyone else's motivations, but simply because only the United States had the power to harm the Soviet Union, and vice versa (Mearsheimer 2001: 36, 256–57, 322, 333; Waltz 1979: 170). Although both parties were security seekers, they were too fearful to cooperate with each other. Furthermore, the two players enacted the noncooperative equilibrium of the models of the previous two chapters. In this equilibrium, all types defect, and, hence, there is no learning or updating of beliefs. Mistrust causes defection, which leaves beliefs unaffected, leading to more defection.

The defensive realist approach accords a greater role to the level of mistrust. As in the offensive realist view, both sides are coded as security seeking and in addition they are fearful of each other's motivations, so they are security seeking/fearful types in the Spiral Game. Contrary to offensive realism, however, they played the spiral equilibrium rather than the noncooperative equilibrium. As a result, their beliefs changed in response to the behavior

---

[3]These distinctions are not clear in the historiographical literature in part because the post-revisionist school was influenced by the earlier realist literature, such as Waltz 1979, in which the distinctions had not yet crystallized.

they observed, and they became more suspicious of each other over time. The Cold War is seen as a tragic spiral in which two states became more fearful of each other despite the fact that they were true security seekers. Defensive realism is explicitly endorsed by Leffler and quite in line with Gaddis's 1973 analysis.

Traditionalism

The traditionalist explanation of the Cold War (also known as the orthodox view) portrays the Soviet Union as an inherently expansionist power, interested in exploiting cooperation, not reciprocating it, that is, untrustworthy. Usually, the blame is laid on communism as an ideology. As a universalistic revolutionary ideology, it provided a motivation to overthrow existing governments in the capitalist world, a justification for totalitarian rule in the Soviet Union and a rationale for Soviet domination of the emerging socialist bloc. However, the continuity with traditional Russian expansionism is also emphasized (Ulam 1974: 5–12). The United States, on the other hand is coded as a security seeker; trusting at first, and then increasingly fearful as time went by. The United States had no desire to conquer the world, but was merely interested in preserving its security from a second possible totalitarian hegemon, having helped defeat the first, Nazi Germany. The Cold War is therefore seen as a nontragic spiral in which a security seeking United States became more fearful of the Soviets in response to noncooperation on their part, but this fear was simply a correct appreciation of Soviet expansionist motivations, not a mistake. This view was prevalent in the United States while the Cold War was getting underway, and remained relatively unchallenged until the 1960s.[4]

Revisionism

The revisionist view is the flip side of the traditionalist view. Here the Cold War is blamed on the intrinsically expansionist nature of the United States.[5] Revisionists argue that the United States staged a confrontation with the Soviet Union in order to generate domestic support for an expansionist foreign policy, and to divert attention from economic disparities at home (Kolko and Kolko, 1972: 6–7, 11–15). The founder of revisionism, William Appleman Williams, traces this expansionist drive to the open

---

[4]Traditionalist works include Acheson 1969; Feis 1970; Ulam 1974; Taubman 1982; Woods and Jones 1991; Gaddis 1997; and Macdonald 1995/96.

[5]Key revisionist works include Williams 1959; LaFeber 1997; and Kolko and Kolko 1972. See Buzzanco 1999 for a review.

door policy of the turn of the century (Williams 1959: 35–39). American expansion, after the war as before, was necessitated by the the fear that without foreign markets, the U.S. economy would languish, which could endanger social stability, or more pointedly, the priviledged position of wealthy elites (Williams 1959: 166–67, 173–79; LaFeber 1997: 8). In this regard, the revisionist historians draw heavily from classical theories of imperialism and the imperialism of free trade (Hobson 1988 [1902]; Lenin 1996 [1916]; Gallagher and Robinson 1953). Thus, the United States is coded as expansionist, unwilling to reciprocate Russian cooperation, but bent on exploiting it. The Cold War is seen as a nontragic spiral in which the Soviets came to believe that the United States was bent on expansion and would not cooperate, and this belief was correct.

Orwellianism

A logical combination of both of the above perspectives contends that both the United States and the Russians were inherently expansionist countries. The most eloquent expression of this view, couched as a warning about the future, is George Orwell's *1984*. In Orwell's distopia, Oceania and Eurasia fight an interminable war that serves to justify totalitarian rule at home. The war and the hate campaigns that accompany it redirect popular frustration outward, propping up inefficient and oppressive regimes. E. P. Thompson, after his break with Stalinism, also adopted this interpretation of the Cold War (Thompson 1957, 1985).[6] Noam Chomsky takes this position when he argues, "for the USSR the Cold War has been primarily a war against its satellites, and for the U.S. a war against the Third World. For each it has served to entrench a particular system of domestic privilege and coercion" (Chomsky 1991: 28, 33, 1982: 192). While Chomsky, like the revisionists, is mostly concerned with criticizing U.S. behavior in the Third World, Mary Kaldor provides a more balanced analysis that fully explores the Orwellian dynamic on the Soviet side as well. She dubs the Cold War an "imaginary war" between "Atlanticisim" and Stalinism, which played the role of a "disciplinary technology" that "serves to maintain social cohesion" (Kaldor 1990: 4).[7] In East Europe, resistance to Soviet rule produced instability that, "was the reason for reproducing the military and police apparatus, for continued preparation for war, and for real wars" (Kaldor 1990: 69). The Cold War, if it was is a spiral at all, was doubly nontragic, since both sides were genuinely expansionist and would only exploit cooperation by the other side.

---

[6]See also C. Wright Mills 1958.

[7]Kaldor even displays a version of Table 4.1 and explicitly locates her theory in the hitherto blank spot I have labeled the Orwellian perspective (Kaldor 1990: 41).

Evaluating the Perspectives

The implications of the Spiral Game from the previous chapter help us identify questions to ask of the historical record that will allow us to make inferences about the relative likelihood of the various perspectives. The central questions are the following.

First, what direct evidence do we have about the parties' motivations and beliefs? Such evidence can come from government documents, memoirs and other reminiscences, as well as public opinion polls in the United States. One of the fundamental asymmetries of the Cold War is that this kind of evidence is much more plentiful for the United States than for the Soviet Union; indeed the dearth of such evidence for the Soviet side provides one of the central rationales for developing other ways to draw inferences on this topic. Nonetheless, there is some evidence available on both sides. Evidence that the United States is a security seeker supports postrevisionism and traditionalism, while evidence that they are expansionist supports revisionism and Orwellianism. Evidence that the Soviets are security seekers supports postrevisionism and revisionism, while evidence that they are expansionist supports traditionalism and Orwellianism. Note that implication 3.7 says that tragic spirals are rare in comparison with nontragic ones. This implies that strong direct evidence that the parties are security seekers will be required to offset the damaging inferences that may arise if the parties defect in a spiral equilibrium. Absent such direct evidence, it will be relatively unlikely that both sides are security seekers if they end up in conflict.

Second, do the beliefs of the parties change in response to defections, or remain the same? Implication 3.8 tells us that if beliefs are static, the parties are likely to be in a pooling equilibrium, the noncooperative equilibrium in which all types are expected to defect. This would strongly support the offensive realist version of postrevisionism against all other perspectives, including the defensive realist version of postrevisionism. If the beliefs change over time in response to defections, however, it undercuts offensive realism and supports the other perspectives that focus on changing beliefs. If beliefs change gradually over time in response to defections, the players are likely to be in the spiral equilibrium, which enables external observers to make inferences about their type from their behavior.

Third, did the parties cooperate or defect, especially in the early Cold War? Provided the parties are in the spiral equilibrium, observing one of the parties defect will lower the other party's level of trust for it according to implication 3.1. We, as external observers, should also grow less trusting of the defecting party, according to implication 3.4. Soviet defections support traditionalism and Orwellianism, U.S. defections support revisionism and Orwellianism. These are the most basic implications of the Spiral Game.

More specifically, do we observe instances where the United States cooperates and the Soviets defect? If so, implication 3.5 tells us that because information about the United States is relatively good and information about the Soviet Union is relatively bad, our level of trust for the Soviet Union should decline even more sharply. U.S. cooperation is evidence that it is a security seeker. Since information on the United States is relatively good, the Soviets are relatively likely to have evidence to this effect. The fact that the Soviets defected anyway casts greater doubt on their motivations than would be the case if information about the United States was bad. Finally, the fact that information about the Soviets is bad increases the likelihood that the United States was misinformed about Soviet motivations, and cooperated due to being mistakenly trusting. Therefore, instances where the United States cooperates and the Soviets defect strongly support traditionalism, and undercut the other perspectives.

Finally we can consider the degree to which beliefs change. Implication 3.2 says that security seekers experience a greater fall in their level of trust if the other side defects than expansionists. This is because security seekers know themselves to be security seekers and therefore think it more likely that the other side is trusting than fearful, whereas expansionists think it more likely that the other side is fearful rather than trusting. Therefore, if one side seems to grow more fearful as a result of defections than the other, the side growing more fearful is more likely to be a security seeker while the side with less belief change is more likely to be expansionist. If the United States experiences a greater belief change, it supports traditionalism against the other perspectives, while if the Soviets experienced a stronger belief change, it would support revisionism.

How do the perspectives fare when confronted with the evidence? As we will see below, offensive realism is undercut by the fact that the United States was very concerned with Soviet motivations and became more fearful in response to Soviet behavior. The United States started out fairly trusting but grew markedly more fearful of the Soviet Union in 1945 and 1946, and the Czechoslovak coup and Korean war raised these fears to new levels. This belief change supports the inference that the parties were in a spiral equilibrium, and, hence, supports the other perspectives in which increasing fear is part of the story.

The defensive realist perspective is also undermined by the evidence. The record indicates several cases of Soviet defection and little independent evidence that the Soviets were security seekers. The postrevisionist historians acknowledge this lack of direct evidence on Soviet motivations, although it would seem to call into question their fundamental assumption that both sides were security seekers. For instance, despite his unequivocal pronouncement about neither side wanting to harm the other, Leffler admits that Soviet motivations "remain unknowable" and are "impossible to state...with any degree of certainty" (Leffler 1992: ix, 132). In the same way, Gaddis, a few pages before making his equally strong claim that both sides sought security, acknowledges that "we have little reliable information about what went on inside the Kremlin...Nor is it now feasible to make final judgments about responsibility for that conflict" (Gaddis 1972: xiii).[8] Moreover, the additional information available today tends to substantiate rather than undercut fears of Soviet expansionism.[9] In particular, evidence such as the reminiscences of Soviet Foreign Minister Viacheslav Molotov, documents relating to Soviet policy in Eastern Europe, and documents indicating Soviet complicity in the outbreak of Korean war all point to an expansionist Soviet Union. Thus, both the record of events and subsequently available information undercut the defensive realist viewpoint.

With both versions of postrevisionism undercut by the evidence, the other three interpretations become more likely. Revisionism, however, is also undercut by Soviet defections. This leaves traditionalism and Orwellianism as the most likely contenders; either the Soviets alone, or both the United States and the Soviets were expansionist. I discuss U.S. motivations in 1945 below; evidence is strong that the United States in this period sought a cooperative relationship with Russia and had little desire to invade or even subvert the Soviet Union. Even George Kennan, in his famous "long telegram" which articulated the policy of containment in February 1946 argued that the Soviet thesis of the inherent incompatibility of communism and capitalism was false, and "experience has shown that peaceful and mutually profitable coexistence of capitalist and socialist states is entirely possible" (FRUS 1946 VI: 698).[10] While expansionist U.S. actions, such as the acquisition of far-flung basing rights, may lower our trust for the United States, they are offset by cooperative actions, at least in the 1945–46 period. Hence, the record of behavior is fairly consistent with a documentary record of a trusting security seeking United States attempting to establish a cooperative relationship with the Soviets after the war.

Thus, an examination of the evidence in conjunction with the implications of the Spiral Game will show that the most likely interpretation of

---

[8] See also Nation 1992: ix–xvi, 158–60.

[9] For a debate over what the newly available archival evidence means, see *Diplomatic History* 21, no. 2, 217–305 (1997), and for a selection and discussion of documents, see the Web site of the Cold War International History Project.

[10] Throughout I will abbreviate the Foreign Relations of the United States series of documents issued by the United States Department of State as FRUS. They are referenced in the Bibliography under United States of Department of State.

the Cold War is the traditional one, followed by Orwellianism, and, more distantly, by postrevisionism and revisionism.

SETTING THE STAGE: MOTIVATIONS AND BELIEFS IN 1945

Before analyzing the record of behavior, we need to set the stage by considering the available evidence about the parties' motivations and prior beliefs in early 1945.

The United States had four essential aims for the postwar period. First was political change in the form of democracy, self-determination, and the destruction of militarism. Second was economic change, meaning the creation of an open world trading system. Third was institutional change in the form of a new international organization founded on great power cooperation and policing. Fourth was military change resulting in an increased American security presence abroad. The first is reflected in the Atlantic Charter, drawn up by Roosevelt and Churchill in August of 1941 before U.S. entry into the war, which declared that the United States and Britain would seek no territorial gains, oppose territorial changes against the will of the inhabitants, and support self-determination and self-government (Gaddis 1972: 12). This commitment harked back to Wilson's emphasis on self-determination and reflected the popular view that the war was a result of militarism and nondemocratic regimes. The second goal, an open world trading system, was believed by Secretary of State Cordell Hull, among many others, to be essential to maintaining peace and ensuring postwar prosperity (Gaddis 1972: 18–23; Kolko and Kolko 1972: 11–28; Pollard 1985: 5–18). This goal was first embodied in the 1944 Bretton Woods accords and would drive economic policy subsequently. The third goal, great power cooperation in policing the world, was essential to Roosevelt's vision of the postwar system. The "four policemen" concept envisioned the United States, Britain, the Soviet Union, and China preventing any recurrence of aggression in concert. Discussed at Tehran, it became the foundation for the United Nations Security Council, with its veto system for the great powers (Feis 1957: 270–71; Luard 1982: 17–32). The fourth goal, an expanded security presence, was embodied in plans for military bases abroad. Roosevelt approved a plan for military bases that would establish U.S. hegemony over the Atlantic and Pacific oceans; this perimeter would subsequently be extended into the Middle East (Leffler 1992: 56).

How can we characterize these goals on the security seeking expansionist dimension? The United States clearly had goals for international change, however they were limited. Territorial expansion was not sought. With respect to weaker powers, the aim was to set up democratic regimes and then encourage them to adopt an open economic system, not to set up puppet regimes that could simply be instructed to do so. U.S. influence would therefore be constrained by the ability to secure majority support for the proposed policy, which meant there had to be something in it for the weaker powers as well. With respect to the Soviet Union, the four policemen concept indicates a desire to achieve a cooperative relationship to police the world in concert, not to undermine or destroy the Soviets.

Turning to the U.S. level of trust for the Soviets, the dominant view in the United States on the Soviet Union in early 1945 was fairly benign.[11] Roosevelt felt that the Russians would cooperate if their security interests were recognized and if they could be brought to trust the Americans and British (Gaddis 1972: 7, 64; Yergin 1977: 42–43). He shared the then-popular belief that Stalin himself was relatively moderate and that Soviet noncooperation was due to Stalin being misinformed or subject to political pressure (Gaddis 1972: 93).[12] This view is now known to be mistaken; in fact, Stalin had occasion to criticize his foreign minister Molotov for his tendency to "picture himself as more liberal than the government" (Pechatnov 1999: 10).[13]

Others in the administration had similar views. A briefing book paper prepared for the Yalta conference argued that the British and Soviets were falling prey to a spiral of suspicion though, "[i]n actual fact these mutual suspicions appear to be unjustified in that it is not a fixed and calculated British policy to support right-wing elements in Europe, nor on the basis of existing evidence can it be said that the Soviet Government is determined to install Communist regimes throughout Europe" (FRUS Yalta: 102). Joint Chiefs of Staff Chief Admiral William Leahy in May of 1944 also analyzed British-Soviet relations as a security dilemma: "The greatest likelihood of eventual conflict between Britain and Russia would seem to grow out of either nation initiating attempts to build up its strength, by seeking to attach to herself parts of Europe to the disadvantage and possible danger of her potential adversary" and urged that U.S. policy should be to promote Anglo-Russian cooperation (FRUS Yalta: 108). Averell Harriman,

[11] For the evolution of U.S. views towards the Soviet Union before the war, stressing the extent to which Americans believed Marxist ideology in decline, see Mark 1989.

[12] Even the suspicious Churchill confided in an optimistic mood, "Poor Neville Chamberlain believed he could trust Hitler. He was wrong. But I don't think I am wrong about Stalin." (Yergin 1977: 65–66).

[13] Molotov was subject to repeated attacks for being too soft, was forced to divorce his wife, who was subsequently arrested and sent to the Gulag in 1949, and feared for his own life by the end of Stalin's reign (Chuev 1991: 313–28). The persistence of the myth is perhaps explainable by the fact that Stalin granted his diplomats no real flexibility, so most concessions would ultimately come directly from him. As Molotov recalled, "We had a centralized diplomacy. Ambassadors had no independence . . . It was impossible for the ambassador to take any initiative." (Chuev 1991: 69).

the ambassador to the Soviet Union, enthusiastically supported a Soviet request for a six billion dollar loan in January 1945, arguing "It is my basic conviction that we should do everything we can to assist the Soviet Union through credits in developing a sound economy. I feel strongly that the sooner the Soviet Union can develop a decent life for its people the more tolerant they will become...I am satisfied that the great urge of Stalin and his associates is to provide a better physical life for the Russian people, although they will retain a substantial military establishment" (FRUS Yalta: 314). This optimism was widely shared in the United States (Gaddis 1972: 34–42). In a March 1945 poll, 55 percent of respondents thought Russia could be trusted to cooperate with the United States after the war, as opposed to 31 percent who thought it could not (Gallup 1972: 492).[14]

Some Western observers had a darker view of the Soviet Union. Adherents to the "Riga axioms" looked to the nature of communist ideology and the previous internal behavior of the Soviets, such as the collectivization of agriculture and resulting famine and the purge trials of the later 1930s, and saw a brutal regime with no moral or legal self-restraint (Yergin 1977: 17–32). The external behavior also gave pause, especially the Molotov-Ribbentrop pact of 1939 and the resulting Soviet invasion of Poland, annexation of the Baltic states, and invasion of Finland (Raack 1995). The head of the military mission to Moscow, General John Deane, endorsed a get-tough policy in December of 1944, arguing, "Gratitude cannot be banked in the Soviet Union....The party of the second part is either a shrewd trader to be admired or a sucker to be despised....Officials dare not become too friendly with us, and others are persecuted for this offense" (FRUS Yalta: 448). These views were widespread among those who spent time in the Soviet Union, but they did not have dominant political influence in early 1945.

Turning to Soviet aims and perceptions, two schools of thought can also be distinguished. One consisted of diplomats with experience in the West, namely Maxim Litvinov, the 1930s foreign minister, Andrei Gromyko, the young ambassador to Washington, and Ivan Maisky, a former ambassador to Great Britain.[15] In documents dating to 1944–45 and released after the Cold War, these three advocated sustained cooperation with the United States and Britain in the postwar world (Pechatnov 1995; Filitov 1996; Zubok and Pleshakov 1996: 28–32). The Soviet Union would certainly acquire a sphere of influence in Eastern Europe; indeed they advocated certain aims that Stalin ultimately failed to achieve, such as trusteeship over Italian colonies and a presence at the Black Sea straits. However, they

---

[14] The average since late 1943 had been around 50 percent, up from the mid-40 percent range in the early part of the war (Cantril 1948: 39).

[15] On the "Litvinov alternative," see Roberts 2002.

advocated development of this sphere within limits imposed by agreement with Britain and the United States and, importantly, the establishment of democratic regimes. Maisky, echoing Wilson, argued that "democratic government is one of the main guarantees of durable peace" (Pechatnov 1995: 4) and, remarkably in light of subsequent events, argued that U.S. and British help in democratizing the countries of Eastern Europe would be welcome. Gromyko argued that the United States would be a force for peace and the establishment of "bourgeois-democratic political regimes," while Litvinov argued that spheres of influence should not be "detrimental to the independence of the states included in them" and noted that Britain would likely insist on this (Pechatnov 1995: 14). The imposition of communism was not seen as a near-term goal, though Maisky alluded to the eventual triumph of socialism within thirty to fifty years.

The other school can be identified with Molotov and Stalin, who had more aggressive designs and took a much darker view of the wartime allies. Molotov, in a series of conversations in the 1970s and 1980s, recalled that his job was to "expand the borders of our Fatherland" (Chuev 1991: 8). His perceptions of Western statesmen are harsh; on Churchill, "That man hated us and tried to use us. But we used him too." On the American leaders, "Roosevelt was an imperialist who would grab anyone by the throat . . . [he] knew how to conceal his attitude toward us, but Truman— he didn't know how to do that at all. He had an openly hostile attitude." The allies were seen as attempting to create a "bourgeois" Poland that would be an "agent of imperialism and hostile to the Soviet Union" (Chuev 1991: 49–54). Molotov even boasts of tricking the allies into an early promise of a second front, which when it was not fulfilled, could be used to shame more assistance out of them (Chuev 1991: 46–47). He retroactively endorsed the 1968 invasion of Czechoslovakia "from a communist position" rather than a power politics point of view, and stuck to his 1926 assertion that the ultimate goal was the triumph of socialism on a world scale. His ambitions reached comic heights when in response to a description of a 1946 army base in the Far East designed as a launch pad for an invasion of the United States he mentioned that he "wouldn't mind getting Alaska back," but that the "time hadn't arrived for such tasks" (Chuev 1991: 71).[16] Late in his life he stuck to the thesis that (nuclear) war was inevitable and that peaceful coexistence was a rightist deviation (Chuev 1991: 376–77).

Stalin appears in a similar light. Milovan Djilas quotes Stalin as asserting in 1945 that "This war is not as in the past; whoever occupies a

---

[16] His insight on American politics was almost as comical, he commented that the United States was the most suitable country for socialism and that it would come earlier there than elsewhere.

territory also imposes on it his own social system. Everyone imposes his own social system as far as his army can reach. It cannot be otherwise." Looking at a map of the Soviet Union, Stalin worried that the Americans and British "will never accept the idea that so great a space should be red" (Djilas 1962: 114, 74). In another map story, Stalin is said to have expressed satisfaction with the expanded borders that had been achieved at the expense of Japan in the East, Finland in the North, and the Eastern European states in the West, but complained, "I don't like our border right here!" pointing to the Caucasus mountains and the border with Iran (Chuev 1991: 8). Stalin confided to the former Comintern head Georgi Dimitrov that though they were currently fighting with democratic capitalists against fascist capitalists, they would eventually turn against the former (Zubok and Pleshakov 1996: 37). Yet, because of Soviet weakness, that day should be postponed, and, hence, the Yugoslavs were constantly urged to soft pedal their revolutionary goals and rhetoric for the time being (Djilas 1962: 27, 31, 44, 73–74, 82). Eduard Mark presents evidence that this policy was not restricted to Yugoslavia; the Soviets pursued a "national front" strategy instructing the European communist parties to cooperate with peasants, intellectuals, and the petite bourgeoisie to acheive power gradually without alarming the British and Americans (Mark 2001; Naimark and Gibianskii 1997: 10).

Whereas in the United States the more benign view held sway, certainly while Roosevelt lived, in the Soviet Union, Stalin held absolute power and Molotov remained foreign minister because his views coincided with Stalin's. The Litvinov-Maisky-Gromyko analysis was peripheral and would ultimately have little influence. Hence, available direct evidence, sparse as it is, increases the likelihood that the Soviets were both more expansionist and more fearful than the United States. The Soviet Union did seek territorial gains. They sought to impose their system as far as their army could reach, regardless of whether their system could be sustained by a democratic majority in the recipient states. They foresaw renewed conflict with capitalism, rather than a period of great power cooperation to police the world. They wished to see socialism supplant capitalism throughout the world, and believed that this was inevitable. And they feared that the the capitalists wished to destroy them, rather than cooperate with them.

Although the evidence suggests that the Soviets were more expansionist and more fearful than the United States, this does not mean that we can assign types to the states with certainty. Each side had goals for international change; if they valued them strongly enough in comparison with the costs of conflict, each could become untrustworthy. Each side had fears of the other, fears which might or might not prevent cooperation—hence, the need to examine the record of behavior. While I will focus mostly on the conflicts relating to Soviet expansionist behavior, I will also more briefly note other issues or events that shed light on Soviet motivations and U.S. perceptions of them. I focus primarily on 1945 and 1946 when the greatest change in perceptions took place, but I also discuss subsequent events that had similar impacts, such as the Czechoslovak coup and the Korean war. I postpone consideration of issues relating to Germany to chapter 6.

THE FATE OF POLAND

In February of 1945 the leaders of the Big Three wartime allies, Churchill, Roosevelt, and Stalin, met at the Black Sea resort of Yalta in what was widely regarded as a cordial and successful summit. Five months later in July the allies met again in the Berlin suburb of Potsdam. The war in Europe was won, and relations between the allies had already deteriorated.

The central cause of this lessening of trust was the accession to power in Eastern Europe, particularly Poland, of communist dominated regimes controlled by Moscow. While there were other conflictual issues, such as German reparations, the peace treaties, and the control of Japan, Eastern Europe appears to have been the "litmus test" of Soviet intentions (Leffler 1992: 34). In March, Churchill wired Roosevelt that Poland was "the test case between us and the Russians of the meaning which is to be attached to such terms as Democracy, Sovereignty, Independence, Representative Government, and free and unfettered elections" (FRUS 1945 V: 148). In the fall, all of these ideals were again at stake in Bulgaria and Romania. The passing of these countries under Soviet domination, so soon after Hitler's expansionist drive was crushed, aroused Western suspicion about where Soviet ambitions ended, and how they might be contained.

With respect to Poland, there were two questions, one territorial and the other political. On the territorial question, the Soviets wanted to shift Poland westwards, taking territory in the East and compensating Poland in the West at Germany's expense. Soviet territorial claims contradicted the Atlantic Charter's emphasis on self-determination and indicated Soviet expansionist desires, but the Americans and British were willing to accede after only mild objections. At the Tehran meeting in 1943 Roosevelt asked Stalin to understand that for electoral reasons he could not openly support Soviet territorial demands in Poland and the Baltics but that Stalin could help him with public opinion by promising plebiscites in the regions he planned to annex (Gaddis 1972: 138–39; Taubman 1982: 67–68). Stalin failed to see the necessity for this and the conversation ended. At Yalta, Roosevelt made a half hearted effort to get the Russians to leave Poland the area around Lvov, but Stalin held fast to the "Curzon line" drawn up by the Allies at Versailles and this too ended the discussion (FRUS Yalta: 667–69).[17]

The political question was much harder fought. The U.S. hope for the political future of Eastern Europe in early 1945 was an "open sphere" of influence in which the Soviets called the shots on foreign policy and security questions but the states of the region were free to govern themselves and have normal trading relations with the outside world (Mark 1979, 1981). In the briefing papers for the Yalta conference, the Soviets are constantly acknowledged to have a "more direct interest" in the countries of the region (FRUS Yalta: 234, 235, 237, 245, 247). However, there is a desire that U.S. influence not be "nullified" and that the countries be free to govern themselves. The signaling logic of the open sphere is emphasized in a U.S. State Department analyst's wartime musing on what Soviet conduct towards Eastern European states would reveal about its intentions:

> I see no reason why we should object to their being within the orbit of Russia, provided we were assured that the U.S.S.R. would not use this power to subvert the governments, and set up a regime of terror and cruelty among the peoples— in other words, deal with the situation as they dealt in the Baltic countries. There should be some basis of adjustment whereby the safety and international interest of the U.S.S.R. will be assured without their claiming to dictate the method of life, cultural development and the type of civilization to be enjoyed by these countries. This is, indeed, the chief distinction which exists between a power which seeks world domination and a power which does not.
>
> (Berle 1973: 401)

The willingness of the Soviets to live with an open sphere would be a key test of their trustworthiness.

With respect to Poland in particular, the United States was careful to assert that it supported, "a strong, free and independent Polish state with the untrammeled right of the Polish people to order their internal exis- tence as they see fit" (FRUS Yalta: 210). The use of the word, "internal," which appears repeatedly, implies that Poland's external independence, i.e., sovereignty in foreign policy matters, was by contrast not supported. The Polish government in exile in London finally got the point, too late, in a statement in which they asserted Poland's right, "to organize her internal life in accordance with the will of the Polish Nation" (FRUS Yalta: 229). This was the solution ultimately achieved by Finland, and assiduously pur- sued by Eduard Benes for Czechoslovakia, and it seems to be what the Maisky-Gromyko-Litvinov school had in mind.

---

[17]Churchill had already accepted the Curzon line. No agreement was reached on the Western frontier.

In January 1945, and over strong U.S. objections, the Soviet government recognized the "Lublin" Poles, handpicked by Stalin, as the new government of Poland (FRUS Yalta: 224). Under pressure, Benes recognized them shortly afterwards on behalf of Czechoslovakia (Mastny 1979: 229). At Yalta, the Polish government was in Churchill's words, "the crucial point of this great conference" (FRUS Yalta: 778; Delzell 1956). Churchill tenaciously defended the rights of small countries to govern themselves (outside the British empire of course) and proposed that the Lublin regime be scrapped and be replaced by a new one favoring the Polish government in exile in London (FRUS Yalta: 590, 668, 778–79). Stalin argued that the Lublin regime should merely be expanded with additions from the London Poles. Ultimately, it was agreed that the Lublin regime would be "reorganized on a broader democratic basis with the inclusion of democratic leaders from Poland itself and from abroad." "Free and unfettered" elections would thereafter be held to determine a new government (FRUS Yalta: 980). Roosevelt insisted repeatedly that the elections must be free and acceptable to the Poles and Stalin explicitly accepted this and agreed that they might take place in a month (FRUS Yalta: 781, 853, 854; Gaddis 1972: 163; Taubman 1982: 93; Mastny 1979: 245–48). The three leaders also endorsed a "Declaration on Liberated Europe" in which they pledged to establish representative provisional governments that would hold free elections in the countries occupied by their armies (FRUS Yalta: 853–54, 972). It appeared therefore, as if the West had conceded to Stalin on the issue of the interim government but prevailed on the eventual political status of Poland. Self-government within an open sphere was provided for, in principle.

In the succeeding months, however, the negotiators in Moscow charged with implementing the Yalta decision could not even agree on a list of Poles to consult with, much less reorganize a government and hold elections. The stalemate hardened ambassador Harriman's attitudes towards the Russians; in March he was still convinced that "the Russians cannot afford to let the Crimea decisions break down," but by April he was arguing that the West was faced with a "barbarian invasion of Europe" (FRUS 1945 V: 136, 232). Churchill pressed for a hard line and Roosevelt, while acknowledging that the Yalta compromise gave the Lublin regime "somewhat more emphasis," sent a strong cable to Stalin saying that a "thinly disguised continuance of the present Warsaw regime would be unacceptable" (FRUS 1945 V: 147–48, 189, 194–96; Gaddis 1972: 172; Leffler 1986: 95).[18]

When Harry Truman succeeded Roosevelt in April 1945, he toughened the stance on Russia at least at the rhetorical level. Truman is usually

[18] Roosevelt also complained about developments in Romania in light of the Declaration on Liberated Europe.

portrayed as less trusting than Roosevelt, but he shared certain common ideas, particularly the myth that Stalin was a "moderating influence" who was often misinformed and faced political pressure from the politburo (Taubman 1982: 100; Larson 1985: 196–97; Leffler 1992: 52–53; Copeland 2000: 165–68).[19] Truman met with Soviet foreign minister Molotov, on his way to the UN conference in San Francisco, and complained about Soviet nonfulfillment of the Yalta pledges (Gaddis 1972: 205; Taubman 1982: 100).

However, Truman still wanted to continue a basically cooperative relationship with the Russians, and saw himself as continuing Roosevelt's policy in this regard. To emphasize this, he sent Harry Hopkins, Roosevelt's old confidante, to Moscow to have talks with Stalin in May. Hopkins emphasized that Soviet policy on Poland was alienating those who had supported Roosevelt's policy of cooperation with the Soviet Union which could render a policy of cooperation impossible to sustain and stressed the need for free elections (FRUS Potsdam I: 26–27, 38, 55). Stalin replied that the Yalta accord had said the Lublin regime would be reorganized and that this meant it would predominate in the new regime, but he had no intention to sovietize Poland (FRUS Potsdam I: 32, 39). He offered to give four or five ministries (about a quarter of the total) to non-Lublin Poles and in June Truman accepted the offer (FRUS Potsdam I: 40). Just before the Potsdam conference, the United States and Britain (more reluctantly) recognized the modified regime (Taubman 1982: 103–08). Harriman warily endorsed the agreement, and reported the hope of a leader of the London Poles that when the security situation improved the Russians would turn to internal matters and allow greater freedom in Poland (FRUS Potsdam I: 728).

The Polish dispute and the conditions in Eastern Europe more generally had begun to diminish Western trust for the Soviets. Churchill, in a letter to Truman in May wrote that he felt "deep anxiety because of their misinterpretation of the Yalta decisions, their attitude towards Poland, their overwhelming influence in the Balkans" and claimed, a year before he made the phrase famous, that "an iron curtain is drawn down upon their front" (FRUS Potsdam I: 9). The United States also complained about the lack of access of Western reporters to the region, and wondered what it signified (FRUS Potsdam I: 318). Hopkins stressed how Poland was the key issue causing a lessening of trust (FRUS Potsdam I: 27). A Potsdam briefing book paper on Britain moved away from Leahy's security dilemma inspired policy of trying to prevent Britain and the Soviets from acquiring spheres of influence and argued that "spheres of influence do in fact

---

[19] Harriman labored under a similar illusion (FRUS Potsdam I: 13, 61; Taubman 1982: 106–07).

exist, and will probably continue to do so for some time. . . . it is not in our interest to deny to the United Kingdom protection against possible dangers from the Soviet Union, especially since the Soviets have established domination of Eastern Europe" (FRUS Potsdam I: 264). Another memorandum argued that the international communist movement had returned to a hard line stance and was still directed from Moscow, despite the apparent dissolution of the Comintern (FRUS Potsdam I: 267–80). Papers on the Balkans argued that "Soviet authorities and local Communist parties are actively engaged in establishing regimes based on the one-party or "one-front" system" (FRUS Potsdam I: 357). The British agreed (FRUS 1945 II: 102).

Public opinion was also turning negative. In August 1945, 31 percent of U.S. respondents still approved of a proposed $6 billion U.S. loan to Russia, about the same as the 27 percent who approved a loan to Britain.[20] In September, 55 percent thought Russia could be trusted to cooperate after the war, up from 45 percent in June possibly as a result of Russian entry into the war on Japan and its quick end. However, on the fundamental question of Soviet motivations and trust, 39 percent thought Russia a peace-loving nation, willing to fight only if she thinks she has to defend herself, while 38 percent thought she was aggressive and might start a war to get something she wants. In Eastern Europe, 29 percent thought that the reason for Russia's "interest in the countries lying along her borders" was to be able to "count on them in case of attack," while 26 percent thought it was to spread communism.[21] All in all, the American public appeared evenly split in its evaluation of Russian motivations.

Despite these developments, there was still some optimism that cooperation with the Russians could be possible if trust were built. An important reflection of this was the U.S. withdrawal of troops from what would become the Soviet zone in Germany. Churchill urged that Western forces advance as far as possible and remain in place as bargaining leverage, but the Americans decided to honor the zonal agreement. Generals Dwight D. Eisenhower and Lucius D. Clay, later to preside over the American zone, believed that more contact with the Russians would facilitate cooperation and that one had to "give trust to get trust" (McAllister 2002: 71).

The dispute over Poland, in conjunction with the implications of the Spiral Game, supports several inferences. First, as just outlined, there is strong evidence of U.S. belief change in response to Soviet behavior: the United States grows less trusting. As implication 3.8 says, this implies that the parties are in a spiral equilibrium rather than the noncooperative

---

[20] An amazing 50 percent favored credits to Russia through private banks. "The Quarter's Polls," *Public Opinion Quarterly* 9, no. 3 (1945): 383.

[21] "The Quarter's Polls," *Public Opinion Quarterly* 9, no. 3 (1945): 387–88.

pooling equilibrium. This undercuts offensive realism and supports the other perspectives that are based on the spiral equilibrium.[22]

Second, Soviet defection from the Yalta agreements should lower our trust for the Soviet Union, supporting the traditionalist and Orwellian perspectives. In the Yalta agreements, particularly the Declaration on Liberated Europe, each side promised to establish democratic regimes that were free to govern their own affairs, and the West acknowledged tacitly that countries in the Soviet sphere would have to heed Russian guidance on security policy. With respect to Poland, Yalta specified that the government be reorganized to include democratic leaders from Poland and abroad, and that it hold free elections. The Soviets stalled on reorganizing the Polish government until after the Hopkins visit in May. In the meantime they entrenched the Lublin Poles and weakened other political groups. Free elections were never held. This is a clear case of Soviet defection from the Yalta agreements.

Third, the United States largely cooperated in the Yalta provisions on Poland and the other liberated countries, supporting traditionalism over Orwellianism. Revisionists and postrevisionists argue that the United States too went back on its Yalta concessions. Harriman realized at the time that the U.S. emphasis on free elections and independence for the Poles must have seemed sanctimonious and even a thin veil over a desire to keep the Soviets out of Europe (FRUS Potsdam I: 61; Gaddis 1972: 234; Leffler 1992: 50). Leffler argues that Roosevelt accepted that the Polish government would be communist dominated and that elections would be rigged, but that the United States attempted to reverse this concession because of its unpopularity and Truman's ignorance of the actual record of what happened at Yalta (Leffler 1986; Messer 1982: 50–51). However, Roosevelt fought as hard for free elections as for anything at Yalta, and accepted that the Lublin regime would form the basis of the provisional government only on assurance from Stalin that free elections would be held soon. The United States and Britain did attempt to get as many noncommunists into the provisional government as possible, but this did not violate the agreement, and they ultimately accepted Stalin's offer for a cosmetic change to the Lublin regime. Finally, the Western sphere of influence was already markedly more open than the Eastern one.

Thus, it appears that the United States abided by the agreement and the Soviets did not. Implication 3.5 says that this should cause our level of trust for the Soviets to decline. Given that information is plentiful about the United States and poor about the Soviets, for the Soviets to not cooperate while the United States does indicates expansionist motivations. Thus, the

---

[22]The fact that trust did not collapse entirely in response to the first defection rules out the cooperative equilibrium.

dispute over Poland supports the traditionalist interpretation of the Cold War over the alternatives.

BULGARIA AND ROMANIA

With Poland essentially out of the way, the main issue at the Potsdam summit in July was Germany, and especially the thorny question of German reparations, which I will discuss in chapter 6. Another important issue in the fall of 1945, which sheds intriguing light on U.S. perceptions of the Soviet Union, was the question of international control of atomic weapons (Gaddis 1972: 244–54; Bernstein 1974). A substantial portion of U.S. opinion held that the new technology was too dangerous to be treated as an ordinary weapon of war. Proposals began circulating for putting atomic energy under some form of international control, in order to head off fruitless and deadly arms races. Two supporters included Secretary of War Henry L. Stimson and Dean Acheson at State. In September 1945 Stimson wrote that "if we fail to approach them now and merely continue to negotiate with them, having this weapon rather ostentatiously on our hip, their suspicions and their distrust of our purposes and motives will increase" (FRUS 1945 II: 42).[23] He acknowledged that cooperation involved a risk, but believed it worth running.[24] Acheson also discussed the risk, but claimed that, "the advantage of being ahead in such a race is nothing compared with not having the race" (FRUS 1945 II: 49). Despite his later hawkishness, he also adhered to a tragic spiral interpretation at this point, arguing, "I cannot see why the basic interests of the two nations should conflict. Any long range understanding . . . seems to me impossible under a strategy of Anglo-American exclusion of Russia from atomic development."[25] Secretary of State James F. Byrnes opposed internationalization, revealing how recent negotiations over Eastern Europe had affected his thinking, "he said that we can't get in to Romania and Bulgaria much less Russia and that it is childish to think that the Russians would let us see what they are doing" (FRUS 1945 II: 60). Truman ultimately endorsed negotiations with Canada and Britain, which led to the "Baruch Plan" for international control of atomic energy the following year. The fact that prominent U.S. policymakers could seriously propose giving up the monopoly on atomic weapons in order to reassure the Russians indicates that there was still a substantial well of U.S. trust towards the Soviets,

---

[23] The British ambassador to Russia had a similar analysis (FRUS 1945 II: 82–84).

[24] His philosophy on trust, remarkable for a Secretary of War: "The chief lesson I have learned in a long life is that the only way to make a man trustworthy is to trust him; and the surest way to make him untrustworthy is to distrust him and show your distrust."

[25] Of course, exclusion was futile as the Manhattan project had already been penetrated by Soviet intelligence (Holloway 1994: 82–95).

enough to make it worthwhile considering relinquishing this great, though temporary, advantage.[26]

The main international controversies of the fall of 1945, however, were the effort to draw up peace treaties for Germany's satellites and the fate of Romania and Bulgaria. At Potsdam, the foreign ministers of the Big Five had been tasked with drawing up peace treaties for Italy and the other enemy states. In the Balkans as in Poland, the Western allies complained, the Russians had imposed communist dominated regimes and restricted access to Western diplomats and journalists (FRUS Potsdam II: 150–55, 228–31; FRUS 1945 II: 102). U.S. officials faced similar pressures to see that the Yalta Declaration on Liberated Europe was fulfilled and representative governments established in these two countries. These issues moved to the front burner in September at the first Council of Foreign Ministers (CFM) meeting in London.[27]

In a tactical mistake on the first day, Molotov agreed that France and China should be allowed to participate in the discussion on all the peace treaties but vote only on those with states with which they had fought (FRUS 1945 II: 114–15). Stalin later decided that this would provide unnecessary opportunities for the West to gang up on the Soviet Union in the negotiations and instructed Molotov to retract this concession, a position supported by the Potsdam accords. Meanwhile, other conflicts arose. Molotov asked for a role in the occupation of Japan and trusteeship over Italian colonies in North Africa (FRUS 1945 II: 164, 167–75). Byrnes opposed dividing up the colonies on the grounds that this would make everyone look expansionist, while the new British Foreign Secretary Ernest Bevin more bluntly acknowledged that the same security concerns that made the Soviets want the West out of Eastern Europe made the British want the Russians out of the Mediterranean (FRUS 1945 II: 189). Byrnes and Bevin criticized Russian policies in Romania and Bulgaria, and Byrnes pushed Molotov to accept a version of the Polish solution (FRUS 1945 II: 196). Molotov rejected this and charged that the United States wanted to install governments hostile to the Soviet Union (Pechatnov 1999; FRUS 1945 II: 194–200, 243–46, 291–98, 300–06). The conference ended in disagreement, hung up on the seemingly procedural issue of who would discuss what peace treaties.[28]

[26] Had the Soviet Union developed the bomb first, it seems unlikely that Molotov, or even Litvinov or Maisky, would have sincerely advocated a program of international control of the weapon.

[27] On the London CFM, see Leffler 1992: 38–39; Gaddis 1972: 264; Pechatnov 1999: 1–8.

[28] Despite Molotov's obedient intransigence and the failure of the conference, Stalin orchestrated an attack on his excessive "liberalism" and concessions to foreigners that placed Molotov in grave danger (Pechatnov 1999: 8–14).

As the fall wore on, conditions worsened in Bulgaria and Romania. Increasingly alarmed, the State Department sent Mark Etheridge, a news-paper publisher, to conduct an inquiry. The Etheridge Report was damning on the political conditions in the two countries, claiming that the Soviets pursued "a policy of... indirect political domination of Romania and Bulgaria through the Communist Party." Even more sinister, while there was no reason to suspect that the Russians had more in mind than a security perimeter, their position in Eastern Europe will "doubtless be used as a means of bringing pressure to bear on Greece, Turkey and the Straits, and could be converted without great effort into a springboard for aggression in the Eastern mediterranean" (FRUS 1945 V: 633–37). Harriman had by now abandoned the tragic spiral interpretation, writing, "We have recognized that the Soviets have deep seated suspicions of all foreigners including ourselves. Our natural method of dealing with suspicion in others is to show our goodwill by generosity and consideration. We have earnestly attempted this policy and it has not been successful" (FRUS 1945 V: 822).

The conflict over Romania and Bulgaria was finally resolved at a meeting of the Big Three foreign ministers in December in Moscow.[29] By meeting as three rather than five Byrnes symbolized his concession on the peace treaties issue. Stalin reciprocated with concessions along the lines of a weaker version of the Polish solution, adding two outside politicians to the existing regimes with promises of elections in exchange for American recognition (FRUS 1945 II: 821–22). A control council for Japan was also created. While Byrnes thought he had struck a reasonable deal, at home he was subject to a firestorm of criticism for appeasing the Russians. Truman criticized Byrnes for keeping him in the dark about what he was doing. Though the United States recognized the objectionable regimes, U.S. suspicions of the Russians had grown.

The disputes over Bulgaria and Romania have the same implications as the Polish dispute. U.S. trust lessened as the fall wore on, supporting the spiral equilibrium over the noncooperative equilibrium and offensive realism. The Soviet imposition of satellite regimes in Bulgaria and Romania constituted defections from the Yalta accords specifying representative governments within an open sphere of influence. Overall, creation of the East European satellite regimes would seem to support traditionalist and Orwellian interpretations. Soviet noncooperation and expansionism seems evident; this diminished Western trust, and should diminish the trust of external observers. Finally, the United States and Britain honored the agreement on open spheres, supporting traditionalism over Orwellianism.

---

[29] On the Moscow conference, see Gaddis 1972: 276–81; Taubman 1982: 125–26.

THE IRANIAN CRISIS

In the first half of 1946 relations between the United States and the Soviets worsened still further and many historians date the beginning of the Cold War to this period (Trachtenberg 1999: 35, Leffler 1992: 100).[30] Policymakers on both sides reflected critically on the past and painted stark pictures of the future relations between East and West. The long simmering dispute over Soviet troops in Iran erupted. Suspicions, already aroused by the fate of Poland, Bulgaria, and Romania, deepened still further.

At a rhetorical level, East-West relations became noticeably chillier. On February 9, Stalin made a rare public speech in which he returned to the thesis that capitalism and socialism were intrinsically incompatible. World War II was caused by the nature of capitalism, and war would be inevitable as long as capitalism remained. Therefore, there must be no relaxation in the Soviet Union; instead there must be a new series of five-year plans to prepare the country for war (Gaddis 1972: 299; Wohlforth 1993: 62–64; and for a milder interpretation see Leffler 1992: 103; Taubman 1982: 133–34). Western observers interpreted this and speeches by other Soviet leaders at this time as a return to isolationism and an attempt to prepare the public for a confrontation with the West. However, given his earlier remarks to Dimitrov, it is not clear that the speech embodied either a change in goals or in perceptions of the West.

Shortly after Stalin's address, George F. Kennan's seminal "long telegram" arrived in Washington (FRUS 1946 VI: 696–709). Kennan had been asked to provide an analysis of Soviet behavior and motivations, and though he had sounded similar themes in the past, (FRUS 1945 V: 853–60), this time his words would be required reading throughout official Washington and would eventually form the basis of his influential *Foreign Affairs* article on the sources of Soviet conduct (Kennan 1947).[31] The main thrust of the argument was that the Soviet Union, like the Tsarist regime before it, was a tyranny that needed conflict with the outside world to maintain its grip on power. Marxism served as a further justification for internal isolation and external hostility. As a result, Russia would remorselessly attempt to weaken the capitalist bloc, infiltrate the third world, and strengthen the Socialist camp. Fortunately for the West, however, the regime was not reckless and could be contained, and it was internally weak because communism had ceased to inspire the masses.

The next month, Winston Churchill gave his famous address at Fulton, Missouri, declaring that an iron curtain had descended over Europe,

---

[30] Some date it as early as August 1945 (Copeland 2000: 146–47) while others postpone it until 1949 (Taubman 1982: 193).

[31] On Kennan's ideas and their impact, see Gaddis 1982: 3–53.

behind which Soviet domination was gradually being imposed. Truman read the speech and tacitly signaled his approval by being present on the platform while it was delivered. Commentators generally approved of the speech, though some objected to Churchill's proposal for an association of the "English speaking peoples" as a potentially entangling alliance. In response to the criticism, Truman backpedalled in public, but his private views were similar to Churchill's.

These speeches and writings reflected a climate of increased suspicion and fears for the future. In such an atmosphere, new conflicts could hardly improve relations, and they were not long in coming.

The first real crisis of the Cold War occurred over Iran (Trachtenberg 1999: 35; Leffler 1992: 80–81, 110).[32] British and Soviet troops had occupied the country in 1941 to secure access to Iranian oil and to create a supply line to Russia. With U.S. prodding, the two powers signed a treaty with Iran in 1942 promising to respect Iran's sovereignty and territorial integrity, and to withdraw six months after the end of the war with Germany and her associates. In 1943, the Big Three met in Tehran and pledged to respect Iranian independence (Kuniholm 1980: 140–43, 167). Soviet prodding for an oil concession and interference in Iranian politics worried the British and Americans, however, and just before Yalta, Churchill wrote Roosevelt that Iran could be a test case of Russian intentions. The foreign ministers discussed the matter at Malta on the way to the Crimea and at Yalta the British pushed for an early joint withdrawal, but the Soviets refused (FRUS Yalta: 337, 500, 738–40). At Potsdam, the Big Three agreed to withdraw troops from Tehran, but failed to agree on an accelerated withdrawal from the country as a whole.

In November an Azeri nationalist movement launched a revolt in the zone occupied by the Soviets and the Russians prevented Iranian troops from quelling it. In December, the Kurds followed suit and there were two autonomous republics in the Soviet zone. At Moscow, Byrnes warned that the issue would likely come before the United Nations in January, and it would be difficult to defend Soviet policy. Stalin claimed that he was concerned with possible attacks on the Baku oilfields, that withdrawing before the March 2 deadline was out of the question, and after that he would have to see. Bevin, always to the point, asked Stalin what he wanted in Iran and Stalin disclaimed any territorial ambitions (FRUS 1945 II: 684–90). No agreement was reached. State department officials warned that any concessions by Britain to Russia in the Near East would lead to further demands (FRUS 1946 VII: 3). In January the Iranians placed

---

[32] See also Harbutt 1981–82; Hess 1974. For a review of the literature on the Near East in the early Cold War, see Jones and Woods 1993.

the matter before the United Nations, and subsequently began bilateral negotiations with the Russians.

The crisis entered a critical phase in March, when the deadline for withdrawal passed and Russian troops remained. The United States protested, and began to receive alarming reports from Tabriz of Soviet troops moving southwards rather than northwards (FRUS 1946 VII: 340–45). Byrnes, newly combative after his chastening over the Moscow conference, vowed to "give it to them with both barrels"(FRUS 1946 VII: 356). The United States publicized the troop movements and supported the Iranians in bringing the matter before the UN Security Council again. Theatrical negotiations in the Council followed, punctuated by a Soviet walkout. Truman told the new U.S. ambassador to the Soviet Union, Walter Bedell Smith, to tell Stalin that he had always considered Stalin a man of his word until he kept troops in Iran past the treaty specified deadline (Kuniholm 1980: 332). After tense negotiations, the Russians and Iranians reached an agreement on April 4 promising a Russian withdrawal within six weeks and the formation of a Russian-Iranian oil company to exploit reserves in the North, subject to ratification by the Iranian parliament. Tension abated as the Soviets appeared to withdraw their forces in May, though controversy remained about how many Russians remained out of uniform.

The effect of the Iranian crisis was to further deepen Western fear. A July review of Soviet foreign policy by the Central Intelligence Group, the forerunner of the Central Intelligence Agency, argued that the Soviets believed in inevitable conflict, but wished to postpone it while building up their forces and weakening the capitalist world. In the meantime their policy would be "grasping and opportunistic" and they wished to include Greece, Turkey, and Iran within their sphere by installing friendly governments (Kuhns 1997: 59, 62). Public opinion in the United States had swung strongly against the former ally. In April, 44 percent thought Russia wanted world power, to expand as much as possible, or the supremacy of communism, while in July 58 percent thought Russia wanted to be the ruling power, while only 29 percent said she wanted protection.[33] Also in July, 71 percent disapproved of Soviet behavior and 60 percent thought the Soviets wanted to rule the world.[34] This provides more support for the spiral equilibrium as opposed to the pooling equilibrium, undermining offensive realism.

The Iranian crisis provides an even more clearcut example of Soviet defection and Western cooperation, which should strongly undermine trust for the Soviets and support the traditionalist interpretation of the Cold War, according to implication 3.5. The Soviets and the British had an explicit

[33] "The Quarter's Polls," *Public Opinion Quarterly* 10, no. 2 (1946): 264–65.
[34] Gallup 1972: 591; see also Gaddis 1972: 315.

agreement to withdraw their troops from Iran by six months after the end of the war. The British and Americans honored this agreement and withdrew their military forces. The Soviets did not, and used their troops to protect secessionist movements, thereby violating their commitment to Iran's territorial integrity. The evidence seems unambiguous that the Soviets defected while the West cooperated.

Postrevisionist historians, such as Leffler and Fred Lawson, nonetheless argue for a tragic spiral interpretation of the Iranian crisis (Lawson 1989). In this view, the Soviets were growing fearful of the United States as a result of its increasingly close ties with Saudi Arabia and the construction of a modern airbase at Dhahran (Leffler 1992: 56–59). Such a base would threaten Soviet oil fields in the Caucasus and industrial plants in the Southern regions of the Soviet Union. In response, the Soviets refused to vacate Northern Iran and fostered separatist movements there in order to move their defense perimeter southwards. The crisis abated not because of the strong stance of the Truman administration, but because of its weakness. The United States merely brought the matter to the attention of the Security Council rather than building up military forces in the region. This reassured the Soviets and made them feel safe enough to withdraw their forces (Lawson 1989: 322). In a related view, Natalia Yegorova argues that the Soviets were mainly interested in oil but feared that without troops on the ground they would have no leverage, and Iranian concessions rather than Western pressure ended the crisis (Yegorova 1996: 7, 8, 17).

Two problems with this interpretation are apparent. First, Western forces had withdrawn from Iran on schedule, and Iran was closer to the Soviet Union than Saudi Arabia. Surely it must have been far more reassuring to the Russians when the United States pulled out in 1945 than when it insisted on raising the issue to the highest levels in the spring of 1946. Yet, the Soviets pulled out only under pressure, not when the U.S. commitment to country was less pronounced. Second, Stalin never attempted to link his withdrawal from Northern Iran with the fate of the U.S. base in Dhahran. If this was the link in the Russian view, it would seem that they would at least attempt to get a quid for their quo (Trachtenberg 1995: 448–50). Finally, even if Yegorova is correct and Stalin's minimal demands for oil were really his maximal ones, the crisis still represents a defection in the model and justifiably raises suspicions. The aftermath of the crisis also supports the claim that U.S. pressure was key, because the Iranians subsequently reneged on the April agreement with no response from the Soviets (Hess 1974: 145). In December the Tehran government sent troops to Tabriz to crush the separatist regime and in 1947 the Majlis refused to approve the Soviet oil concession. The Soviet nonresponse to this defection from Iran seems due to a reluctance to engage the United States again, since as Smith wrote from Moscow, "Iran is no stronger than the UN and UN, in last analysis, is no stronger than USA" (FRUS 1946 VII: 566).

After the Iranian crisis, Western fears received remarkable confirmation from an unpublished interview with Litvinov. In June 1946, Litvinov was on his way out again, and was growing disillusioned with his country's policy. A reporter asked "Suppose the West were suddenly to give in and grant all Moscow's demands . . . Would that lead to good will and the easing of the present tension?" Litvinov's answer, stunning coming from someone who still worked for the Soviet Foreign Ministry: "It would lead to the West's being faced, after a more or less short time, with the next series of demands." (Taubman 1982: 133). It was this interview, among other indiscretions, which led Molotov to comment that Litvinov "remained among the living only by chance" (Chuev 1991: 69). At the same time the Soviets were planning for the creation of a new international communist organization, what would become the Cominform in 1947. This step, often portrayed as a reaction to the Marshall Plan, was being planned in May 1946 and was consciously delayed to avoid a negative impact on upcoming elections in France and Czechoslovakia, and on East-West relations in general (Békés 1998).

THE TURKISH CRISIS

The next major dispute to come to a head was the conflict over Turkey and the Dardanelles. At the 1943 Tehran conference Stalin had raised the issue of revising the Montreux convention regulating access to the strategically important straits linking the Mediterranean and Black seas (Mastny 1979: 125). The convention gave Turkey control over the straits; Russia wanted control for herself, comparing the case to British control over Gibraltar and Suez, and the U.S. control over the Panama Canal. At Yalta the issue was discussed again (FRUS Yalta: 910), and in June Stalin added new demands for pieces of Turkish territory adjacent to the Soviet Union and military bases on the straits (Mark 1997: 388; Yergin 1977: 234; Taubman 1982: 109). At Potsdam the Western allies made it clear they supported free Soviet navigation of the straits but not bases or territorial changes, but Stalin rejected this offer (FRUS Potsdam II: 256–59, 301–04, 365–66). Truman began to fear a possible Soviet invasion by December (Mark 1997: 389; Trachtenberg 1999: 38). Soviet troop levels in Romania and Bulgaria were monitored closely and seemed to be in excess of occupation requirements. The United States began planning for war and even coordinated with the British for the defense of the region. In February, the Soviet ambassador to Turkey made the Eastern European analogy explicit by telling the Turkish Foreign Minister, "We waited long time regarding arrangement we wanted with Poland and finally got it; we can wait regarding Turkey" (FRUS 1946 VII: 816). In March, during the Iran crisis, the U.S. ambassador to Turkey warned of military preparations in Bulgaria and argued that the straits issue was secondary to a desire to install a "friendly" government subservient to Moscow (FRUS 1946 VII: 818, 821). In early June 1946 top U.S. officials met and agreed that war was certainly possible, but tension abated slightly with subsequent reports of Russian troop withdrawals.

Tension peaked again in August, when the Soviets finally presented Turkey with an explicit demand for revision of the Montreux convention. The Soviets made five demands, three regarding use of the straits and two designating the Black Sea powers as solely responsible and giving the Soviets joint custody, an implicit demand for bases (the issue of the Eastern provinces was dropped) (FRUS 1946 VII: 827–29). The United States reacted with alarm, a memo approved by the President on August 15 argued that the "primary objective of the Soviet Union is to obtain control of Turkey," and that granting it bases would lead to this result, cutting off the Eastern Mediterranean from the Western world. The Russians could only be deterred by "the conviction that the United States is prepared, if necessary, to meet aggression with force of arms," and fostering this conviction was the best chance of peace (FRUS 1946 VII: 841–82). The United States had decided to fight for Turkey, if necessary. A Central Intelligence Group (CIG) analysis maintained that several factors indicated an elevated risk of war, though, on balance, the Soviets would probably not attack (Kuhns 1977: 71, 77–80).

The United States cabled Moscow to reject the fourth and fifth points and said that if the straits should come under attack it would be a threat to international security that would be "a matter for action on the part of the Security Council" (FRUS 1946 VII: 847–48). The United States also dispatched a naval task force to the Eastern Mediterranean, making the Turkish crisis the first in which U.S. military forces were overtly used. The crisis continued until September 24 when Stalin gave an interview with a friendly British journalist dismissing the likelihood of war and sent a less confrontational note to Turkey. No further steps were taken to press Soviet demands (Taubman 1982: 150). Eduard Mark argues that one of the key factors convincing Stalin to back down was a report from Donald Maclean, the British spy in Washington, indicating that the Americans would fight (Mark 1997: 408). Molotov later recalled that Stalin was pushing too far with the demand for bases and was in danger of provoking war (Chuev 1991: 73).

In the end, the Turkish crisis, like the Iranian crisis early in the year, cemented the American perception that the Soviets were hostile, but that they could be forced to give up their demands by an adequate show of force short of war. Planning for war with Russia was initiated, with the most likely scenario being the Soviets attacking a weak power under the impression that the United States would not respond.

Two documents highlight the negative perceptions each side had of the other. In July, Truman commissioned a report on Soviet noncompliance with its international agreements and the document, known after its authors as the Clifford-Elsey report, was completed in September, during the Turkish crisis (Krock 1968: 419–82). The Soviets are portrayed as believing in inevitable conflict and bending all their efforts to weaken the West. Their record of violating agreements is discussed at length, focusing on unilateral actions and the establishment of satellite regimes in Eastern Europe, as well as preventing Iranian troops from putting down the secessionist movement in Northern Iran, in contravention of the agreement to respect Iranian sovereignty (Krock 1968: 446–47).[35]

Soviet perceptions are reflected in a telegram commissioned (and "coauthored") by Molotov from the Soviet ambassador in the U.S. Nikolai Novikov on September 27. The Novikov telegram portrays a United States in the grip of monopoly capital which is building up military capability "to prepare the conditions for winning world supremacy in a new war."[36] The analysis is relentlessly ideological but at least serves to identify developments that were viewed with concern by the Soviets at the time, including U.S. military bases and Anglo-American cooperation.

The Turkish crisis is another case where the Soviets attempted to expand at the expense of a weaker state on their periphery, constituting a defection in terms of the Spiral Game. Although there is no parallel sense in which the United States cooperated, implication 3.4 still holds that such an event strengthens the traditionalist and Orwellian perspectives by lowering our level of trust for the Soviets. Postrevisionists counter that Stalin had legitimate security interests in the Dardanelles and that Soviet actions to press their claim were not especially aggressive. The U.S. military response is portrayed as an overreaction because the Soviets are claimed to have never contemplated the use of force (Yergin 1977: 235; Leffler 1985, 1992: 124). However there is little direct evidence of Soviet intentions, certainly not enough to rule out the possibility of invasion (Mark 1997: 412; Trachtenberg 1995: 442–44, 448). Soviet demands were accompanied by a propaganda war against Turkey that seemed to be preparing Russians for war. Though there was no verbal threat of invasion, there had been troop movements in the Balkans and other more subtle threats, which, in the context of the vast power disparity between the Soviet Union and Turkey,

---

[35] For a critique of the report's biases, see Leffler 1992: 130–38.

[36] The telegram, along with commentary, can be found in *Diplomatic History* 15, no. 4 (Fall 1991): 523–63.

could hardly be reassuring for Turkey. Finally, the Soviets again seemed to back down under pressure, rather than be provoked by it.

The year 1946 saw the beginning of the Cold War. The essential components were in place. The Soviet installation of puppet regimes in Poland, Bulgaria, and Romania fostered Western suspicions, as did Soviet challenges in Iran and Turkey, generating fears of war through miscalculation, and the first efforts to plan for war with the Soviet Union. The doctrine of containment had been formulated in the long telegram. However, it was still unclear just how expansionist the Soviets were, what a policy of opposing Soviet expansionism would entail, how much it would cost, and whether the U.S. public would be willing to pay for it. The following year would begin to answer these questions.

THE TRUMAN DOCTRINE

The major developments of 1947, the Truman Doctrine and the Marshall Plan, were not so much a result of Soviet provocations or even disagreements with Russia as of feared crises within what had come to be thought of as a Western camp. In the context of a threat from the East, the reality of which had been demonstrated in 1945 and 1946, strong steps needed to be taken to shore up regimes on the Western side of the line. How strong and how costly those steps would need to be, and who would pay for them, became clearer in 1947. Here I will discuss the Truman Doctrine. I leave the Marshall Plan, which involved a greater degree of intra-European cooperation, for chapter 6.

In early 1947, Great Britain decided that it could no longer shoulder the burdens of empire. In a short space of time Britain decided to withdraw from Burma, Palestine, and most importantly, India itself, the heart of the imperial system (Kuniholm 1980: 406). In the Eastern Mediterranean, Britain was unable to maintain its support for Greece and Turkey. The Greek government was threatened by an indigenous communist insurgency, as it had been since 1945. The British had supported the noncommunist regime in pursuance of its traditional efforts to prevent Russian encroachment on the Eastern Mediterranean, and in accordance with the famous percentages agreement with Stalin giving the British a "ninety percent" say in Greece. By 1947, however, the domestic economic crisis made British predominance in the Eastern Mediterranean a luxury that could no longer be afforded.

The Truman administration decided quickly that the United States could not afford to stand aside (Kuniholm 1980: 410). To cut the Greeks loose would be to shift the momentum in that civil war, bringing the communists to power (Kuhns 1997: 101). A communist Greece, even if the Soviets had not brought it about directly, would serve Soviet interests by giving them a tremendous naval presence in the Eastern Mediterranean, allowing them to put additional pressure on Turkey and threaten Western access to Middle Eastern oil-producing regions via the Suez canal. Inspiration would also be given to communist parties in Italy and France. Turkey, while no longer on the front burner diplomatically, should be given aid as well, for who knew when Soviet pressure might be ratcheted up again.

The administration then set about obtaining Congressional and popular support for a foreign aid package to the two countries. In a meeting with Congressional leaders, Secretary of State George C. Marshall made the case in moderate terms only to be met with complaints about pulling British chestnuts out of the fire. Dean Acheson then took the floor and painted an apocalyptic picture of the future should Greece or Turkey fall to the communists. In a world divided into two irreconcilable camps, one loss in the Near East would lead inevitably to further collapses in Southern and Eastern Europe, gravely endangering the security of the United States. Only prompt aid to Greece and Turkey could prevent this bleak future (Gaddis 1972: 349; Kuniholm 1980: 411; Leffler 1992: 145). The assembled Congressmen were duly impressed and the administration learned the lesson that to gain public support, rhetoric must be "clearer than the truth," as Acheson would later put it. On March 12, Truman addressed a joint session of Congress to present the administration's aid package, and justified them in stark, Achesonian terms. Congress was swayed, and on May 12, Truman signed the aid package into law and the doctrine bearing his name was born.

What inferences can we make from the Truman doctrine episode? I argue that neither side defected in a clear cut way and so the event is not very informative. Postrevisionist historians correctly point out that the Russians had done little if anything in the immediate run up to the Truman Doctrine (Leffler 1992: 143–45). The United States was worried by events that were not Soviet actions, such as insurrections in Greece and China, economic paralysis, and the strength of communist parties in France and Italy. The United States is portrayed as taking the initiative in response to these events while the Soviets reacted defensively. (Leffler 1992: 513). While this is true, the United States had little doubt that a communist Greece would shift immediately to the Soviet camp, regardless of how it came into being. U.S. suspicion of the Soviet Union had hardened to the point that active steps needed to be taken to shore up the Western bloc, even if the Russians were merely in a position to take advantage of trouble, rather than instigating it. Can the Truman doctrine be counted as a U.S. defection? It was certainly an effort to support the Greek regime against domestic opponents with some level of popularity, and to that extent constituted an interference in the affairs of a weaker nation. The size of the defection is reduced by the fact that the government side, as well, had domestic support, and so cannot be considered a puppet regime.

Vojtech Mastny points out that Soviet reaction to Truman Doctrine was mild. "Its internal assessments showed no sense of alarm, and the lack of any response on its part other than verbal condemnation showed Stalin correctly understood the presidential doctrine as not applying to the part of Europe he already controlled. In its effects on Soviet policy, it was not the turning point it was later made out to be" (Mastny 1996: 26). Indeed, while the Truman doctrine marked a large rhetorical break, it was not a great substantive break (Gaddis 1974). At the rhetorical level it was an innovation in that the President firmly endorsed Churchill's Fulton message about the Soviet threat that he had waffled on when it was first enunciated the previous year. This was necessitated by the requirement of Congressional approval of the aid package, and it sparked a great debate in the United States (Gaddis 1974: 389). However, at the practical level, the Truman Doctrine was not to be taken quite literally. Despite the promise to "support free peoples who are resisting attempted subjugation" the United States acquiesced in the "loss" of China two years later. In the end, the Truman doctrine is perhaps best conceived of as a reallocation of the defense burden within the Western bloc from Britain to the United States, which had little effect on the U.S.-Soviet relationship, or on the relative likelihood of the various perspectives on the Cold War.

HUNGARY AND CZECHOSLOVAKIA

Relations between East and West continued to deteriorate in the fall of 1947 with conflicts over the Marshall Plan. In early 1948, they took yet another turn for the worse. Two key developments in this period were the final extinction of pluralism in the two Eastern European states that held out longest, Hungary and Czechoslovakia.

Hungary was perhaps the best executed example of the national front strategy, in that the road to satellite status was smooth and unmarked by sudden crises that could serve as alarm bells for the West. Stalin is reputed to have warned the Hungarian communists that their goals might have to wait ten to fifteen years (Gati 1986: 21). Soviet economic penetration, however, was immediate and under the aegis of reparations and joint companies, Russia swiftly took over the Hungarian economy beginning in 1945 (Borhi 2000). In the fall of 1945, Hungary had free elections won by the noncommunist Smallholders party, but the Russians intervened to secure key cabinet posts for communists. In the course of 1946 the Smallholders were infiltrated and discredited, but elections held in August 1947 gave the communists only 22 percent of the vote. In 1948 the social democrats were annexed by the communists and the remnants of the private economy were eliminated. The gradual character of Hungary's incorporation into the Soviet bloc, however, combined with the drama of events elsewhere, prevented Hungary from becoming a center of East-West tension.[37]

The case of Czechoslovakia was far more dramatic. The Czechoslovakian government had hitherto managed to tread a fine line, maintaining a democratic polity while accommodating Soviet preferences internationally on such issues as the Marshall Plan. The balancing act was unstable, however, and in February 1948 the end of the line was reached. In a fatal error, several noncommunist ministers resigned from the cabinet. This enabled the communists to take control of the government and by March they had consolidated a dictatorship (Leffler 1992: 205).

The Czechoslovak coup increased Western fears of Soviet intentions, once again supporting the spiral equilibrium over the noncooperative equilibrium and offensive realism. The Central Intelligence Agency (CIA) opined that the coup, "reflects the refusal of the communists to settle for anything less than complete control" (Kuhns 1997: 174). In March, 73 percent of the public thought U.S. policy towards Russia was "too soft" up from 62 percent the preceding October.[38] The U.S. began to ponder increases in military spending and personnel (Leffler 1992: 209). General Clay in Germany thought that war might be imminent, and the administration proposed universal military service. Truman compared the situation to that facing Britain and France in 1938–39, a comparison made all the more salient by the fact that it was once more Czechoslovakia that was succumbing to totalitarian aggression (Taubman 1982: 168–69). The Italian foreign minister made the same comparison. A French diplomat inferred that Russia's main preoccupation was to prepare for a possibly imminent war (Trachtenberg 1999: 79). French foreign minister Georges Bidault worried that in Italy and Austria internal subversion could be accompanied by external invasion, and appealed for an alliance (Wall 1991: 133). Bevin believed that Russia was "actively preparing to extend its hold over the remaining part of continental Europe and subsequently, over the Middle East and no doubt the Balkans and Far East as well" (Mastny 1996: 43).

While developments in Czechoslovakia were disturbing, the West scored a victory in its own camp when the communists were defeated in the April 1948 Italian elections. The United States had aided the noncommunist

[37] Although it was carefully monitored by the United States and covered in the CIG weekly intelligence summaries (Kuhns 1997: 54, 68, 86, 91–92, 99, 114).

[38] "The Quarter's Polls," *Public Opinion Quarterly* 12, no. 2 (1948): 354. However, the percentage saying that Russia wanted to be the "ruling power of the world" remained flat, 76 percent in October, to 77 percent in March, though the number saying Russia wanted protection declined from 18 percent to 12 percent (Gallup 1972: 721).

parties both covertly and overtly, and were extremely worried about the outcome. It was hoped that a democratic defeat of the Italian communists would help weaken their cause in France and strengthen the overall argument that communism was unpopular and had to be imposed on a country by military force or machinations like those in Hungary and Czechoslovakia. Thus, by mid-1948, the lines between the blocs had become clear. Aside from Finland, no democracy remained east of the Iron Curtain, and west of it, the communists had been decisively defeated in reasonably free elections.

The contrast between Hungary and Czechoslovakia on the one hand, and Italy on the other once again illustrates the relative openness of the Western sphere in comparison with the Eastern one. The Soviet defection and Western cooperation again supports the traditionalist interpretation, in line with implication 3.5 of the Spiral game. In the East, the Soviets sponsored minority parties which subverted and annexed other parties, and eventually seized power. In the West, the United States aided non-communist parties, which were able to win elections and form coalition governments with popular support. The consolidation of Soviet domination in the Eastern bloc and the extinction of political freedom cemented their reputation as an expansionist power. The Europeans would live with this contrast for the next forty years.

The first half of 1948 also saw significant events in Germany, with the London Accords on the creation of the Federal Republic of Germany and the subsequent Berlin crisis in June, discussed in chapter 6. In the fall U.S.-Soviet tensions were high, and a CIA report argued that the Soviet Union was "essentially and implacably inimical towards the United States," and though it was "unlikely to resort deliberately to war to gain its ends within the next decade," the fundamental hostility of the Soviet Union required that the United States be prepared for war. In the spring of 1949, a CIA report on the likelihood of war stated that "international tension has increased in 1948. It will probably increase further during 1949. In these circumstances, the danger of an unintended outbreak of hostilities through miscalculation on either side must be considered to have increased" (Kuhns 1997: 243, 309).[39]

Another development in the wake of the Berlin crisis, which reflects the growing militarization of the Cold War, is the discovery that the Soviets had exploded an atomic bomb and the subsequent drafting of NSC-68. In September 1949, the United States obtained evidence that the Russians had exploded a nuclear weapon, the atomic monopoly was over. In response the United States undertook a policy review, directed by

---

[39] After the conclusion of the Berlin crisis, however, the CIA believed the chance of war had declined (Kuhns 1997: 326).

Paul Nitze in the State Department. The resulting document, NSC-68, called for greatly increased funding for the military to meet the challenges of containing and eventually rolling back Soviet power (Gaddis 1982: 93–94, 99). More bombs and stronger conventional forces were required, to defeat the Soviets wherever they chose to attack (Leffler 1992: 355–60). In April of 1950, the CIA produced a report minimizing the likelihood of any Soviet policy change in response to acquiring nuclear weapons, but the State Department and military dissented strongly, arguing that possession of the bomb would encourage the Soviets to be more aggressive than they were when the United States had a monopoly on atomic weapons (Kuhns 1997: 367–79). However, NSC-68 would remain a study on the shelf until the next great crisis of the Cold War.

The Korean War

The final case of Soviet expansionism, which played a significant role in generating U.S. fears, was the outbreak of the Korean war. In 1945 the Russians and Americans had agreed to divide Korea at the thirty-eighth parallel into occupation zones. The Soviets immediately closed off their zone to the south and redirected its economy northwards. At Moscow in December the foreign ministers agreed on a trusteeship arrangement for Korea with a view towards creating a unified government (FRUS 1945 II: 820). This proved extremely unpopular in the Southern zone, smacking as it did of Japanese colonization (Weathersby 1993: 21). Thereafter, the status quo congealed. In 1948 governments were set up in the two zones, both dependent on external powers. By 1949 both sides had withdrawn their military forces. Many policymakers believed that the United States would eventually have to abandon South Korea but should attempt to arrange some face-saving way of doing so (Taubman 1982: 211–12; Mastny 1996: 90). Acheson had even publicly failed to include South Korea within the U.S. defense perimeter.

The CIA continually discounted the likelihood that the North would invade, and in January 1950 attributed troop movements towards the border as defensive precautions. As late as June 19, the CIA acknowledged Northern military superiority, but downplayed their ability to take over the South (Kuhns 1997: 349, 390). Nonetheless, on June 25, 1950, the North Korean army invaded the South along a broad front. The offensive was a dramatic success—in days Seoul fell and South Korean forces were in full retreat. The United States, despite its earlier disinterest, responded quickly, taking advantage of a Soviet walkout to pass a UN resolution in favor of repelling the attack and ultimately committing ground forces to fight the North Koreans (Leffler 1992: 361–80).

The effect of the Korean attack was to greatly increase Western fears and promote the militarization of the Cold War (Jervis 1980). The percentage of Americans thinking the Soviets wanted to rule the world jumped from 70 percent in November of 1949 to 81 percent in November 1950 (Gallup 1972: 881, 949). In July of 1949, Truman forced the military to accept a budget of $13 billion; in December of 1950 the administration proposed to spend $140 billion on defense in the period from 1951 to 1952 (Leffler 1992: 276, 402). The dreams of NSC-68 became a reality (Gaddis 1982: 109; Leffler 1992: 355–60).[40] Americans worried about the possibility of a Soviet strike westward in Germany, perhaps motivated by preventive considerations relating to the U.S. military buildup. This led them to focus more seriously on the defense of Germany. Germany could best be defended with the participation of the Germans, which implied German rearmament, hitherto a taboo subject because of French fears (Trachtenberg 1999: 100–02). Overall, the reaction to the Korean war supports the spiral equilibrium and the perspectives based on it, rather than the noncooperative equilibrium and offensive realism.

The North Korean attack seems like an unambiguous case of Soviet defection and Western cooperation. The Soviet proxy prepared a secret invasion and launched it, while the American proxy did not. Implication 3.5, once again, would indicate that it provides dramatic support for the traditionalist view, over other spiral equilibrium based views. However, some revisionist historians have argued that the war was entirely of native origin and that it is difficult to determine who even started it.[41] Both North and South Korea can certainly be coded as expansionist and fearful; both sides wanted to unify the peninsula and this was common knowledge. Syngman Rhee, the Southern leader, even confessed to visiting Americans that he planned to invade the North in the coming year (Leffler 1992: 365).

Recently released documents however, uncover the direct Soviet role in approving and planning the invasion.[42] North Korea was unable to take any meaningful step without Soviet approval; Kim Il Sung even sought the Soviet ambassador's approval for the agenda of the North Korean assembly (Weathersby 1995/96: 36). In particular, Kim sought Soviet permission for an attack in March 1949, but was turned down because Stalin thought the North Koreans did not have military superiority, and U.S. troops, still on the peninsula, would intervene (Weathersby 2002: 3–4). In September he sought permission for a limited offensive to seize

---

[40]The CIA, seemingly unfazed by its failure to anticipate the attack, maintained its skepticism that the Soviets would pursue further ventures though they did begin to consider the possibility. CIA also predicted that China would not intervene in force (Kuhns 1997: 412, 450–51).

[41]The main revisionist work on the Korean war is Cumings 1981, 1990.

[42]See Weathersby 1993, 1995, 1995/96, 2002.

the portion of the Ongjin peninsula south of the thirty-eighth parallel, but was again turned down because of fears that it would lead to a general war that the North would not necessarily win and that might attract U.S. intervention (Weathersby 2002: 6–7, 1995: 6–8). Finally, in January, encouraged by the example of the recent Chinese triumph, Kim again requested permission to attack, and this time Stalin indicated that he was "willing to help him in this matter" (Weathersby 1995: 9). In the succeeding months, the Soviets sent military advisors to draw up the plan of attack, along with military supplies necessary to equip the forces. Kim traveled to Moscow in April to receive final approval. At the meeting, Stalin indicated why he had changed his mind, telling Kim:

> The Chinese victory is also important psychologically. It has proved the strength of Asian revolutionaries, and shown the weakness of Asian reactionaries and their mentors in the West, in America. Americans left China and did not dare to challenge the new Chinese authorities militarily.
>
> Now that China has signed a treaty of alliance with the USSR, Americans will be even more hesitant to challenge the Communists in Asia. According to information coming from the United States, it is really so. The prevailing mood is not to interfere. Such a mood is reinforced by the fact that the USSR now has the atomic bomb and that our positions are solidified in Pyongyang.
>
> (Weathersby 2002: 9)

Stalin also required Kim to get Mao's permission as well as his own, in part because he wanted Chinese rather than Soviet troops to backstop the North Koreans in case things went badly (Mastny 1996: 95; Gaddis 1997: 73–74; Kramer 1999: 541).

It is therefore clear that the traditionalist interpretation of the Korean war as an attempt at expansion by a more or less unified communist bloc is substantially correct. It is also clear that the the invasion was an effort to take advantage of weakness, rather than respond to a threat. Stalin permitted Kim to move as soon as he thought that the United States would not respond, and this belief was a result of the U.S. nonresponse to the fall of China.

CONCLUSION

Thus, the Korean War completed the process begun in 1945 with the disputes over the governments of Poland, Romania, and Bulgaria. Trust had sunk to a low from which it would take decades to recover. The United States image of the Soviets had shifted from prickly but businesslike partners in war, to cautions expansionists imposing their will on their weak neighbors in Eastern Europe and the Near East, to more aggressive expansionists willing to use outright war, albeit through a satellite, to expand their domain. In parallel to this pattern, U.S. policy shifted from a willingness to negotiate with the Russians, to a desire to contain them primarily with economic resources, to a policy of military containment via standing alliances with permanent U.S. military forces stationed in Europe. This evidence for Soviet expansionism supports traditionalist and Orwellian views of the Cold War. When evidence of the U.S. cooperation is added, the traditionalist viewpoint receives the most support. The most likely set of motivations and assumptions at the outset of the Cold War is that the United States was security seeking and trusting, while the Soviets were expansionist and fearful. The United States attempted to cooperate initially, while the Russians engaged in expansionist behavior. The United States subsequently revised its level of trust downwards and reduced its level of cooperation.

An interesting question which I have not focused on is whether the Soviets were reassured by early U.S. behavior and became any less fearful. Evidence about actual Soviet perceptions, as opposed to propaganda positions, is scarce. As I will discuss in chapter 7, one cannot take public statements about a state's perceptions of its adversary's intentions any more seriously than those about its own motivations. Expansionist states have every incentive to claim to be security seekers who are fearful of the other side, in order to get the other side to lower their guard. That said, it appears that the Soviets interpreted restraint as a sign of weakness, rather than trustworthiness. A more complicated model that incorporated uncertainty over strength in a bargaining context, as well as uncertainty over trustworthiness, would be required to fully capture this pattern of updating. Such a model would integrate the crisis bargaining literature with the models of trust developed here, and would be an interesting avenue for future research.

The model of the previous chapter and the discussion of this one have largely focused on the actions and beliefs of two parties, the United States and the Soviet Union. However, to deal fully with the origins of the Cold War system in Europe, it is necessary to take into account the other states, especially Britain, France, and Germany. This requires us to go beyond the two-actor framework of the previous chapter. In the next chapter I present an n-person model of trust in international relations that will allow us to explore these issues.

PART III

European Cooperation
and the Rebirth of Germany

CHAPTER 5

Trust, Hegemony, and Cooperation

INTERNATIONAL RELATIONS are sometimes unavoidably multilateral, and some issues are best handled in a multilateral fashion. Consider the 1987 Montreal Protocol, which severely limited production of chloroflouro-carbons (CFCs) which are suspected of thinning the stratospheric ozone layer that helps protect the surface of the earth from ultraviolet radiation (Haas 1992). Many countries were involved in negotiating the treaty and it has resulted in the virtual elimination of CFC production in the developed world, and substantial inroads on production in the South. In the security realm, NATO formalized an alliance between the United States, Canada, and most countries of Western Europe in 1949. While the United States plays a strong role, the alliance involves mutual cooperation between all the members, and hence cannot be broken down into a simple set of bilateral arrangements.

Mistrust can hinder cooperation among groups just as it can between two individuals. If a country is convinced that a certain number of other countries are insincere in their pledges to reduce air pollution or open their borders to trade, it may be too mistrustful to take these steps itself. Reducing one's military forces may make no sense if one interacts regularly with states who are believed to cheat on their arms control commitments. The mistrust problem, therefore, is just as strong if not stronger in multilateral contexts as it is in bilateral ones.

To understand how trust works in multilateral contexts, we need a theory based on a multilateral model. This chapter extends the framework for thinking about trust developed in chapter 2 to the multilateral context. I develop an n-person model with uncertainty over preferences that can be applied to multilateral agreements of all kinds, from arms control to trade agreements. The model has implications for the question of whether hegemony promotes cooperation. A standard argument in international relations theory is that a system with one preeminent state, the hegemon, is more likely to experience international cooperation than one where power is more equally divided among the various states. Models of public goods provision are often invoked to support this claim. I investigate hegemony in the context of mistrust and examine when hegemony will promote cooperation in the face of mistrust and when it will not. The key implication of the model is that hegemons must be *trustworthy* to promote cooperation.

Untrustworthy hegemons not only fail to promote cooperation but may prevent it from occurring between trustworthy states.

MULTILATERAL COOPERATION

Cooperation among groups of actors is often thought to be more difficult to achieve and sustain than cooperation in pairs. Two problems in particular are thought to prevent cooperation, the tendency of individuals to *free ride* on the efforts of others and the difficulty of overcoming *coordination problems* among groups of actors. I discuss each in turn and then show how they combine to form a multilateral trust problem.

The free rider problem arises in situations where the benefit of group cooperation is shared by all, but the cost of cooperating is borne by the individual. In the atmospheric pollution example, a strong ozone layer reduces cancer rates around the world, but each country pays the economic costs of shifting to alternative refrigerants individually. Under certain assumptions about preferences and the costs of cooperating, countries will be tempted to free ride, or continue to use harmful chemicals while enjoying the reduced cancer rates produced by the efforts of others. In typical public goods models, the most basic result is that provision of the good will be not be Pareto optimal, that is, all could benefit if everyone contributed more, but each faces an individual incentive to shirk (Cornes and Sandler 1996). This situation is analogous to a multilateral Prisoner's Dilemma, where defection corresponds to the individually optimal level of contribution, while cooperation is an increased contribution at the Pareto optimal level. All players have a dominant strategy to defect, or contribute at the Nash level.

One potential solution to the free rider problem is the presence of a "large" or hegemonic actor. Mancur Olson argued that public goods will not be provided unless there is a single, presumably large, actor for whom the benefits outweigh the costs (Olson 1965). This argument was very influential in the international political economy literature. Charles Kindleberger argued that the depression of the 1930s was due to the fact that the international economy needed a stabilizer, and Great Britain could not, and the United States would not fulfill that role (Kindleberger 1973). Stephen Krasner argued that periods of trade openness correlated with the existence of a powerful country, Britain in the nineteenth century, the United States in the twentieth (Krasner 1976). Regime theorists argued that hegemons set up cooperative regimes in their heyday that, in turn, sustain cooperation after the hegemon declines (Keohane 1984; Krasner 1983). Hegemonic stability theory, as it came to be known, always had its detractors (Conybeare 1984), but it remains an important theoretical strand in international relations (Gowa 1989; Lake 1993; Pahre 1999).

Hegemony is thought to overcome the free rider problem in one of two ways, corresponding to "benign" and "coercive" theories of hegemony (Snidal 1985). The benign hegemon, as in Olson's theory, provides the public good unilaterally even though the other states are free riding. Of course, this does not really solve the free rider problem per se, in that the followers are not induced to cooperate, but at least more of the public good is provided. A problem with this analysis, despite the tremendous influence of Olson's book, is that in many models of public goods provision, an increased concentration of resources in one actor—hegemony—does not actually increase the level of public goods production, it merely reallocates the burden of producing it (Pahre 1999: 29). In contrast, the coercive hegemon really solves the free rider problem directly by forcing the followers to contribute more than they would if left to their own devices, presumably by threatening to withhold private goods or inflict private costs if they do not comply. Coercive hegemony corresponds more closely to structural realist or Marxist notions of how the global political economy functions (Gilpin 1981).

The second problem thought to impede cooperation in groups is the coordination problem. The coordination problem involves getting everyone in a group to choose a certain outcome, in a context where there are costs associated with failing to agree. For instance, if a dictator is to be overthrown, all (or a big enough subset) of his henchmen must agree to stop supporting him at a certain time. No follower wants to support the dictator if all the others have launched a coup, but no follower wants to launch a coup all by himself either. Schelling (1978) introduced the tipping game to analyze such situations.[1] In tipping games, there are two choices, *A* and *B*. If everyone else chooses *A*, then each player wants to choose *A* as well, and the same for *B*. The all-choose-*A* outcome may be preferred to the all-choose-*B* outcome, leading the players to try to coordinate on *A* rather than *B*. The tipping point is the point at which each player is indifferent between the two options; if a few more choose *A*, then *A* becomes the preferred choice, whereas if a few more choose *B*, then *B* becomes what everyone wants to do.

The tipping game is an *n*-person version of the Assurance Game. The difference, in the *n*-person context, is that each player must be assured, not just that one other player will cooperate, but that several others will, in order to be willing to cooperate itself. This may pose greater difficulties for achieving cooperation than are found in the two actor case. The problem is

[1] See Laitin (1993, 1994) for an application to language choice and Karklins and Peterson (1993) for an application to the eastern European revolutions of 1989.

one of coordinating everyone's expectations—getting everyone to believe that everyone will cooperate—so that they will be willing to cooperate. Beliefs need to be coordinated on the better, cooperative equilibrium, rather than on the not so good non-cooperative equilibrium. The tipping point will vary from situation to situation, but the basic coordination problem is the same, convince everyone that the number of cooperators will exceed the tipping level, so that everyone will then be willing to cooperate, fulfilling the expectation. This process is aided by the fact that the cooperative equilibrium is everyone's favorite equilibrium, making it a "focal point" in the game (Schelling 1960: 54).

In some contexts this coordination problem may be a daunting one. One possible reason for a failure to cooperate in such games is a lack of communication among the players. If the players cannot communicate with each other, perhaps they will not be able to fix their expectations on the cooperative outcome and will defect instead. For instance, in the coup example, if all the henchmen prefer that the dictator is overthrown, it might seem easy for them to coordinate on doing so, given that the dictator depends on their support. But in order to do so, they need to shift from the equilibrium in which they all support him to one in which they all do not support him. This involves some communication, to set a date on which support will end, and get some agreement on what should happen next. But of course, dictators get where they are precisely by being better at this kind of plotting than the average person. Any henchman who tries to alter expectations towards removing the dictator is likely to find himself reported to the dictator by another henchman and killed. The severe penalties for being wrong—opposing the dictator while everyone else still supports him—will reinforce this problem.[2]

In the context of international cooperation, however, this explanation for ending up in the inferior noncooperative equilibrium is weak. International cooperative ventures are usually the product of long bouts of negotiation that result in a fairly explicit understanding of what cooperation entails and what everyone's obligations are, whether it is so many tons of greenhouse gas reductions or so many tanks decommissioned. In the case of the Montreal Protocol, for instance, CFC's had been on the international agenda since the mid-1970s when scientists first advanced the hypothesis that they might be responsible for a thinning of the ozone layer (Haas 1992: 197). Individual states and the European Community took steps to limit or ban CFC production and use in the late 1970s and international negotiations for a global treaty began in 1985, leading to

---

[2]As a result, actors may engage in extensive preference falsification to hide their true feelings, further encouraging the idea that no one will cooperate. Kuran (1991) argues that this explains why revolutions can be surprising, no one will know the true state of discontent with an oppressive regime until it is overthrown.

the Montreal Protocol in 1987. It is simply not credible to suggest that a failure to cooperate after such a lengthy process of communication can be blamed on an inability to focus everyone's expectations on the cooperative equilibrium. The parties were fully aware what the cooperative outcome was, and what was required of them to bring it about (and did, in fact, cooperate in this case).

Cooperation in international tipping games or n-person assurance problems would be more difficult, however, if there were uncertainty about the preferences of the players. In particular, if the actors feared that some of the other actors preferred to free ride on any agreement rather than cooperate, this could make it hard to get past the tipping point. If some actors would prefer to defect regardless of how many others are cooperating, it may make the actors who really do want to cooperate too fearful to do so. This is the mistrust problem in a multilateral guise. Uncertainty about whether everyone actually does want to cooperate may make those who do want to cooperate hesitate to do so.

The trust problem has been overlooked in the literature on multilateral cooperation. Yet trust would seem to be central to many episodes of international cooperation, particularly the post-World War II era as will be discussed in the next chapter. The next section develops a model of multilateral cooperation in the face of mistrust. The model combines in one framework a public goods provision problem similar to a multilateral Prisoner's Dilemma and a multilateral Assurance Game, just as the bilateral trust game combined the two player versions of these games. Thus, it enables us to examine how fears of free riding can impede cooperation among states who would prefer to cooperate if others could be trusted to do so. The model also offers a novel analysis of how hegemony can overcome mistrust and facilitate cooperation.

THE MULTILATERAL TRUST GAME

Consider a model with n players, designated $1, 2, 3, \ldots n$. They face a multilateral social dilemma in which their decision to cooperate or defect will affect some or all of the other players.

The Player's Characteristics: Power and Geography

With n players, the model must make some assumptions about how much each state cares about the cooperation of each other state. In a group of states, how much does state 1 care about state 2's cooperation, state 3's cooperation, etc.? The simplest assumption to make would be that the states all care about each other equally, so that the model is completely symmetric. In many public goods games all actors care equally about the public good and face the same costs for contributing. However, this assumption would be unduly restrictive; states clearly care more about the cooperation of some states than about others. Peru cares more about the cooperation of Chile than it does about Namibia; the United States cares more about Canada than about Estonia. It also would prevent any investigation of hegemony, geography, or asymmetry among the actors of any kind.

To capture these factors, I will assume that each state's utility is affected by each other state's behavior by a certain amount that is specific to those two states. Specifically, I incorporate two characteristics of the actors into the model, their *relative power* and their *geographic location*.

States that are more powerful will have greater impact on the utility of other states. The cooperation or lack thereof of a powerful state matters more for others than that of weak states. To model this, posit that state i has a stock of resources, $\rho_i > 0$. This could be its GDP, military expenditures, population, or some other metric of power. The world total of resources is denoted $\rho = \sum_{i=1}^{n} \rho_i$ and state i's share of world resources or relative power is denoted

$$r_i = \frac{\rho_i}{\rho}.$$

(Wagner 1986; Niou Ordeshook and Rose 1989). We can define a column vector for all the r_i's as follows:

$$\mathbf{r} \equiv \begin{bmatrix} r_1 \\ r_2 \\ \vdots \\ r_n \end{bmatrix}.$$

Notation in the game is summarized in Table 5.1.

States will also care more about the cooperation of nearby states than about states far away, other things being equal. States usually have more interactions, and, hence, more need for trust with their neighbors than with more distant states. This underlies the intuition that Canada and the United States loom large for each other, as do Peru and Chile, but not Peru and Namibia.[3]

To capture this, posit a measure of nearness, $n_{ij} \in (0, 1]$, which indicates how near state j is to state i. This measure could be a function of the inverse of the distance between the capitals, a measure of contiguity (are the two

---

[3] These considerations have led to a focus on "politically relevant dyads"—those in which the states are contiguous or at least one state is a great power—in the quantitative international relations literature (Lemke and Reed 2001).

TABLE 5.1
Notation in the Multilateral Trust Game

ρ_i	Player i's absolute resources.
ρ	The world total of resources.
r_i	Player i's relative power.
$\mathbf{r}$	The vector of players relative power.
n_{ij}	Player i's nearness to player j.
$\mathbf{n}_i$	Player i's nearness to all the other players.
w_{ij}	Player i's weight on player j.
$\mathbf{w}_i$	Player i's weights on all the other players.
$\mathbf{W}$	The global weight matrix.
p_i	Player i's benefit from the public good.
q_i	Player i's benefit from the club good.
c_i	Player i's cost of cooperation.
$F_i, (f_i)$	The CDF (PDF) of player i's costs of cooperation.
τ_i	Player i's likelihood of cooperating.
τ	The vector of likelihoods of cooperating.
$\mathbf{A}$	A modified version of the weight matrix.

states neighbors or not), or any other indicator of nearness, such that states closer together get higher scores. The closest possible state(s) gets a score of 1 ($n_{ij} = 1$) and the farthest away get scores near zero ($n_{ij} \approx 0$). I code a state's nearness to itself as zero ($n_{ii} = 0$), because the nearness scores will be used to construct a measure of the importance of *other* states, not the state itself. The row vector

$$\mathbf{n}_i \equiv [n_{i1} \quad n_{i2} \quad n_{i3} \quad \dots \quad n_{in}].$$

contains the nearness scores of each other state to state i.

These two features of states, their power and proximity, can be combined to form an overall index of how much they care about each other's cooperation. We can think of this as a weight that each state assigns the other in its utility function, the amount by which the other state's cooperation or noncooperation affects the state's well being. In combining power and proximity to form the overall weight, a multiplicative relationship seems appropriate. The farther away a state is, the less its power matters. Germany is far from Indonesia; hence, an increase in German power caused by reunification matters little in Jakarta. Conversely, the weaker a state is, the less its location will matter. It doesn't matter to the United States whether Greece is in Europe or Central America; it is weak and, hence, has a limited impact on the utility function of the United States. To represent this kind of relationship we can define a weight that state i assigns to state j, w_{ij}, as follows:

$$w_{ij} \equiv \frac{n_{ij} r_j}{\mathbf{n}_i \mathbf{r}}.$$

Thus, the weight accorded by state i to state j increases with state j's relative power, r_j and with its nearness to state i, n_{ij}. (The denominator simply normalizes the weights so that they add to one.) Power will matter less the farther away a state is, and proximity will matter less the weaker a state is. The greater w_{ij}, the more player i cares about whether or not player j cooperates. The less w_{ij}, the less impact on player i's utility player j's behavior has. Each weight is bounded by zero and one, $w_{ij} \in (0, 1)$, so that it represents the fraction of importance that country has in player i's utility function (this will be made explicit later on). A state's weight on itself is zero, $w_{ii} = 0$.[4]

Note, these weights are directional, not just dyadic. Player i may care more about player j's behavior than player j does about player i, if $w_{ij} > w_{ji}$. If player 1 is a strong state with the ability to project its power abroad and player 2 is a weak state with only regional influence, player 1 might care less about whether or not player 2 cooperates than vice versa, so w_{12} would be less than w_{21}. For instance, if player 1 were the United States and player 2 were Belgium, and the issue were security cooperation during the Cold War, U.S. behavior would figure more prominently in Belgium's utility function than vice versa. In general, hegemons will care less about each individual follower in the system than the followers care about the hegemon, because the hegemon distributes its concern across many states, while the followers concentrate their concern more on the hegemon.

The row vector

$$\mathbf{w}_i \equiv [\quad w_{i1} \quad w_{i2} \quad w_{i3} \quad \dots \quad w_{in} \quad]$$

is defined so as to contain player i's weights on all the players. The weights each player accords to all the players sum to 1, $\sum_{j=1}^{n} w_{ij} = 1$ for all the players. Thus, the w_{ij} represent a way of adding up the level of cooperation that player i is receiving from the other states. The matrix containing all the weights is denoted $\mathbf{W}$.

To get a better intuitive grasp on how this weighting system works, it will help to consider two special cases. First, consider a perfectly symmetrical

[4]See Snidal 1991 for another use of this modeling device.

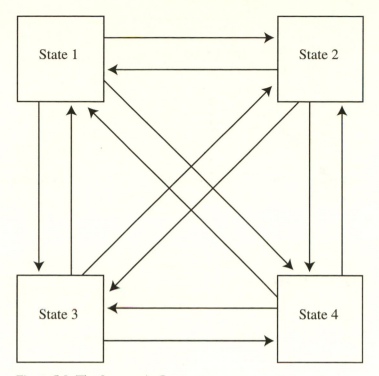

Figure 5.1 The Symmetric Case

system in which each state weights each other state equally. This ideal is approximated by classical balances of power in which there is a group of powers in a region with roughly equal capabilities that can threaten or support each other, such as eighteenth-century Europe. The symmetrical system is illustrated in Figure 5.1 for the case of four actors. Each state considers each other state of roughly the same importance and so weights each other actor the same.

If each state is equally near ($n_{ij} = 1$, $\forall i,j$), and all states are equally powerful ($r_i = \frac{1}{4}$, $\forall i$), then the weighting matrix for the symmetric case looks like the following:

$$\mathbf{W} = \begin{bmatrix} 0 & \frac{1}{3} & \frac{1}{3} & \frac{1}{3} \\ \frac{1}{3} & 0 & \frac{1}{3} & \frac{1}{3} \\ \frac{1}{3} & \frac{1}{3} & 0 & \frac{1}{3} \\ \frac{1}{3} & \frac{1}{3} & \frac{1}{3} & 0 \end{bmatrix}.$$

Each state weights each of the other three states equally, so that $w_{ij} = \frac{1}{3}$.

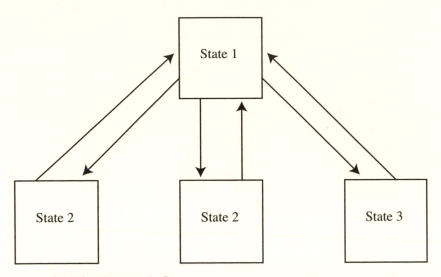

Figure 5.2 The Hegemonic Case

A second polar case worth considering is the hegemonic system. If we imagine an extremely powerful hegemon, such as the United States after World War II, the followers may care mostly about what the hegemon does and very little about each other's behavior. The hegemon will also care less about the followers, but will distribute that concern equally across the followers. This case is illustrated in Figure 5.2. State 1 is the hegemon; the other three states are heavily focused on the hegemon's behavior and less concerned about each other.

If the hegemon has two-thirds of the power and the followers one-ninth each $\left(r_1 = \frac{2}{3} \text{ and } r_i = \frac{1}{9}, i \neq 1 \right)$ and the hegemon is further from the followers than they are from each other $\left(n_{1j} = n_{j1} = \frac{1}{2}, \forall j \text{ and } n_{ij} = 1, \forall i,j \neq 1 \right)$, the weight matrix for a hegemonic case looks like this:

$$
\mathbf{W} = \begin{bmatrix}
0 & \frac{1}{3} & \frac{1}{3} & \frac{1}{3} \\
\frac{3}{5} & 0 & \frac{1}{5} & \frac{1}{5} \\
\frac{3}{5} & \frac{1}{5} & 0 & \frac{1}{5} \\
\frac{3}{5} & \frac{1}{5} & \frac{1}{5} & 0
\end{bmatrix}.
$$

The hegemon weights the followers at $w_{hf} = \frac{1}{3}$ each. The followers weight the hegemon, $w_{fh} = \frac{3}{5}$ because the hegemon is stronger than the other followers, and weight each other at $w_{ff} = \frac{1}{5}$.

The Payoffs and Beliefs

With a means of representing how much the various states care about each other's behavior, we can now define utility functions for the players. I normalize the payoff for universal noncooperation to zero for all players. There is a cost of cooperation c_i for each player. Cooperation provides two kinds of benefits, a public good that is available to all regardless of whether they cooperate and a club good that is shared only among the cooperators. In the case of postwar European security cooperation, the public good could be a general moderation in Soviet foreign policy produced by a countervailing bloc, while the club good would be more specific benefits accruing to members of the alliance, such as greater security against Soviet pressure or invasion, economic and political gains from being a member of a powerful group, etc. Player i produces a public good, $r_i p_i$, from its own cooperation; this is proportional to her relative power, so stronger countries produce more benefits by cooperating. In addition, player i receives an additional $(1 - r_i)w_{ij}p_i$ from each other player who cooperates. Thus, if only player i cooperates, player i gets $r_i p_i$, and if all other states cooperate, state i receives a benefit equal to $r_i p_i + \sum_j (1 - r_i)w_{ij}p_i$ or just p_i. Player i also produces a club good from its own cooperation, $r_i q_i$, and receives $(1 - r_i)w_{ij}q_i$ from other cooperators. These benefits do not accrue to noncooperators.[5]

If we consider variations in the cost of cooperation, c_i, we can distinguish three types of player in the model. If no one else is expected to cooperate, cooperation yields a payoff of $r_i(p_i + q_i) - c_i$, while defection yields zero, so, if $c_i < r_i(p_i + q_i)$, then the player is willing to cooperate even if it is the only state to do so. Such a player has a dominant strategy to cooperate, so I label them the *certain cooperators*. The more powerful a state is, the greater r_i, the more likely it will be in this category and have an incentive to cooperate even if others do not. If everyone else is expected to cooperate, the players receive $p_i + q_i - c_i$ if they cooperate and $(1 - r_i)p_i$ if they do not, so, if $r_i(p_i + q_i) < c_i < r_i p_i + q_i$, then a state will prefer not to cooperate if it is the only one to do so, but it will wish to cooperate if all other states in the system are expected to do so. I label such states *contingent cooperators* because they will cooperate if enough others will do so. Finally, if $c_i > r_i p_i + q_i$, a state will prefer to defect even if all other states are expected to cooperate, it has a dominant strategy to defect. I label such states *noncooperative* types.

For example, consider an eleven state world in which all states weigh each other equally. The payoffs for the noncooperative types are shown in

---

[5] The club good can also be thought of as a selective incentive, an additional excludable good available only to cooperators.

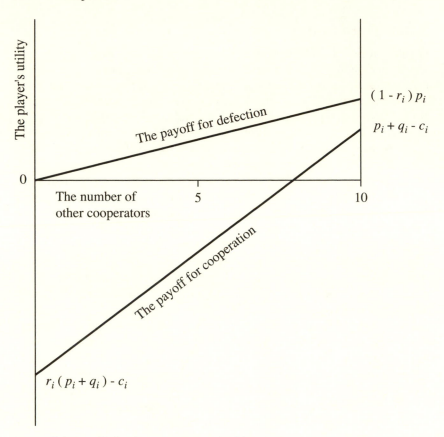

Figure 5.3 Payoffs for the Noncooperative Types

Figure 5.3. The payoff for cooperation increases linearly from $r_i(p_i+q_i)-c_i$ to $p_i+q_i-c_i$ as more other actors cooperate, while the payoff for defection increases linearly from 0 to $(1-r_i)p_i$. Notice, the noncooperative type is always better off defecting; regardless of how many other players cooperate, their payoffs resemble a multilateral Prisoner's Dilemma.

The payoffs for the contingent cooperators are represented in Figure 5.4. For the contingent cooperators, if enough others are expected to cooperate, cooperation is preferred to defection. The tipping point here is five players, if five others cooperate, a player is indifferent between cooperating and defecting; if six or more cooperate, the player prefers to cooperate as well. If fewer than five cooperate, the player prefers to defect.

Figures 5.3 and 5.4 illustrate symmetrical cases where all players weigh each other equally. The payoffs work similarly if the weights are unequal. In

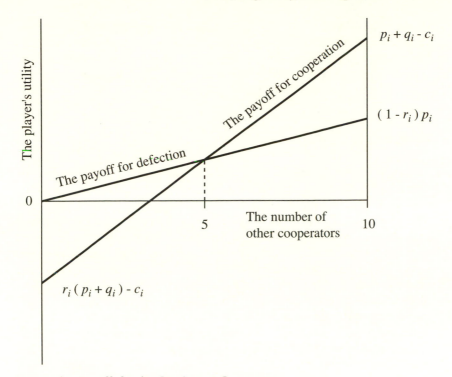

Figure 5.4 Payoffs for the Contingent Cooperators

a three state world, if player 1's relative power is $r_1 = \frac{1}{4}$ and player 1 cares more about player 2 than about player 3's cooperation, so that w_{12} is equal to $\frac{3}{4}$ and w_{13} is only equal to $\frac{1}{4}$, then if only player 2 cooperates, player 1's payoff for cooperating is $\left(\frac{1}{4} + \left(1 - \frac{1}{4}\right)\frac{3}{4}\right)(p_1 + q_1) - c_1$, while if only player 3 cooperates, player 1's payoff is less: $\left(\frac{1}{4} + \left(1 - \frac{1}{4}\right)\frac{1}{4}\right)(p_1 + q_1) - c_1$. The same linear payoff relation holds as in Figures 5.4 and 5.3, but states that one cares about more push one further along the horizontal axis towards total cooperation than states that one cares less about. Thus, if the United States is the most important country for Canada, and if the United States cooperates, this alone may push Canada over the tipping point, enabling Canada to cooperate as well. If another state that Canada cares less about, such as Argentina, cooperated, this would only push Canada part of the way towards the tipping point, making it still reluctant to cooperate (Snidal 1985: 601).

Nature begins the game by determining the types of each of the players. Let each player's costs for contributing be distributed according to a probability density function (PDF) f_i on the positive real numbers with a cumulative distribution function (CDF) F_i.[6] The types of the players are uncorrelated with each other. The distribution functions are common knowledge among the players. Each player is informed of its type but not that of any other player. With this notation in hand, we can proceed to analyze the Multilateral Trust Game.

EQUILIBRIA IN THE GAME

The players face a simple binary choice as before, to cooperate or defect. They choose in ignorance of what others are choosing, so they must make their decisions based only on their type and their beliefs about the other players' types and what they might be doing. How should they choose? Noncooperative types will defect regardless of their beliefs about the types of the other players. Given that they prefer to defect regardless of how many others are cooperating, they have a dominant strategy to defect. Similarly, certain cooperators will cooperate regardless of their beliefs. The choices of the contingent cooperators depend on the probability distributions over the player's costs of contributing.

For each state there will be a threshold level of costs $c_i^* \in [r_i(p_i + q_i), r_i p_i + q_i]$ below which player i will cooperate and above which player i will defect. The threshold is illustrated in Figure 5.5. The likelihood that any player will cooperate, denoted τ_i, is $\tau_i = F_i(c_i^*)$. Note τ_i is not the same as the level of trust. Since all types with $c_i \leq r_i p_i + q_i$ would be willing to cooperate if certain that everyone else would, all such types should be counted as trustworthy according to the definition of chapter 1. The level of trust is therefore $t_i = F_i(r_i p_i + q_i)$. Not all such types will be able to cooperate in equilibrium, however, because not everyone is certain to cooperate. Instead, τ_i is an expectation about behavior, how likely the other side is to cooperate in the equilibrium. I define a column vector of these expectations as follows:

$$\tau \equiv \begin{bmatrix} \tau_1 \\ \tau_2 \\ \vdots \\ \tau_n \end{bmatrix}.$$

To find out when a contingent cooperator is willing to cooperate in equilibrium, we compare their payoffs for cooperation and defection, assuming that the other players will cooperate if $c_j \leq c_j^*$. First, we need the expected

[6]See the literature on global games for a set of related models, e.g., Morris and Shin 1998, 2003.

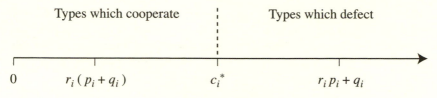

Figure 5.5 The Threshold between Cooperation and Defection

value of cooperation. The payoff for cooperation is $r_i(p_i + q_i) - c_i$ if no one cooperates, and an additional $(1 - r_i)w_{ij}(p_i + q_i)$ for every other state j who cooperates. The likelihood that state j cooperates is τ_j. If state j does not cooperate, which will happen with likelihood $1 - \tau_j$, then player i will reap no benefit. The benefit to be expected from each other player is therefore equal to $\tau_j(1 - r_i)w_{ij}(p_i + q_i) + (1 - \tau_j)(1 - r_i)w_{ij}(0)$ or just $\tau_j(1 - r_i)w_{ij}(p_i + q_i)$. Summing up over all the players, the expected value of cooperation for the contingent cooperator is therefore $r_i(p_i + q_i) - c_i + (1 - r_i)w_{i1}\tau_1(p_i + q_i) + (1 - r_i)w_{i2}\tau_2(p_i + q_i) + \cdots + (1 - r_i)w_{in}\tau_n(p_i + q_i)$. This can be more concisely expressed as $r_i(p_i + q_i) - c_i + (1 - r_i)\sum_{j=1}^{n} w_{ij}\tau_j(p_i + q_i)$ or just $r_i(p_i + q_i) - c_i + (1 - r_i)\mathbf{w}_i\tau(p_i + q_i)$.

The vector product, $\mathbf{w}_i\tau$, is just the sum of the likelihoods that the players will cooperate, τ_j, weighted by how much player i cares about them, w_{ij}. For Canada, say, we take how much it cares about the United States times the likelihood the United States will cooperate, plus how much it cares about Great Britain times the likelihood that Great Britain will cooperate, etc. through all the countries that Canada cares about. Thus, it is a weighted average of how likely the other players are to cooperate, where the states that player i cares about more are weighed more heavily and those that player i cares less about are weighed less heavily.

The payoff for defection can be derived in an analogous way and is equal to $(1 - r_i)\mathbf{w}_i\tau p_i$. Cooperation beats defection for the contingent cooperators if $r_i(p_i + q_i) - c_i + (1 - r_i)\mathbf{w}_i\tau(p_i + q_i) > (1 - r_i)\mathbf{w}_i\tau p_i$, so player i's threshold level of costs is as follows:

$$c_i^* = r_i(p_i + q_i) + (1 - r_i)\mathbf{w}_i\tau q_i. \tag{5.1}$$

Equation 5.1, along with the fact that $\tau_i = F_i(c_i^*)$, establishes a set of n equations in the cutoff points c_i^* that must be satisfied in equilibrium. In general, the equilibrium need not be unique, however the following theorem is proved in the Appendix.

Theorem 5.1 *There exists a unique best equilibrium in the Multilateral Trust Game in which each player's likelihood of cooperation is maximized. In this equilibrium, the likelihood that each player cooperates increases with any player's public goods payoff, p_i, club goods payoff, q_i, and likelihood of cooperation, τ_i.*

By specifying the cost distributions, $F_i(\cdot)$, we can solve explicitly for an equilibrium. For instance, consider the case where c_i is distributed uniformly over $[0, \bar{c}_i]$. In this case, $f_i(c_i) = \frac{1}{\bar{c}_i}$ and $F_i(c_i) = \frac{c_i}{\bar{c}_i}$. We can rewrite equation 5.1 as follows.

$$\mathbf{w}_i \tau - \frac{c_i^*}{(1-r_i)q_i} = -\frac{r_i(p_i + q_i)}{(1-r_i)q_i}. \tag{5.2}$$

We know that $\tau_i = F_i(c_i^*) = \frac{c_i^*}{\bar{c}_i}$, so if we define $a_{ii} = -\frac{1}{(1-r_i)q_i}$, $a_{ij} = w_{ij}f_j = \frac{w_{ij}}{\bar{c}_j}$, $\mathbf{c}^*$ as the column vector of cutoff values and $m_i = -\frac{r_i(p_i + q_i)}{(1-r_i)q_i}$, then we can re-express equation 5.2 as $\mathbf{a}_i \mathbf{c}^* = m_i$ and, letting $\mathbf{m}$ represent the column vector of the m_i, the set of n equations is $\mathbf{Ac}^* = \mathbf{m}$. This is a set of n linear equations in n unknowns, so, if we define $\mathbf{A}_i$ to be the $\mathbf{A}$ matrix with the ith column replaced by $\mathbf{m}$, then the solutions for the cutoff points are given by Cramer's rule as

$$c_i^* = \frac{|\mathbf{A}_i|}{|\mathbf{A}|} \tag{5.3}$$

provided that $|\mathbf{A}| \neq 0$ (Silberberg 1990: 143). This equilibrium is unique.

In the analysis that follows, I will use a linear numerical example to generate the illustrations. However, the comparative static results apply in the general case to the equilibrium identified in Theorem 5.1, as shown in the Appendix. I turn first to the payoffs for the public and club goods.

The Payoffs and Cooperation

How do the payoffs, p_i and q_i, affect the likelihood that the states will cooperate? Raising a state's payoff for the public and club good increases the likelihood that they will cooperate, and this, in turn, raises the likelihood that other states will cooperate. Consider the example illustrated in Figure 5.6. There are five states, arranged in a line so that states farther away are weighted less heavily.[7] The vertical axis is τ_i, the likelihood that each state cooperates. The states have equal relative power and their costs are distributed uniformly with an upper bound $\bar{c}_i = 10$. The baseline case

---

[7] The distance function is $n_{ij} = \frac{1}{|i-j|}$.

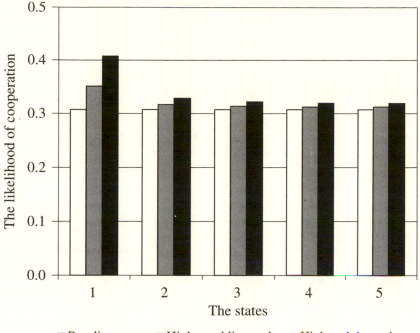

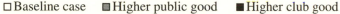

Figure 5.6 The Effect of Player 1's Payoffs

is when all states have the same public good and club good payoffs, $p_i = 2$ and $q_i = 6$. In this case each state has roughly a 31 percent likelihood of cooperating, $\tau_i = 0.31$.

If we increase player 1's public goods payoff to $p_1 = 4$, all states become more likely to cooperate as illustrated by the middle bar. The effect is strongest for player 1, whose likelihood of cooperate increases to 35 percent. However, the fact that player 1 is more likely to cooperate makes the other states more likely to cooperate as well. This effect tapers off with distance, so player 5 feels the smallest impact of the increase. If instead we increase player 1's club good payoff to $q_1 = 8$, the effect is similar but more pronounced as shown in the right hand bar in each set. The likelihood that player 1 cooperates goes up to 41 percent, and the likelihood that the other players cooperate also increases. Once again the effect tapers off with distance, but is still felt even by player 5.

The impact on cooperation of increasing the club good payoff is greater than that for increasing the public good. This is because the public good produced by others is received whether or not one cooperates. Therefore, cooperation becomes more attractive than defection only to the extent that one's own public good production becomes more valuable. With the club good, one receives the benefit of others' cooperation only if one cooperates as well, so that increasing the club good payoff increases the payoff to cooperation substantially and the payoff for defection not at all.

GEOGRAPHY AND MISTRUST

Now consider how geography and mistrust affect cooperation in the Multilateral Trust Game. States care more about states closer to them and less about ones that are farther away. If some states are more trustworthy than others, states nearby the less trustworthy states may find it harder to cooperate than those farther away.

This relationship is illustrated in Figure 5.7. As before, we have five states in a line and their likelihood of cooperation on the vertical axis. The base line case is the same as before; each state is equally trustworthy, with the same upper bound on costs $\bar{c}_i = 10$. In this case, each state has a 31 percent likelihood of cooperating. In the comparison case, we make player 5 less trustworthy, by increasing its upper bound to $\bar{c}_5 = 20$. This

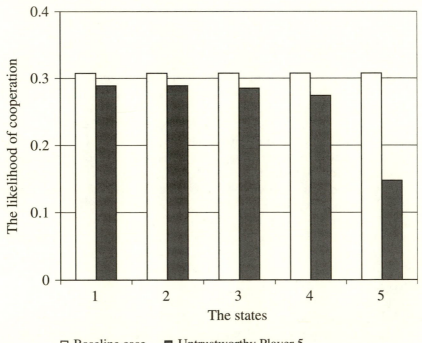

□ Baseline case   ■ Untrustworthy Player 5

Figure 5.7 The Effect of Geography and Mistrust

shifts player 5's cost distribution towards higher costs, making player 5 more likely to be a noncooperative type, and, hence, untrustworthy.

The effect is to make all the players less likely to cooperate, with the effect growing stronger the closer one gets to player 5. Player 5's likelihood of cooperation drops in half, to 15 percent. Player 4's likelihood of cooperation drops to 27 percent, while player 3 drops to 28 percent and players 1 and 2 to 29 percent. Player 5's untrustworthiness has made it harder for the others to cooperate, convincing some borderline types to defect instead. Geographical considerations mandate that this effect is strongest on states closest to the untrustworthy state. This is summed up in the following implication of the model.

Implication 5.1   *States closer to less trustworthy states, other things equal, will be less likely to cooperate.*

HEGEMONY AND COOPERATION

Finally, we can use the model to investigate the issue of whether international cooperation is aided by hegemony. Hegemons are typically thought of as states at the top of the international power hierarchy with a substantial gap between themselves and number two. In the model we can represent this idea through the relative power variable, r_i. Let state 1 be the most powerful state in the system, $r_1 > r_i, \forall i > 1$. We can think of state 1 as the hegemon and the degree to which its power exceeds the second ranked power as a measure of the extent of its hegemony.

The impact of hegemony on cooperation is illustrated in Figure 5.8. Once again we have five states with the likelihood of cooperation on the vertical axis. I consider five cases. The base line case is the same as before, with each state equally powerful and trustworthy, and each state has a likelihood of cooperation of 31 percent. In the second case, player 1 has been made more trustworthy by reducing $\bar{c}_1$ to 8. This has the effect of making all the players more likely to cooperate. Player 1 becomes 39 percent likely to cooperate and even player 5's likelihood of cooperation goes up by a percentage point. If player 1 is then made hegemonic as well, by increasing its relative power to 40 percent ($r_1 = 0.4$), this further increases the likelihood of cooperation in the system. The hegemon becomes 55 percent likely to cooperate and the nearby states, 2 and 3, also become more likely to cooperate. Thus, the presence of a trustworthy hegemon can foster cooperation. Increased power makes the hegemon more likely to cooperate, which makes states close to the hegemon also more likely to cooperate.

The next two cases are more problematic, however. The third case returns player 1 to an equal power level but makes it less trustworthy,

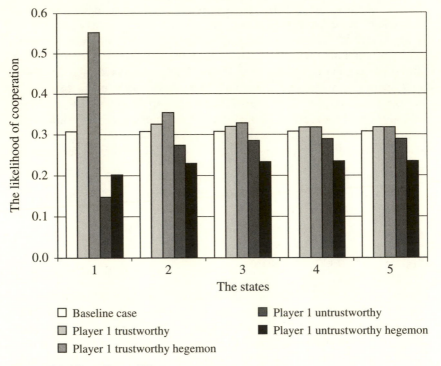

Figure 5.8 The Effect of Hegemony

increasing $\bar{c}_1$ to 20. This has a negative effect on cooperation across the system, as was shown in the previous section. Player 1 becomes only 15 percent likely to cooperate and the other states also suffer declines in their cooperation rates. Will hegemony solve this problem by making player 1 more willing to cooperate? In fact, as the last bar shows, hegemony only makes the problem worse. If player 1 is returned to a relative power of 40 percent it does become more likely to cooperate, up to 20 percent. However, the other states suffer further declines in their willingness to cooperate; their likelihood of cooperation declines to about 23 percent. The presence of the untrustworthy hegemon therefore *reduces* the likelihood of cooperation of the followers from 31 percent to 23 percent, rather than increasing it.

Why does the presence of an untrustworthy hegemon fail to promote cooperation? Making an untrustworthy state more powerful has two negative effects on the willingness of others to cooperate. First, making a state more powerful means that other states place more weight on it since relative power is a key component of the weighting function. Placing more weight on the relatively untrustworthy player 1 than on the other players, who are more likely to cooperate, makes the followers less willing to cooperate. If Belgium is untrustworthy, it will have little impact on the ability of other European states to cooperate. If Germany is untrustworthy, it will have a much more significant impact, because Germany's power makes it more important to the other states.

Second, hegemony reduces the followers' relative power, and this directly reduces their willingness to cooperate. The payoff for cooperation is a direct function of a state's relative power. Stronger states produce more public and club goods when they cooperate, so, the weaker a state is, the less it will want to cooperate. Making one state hegemonic makes the other states relatively weaker, which lowers their interest in cooperation. In a world of five equal states, each state has 20 percent of the power and therefore produces a significant amount of public goods. If one state grows to have 60 percent of the power, the others fall to 10 percent each, reducing their power in half, which reduces their ability to produce significant quantities of the public goods.

The standard claim of hegemonic stability theory, that increasing the power of one state will promote cooperation, therefore needs further refinement. The Multilateral Trust Game shows that a hegemon that is relatively trustworthy can indeed promote cooperation among the followers. However, a hegemon that is relatively untrustworthy can inhibit cooperation among the followers, preventing states from cooperating that would have cooperated in the absence of hegemony. This insight is summed up in the following implication.

Implication 5.2   *For hegemony to increase the likelihood of cooperation among the followers, the hegemon must be relatively trustworthy.*

As I will explore in chapter 6, this implication sheds light on the situation of the United States vis a vis Europe in the post–World War II period. The United States was certainly hegemonic; with half the industrial capacity of the world and a monopoly on atomic weapons, few could challenge it. The Europeans also trusted the United States more than they did each other. The terrible toll of two world wars had left a legacy of bitter distrust, especially towards Germany, but also of the other European countries. The United States stood above this legacy. The United States was a trustworthy hegemon, and that helped make cooperation possible in postwar Europe.

CONCLUSION

This chapter has shown that the analysis of trust presented in the Security Dilemma Game of chapter 2 can be easily generalized to more than two players. The Multilateral Trust Game has implications for the study of the effects of hegemony on international politics. The usual explanation of why hegemony produces cooperation is that hegemons are supposed to be privileged providers of public goods, willing to bear the costs while others shirk. I advance an alternative theory of hegemony based on trust. Hegemons can help resolve trust problems among their followers, enabling them to cooperate. For hegemons to carry out this role, they must be relatively trustworthy. The case of U.S. hegemony after the Second World War is an example of this kind of hegemonic cooperation at work, as I will explore in the next chapter.

APPENDIX

We have a system of n equations:

$$c_i^* = r_i(p_i + q_i) + (1 - r_i)q_i \sum_{j=1}^{n} w_{ij} F_j(c_j).$$

We assume the following about the basic parameters of the model: $c_i \geq 0$, $r_i \in (0,1)$, $\sum_{i=1}^{n} r_i = 1$, $p_i > 0$, $q_i > 0$, $w_{ij} \in [0,1]$, $w_{ii} = 0$, $\sum_{j=1}^{n} w_{ij} = 1$, and F_i is a strictly increasing CDF defined on $[0, +\infty)$.

If we think of these equations as a function from R^n to R^n, we can see that it is strictly increasing since each cutoff point is an increasing function of the other ones. Therefore, by Tarski's fixed point theorem there is a greatest fixed point that corresponds to the equilibrium identified in Theorem Five (Topkis 1998: 40).

We also know that the function is increasing in the values of the public goods, p_i, club goods, q_i, and likelihood that the each player is trustworthy, F_i. Milgrom and Roberts show that the greatest fixed point is therefore increasing in these parameters, establishing the comparative static results (Topkis 1998: 41; Milgrom and Roberts 1994). The function is not increasing with respect to the hegemon's power, r_1, so no general comparative static result is possible for this parameter. By example, we have shown that if a state is relatively trustworthy, increasing its power can raise the level of cooperation, and if it is relatively untrustworthy, raising its power can decrease it.

For those not familiar with the theorems cited, consider the following proof. Consider n sequences $\hat{c}_i^r$, (where the superscript r stands for "round," not relative power) constructed as follows. In the first round, we set $\hat{c}_i^1 = r_i p_i + q_i$. In the second round, $\hat{c}_i^2$ is adjusted downward until it equals c_i^* holding the other cutoff points at their previous round levels. (It must be adjusted downwards because $c_i^* = r_i p_i + q_i$ is the solution if the $c_j = \infty$, but the c_j are only $r_j p_j + q_j$ so c_i^* must be less.) Repeat for indefinitely many rounds. Since $F_i(c_i)$ is increasing in c_i, the sequences $\hat{c}_i^r$ will be declining monotonically, $k < l \Rightarrow \hat{c}_i^k > \hat{c}_i^l$. The sequences are bounded below by $r_i(p_i + q_i)$. Therefore the sequences have a limit, and an equilibrium will exist:

$$c_i^* = \lim_{r \to \infty} \hat{c}_i^r.$$

To see that it is uniquely best, note that each term in each sequence is an equilibrium reaction to values for the other solutions that are always higher than any possible equilibrium level. It is therefore itself higher than any possible equilibrium value. Thus, the limits are lower bounds of sequences which are all higher than any possible equilibrium and so the equilibrium must be greater than any other.

For the comparative static results, consider two values of player 1's public goods, p_1 and p_1' where $p_1 < p_1'$. Construct a sequence to find the solution in the p_1' case, but this time begin the sequences at the solution corresponding to p_1, so that $\hat{c}_i^{1'} = c_i^*$. For player 1, since $p_1' > p_1$, it must be that $\hat{c}_1^{2'} > c_1^{1'} = c_1^*$. For the other players, the second round values will be unchanged, $c_j^{2'} = c_j^{1'}$. In the third round, however, all values will be bigger than the previous round value, because player 1's is larger, and the other's are an increasing function of player 1's, so $c_i^{3'} > c_i^{2'}$, and so forth for subsequent rounds, $k < l \Rightarrow \hat{c}_i^{k'} < \hat{c}_i^{l'}$. The sequences are bounded above by $r_i p_i + q_i$ and the limits to the sequences will be strictly greater than the starting points, so $c_i^{*'} > c_i^*$. Therefore, each player's cutoff point will increase with any player's value for the public good. The other comparative statics can be similarly derived.

CHAPTER 6

European Cooperation and Germany, 1945–55

> French policy is based not simply on the fear of future German aggression but equally, if not more, on the fear that the United States will lose interest, eventually withdraw from Germany, and that some fine morning they will wake up and find themselves face to face with the Russians on the Rhine.
>
> —Robert Murphy (U.S. State Department)

IN 1939 NAZI Germany launched a war of aggression after every effort had been made to satisfy its demands. During the conflict, Germany implemented, as a matter of national policy, a program of genocidal extermination. Millions of Jews, Gypsies, and other minorities were annihilated. However, at a price in excess of twenty million dead, paid largely by the Russians, Germany was defeated in 1945 and Berlin was occupied. Even the supposedly naive and incorrigibly optimistic Americans indulged in fantasies of revenge. Treasury Secretary Henry Morgenthau proposed a plan calling for the "pastoralization" of Germany, the destruction of its factories, steel mills, and mines, so that Germany could never again threaten its neighbors. At the Tehran conference when Stalin called for the liquidation of fifty to one hundred thousand officers in the German army, Roosevelt quipped that he would settle for forty nine, disgusting even Churchill (Gaddis 1972: 102).

Ten years later, Germany was partitioned into two states along the boundaries separating the Soviet from the Western zones of occupation. West Germany was recovering economically, and had just entered a military alliance with the United States, Britain, France, and other Western European nations only recently liberated from German occupation. Furthermore, its allies had just approved a plan for West German rearmament and a German army was once more being created.

The rehabilitation of Germany was only part of a larger development, the creation of a Western bloc. The early Cold War saw a remarkable series of cooperative institutional developments. In 1947, Britain and France formed an alliance embodied in the Treaty of Dunkirk. In 1948, they joined the Benelux nations (Belgium, Netherlands, and Luxembourg) in the Brussels Pact alliance. That same year the Marshall Plan was passed and the Organization for European Economic Cooperation (OEEC) was born. In 1949, the North Atlantic Treaty Organization (NATO) linked the United States and Canada to the European states in a grand alliance. In 1951, the continental states formed the European Coal and Steel Community (ECSC) and the next year signed a treaty establishing a European army and a European Defense Community (EDC) providing for the rearmament of Germany. This last proved to be a community too far, however, but after the French assembly failed to ratify it, Germany was brought into the Brussels Pact and NATO and rearmed anyway.

How should the revival of Germany and the creation of a Western bloc be understood? This chapter will argue that the theory of trust under hegemony offered in the last chapter sheds considerable light on the process. The existence of the United States as a powerful, trusted, hegemonic actor made it possible for the European states to cooperate with each other, when otherwise it would have been difficult or impossible. The chapter has two sections. First I lay out my explanation for European cooperation in the light of the Multilateral Trust Game of the previous chapter, alongside two alternative explanations that are common in the literature. Second, I trace the development of European security cooperation from 1945 to 1955, and assess how the competing perspectives account for the emergence of institutionalized European cooperation and the restoration of Germany in the early Cold War. Though this chapter covers some of the same ground as chapter 4, my focus here is on Germany and the policies of the European governments, particularly Britain, France, and, after 1949, West Germany itself.

Explaining European Cooperation

The European states faced several public goods problems after the war even apart from any threat from the Soviet Union. Their economies were devastated and inward looking and international economic cooperation was needed to foster recovery and growth. German power might one day be a threat again, so security cooperation could produce important benefits for its former victims. If the Soviets had been trustworthy, they might have participated in multilateral cooperative efforts to address these problems. The growing threat from the East, however, presented the Western powers with an additional public goods challenge: providing for mutual defense and deterrence. This new issue eventually came to set the context in which all other cooperative ventures would be played out. The potential players would be the states west of the iron curtain, the ultimate goal would be to strengthen their ability to resist Soviet expansion. Thus, the failure of the United States and Soviets to cooperate, detailed in Chapter 4, created an acute need for cooperation between the United States and the Western European states for the common defense.

A common threat is at the core of realist theories of cooperation. Offensive realist explanations for cooperation focus on the existence of common threats in the form of powerful third parties which lead states to ally with each other (Mearsheimer 2001: 52–53). Waltz argues that states balance against power, "Secondary states, if they are free to choose, flock to the weaker side, for it is the stronger side that threatens them" (Waltz 1979: 127). Mearsheimer argues that states prefer to buckpass, or free ride off the efforts of others to oppose aggressors, unless the aggressor is a potential hegemon, in which case they balance against it (Mearsheimer 2001: 270).[1]

Yet balance of power theory has difficulty accounting for certain aspects of postwar European cooperation. The global balance of power favored the United States, but the Europeans aligned with the United States against the weaker Soviet Union. If instead we consider the European balance, it is true that it strongly favored the Soviets (Karber and Combs 1998). However this imbalance was *voluntarily* produced by the thorough demobilization of the U.S. military. That is, since U.S. potential power was greater than that of the Soviets, the fact that its power in being in Europe was much less can only be the result of a conscious choice on the part of the United States to build less power than its rival. This is a serious anomaly for offensive realism. Why build less power than your rival when you assume from the start it will use every means up to and including offensive war to achieve hegemony in Europe? Also, the U.S. decision to opt for military inferiority was made in 1945 but the balancing reaction on the part of the Europeans did not begin until 1947, and was not militarily significant until 1950 with the militarization of NATO. Such a lag seems difficult to explain within the theory.

Defensive realists refine balance of power theory by arguing that states balance against the most *threatening* state they perceive, where threat is defined as a composite of power, intentions (motivations), geography, and offensive capabilities (Walt 1987: 274–80). Balance of threat theory can account for the lag between cause and effect by arguing that the Soviets were initially not especially distrusted, certainly compared to Germany. However, Soviet behavior made the European states more suspicious of Russian motivations, which, in turn, made the Soviet Union more threatening as time went by. This increased threat from the Soviet Union posed a grave security problem for the United States and the European states. Defending the West against Soviet expansionism became a more and more important public good.

---

[1] A similar result is found in formal models of balance of power systems, in that stability is attained when one power has half the system's resources because the others then balance, see Wagner 1986; Niou, Ordeshook, and Rose 1989.

However, balance of threat theory does not provide a very compelling explanation of when states will balance against a threat and when they will pursue alternative strategies (Larson 1991; Schweller 1994; Powell 1999: 179). States may wish to free ride off the efforts of others, join the expansionist state to realize their own expansionist ambitions, or capitulate to the threat in hopes of currying favor, among other possibilities. As the quotation that begins this chapter indicates, Europeans feared that the United States would abandon them to face the Russians by themselves, as the United States had left them to face Germany after the First World War. American policymakers feared that European states would capitulate in an effort to appease the Russians. Stephen Walt argues that weak states are more likely to bandwagon with the threatening power, but the European states, aside from Britain, were quite weak in comparison to the Soviet Union, yet they managed to balance in the end. In sum, balance of threat theory identifies a public good, collective defense against a powerful, expansionist state, but fails to offer a well-developed theory of when it will be provided and when it will not be.

An obvious place to look for such a theory is the literature on collective action in international relations, particularly hegemonic stability theory. I will contrast my take on hegemony drawn from the previous chapter with two approaches common in the literature.

Hegemonic Assurance

In the hegemonic assurance perspective, mistrust is seen as the main barrier to cooperation and U.S. hegemony solved this problem. The European states faced a multilateral trust problem after the war. The rise of the Soviet threat created a situation in which it behooved the Europeans to cooperate with each other, the United States, and with Germany. Fail to cooperate, and each state would have to come to an understanding with the Russians on their terms. Each of the European states preferred to cooperate if the others would; however, they were all uncertain about whether the others shared this preference ordering. In the words of Martin H. Folly, they faced a "vicious circle" in that each side would cooperate if the other side would go first, but each side was afraid to go first (Folly 1988). No one wanted to be the lone cooperator if the enterprise failed and Russian wrath had to be faced. The United States also preferred to cooperate if it could be assured that the Europeans would as well, but feared that European mistrust might prevent cooperation, rendering their investment in Europe a waste of resources.

This problem was solved by U.S. hegemony. U.S. hegemony made its behavior highly salient to the European states. The United States was also comparatively trustworthy. The main fear was not of U.S. aggression but of U.S. indifference or withdrawal. This was a very real fear; Roosevelt made it plain that the United States would not keep troops in Europe for long, gravely worrying Churchill (FRUS Yalta: 286–87). Much of U.S. early Cold War policy, including the strategy of encouraging European unification, had the goal of building up Europe to the point where it could deter the Soviets without further U.S. assistance (Sheetz 1999; Creswell 2002; McAllister 2002). The United States had to overcome European mistrust with firm commitments to European security. By making such commitments, the United States was able to create sufficient incentives for the Europeans to make cooperation worthwhile in the face of the lingering mistrust.

Two main hypotheses can be derived about the possibility for European cooperation, following from the implications of the previous chapter. First, implication 5.1 from the previous chapter tells us that being closer to an untrustworthy state will make it more difficult for a state to cooperate; those further away will find it easier. The most distrusted state by far is Germany and the most trusted is the United States. If we compare the two key West European states, France and Britain, we can say that they are both roughly the same distance from the United States, but France is closer to Germany than Britain is. This implies that France will have a harder time than Britain in cooperating in multilateral endeavors that involve Germany. Of course, in the early postwar years, Germany was not a full-fledged independent actor. However, it was clear that Germany could not be occupied indefinitely and so would eventually regain its sovereignty. France and the other states therefore faced a similar trust problem with respect to Germany, particularly when they contemplated moves that involved reviving Germany economically, politically, and especially militarily. Though Germany could not defect immediately after the war, eventually it would be able to and its motivations at that point would be crucial.

Second, from implication 5.2, guarantees from the trusted hegemon will be required to overcome mistrust problems in the most difficult cases of European cooperation. The other European states are more trustworthy than Germany but not perfectly so. This indicates that cooperative enterprises between the European states excluding Germany, or for the purposes of restraining Germany, will be relatively easy to accomplish, and will not necessarily require U.S. participation. However, cooperative enterprises that involve Germany, and particularly those that tend to foster German revival, will be more difficult to achieve. The United States is relatively trusted, compared to most states, and is hegemonic. As a result, it can function as a trusted hegemon, making cooperation possible where it otherwise would not be. Therefore, in cooperative ventures designed to revive German power, U.S. participation or guarantees will typically be necessary.

The theory of hegemonic assurance is, of course, not the first to link U.S. power and European cooperation after the war. However, the mechanisms that link these two variables in traditional explanations are different from the one I focus on. There are two principal alternative conceptions of the role of hegemony in postwar Europe. Some theorists argue that the United States was so powerful that the European countries could free ride off U.S. public goods provision. An alternative approach to hegemony argues instead that the United States coerced cooperation, so the European states had little choice in the matter.

Benign Hegemony and Free Riding

The first alternative theory of hegemony holds that U.S. power made European cooperation irrelevant, and, hence, no trust was necessary. Sometimes it is said that the United States provided security for the allies, so they did not have to provide it for themselves, or that they were able to escape the security dilemma or even anarchy itself because U.S. hegemonic influence was so powerful. Hegemonic stability theory holds that hegemons provide public goods such as security or institutions supporting free trade, while smaller powers free ride, not contributing or contributing little, while taking advantage of the hegemon's provision (Olson and Zeckhauser 1966; Kindleberger 1973; Keohane 1984; Snidal 1985; Pahre 1999). In this view, European postwar good relations are a product of American hegemonic power relieving European states of the necessity of making important security choices (Mearsheimer 1990: 47; Waltz 1979: 70–71).

The key assumption about preferences in this story is that the Americans prefer to provide the public good, security, even if the Europeans fail to contribute. The United States, in effect, has "Harmony" preferences, in which they have a dominant strategy to cooperate regardless of what the Europeans do. Knowing this, the Europeans are able to free ride, certain that the United States will pick up the slack. Europeans have Prisoner's Dilemma payoffs, preferring to defect even if the other side is expected to cooperate. Thus, the game features complete information about preferences, and the only equilibrium is for the United States to cooperate and the Europeans to defect. In more complicated versions of the game with continuous strategy spaces, the central result is that smaller powers undercontribute, they may not defect completely (Sandler and Hartley 2001).

Implicit in this perspective is the notion that any seeming cooperation one might observe among the Europeans is a mere multilateral veneer over U.S. provision of public goods. Treaties are signed and institutions created, but the underlying reality is that the Europeans make no meaningful contribution to their own security, which is taken care of by the United States.

Coercive Hegemony and U.S. Domination

The second alternative interpretation of hegemony argues that the Europeans cooperated because the United States had predominant power and wanted them to. A favorite of Marxists as well as realists, this theory posits European states, weakened by war and defeat, succumbing to American control. In the Marxist version, the United States used its economic and military power to coerce adherence to a Western capitalist bloc, preventing any drift to the left. As the Kolkos would have it, "American business could operate only in a world composed of politically reliable and stable capitalist nations, and with free access to essential raw materials. Such a universal order precluded the Left from power, and necessitated conservative, ultimately subservient, political control throughout the globe" (Kolko and Kolko 1972: 2). Or, in Robert Gilpin's realist version, "In every international system the dominant powers in the international hierarchy of power and prestige organize and control the processes of interactions among the elements of the system. . . . These dominant states have sought to exert control over the system in order to advance their self-interests" (Gilpin 1981: 29). U.S. hegemony is once again seen as the key variable, but for a different reason than the hegemonic assurance theory I advance or the public goods provision approach of benign hegemony theory. The main implication of this theory is that European states cooperate when instructed to do so by the United States, because so-called cooperative arrangements are really window dressing for U.S. exploitation. Note, coercive hegemony, unlike benign hegemony, does argue that the Europeans actually cooperate, rather than merely free ride off the Americans. However, this is explained by American domination rather than European initiative. A second implication is that in any disagreement between the United States and the European allies, U.S. preferences prevail. This is a result of the bargaining leverage of the parties; U.S. preferences win out because of U.S. power.

Evaluating the Perspectives

In evaluating the perspectives, we are handicapped by having one historical era to consider, the post–World War II period, and, therefore, one hegemon and one set of followers to deal with. We cannot compare what happened with what would have happened with an alternative hegemon, no hegemon, different followers, etc. However, we can break up the overall case into several subcases, and analyze the pattern of events in each subcase for clues about which perspective is most supported by the evidence. The decade between 1945 and 1955 contains many efforts at U.S.-European cooperation, some successful and some unsuccessful, and each is informative about the conditions that facilitated cooperation or hindered it.

When interpreting the historical record to evaluate the perspectives, three questions are crucial. First, did the European states genuinely cooperate in postwar security and economic affairs, or did they free ride off U.S. provision of public goods? If the Europeans cooperate, this supports hegemonic assurance and coercive hegemony, if they free ride, it supports benign hegemony. Second, if the European states cooperated, did they do so only in response to U.S. instructions, or did they do so on their own, with each other, and in an effort to draw in U.S. participation? If the Europeans are reactive or passive, this supports coercive hegemony, if they are active and initiate cooperation, this supports hegemonic assurance. Finally, in bargaining over the terms of cooperation, does the United States get its way most or all of the time, or do the preferences of the European states have a significant impact on the final deal? The more often the United States prevails, the better coercive hegemony looks; the more often European preferences matter, the weaker it looks.

The narrative that follows will make it clear that the historical record supports hegemonic assurance over benign and coercive hegemony. Recent historical scholarship has emphasized that the formation of the Western bloc was a truly multilateral affair. The leading British role in the origins of the Cold War and the formation of the Western alliance is now well documented (Best 1986; Deighton 1990; Baylis 1993). France, once thought to have been largely ineffective in fighting a losing battle to control Germany, is now recognized to have successfully resisted U.S. pressure and affected the terms and pacing of European cooperation (Wall 1991; Hitchcock 1998; Creswell and Trachtenberg 2003). Historian Geir Lundestad has called the U.S. relationship with Europe an "empire by invitation" and indeed the U.S. role was not only invited but also closely circumscribed by the European states (Lundestad 1990). This new historiography casts doubt on the idea that postwar security institutions were a U.S.-provided public good or a mechanism for enforcing obedience based on coercion.

In the sections that follow, I will trace the evolution of Western security and economic institutions and how they ultimately formed a lasting and mutually beneficial solution to the twin problems of Russian threat and German untrustworthiness that confronted the West in 1945.

THE ROAD TO BIZONIA

The question of what to do with Germany after it had been defeated generated a fair amount of discussion but little agreement before the end of the war (McAllister 2002: 49–55). On the U.S. side, the Treasury department put forward a plan for pastoralization of the economy which Roosevelt temporarily embraced. The State Department was concerned that these policies would alienate the Germans and lead to a recurrence of war in the future. Instead, the State Department wanted to keep Germany united and democratize the country, believing that the benefits of democracy and free trade would suffice to keep Germany peaceful. As the war drew to an end, State Department views began to win out over harsher recommendations, and pastoralization and permanent partition faded away as options (FRUS Yalta: 155; Trachtenberg 1999: 21). As a temporary expedient, however, it was agreed in late 1944 that Germany would be divided into zones parceled out among the Big Three and, at Churchill's insistence, France. Berlin, within the Soviet zone, would itself be divided in four as well. An Allied Control Council (ACC) would be set up to deal with matters affecting all of Germany, while most things would be run in each power's zone as the power saw fit.

One implication of the location of the zonal boundaries is that the Western powers had relatively little to gain from seeing Germany eventually united. The Western zones were by far the richest portion of Germany and contained over two-thirds of the population and the all important Ruhr industrial area, the foundation of German military power. The Soviets, in contrast, had a smaller and more agricultural section of Germany (and had handed over the area east of the Oder and Niesse rivers to Poland). As a result the West had comparatively little to gain from trying a cooperative agreement over Germany. Partition would lead to a West Germany firmly locked in the Western bloc, unable to cause trouble on its own and possibly armed against Russia. Mutual cooperation would produce a neutral Germany which might become a loose cannon, playing the two superpowers off against each other. If the other side defected successfully, the result could be a united Germany in the camp of the adversary. Given the mistrust that was fostered in 1945 by the fate of Eastern Europe, it is not surprising that the West gradually gave up on its efforts to run Germany on a unified basis and began to take steps towards partition in 1946 (Wagner 1980).

At the end of the war, two key issues were reparations and whether Germany would be treated as a unit or run on a zonal basis. At Yalta the Russians secured agreement from the United States (but not the British) on a total of $20 billion in reparations with half going to the Soviet Union as a "basis for discussion" (FRUS Yalta: 901–03, 979; Snell 1956: 63). After Yalta, the Americans began to back away from this idea. U.S. policymakers wanted above all to prevent a reprise of the post-World War I experience in which fixed reparations were imposed upon a Germany that had little desire or ability to pay, Americans ended up loaning Germany the money to pay its responsibilities to Britain and France, and the United States was ultimately left holding the bag (McAllister 2002: 78–84). The British were even more adamantly opposed to a fixed sum of reparations, as their stance at Yalta made plain. The reparations issue could not be considered alone, however, because it was fundamentally linked to the question of how the Germany economy would be run. If Germany were run on a unified basis economically, then reparations taken from one zone would effectively be subsidized by the other zones, unless equally harsh reparations were imposed on all zones. This exposed a disagreement over how harshly Germany should be treated. Russia wanted high levels of reparations, both to cripple Germany and to aid Russian economic recovery. They seemed willing to have this lead to poverty and chaos in Germany. The Western powers preferred to minimize occupation costs by restoring the German economy, at least to some reasonable level, and taking reparations only if there was a surplus after imports were paid for. On the other hand, Germany could be run on a zonal basis, in which case each power could do what it liked with its own zone. But this would indicate a failure to cooperate among the wartime allies and have serious implications for the future of Germany.

At the Potsdam conference, Germany and the reparations question were center stage. The Russians pressed hard for a fixed amount of reparations on a Germany-wide basis, but the Western powers resisted.[2] Byrnes instead proposed a curious hybrid system that ultimately was agreed upon. Each side would take whatever it wished from the occupation zone it controlled. In addition, the United States and Britain would give the Russians from their zones 10 percent of an amount of industrial equipment that was deemed "surplus" to the requirements of the German peacetime economy, and an additional 15 percent of this surplus equipment would be traded to the Russians for food from the primarily agricultural Russian zone (FRUS Potsdam II: 1485–86; Gaddis 1972: 241). At the same time, the parties agreed that "during the period of occupation Germany shall be treated as a single economic unit" and provided for the creation of central administrative agencies to control finance, transportation, communication, foreign trade, and industry (FRUS Potsdam II: 1483–84). The two provisions were in some tension, for if the Russians stripped their own zone to the point of economic paralysis, the Allied Control Council in charge of the German economy would have to remedy the situation with resources from the Western zones, ultimately financed by the United States—the interwar scenario once more. Only by privatizing the zones would the Russians have no ability to draw on U.S. resources, but this would negate the provisions on unified treatment. The strangeness of this hybrid leads Mark Trachtenberg to argue that Byrnes and Stalin agreed upon an "amicable divorce" in which each side would do as it saw fit in

---

[2] Belying his reputation for intransigence, Molotov eventually came down to a mere $800 million, a considerable reduction from the original $10 billion (FRUS Potsdam II: 486).

their own zone (Trachtenberg 1999: 18–34). Lip service would be paid to the idea of four-power cooperation and control, but in reality each side would go its own way. The Soviet zone would be subject to heavy reparations and be isolated from the rest of the country. The three Western zones would be much more closely integrated with each other and much more lightly treated, with reparations only taken after imports were paid for.[3] However, if this truly was Byrnes's intention, he overstepped the bounds of the domestic political consensus in the United States which still favored treating Germany on a unified basis. American diplomats and the U.S. military governor Lucius Clay took the provisions for unified treatment seriously, and Byrnes did little to correct this (Trachtenberg 1999: 42).

Along with the United States and Soviet Union, Britain and France were also formulating policy for the postwar world at this time. Churchill had openly worried about what would happen when American troops left and pursued a policy of building up France (FRUS Yalta: 286–87, 617). While the Potsdam conference was in session, Churchill's Conservative Party was voted out of office and a Labor government led by Clement Attlee took over, with Ernest Bevin as Foreign Minister. British policy by this point was motivated by increasing suspicion of the Russians and ambivalence on Germany. With respect to Germany, some British military officials and diplomats had argued as early as 1944 that after the war Russia would become the chief enemy and Germany would need to be revived to cope with the new threat (Deighton 1990: 18–20, 25–27). Bevin and Attlee favored partition during the war, but came around to support unified institutions by the time of Potsdam (Trachtenberg 1999: 32). Bevin also rejected Soviet desires for four-power control of the Ruhr, the heartland of Germany's industrial power which fell within the British zone (Deighton 1990: 32). However, the British were not prepared to abandon four-power cooperation in general, and feared provoking the Russians. With respect to European policy more generally, Bevin favored an alliance with France both to contain Germany and as a tacit force against Soviet domination, which would act as a foundation for a broader Western group, though the details of what this would entail were not clear (Young 1984: 14).

France, under General Charles De Gaulle, also favored creation of a Western group and a possible British alliance, but differed from Britain over German policy. As early as 1944 De Gaulle had made a speech proposing a Western group and French officials studied the possibility of

---

[3] Evidence for Trachtenberg's argument can be found in Byrnes's arguments that the plan would leave the zones basically independent (see FRUS Potsdam II: 275, 297, 430, 450, 491) and his more dubious claim that there would nonetheless be no impairment of unified institutions, 474, which Bevin found hard to fathom, 521. For further support, see McAllister 2002: 84–98. Eisenberg (1996) pushes this analysis further, perhaps too far, to argue that the eventual partition was a U.S. decision made because of excessive unwillingness to compromise.

a customs union (Young 1990: 13). However, he was not willing to align solidly with the West yet, and signed an alliance with the Soviet Union in December 1944.[4] De Gaulle also felt that France should extract concessions in return for an Anglo-French alliance, particularly over a colonial dispute in Lebanon and Syria, and over German policy. French policy on Germany was much harsher than British views, as the model of the previous chapter predicts. France supported the policies of demilitarization and denazification agreed upon at Potsdam, but strenuously opposed unified institutions of any kind. While fearing that imposed partition would lead to a nationalist backlash, France favored a very loose confederation of German provinces, with only weak federal institutions. Other key demands related to three important regions, the Saar, the Rhineland, and the Ruhr. The Saar, a coal rich province bordering France, was to be economically tied to France with a view towards possible future annexation, in a replay of French post–World War I efforts.[5] The Rhineland, north of France and west of the Rhine, would be permanently occupied by allied troops. Finally, the all important Ruhr Valley would be separated from Germany and its industrial resources subject to international control and managed for the benefit of Europe (Young 1990: 25–27, 46–49, Hitchcock 1998: 43–45).

After the Potsdam conference, the implementation of the provisions related to Germany quickly broke down. General Clay became increasingly concerned about the economic conditions in his zone and the potential political implications of continuing German poverty. Clay and the State Department, therefore, pushed to get all-German institutions up and running to promote economic recovery. He attempted to get approval for unified institutions in the Allied Control Council only to have them vetoed by France (Young 1990: 82–83; Hitchcock 1998: 51–54). Clay wanted to go ahead without the French, but Byrnes and Bevin were still reluctant to take this step, or to put too much pressure on France, in part for fear of strengthening communist influence in an election season (McAllister 2002: 98–107). During the fall of 1945, then, French preferences prevailed on the question of central institutions, despite the fact that France was by far the weakest of the four powers involved. On the question of the separation of the Ruhr and Rhineland, however, French proposals gained only a lukewarm response in a series of meetings with Britain, the United States, and Russia.

Facing resistance from the French and Soviets, Clay began to use the reparations issue as leverage to get the institutional cooperation he wanted.

---

[4]The West, in the person of Roosevelt, was not very enthusiastic about De Gaulle either, having initially cooperated with the Vichy regime and later attempted to derail his rise to leadership (Wall 1991: 20–34).

[5]The Saar was controlled by France until a 1935 referendum resulted in return of the province to Germany.

In April 1946, shortly after the Iranian crisis, and with approval from the highest levels, Clay insisted on a common import-export plan, or the Russians would get no more reparations from the American zone (FRUS 1946 V: 538).[6] The idea was to test Russian fidelity to the Potsdam agreement; if the Russians refused, they would stand revealed as being opposed to treating Germany as a unit (McAllister 2002: 114). At the same time and with similar intent, Secretary of State Byrnes formally proposed a treaty between the United States, Britain, France, and Russia to keep Germany disarmed for twenty-five years (FRUS 1946 II: 62, 190–93). Such a treaty should answer all of Russia's security needs by protecting them from German revanchism; for Russia to reject it would be to signal that they were expansionist instead (Gaddis 1972: 328–29).[7] The Russians balked at both of these initiatives, refusing the treaty on German demilitarization and demanding the resumption of reparations. The Americans blamed the Russians for the emerging partition before both German and American public opinion (Trachtenberg 1999: 41–46).

In this period, Britain's policy began to react to two linked economic factors. First, conditions continued to deteriorate in the British zone of occupation, which, being heavily industrial, was incapable of feeding itself. Consequently, the costs of occupation for Britain proved to be large and growing. Pushed by these factors, and continued French and Russian objections to economic recovery and unified institutions, Britain began to consider organizing its own zone in isolation from Russia, and, hence, abandoning Potsdam. By fostering economic recovery in their own zone, British occupation costs could eventually be reduced and the appeal of communism diminished. An additional advantage of such a "Western strategy" would be that since the British zone included the Ruhr, separating it from the rest of Germany would prevent Germany's military might from falling under Soviet domination. The danger would be the reaction to be anticipated from the Russians; hence, the British saw a need to bring the Americans on board (Deighton 1990: 79, 80).

France at this time also suffered economically, especially from shortages of food and coal, and was economically dependent on the United States. In December 1945, France received a U.S. loan for $550 million. In the spring of 1946, France was still able to play the superpowers off each other, receiving a shipment of wheat from the Soviet Union and lend lease debt writeoffs and additional loans from the United States (Wall 1991: 49–56; Young 1990: 101–03). France's Russia card, in addition to her internal weakness and importance to the United States, enabled her to

---

[6] He also wanted to use food aid to France as a lever to secure their agreement, FRUS 1946 V: 540.

[7] Given Byrnes's half hearted support for German unity, the test was probably meant to enlighten others rather than clear up any uncertainty on his own part.

resist pressure for central German institutions. However, this policy had become controversial within France; Bidault was under pressure from the Socialists to adopt a more realistic policy on Germany (Hitchcock 1998: 59). There was a renewed flurry of interest in a Franco-British alliance given that two conditions blocking it were disposed of: the dispute in the Levant was resolved and De Gaulle resigned in January 1946. However, the remaining obstacle, German policy and, in particular, whether the Ruhr should be separated from Germany, remained, and no agreement was reached.

Matters came to a head in the Paris Council of Foreign Ministers (CFM) meetings in July 1946. The meetings had been going on, without success, since April, and in a recess beginning in mid-May the British decided to deliver an ultimatum. If Germany was not treated as an economic unit, and any surplus used to pay balance of payment deficits before being available for reparations, the British would organize their own zone. In July, Bevin presented his demands, the Russians once more reverted to the issue of reparations, and Byrnes announced U.S. willingness to merge its zone with other zones (Deighton 1990: 93–97, Leffler 1992: 119). No agreement was reached with the Russians and the conference broke up. In the fall of 1946 the Americans and British negotiated a deal to merge their zones, while the French remained on the sidelines. In September Byrnes gave a speech in Stuttgart and warned that the United States supported German unity, but would not fail to unify the Western zones because of an inability to agree with the Russians, and that U.S. troops would remain in Germany as long as those of any other power, a position that drew 80 percent support from the public.[8] In December, France, after sounding out Byrnes and Bevin, set up a customs frontier around the Saar, thereby separating it economically from the rest of Germany (Young 1990: 129). Molotov criticized the French move. Finally, in January 1947, the British and American zones were combined and Bizonia was born.

The German issue, along with Eastern Europe and the Near East discussed in chapter 4, generated increased fears. Russians blamed the United States for stopping reparations, in violation of Potsdam. Soviet fears of a Germany embraced by the West and turned against Russia were beginning to be realized. From the American perspective, the Soviets had refused to establish the central institutions specified in the Potsdam accords. While the French did as well, they were not party to the accords and were not bound by them. The Soviet refusal indicated a desire to keep Germany in chaos with a view towards ultimately incorporating the whole country into the Soviet bloc (Zubok and Pleshakov 1996: 48). Djilas claims that Stalin said in the spring of 1946 that all Germany would be communist and the

---

[8] "The Quarter's Polls," *Public Opinion Quarterly* 10, no. 4 (1946): 618.

United States was coming to believe that this was, in fact, Moscow's goal (Djilas 1962: 153).

How does the theory of hegemonic assurance fare? Creating the bizone involved a limited economic revival of Germany, so the fact that the Americans and British favored this, but the French were opposed supports the claim that France, being closest to Germany, will be least willing to cooperate with it. The fact that France was not willing to throw in its own zone at this point, despite U.S. participation, seems to contradict the argument that U.S. participation should generate enough reassurance to produce cooperation, but this raises the question of what the U.S. offered in the way of guarantees in order to secure French participation. The most explicit statement was Byrnes's September 1946 Stuttgart speech, in which he pledged that the United States would not withdraw from Germany or "shirk our duty" (Leffler 1992: 120). This was the first assurance to contradict Roosevelt's statement at Yalta that the U.S. troops would remain for at most two years after the war. As the theory predicts, French opposition to central institutions was motivated in part, as their representatives in Berlin told the Americans, by the "fear that the United States will lose interest, eventually withdraw from Germany, and that some fine morning they will wake up and find themselves face to face with the Russians on the Rhine" (FRUS 1946 V: 506; Creswell and Trachtenberg 2003: 12). The assurance provided up to this point that this would not happen was clearly not enough for the French who still hoped for separation of the Ruhr and Rhineland.

Benign and coercive hegemony have difficulties explaining certain aspects of the establishment of the Bizone. According to benign hegemonic theory the Americans should have provided a free ride, but in the bizonal arrangement for financial cooperation, the British agreed, reluctantly, to foot 50 percent of the external deficit (Deighton 1990: 110–13). Further if the bizone was a public good, France should have joined in order to free ride. Coercive hegemony fares no better, since British preferences were aligned with U.S. preferences and, hence, they did not need to be coerced, whereas the French, who were opposed, were not coerced into participating. One could argue that this represented an indirect coercion of France, since the United States and Britain went ahead with policies in their zones that France disapproved of, but this is perhaps better conceived of as a French failure to coerce the Americans and British, rather than a successful U.S.-British coercion of France.

THE ORIGINS OF THE WESTERN BLOC: 1947

The year 1947 saw the consolidation of a Western bloc to oppose Soviet expansionism. The four key developments were the belated realization of an Anglo-French alliance, the Moscow Council of Foreign Ministers which pushed France further into the arms of the West, the beginning of the Marshall Plan and the associated closer economic cooperation of Western Europe, and the final breakdown of four-power cooperation over Germany at the London Council of Foreign Ministers meeting in December.

The Treaty of Dunkirk

Progress in British-French cooperation resumed early in the year. In January, a short-lived Socialist government in France was able to pursue a more anglophilic policy. Prime Minister Leon Blum wrote Bevin proposing a treaty of alliance and visited Britain to discuss the idea. In doing so, France abandoned the demand that Britain support French policy on Germany in exchange for an alliance (Young 1984: 47, 1990: 132). At the same time, French policy on the Ruhr began to evolve. No longer did France explicitly demand political separation; economic controls were now the focus (Young 1990: 130). Negotiations on an alliance came to a successful conclusion in March with the signing of the Dunkirk Treaty (Baylis 1984: 618). The treaty was aimed explicitly at a revival of Germany but many policymakers also considered it a hedge against Soviet power.[9] It represented a considerable evolution in British strategic thought, in that it was a peacetime alliance with a continental power. However, it did not settle the British debate over the continental commitment; indeed the Chiefs of Staff still planned to abandon the continent in the event of a war and opposed staff talks with France because they feared a true appreciation of how bleak the situation was would alarm rather than reassure the French (Baylis 1993: 84, Young 1984: 75). For the French, however, the treaty represented an added bit of security that would permit a more cooperative attitude towards German issues, and a shift towards taking sides with the "Anglo-Saxons" against the Russians.

In March and April 1947 at the Moscow Foreign Minister's conference, the Western powers and Russia made one more attempt at an agreement over Germany. Britain had already decided that the negotiations must fail at all costs, and that the blame must be cast on the Russians. They were firmly looking forward to building up the Western zones until they would be regarded by the Germans as the real Germany while the Eastern zone would be provinces to be regained (Deighton 1990: 134). The key task, according to the British, was to bring this about while inducing the United States to see the situation their way and remain committed to the Bizone.

---

[9]Trachtenberg argues that the Treaty of Dunkirk was aimed at the new Soviet threat and the German threat was a "convenient myth." See "The German Threat as a Pretext for Defense against Russia," http://www.polisci.ucla.edu/faculty/trachtenberg/appendices/appendixII.html and Creswell and Trachtenberg 2003.

The new U.S. Secretary of State, George Marshall, was undecided on Germany and several important figures on the U.S. side (including Clay) were amenable to a deal involving reparations from current production, anathema to the cash-starved British (Deighton 1990: 140–41; McAllister 2002: 124–29).[10]

France went into the Moscow CFM still entertaining hopes of mediating between the blocs, and benefiting by concessions from each side. The Russians apparently hoped to gain French support as well; Stalin even told French Foreign Minister Bidault in private that "It is better to be two against two than three against one" (Young 1990: 143). While this was obviously true for Stalin, the potential "one," whether it was true for France depended on what the Russians had to offer, and the Russians apparently thought they could buy French support on the cheap by acceding to their wishes on the Saar. The French thought they did not need Russian approval for their plans for the Saar, and held out for more substantial concessions. When these were not forthcoming, and Russia refused to discuss the Saar without French concessions, Bidault effectively broke with Moscow (Wall 1991: 66).[11] This break was further widened by a three-power (Western) agreement to increase French coal imports from Germany, a vital concern for France (Young 1990: 144–45; Hitchcock 1998: 62–71). In May, after the French communists refused to support the government on a vote of confidence, they were ejected from the coalition government.[12]

With respect to the United States as well, Russian behavior led to a harder line approach. In a private talk with Marshall, Stalin temporized and made light of the issues, indicating no desire to come to an agreement any time soon. This attitude worried the Secretary of State who felt that the Russians were playing for time while the economic situation deteriorated, in hopes of profiting from the resulting unrest. These considerations led ultimately to the Marshall Plan.

The Marshall Plan

The economic crisis, which forced Britain to retrench from its imperial commitments in the spring of 1947, was not unique to Britain, the other countries of Western Europe were also at risk. Economic production had by and large returned to prewar levels (Milward 1984: 7–19). However, the

---

[10]Trachtenberg (1999: 69) argues Bevin was still hoping for an eventual agreement at this point, but the agreement would have to be entirely on British terms, there was no room for compromise.

[11]Bidault confessed to Bevin after the conference that he had given up on cooperating with the Russians, and was now willing to cast France's lot with the West (Young 1984: 61).

[12]At about the same time, the communists were ejected from the Italian government. See Wall 1991: 67–71 for a refutation of the claim that the United States orchestrated the ejection of the communist parties.

recovery was based on an unsustainable level of imports from the United States, and the result was a balance of payments crisis. European countries simply did not export enough to the United States to earn the dollars they needed to pay for their imports. Further, their exports to the third world, which earned dollars from the United States via raw materials exports, could not make up the difference. Hence, Europe found itself faced with a dollar gap, not enough dollars to pay for needed imports. Curtailing imports from the United States would harm productivity by lessening capital investment, and also harm consumption, leading to political unrest (Leffler 1992: 160).

From the Soviet perspective, the economic health of the West was of crucial importance. A central component of the Marxist paradigm was that capitalism was subject to recurrent crises that would either drive it to wage war or to collapse.[13] Stalin himself maintained an avid interest in the possibility of eventual Western collapse; in April 1947 he quizzed Republican presidential candidate Harold Stassen at length about economic prospects in the United States and Western Europe (Taubman 1982: 137–39). As a result, Western policymakers were convinced that economic stagnation played into the hands of communism and could lead to one or more countries joining the Soviet bloc.

In June, Marshall proposed a program to address the economic crisis.[14] If the Europeans would agree among themselves on a unified plan for economic reconstruction, the United States would fund it. The program would be open to the countries of Eastern Europe, and the Soviet Union itself. The proposal was politically brilliant in several respects. First, by placing the onus on the Europeans to come up with a plan, it would increase the pressure on a parsimonious Congress to fund it. Second, by insisting on a unified plan, it would promote Western European integration, which the United States viewed as essential to creating a counterweight to the Soviet Union. As regards the East, the plan would have beneficial effects whether or not the Eastern Europeans participated. If they participated it would drive home the message that the United States had the resources to help while their Soviet masters did not, and help to wean them away from Russia economically. If, as expected, the Russians kept them from participating, the resentment against Russia would be all the greater (Taubman 1982: 173; McAllister 2002: 130).

---

[13]This tenet was challenged between 1946 and 1948 by the Soviet economist Eugen Varga who argued that U.S. hegemony would dampen intracapitalist rivalries and that the experience of the great depression had taught the capitalists how to stabilize their economies. Varga also argued that Soviet military power would deter a Western attack. This essentially correct analysis was rejected by Stalin (Wohlforth 1993: 77–87).

[14]The literature on the Marshall Plan is large; for a start, see Milward 1984; Pollard 1985; Hogan 1987; Eichengreen 1995; DeLong and Eichengreen 1993.

The Russians initially considered participating, and Poland and Czechoslovakia expressed great interest in the possibility as well. Stalin soon smelled a rat, however, and quickly brought the satellites to heel. The response was a barrage of propaganda against the plan, a wave of communist led strikes, and the establishment of the Cominform, a replacement for the prewar Comintern planned in 1946 but postponed for tactical reasons (Békés 1998; Parrish and Narinsky 1994).[15]

The Marshall Plan was the first embodiment of the idea of a West European solution to the complex of interlocking problems of the beginning of the Cold War. The Soviets were threatening, Germany might be a threat when it recovered, France was insecure, Europe was suffering economic problems. The Marshall Plan, once the Soviets rejected it, would unite the West, foster economic recovery, tie Germany to the West and reassure the French, all the while strengthening the West vis a vis the Soviets. In the Marshall Plan is the germ of the idea that would later be institutionalized in the European Coal and Steel Community (ECSC) and ultimately the European Economic Community (Trachtenberg 1999: 62–65). U.S. support for this aspect of the plan was universal. A united Europe could stand up to the Soviets without American aid; a divided Europe would continue to be a drain on the United States. Though some, such as John Foster Dulles, worried that the Marshall Plan might actually retard European unification by shielding Europe from the harsh realities of life, all agreed that European unity was in the U.S. interest (McAllister 2002: 135–41).

For Britain, the Marshall Plan was practically free money. Britain and the United States agreed on the essential issues, so no great sacrifices were required. The only real difference of opinion was that the United States wanted to use Marshall aid as leverage to bring about the closest European economic cooperation possible, up to an including a customs union. Bevin was willing to consider the idea, but ultimately Britain rejected it (Young 1984: 67). France supported the customs union idea, but aimed to minimize German production levels. Britain, however, was determined that Germany be revived, and France, though gaining some sympathy from the Americans, could not prevent this from happening (Deighton 1990: 195–96; Young 1990: 160–61).

---

[15] Parrish adopts a tragic spiral interpretation of the Marshall Plan and the Soviet reaction, and sees it as a turning point in the Cold War (1994: 5). However, he presents no evidence that Soviet views of the West, as opposed to tactics, changed. Zhdanov's warning at the founding meeting of the Cominform that the American plan was aimed at depriving the east Europeans of their political independence (37), which must have seemed a bit rich to the obedient communist delegations, hardly counts as evidence of a change of beliefs on Stalin's part, since he appears to have believed this to be U.S. policy since the Polish dispute got underway in 1944.

Towards the end of the year, the German question returned to the forefront. France resolved to move ahead towards merging with the bizone in the event that the next Council of Foreign Ministers meeting failed. In talks with the British and Americans, France outlined its desires, headed by international control of the Ruhr and security guarantees for France, due to the increased security risk caused by aligning overtly with the West against Russia (Young 1990: 170–71). France also endured a wave of communist-led political strikes, blessed by the Soviets in a return to militancy orchestrated in Poland at the founding of the Cominform.

At the London Council of Foreign Ministers in December 1947, the final break came over Germany (Trachtenberg 1999: 70). Bevin felt even more secure that British public opinion backed a hard line policy, and that no real effort at compromise was necessary; indeed even Soviet agreement to Western terms would be unfortunate (Deighton 1990: 206). The French had already agreed to begin talks on merging their zone, and were also primarily concerned with casting blame for the break on the Soviets (Young 1990: 172–73). If the Americans could be held firm, all would be well. In the conference itself, the Russians tried belligerence, and then made a series of concessions. These were viewed as too little too late, and the conference was suspended on December 15 (Deighton 1990: 214).

The events of 1947 lent support to the hegemonic assurance perspective. Britain and France engaged in real security cooperation, forming a bilateral alliance against Germany and implicitly against Russia as well. The Treaty of Dunkirk was not a public good provided by the United States nor a product of U.S. coercion, undercutting benign and coercive hegemony. The Marshall Plan supports the hegemonic assurance perspective as well. The Americans very much wanted some demonstration of European ability to work together in a multilateral fashion for the common cause before committing to funding the plan; indeed this was Marshall's main prerequisite (Hogan 1987: 35–43). The European countries agreed to cooperate multilaterally, and to further German revival with the United States as part of the deal. Thus, both the United States and the Europeans wanted to cooperate if the others would, and the U.S. role as a trusted hegemon enabled that cooperation to take place. Coercive hegemony is undercut, since the Western Europeans freely participated in the Marshall Plan; it was the Eastern European states that had to be coerced into not participating. Coercive hegemony is further undercut by the failure of the United States to get the British to agree on a customs union for Europe. Marshall Plan aid did enable the United States to influence French fiscal policy, but American leverage was limited by the very real concern for French political stability in the face of communist unrest and by the centrality of France in the plan for European recovery (Wall 1991: 169–72, 179–80; Hitchcock 1998: 82–87). Benign hegemony does get a big part of the story here, since the United States alone provided the financial resources for the plan.

THE BRUSSELS PACT AND THE LONDON ACCORDS

In the first half of 1948, the logical implications of the Western strategy chosen in 1947 were pursued in two key areas. A Western group would need a security component, and so Britain and France began to think of extending their alliance to include the Benelux states. At the same time, a Western group would be much stronger if it included the resources of the Western zones of Germany and was defended as far east as possible, on the Elbe as opposed to the Rhine. This implied a political as well as economic rehabilitation of Germany, for otherwise German support for the defense of the West could hardly be expected. Hence, these six months saw the creation of the first multilateral Western security alliance, the Brussels Pact, and the creation of a plan for the establishment of a West German state.

After the London CFM, Bevin met with Marshall and discussed a possible Western European "spiritual union" and the possibility of U.S. military support for such an enterprise.[16] Marshall urged him to proceed with a European alliance first, then ask for support from the United States, so that Americans would see the Europeans acting together and willing to stand firm (Young 1984: 79). The nature of the proposed Western Union was somewhat vague, but British officials were considering a customs union and a military alliance component. Belgium had expressed an interest in a military alliance with Britain and France, and France proposed a system of bilateral treaties modeled on the Dunkirk treaty, which might also include Holland and other countries. The advantage of the Dunkirk model would be that the treaties would still be explicitly anti-German, and so less provocative to the Russians. However, the United States, though not directly involved, opined that the Rio pact, a regional collective security agreement, provided a better model, and the Benelux states strongly agreed. Negotiations commenced between France, Britain, and the Benelux countries with France advocating bilateral Dunkirk style treaties, Benelux advocating the Rio model, and Britain anxiously trying to mediate. The Czech coup in February increased fears of the Russians and lessened concern for provoking them, leading Britain to plump for the Rio model and France to acquiesce (Young 1984: 82–85, 1990: 179).

---

[16] In January 1948 Bidault asked for a U.S. alliance to alleviate the fear that France would be abandoned if the Russians invaded (Wall 1991: 132).

In March, Britain, France, and the Benelux countries signed the Brussels pact (Ireland 1981: 68; Baylis 1984). The treaty provided for a collective security system that would be potentially expandable to include a West German state, but would still act to constrain such a state by being directed at internal aggression as well as external aggression, in true collective security fashion (Ireland 1981: 64–74). The Rio format was also believed to maximize the chances of U.S. support, which was earnestly desired by Britain and France (Baylis 1984: 621–25; Young 1990: 180). Truman duly expressed support for the treaty, and Bevin immediately went to work on a North Atlantic pact that could express this support in concrete terms. The British Chiefs of Staff still balked at a serious continental commitment, however, modifying their strategy only to the extent of having the occupation troops fight on the Rhine, unreinforced, until they were pushed out or overrun (Baylis 1993: 88).

Meanwhile, three power negotiations over the creation of a West German political entity got underway. In January, the Western powers began negotiations that would draw the French zone into the bizonal arrangement and incorporate Western Germany into the Marshall Plan. Things got off to a bad start when the British and Americans went ahead with new institutions in the Bizone that France vehemently objected to as a proto-government, but once more France was unable to influence policy in Bizonia (Hitchcock 1998: 87–91; Young 1990: 176–77). France wanted security against Germany in exchange for trizonal fusion and the creation of a German government. As before, France argued for a weak, decentralized Germany with international control of the Ruhr (Young 1990: 188–89). In the London talks that opened in Feburary, British and American preferences typically aligned in favor of a stronger German state, created sooner, with fewer safeguards, while France argued for a more federal structure, created later, with more restrictions. The bargaining leverage lay with the British and Americans because they could (and did) threaten to implement anything they agreed upon in the Bizone without French approval. However, France did succeed in securing an International Authority in the Ruhr (IAR), a Military Security Board to maintain German demilitarization, and a strong role for the *Länder* in drafting the new constitution (Young 1990: 197; Hitchcock 1998: 94–98).

To further reassure the French, the Americans accepted French temporary control over the Saar, and renewed the pledge that they would remain in Germany for the forseeable future. The French continued to drag their heels on German reconstruction, however, asking for a strong U.S. security commitment, and fearing, quite correctly as it turned out, that the Soviets would not passively accept the political revival of Western Germany. The Americans, while threatening to go it alone if necessary,

saw the logic of the French position and attempted to further accommodate it within the realities of U.S. domestic politics. Negotiations on the
North Atlantic Pact were underway, and as momentum towards a formal treaty linking the United States to Western Europe grew, the State
Department began to bring the Senate on board. The result was the
Vandenberg resolution, named for the powerful Republican senator who
was the Congressional partner in the Truman era's bipartisan foreign policy initiatives. To satisfy Vandenberg and the Senate, the resolution was
suitably vague, but the general idea, an endorsement of U.S. participation in an alliance designed to defend Western Europe, was clear enough.
The Vandenberg resolution, along with continued assurances of American
commitment and intention to move towards a security treaty, provided the
assurance needed for the French to accept the London Accords reorganizing Germany in June 1948 (Ireland 1981: 92–100). Though the plan
was controversial in France, indeed Bidault soon lost his job over the issue,
the French Assembly approved the accords by a narrow margin (Young
1984: 95). Thus, a deal was finally struck on the economic and political
reconstruction of Western Germany, in exchange for verbal assurances of
U.S. commitment and promises that these assurances would eventually be
formalized in a treaty.

The Brussels Pact supports the hegemonic assurance hypotheses. It was
in part motivated by a desire to demonstrate, as in the Marshall Plan, that
the Europeans were conditional cooperators, and, hence, were worthy
of U.S. support. French preferences for keeping anti-German clauses in
the treaty, against the wishes of the Britain is explained by geography,
as the theory predicts. Finally, since German revival was not at issue, the
Europeans could cooperate without U.S. participation. Contrary to benign
and coercive hegemony, the West European states cooperated without U.S.
provision of a public good, and without being forced to do so by the United
States.

The London Accords also support the hegemonic assurance hypotheses.
Reviving Germany was a risky enterprise, but the states were willing to do it
if they could be assured that others would cooperate. As the theory predicts,
France was the most hesitant about reviving Germany and required the
most reassurance. French cooperation on the political revival of Germany
was secured with U.S. security commitments, albeit not amounting yet to a
formal treaty (McAllister 2002: 150). Benign hegemony is not supported
since the London Accords did represent serious cooperation by the West
Europeans, not a free ride. Coercive hegemony gets mixed support since
the British were strongly in favor of the revival policy and did not need
to be coerced to support it, while France did object and agreed only with
considerable arm twisting, as well as reassurance, so that U.S. (and British)
preferences prevailed in the main disputes.

THE BIRTH OF NATO AND WEST GERMANY

The London agreements on a German government led immediately to the Berlin blockade, which, in turn, gave increased impetus to the negotiations over an Atlantic alliance. This complex of issues remained center stage for nearly a year, from the summer of 1948 through the spring of 1949. From the perspective of this chapter, the main items of interest are the negotiation of the North Atlantic Treaty and the birth of West Germany.

When Clay began the process of implementing the London Accords by introducing a new currency for the Western zones, the Soviets sealed off access to Berlin and the most severe crisis of the Cold War to date was on (Leffler 1992: 217; Trachtenbeg 1999: 80). The United States and Britain responded with the famous airlift in an effort to keep the city alive without provoking a war, though military experts did not believe enough supplies could be transported by air. As usual, there is some debate about exactly what Stalin wanted or would have been willing to accept out of the crisis. At one point he told Western ambassadors that economic integration of the Western zones was not the problem, just the establishment of a German state (Trachtenberg 1999: 80). However, Milovan Djilas claims that earlier in the year Stalin told him that, "The West will make Western Germany their own, and we shall turn Eastern Germany into our own state" (Djilas 1962: 153).

The effect of the crisis was to further spur Western negotiations towards the creation of a trans-Atlantic alliance. The military aspect of the Cold War became yet more salient (Mastny 1996: 58). A preliminary round of talks limited to Britain, Canada, and the United States had taken place in the spring, and produced the "Pentagon paper."[17] It was decided that there would be a new treaty, that is, the United States would not simply accede to the Brussels Pact or give a unilateral endorsement of it. The treaty would cover the North Atlantic area, and possible members were discussed (Baylis 1993: 94–97). The Pentagon paper was kept secret, however, to avoid offending those who were not invited, and to minimize domestic opposition, especially in the United States where support for a treaty was not uniform, even within the State Department, let alone Congress. American military officials, meanwhile, had become uneasily aware that a reconstructed Europe could no longer be abandoned to the Soviets in the early period of a war without seriously endangering U.S. chances of ultimately prevailing, and, in May 1948, they began planning to fight the Soviets at the Rhine alongside the British and French (Leffler 1992: 216).

---

[17]The French were excluded on the excuse that they were believed to be a security risk, all the while Donald Maclean kept the Russians fully informed from his post at the British embassy.

With the Berlin crisis in progress, negotiations began in July in Washington that would lead to a draft treaty in December 1948. The U.S. delegation still hung back, seemingly unsure of what it wanted. The French, supported on some issues by the Benelux countries, pressed for military aid (Young 1984: 100). The Berlin blockade seemed to confirm French fears that the London Accords could provoke a Soviet invasion; hence, they wanted immediate and strong results. They asked for direct military assistance, U.S. troops in France, a restricted alliance focused on Western Europe, and an automatic commitment to fight, as in the Brussels Treaty. The Americans were unable to provide large scale military aid, favored a wider alliance, and could not give automatic commitments in deference to the Congressional warmaking power (Young 1990: 215–16). However, the Americans did respond to French fears and manage to provide some military aid. After the Brussels Treaty powers set up a Western Union Chiefs of Staff in September, U.S. military equipment flowed to French occupation forces in Germany (Ireland 1981: 107). The British pressed France to take the long view, and be content to get a U.S. alliance commitment as a first step. They also succeeded in persuading the Americans that a pact would help the Europeans psychologically, by assuring them that mutual cooperation was feasible.

The eventual compromise in December favored the U.S. position. The treaty would be broad, and the guarantee would not be automatic. However, the Europeans did win some important points. In exchange for including Norway in the talks, France secured the eventual admission of Italy, over British and initial American objections, and coverage for French Algeria (Wall 1991: 146–47). The United States began preparing a Military Aid Program (MAP) for implementation after the alliance was in place. The treaty was signed in April 1949. The Russians then offered to end the Berlin blockade in exchange for an end to the Western counterblockade of Eastern Germany and a four-power conference to discuss the German question. The United States agreed, provided the blockade would end before the conference. The next month the Soviets ended the blockade of Berlin, the Federal Republic of Germany was born, and the conference produced no results (Leffler 1992: 282–85).

The connection between the signing of the treaty and the end of the blockade was not lost on treaty proponents in the Senate debate on ratification, who touted the important role the treaty had already played in reassuring French fears and permitting progress on Germany (Ireland 1981:139). The debate in the Senate revealed just how far the United States had to go, however. The administration had to postpone consideration of the MAP, and, indeed, even Vandenberg asserted that if the North Atlantic Treaty was going to be a "permanent military alliance" there would not be enough votes to approve it (Ireland 1981: 136). A final impact of the alliance was to help tip the balance in British military thinking towards a continental commitment. In 1950 the strategy finally privileged the defense of Western Europe over the Middle East and a decision was made to send two divisions to the continent in case of war. (Baylis 1993: 89–90, Dockrill 1991: 9).

The other major issue of this period was the implementation and further elaboration of the London Accords on Germany. By this point, France had largely abandoned its previous punitive policy and fully endorsed the Western strategy (Creswell and Trachtenberg 2003: 16).[18] The difficulty of wringing concessions from the British and Americans designed to keep Germany under control was apparent. The heightened level of threat from the Soviet Union led some French officers to propose the radical step of rearming Gemany. European federalism was genuinely popular in France, as well as in other European countries, which led to experiments such as the Council of Europe, an assembly with federal ambitions kept in check by the skeptical British (Young 1984: 108–17). British and U.S. security guarantees were far stronger than after the First World War. All these factors pointed towards a policy designed to embrace Germany in a supranational structure rather than dominate it, though a specific plan for accomplishing this was not yet in hand.[19] The disputes over implementation of the London Accords were, therefore, muted in comparison to the ones involved in its negotiation. A scuffle broke out when U.S. and British occupation authorities once again jumped the gun by decreeing German ownership of the Ruhr firms, but the French were mollified by admission onto the "Essen group," which controlled Ruhr industries, and by joint pressure on the Germans to emphasize the federal aspect in the new Basic Law (Hitchcock 1998: 106–07). The British and French squared off against the Americans, who wanted an end to reparations. The new French approach also was apparent in French agreement for a looser Occupation Statute than they originally favored (Young 1990: 204–11). Acheson believed that the final deal, negotiated in May, was aided by the signing of the North Atlantic Treaty (Leffler 1992: 282). Elections were held in the summer of 1949 and the first government of the Federal Republic of Germany took office in September.

The hegemonic assurance perspective is strongly supported by the origins of NATO. U.S. policymakers made many statements about their willingness to cooperate if they could be assured the Europeans would.

---

[18] At the same time, ironically, some U.S. and British officials briefly advocated reconsidering the accords in light of the Berlin crisis, but the momentum was too great to stop (McAllister 2002: 156–69).

[19] The French rejection of a U.S. idea to extend the IAR's authority to French industry indicated their determination to retain control of the process.

Europeans made similar statements and argued that they had already made themselves vulnerable through cooperation in the Brussels Pact and awaited reciprocation from the United States. Benign hegemony is disconfirmed by the U.S. preference to cooperate if the Europeans did, but not otherwise, because benign hegemons cooperate in the absence of reciprocation. Coercive hegemony is also disconfirmed in that the origins of NATO lie in Europe, in an effort by Britain, especially, to encourage greater U.S. security commitments to the continent. NATO cannot be fairly interpreted as a U.S. scheme for the domination of Europe, given the eagerness with which the Europeans sought the alliance (Wall 1991: 128). The United States did prevail on many disputes on the shape the alliance would take, but this is secondary to the main issue of the existence of the alliance itself, which was sought by all the eventual members.

The birth of the Federal Republic also supports the hegemonic assurance perspective, in that French approval was greatly facilitated by U.S. security commitments, especially in the North Atlantic Treaty. Benign hegemony is undermined by the seriousness of the cooperation required of the allies; this was no free ride, certainly for France.

German Rearmament

By mid-1949 the French had agreed to the economic and political rehabilitation of Germany, but importantly, not rearmament. This had been made possible by commitments from Britain in the Dunkirk Treaty and Brussels Pact, and a subsequent commitment from the United States via NATO. However this commitment was still not of a substantial military nature; indeed, the U.S. Congress had been promised that it would not take on this character. The final, most difficult hurdles in the way of U.S. and European cooperation, German rearmament and a solid U.S. military presence in Europe, remained ahead.

In the summer, the Senate took up the Military Aid Program, and with added impetus from the Soviet explosion of a nuclear device, passed a package of aid the distribution of which would be contingent on the establishment of the North Atlantic Council as envisioned in Article 9 of the treaty. This was in part motivated by Congressional desires to set up NATO organizationally in order to further reassure the French while paving the way for the ultimate rearmament of Germany, which would save costs for the United States (Ireland 1981: 157).

That fall and into the spring of 1950 momentum continued to build to take two additional steps vis a vis West Germany. First, to integrate it into the Western organizations, such as NATO and the Western Union, and second, to rearm it. Military men, especially in Britain but even in France, saw the difficulty of attempting to defend Western Europe at the Rhine and the difficulty of attempting operations within Germany without the support of the people, and indeed participation of German forces (Ireland 1981: 169). To allow Germany into Western institutions, however, France (and Britain) wanted stronger participation by the Americans, but in late 1949 and early 1950 this was still not forthcoming (Dockrill 1991: 13). France and Britain differed, however, on the question of how supranational Western institutions should be. French support for European federalism, and British opposition, had been manifested earlier in disputes over the formation of the Council of Europe (Young 1984: 115). This episode represented a parting of the ways between Britain, in favor of cooperation with Western Europe but opposed to any merging of sovereignty for fear of jeopardizing ties with the Commonwealth and the United States, and France, which took a much more federalist line.

The federalist line achieved its first real success in connection with the perennial issue of the control of the Ruhr industries. The allies retained a degree of control over the Ruhr, in the IAR, but these controls would inevitably have to be given up over time if Germany were to be fully rehabilitated. Yet this would result in unconstrained German power once more. France's answer to this dilemma was to propose a supranational body that would control these industries in *both* countries, and others as well. This would enable controls to be maintained while according Germany equal status, at the price of accepting controls over one's own industry. These ideas were embodied in the Schuman Plan in May 1950, which led to the creation of the European Coal and Steel Community (ECSC) (Hitchcock 1998: 126–32; Lovett 1996).[20] Konrad Adenauer, the new German Chancellor, responded positively to Schuman's proposal. The British considered participation in the talks, but France made the principle of supranationality a precondition of entering discussion, and it was just this principle which the British wanted to dilute. In the end, the talks took place between the "six," France, Germany, Italy, and the Benelux states, highlighting the Franco-British rift (Young 1984: 142–66).

Meanwhile, a NATO communique promised West Germany that though she was not a NATO member, an attack on Western occupation forces in Germany would trigger Article 5, and, hence, that as long as occupation continued, Germany was covered by NATO. The fifty caliber bullet of German rearmament was not yet bitten, however, when the Korean War broke out in June 1950. As mentioned in chapter 4, this greatly ratcheted up the level of tension in the Cold War and raised the profile of the military aspect. Fears became widespread that the Soviets could conceivably contemplate a straightforward invasion of Western Europe, since they had

---

[20]For an overview, see Gillingham 1991.

taken such a gamble in the East. Perhaps the Korean move was but a gambit to draw Western forces away from the crucial theater. Walter Ulbricht, the East German leader, began making belligerent statements about following the Korean example and East German paramilitary formations became a source of concern (Large 1996: 66; Dockrill 1991: 22).

The United States and European countries began to undertake individual and joint efforts to strengthen their defenses. The U.S. defense budget was substantially increased and Truman asked Congress for an additional $4 billion for the Military Aid Program for Europe. Britain increased defense spending and sent an additional division to reinforce the British Army of the Rhine (BAOR). France almost tripled its defense spending between 1950 and 1952 and lengthened the term of service from a year to eighteen months (Hitchcock 1998: 148). The smaller countries announced similar initiatives or a willingness to undertake them if NATO so decided (Fursdon 1980: 72).

At the same time, pressure grew steadily for a move to rearm Germany. The U.S. military advocated simultaneously sending American forces to the continent and creating German forces, both of which would be integrated into the NATO command. Acheson attempted to stem the tide out of concerns for French fears, but was ultimately forced to go along (Ireland 1981: 190–95; McAllister 2002: 188). In September of 1950 a joint Foreign/Defense ministers meeting of NATO was held at which the French came under strong pressure to accept an initiative along these lines. The Americans indicated some willingness to compromise, but the pressure to agree in principle that rearmament would come was strong (Dockrill 1991: 37). The French remained opposed to German rearmament, but began to cast around for a positive counterproposal (Hitchcock 1998: 134–45).

The result, presented in October, was the Pleven Plan for a European Army and a European Defense Community (EDC).[21] The essence of the idea was to create a unified European army, supervised by a European parliament, paid for by a European defense budget. German troops would be integrated into the European army, hopefully at the lowest possible unit level, so that there would be no all-German divisions, much less army corps, which could threaten to act independently. It was a radical extension of the ECSC concept, to render Germany harmless by enfolding it in the tightest possible embrace (Fursdon 1980: 86–90).

The initial British and American reaction to the Pleven Plan was negative. The plan was viewed as a means of postponing German rearmament rather than facilitating it, and French officials admitted as much to the British

[21] For overviews of the EDC and its time, see Ruane 2000; Mawby 1999; Schwartz 1991; Fursdon 1980; Large 1996.

(Trachtenberg 1999: 111; McAllister 2002: 194). Bevin thought the plan unrealistic, though public commentary was more restrained (Dockrill 1991: 41–44). Very rapidly, the British came to the position that they would hold throughout the EDC debate, they publicly supported it for the Continentals, declined to join it themselves, and privately believed it would ultimately fail and have to be replaced with something like German membership in NATO. This did not end Continental hopes that the British might be persuaded to come in, however, and the precise nature of the British relationship to the European army would be a key issue in the subsequent debates.

In the wake of the impasse over the Pleven Plan, the American representative on the North Atlantic Council, Charles Spofford, worked out a compromise with the NATO allies. The Spofford Compromise gave each side what it most wanted, at the price of failing to reconcile the conflicting visions of how to proceed with German rearmament. The Germans would begin raising troops organized in brigades, not divisions, that would be limited in their armaments and without a general staff. The French would convene a conference to discuss the Pleven Plan. A parallel set of negotiations would discuss the details of raising German contingents and incorporating them into NATO. At the same time, NATO approved the plan for the United States to appoint a supreme commander for NATO and commit troops to Europe, as in the earlier package deal (Fursdon 1980: 92–100).

The British and French went along with the Spofford Compromise, the French after pressure and a promise of continued U.S. involvement on the continent (Large 1996: 96–97). However, Adenauer rejected the plan, arguing that the level of discrimination against Germany in the plan was unacceptable, and that he would not permit German troops to serve as mere cannon fodder (McAllister 2002: 199; Large 1996: 104). This marked a crucial turning point, for the first time the new German government asserted preferences in serious conflict with those of the occupying powers and would be allies against the Soviet Union. Adenauer faced strong political pressure domestically to assert himself, however. Socialists on the left and nationalists on the right both rejected Adenauer's strategy of favoring an alliance with the West over the goal of reunification. Hence, Adenauer had to demonstrate that his policy brought results in the form of economic development and political rehabilitation for Germany. The link between lifting occupational controls and German rearmament would become another key feature of the subsequent negotiations.

The result, therefore, was very much in accordance with French and German preferences, rather than U.S. preferences. The United States agreed to appoint a supreme commander of NATO, Dwight Eisenhower, and to send four divisions to Europe (Ireland 1981: 204–07). The negotiations over the Pleven Plan got underway in Paris in February 1951.

The other set of negotiations were held in Petersburg, near Bonn, but given the German refusal to go along with the discriminatory elements of the Spofford Compromise, and the French refusal to abandon them, negotiations bogged down (Fursdon 1980: 107–11). Attlee, meanwhile, announced that German rearmament should take place only after the European NATO allies themselves had rearmed, supporting the French policy of delay (Dockrill 1991: 56). The United States also strongly supported the French position in the negotiations over the ECSC, however, and American leverage was key in getting the Germans to partially decentralize ownership of the Ruhr industries (Hitchcock 1998: 152; Lovett 1996: 449). The treaty was signed in March 1951.

The next year was taken up with the negotiation of the EDC treaty. There were three important developments in the negotiations. First, the discriminatory elements of the Pleven Plan were gradually jettisoned in favor of equal treatment for Germany and the other states.[22] Second, the occupying powers agreed to the fundamental German demand that rearmament would spell the end of the Occupation Statute (Large 1996: 132). Finally, the French became increasingly uncomfortable with their own creation, and began to seek guarantees from Britain and the United States against Germany ever leaving the EDC (Large 1996: 130).

The negotiations over the EDC were not ignored by the Russians. In March 1952, Stalin floated a plan to reunify Germany that seemed to meet most Western demands. Germany would have genuinely free elections, would reunify, and would thereafter be neutral, belonging to neither alliance. The plan was essentially a ploy to derail the EDC; Stalin only approved it when assured that it would be turned down by the Americans (Gaddis 1997: 127). Western leaders were put on the spot and needed to come up with a way to up the ante to levels the Russians would reject without alienating German opinion. The answer was to demand that Germany be free to choose to join an alliance if it wanted to, in effect a demand that Germany would be free to join NATO if it so chose (Trachtenberg 1999: 129).[23]

Despite Russian temptations, in May 1952, the EDC treaties were signed along with the General Treaty relaxing occupational controls, to go into effect on ratification of the EDC. It was arranged that the American general commanding NATO forces, SACEUR, would also command EDC forces. The United States and Britain even gave the French an approximation of what they had wanted in terms of a guarantee against German secession

[22]The one exception being that colonial troops, such as the French forces in Indochina, would not be under the EDC.

[23]It was this demand that was finally agreed to by Gorbachev in 1990. For the debate over the sincerity of the Stalin note, see Steininger (1990), who argues it was a missed opportunity and Van Dijk (1996), who argues it was meant as propaganda and responded to in kind.

from the EDC, which persuaded a skeptical French cabinet to approve the treaty (Hitchcock 1998: 168).

How do the alternative theories of hegemony fare in light of the first phase of the rearmament saga? The European Coal and Steel Community was an instance of French cooperation with Germany without Britain or America. This might seem to contradict the hegemonic assurance perspective; however, in this case, the cooperation was a way of maintaining restrictions on Germany, not removing them. Benign and coercive hegemony fare poorly since it was a French initiative, not a U.S. public good or imposition. The EDC proposal offers support for hegemonic assurance. French geography explains why France preferred a rearmament solution with more limits on Germany than did the United States and Britain. Also, U.S. and British guarantees enabled the French cabinet to approve the treaty. The EDC sharply undermines coercive hegemony, since it was proposed against U.S. wishes. The Spofford Compromise episode is an even starker refutation of coercive hegemony, since the weakest power, Germany, prevailed over all the rest. Benign hegemony gets little support here, because the U.S. aid was accompanied by European efforts, such as the British commitment of an additional division to the BAOR and French and British military spending increases. The hegemonic assurance perspective is supported, since France and Britain accepted the Spofford deal, with its promise of U.S. leadership.

THE DEATH OF THE EDC AND THE NATO SOLUTION

The signing of the EDC failed to resolve the issue of German rearmament and it would be two years before a solution could be found.

Ironically, given their initial opposition, the Americans quickly warmed up to the EDC, and even became fervent supporters by the end. Eisenhower, in his term as SACEUR, became convinced that it would be the only politically feasible way to attain German rearmament (McAllister 2002: 208–15; Large 1996: 125; Hitchcock 1998: 155, 173). The new Secretary of State, John Foster Dulles, was also a passionate supporter. The EDC fit with their goal of building a strong Europe that could eventually deter the Russians without further American assistance. For this very reason, the British were hostile to the idea, and to American pressure on them to join in. The British still viewed themselves as a global power with broad responsibilities and a special tie to the United States. They were quite skeptical of the notion that Europe could ever stand on its own against the Soviet Union, and, hence, wanted to avoid anything that gave the Americans the impression that this was possible. Instead they wished to strengthen the trans-Atlantic bond. As a result, they declined to get involved in EDC, but felt they could not openly oppose it for fear of alienating the Americans (Trachtenberg 1999: 114–17).

The key players, however, were not the United States and Britain, but Germany and France. The ratification process in Germany developed into an extraordinarily complicated political-legal battle. Before the treaty was even signed, the Socialists sued before the Supreme Court on the grounds that remilitarization violated the Basic Law. Lacking the votes necessary to amend the constitution, Adenauer engaged in a series of overly clever shenanigans aimed at manipulating the President, the Supreme Court, and the Bundesrat. The Bundestag approved the treaty in the spring of 1953, but the constitutional issues still were undecided. Fortunately for Adenauer, elections in the fall of 1953 gave his government a larger majority, big enough to put through constitutional amendments explicitly authorizing military forces in the early spring of 1954 (Large 1996: 154–75).

In March 1953 Stalin died, and a power struggle began among his successors, Lavrenti Beria, Georgi Malenkov, and Nikita Khrushchev. Malenkov and Beria, temporarily in the lead, made overtures to the West to renew negotiations. Churchill seized the opportunity to propose a summit that would discuss a settlement of the German question involving reunification and neutralization, thinking that perhaps the Soviet leadership transition provided an opportunity to end the Cold War. French support for the EDC dropped still further, as hopes of a unified but disarmed Germany flared once more. France supported the call for four-power talks and the United States reluctantly went along. Talks were held in January 1954, but produced no results. Deborah Larson portrays this period as a "missed opportunity" for peace, in which a deal on German unification and neutralization was prevented not because both sides did not want it, but because of mistrust (Larson 1997: 40–57; for a contrary view see Richter 1993). However, Beria, the main advocate of unification, was one of four players (if we include Molotov) in a very fluid transitional period. His initial move to abandon socialism in the German Democratic Republic (GDR) was overruled by Khrushchev and Molotov (Chuev 1991, 333–37). After the East German uprising on June 17, he was arrested and ultimately executed. His policies, including towards Germany, were discredited.[24] It seems unlikely, therefore, that a stable Soviet preference for trading away the GDR existed.

French support for the EDC continued to decline (Hitchcock 1998: 170–74). Throughout the negotiation process, France had succeeded in getting many concessions out of its allies, in a tribute to the negotiating leverage that can be generated by domestic constraints (Ripsman, 2000/2001; Dockrill 1991: 114–20). In a final effort to boost support,

---

[24]For new documents on this episode, see Ostermann 1998.

Britain promised not to remove its troops while the threat to Western Europe remained, and to closely integrate her own forces with the EDC, even including one of the armored divisions of the BAOR under the EDC (Dockrill 1991: 136). In the summer of 1954, after French forces were defeated in Indochina, French Prime Minister Mendès-France went to the well one more time for modifications that would lessen the supranational quality of the treaty, but was rebuffed (Hitchcock 1998: 190–94; Large 1996: 211). For over a year the United States had exerted tremendous pressure on France to ratify the EDC, using every economic lever at its disposal (Wall 1991: 266–86). In the end, nothing would suffice to win over French public opinion and in August 1954, the French assembly rejected the EDC treaty. An alliance of Gaullists, opposed to the diminu-tion of sovereignty, and communists opposed to strengthening the West, outvoted the centrist parties who supported the treaty. Thus, the boldest move towards European integration of the early Cold War period ended in failure.

Dulles had threatened an "agonizing reappraisal" of the U.S. commit-ment to Europe in case the EDC should be defeated, but such threats were empty as was quickly demonstrated. Instead, with remarkable rapidity, an alternative framework was agreed upon which brought Germany into the Western Union and NATO, a solution reflecting the British ideal all along. The benefits for France would be no diminution of her sovereignty and a full British commitment.

Foreign Minister Anthony Eden began advocating a Western Union option in September in a tour of European capitals. France opposed it because of a lack of safeguards and Dulles did as well, still angry over the French abandonment of the EDC and wondering if Congressional support for Europe could be maintained in the face of such spineless behavior. A conference was called in London, however, at which support rapidly built up for the British proposals. To bring France around, Britain made a pledge that went somewhat beyond what had earlier been agreed, that British forces on the continent would be maintained at their present level unless a majority of Brussels Treaty nations agreed to a reduction (Hitchcock 1998: 199; Dockrill 1991: 145).

The resulting Paris Accords provided for increases in German sovereignty with certain remaining limits, along with German rearmament in the context of NATO and a strengthened SACEUR (Trachtenberg 1999: 125–28). The allies formally abandoned, but tacitly retained, the right to intervene in case of a German relapse into authoritarianism in the guise of a right to defend their troops. Germany was denied the right to use force to attain unification, or even to negotiate towards this end. Germany also had no right to evict the troops of its NATO partners, in spite of their new role as defending allies rather than occupying army. Germany would also be forbidden to develop nuclear weapons, which Britain had already accomplished and France was beginning a program to do. Germany would, however, be admitted both to NATO and to the Western Union (Brussels Pact). A German army would be created, and German divisions would once more exist in Central Europe. To be sure, they would be part of a unified NATO command structure, led by an American general, but nonetheless, they would exist. The French Assembly initially rejected the accords, but after Britain threatened that its commitment to remain on the continent depended on approval and Mendès-France made it a vote of confidence, the Assembly reversed itself and approved them (Large 1996: 223; Hitchcock 1998: 201).

The ease with which this system was adopted reflected how far the strategic situation had come since 1950. In that year, the Soviets had struck east by proxy, and it was greatly feared that they would strike west for preventive reasons, to anticipate a Western buildup and in particular the rearmament of Germany. Over four years, the Western buildup had been accomplished with a solid commitment of U.S. forces to the continent. Thus, German rearmament would take place in the context of a strengthened U.S. presence that made it harder to imagine that the Soviets would lash out preventively to stop it. French fears remained, but the post–Korean War American and British commitments went a long way to calming them.

As a postscript, the dream of European unity, of course, did not die with the European Defense Community. Within four years it had led to the Treaty of Rome and the founding of the European Economic Community. Beginning as a customs union, the EEC began a process of integration that took up from the ECSC and lead to today's European Union. The question of German power, French fear, and the use of international institutions remained at the heart of this development. Germany used acquiescence in European structures to reassure others, France used European structures in an effort to contain the consequences of German power, and ultimately, in 1990, German reunification. The Maastricht Treaty and the move to a single currency can be seen as a continuation of this trend.

The defeat of the EDC certainly reflected French fears of rearming Germany, as the hegemonic assurance perspective indicates. It might seem to undermine this perspective because France was unwilling to cooperate even with U.S. and British support; however at a deeper level this is not the case. The French were uncomfortably aware that the EDC was embraced by the Eisenhower administration precisely because it seemed to offer promise of an exit strategy for the United States. Dulles threatened an American withdrawal from Europe if the EDC should be defeated, but Europeans foresaw that the opposite was the case, approving the EDC would lead to a more rapid American pullout. The WEU-NATO solution adopted in the end involved both the British and Americans in a continental commitment, also supporting the hegemonic assurance perspective. Though the United States sought in vain for a way out for the rest of the Eisenhower administration, there was, in James McAllister's phrase, "no exit" if European stability was to be preserved (McAllister 2002).

The fall of the EDC undermines coercive hegemony. Great Britain strongly supported French ratification and the United States threatened to terminate economic aid and abandon its commitment to defend France if the treaty was not ratified. France rejected the treaty nonetheless. Benign hegemony is undermined by the Paris Accords because Eden was the prime mover behind them, not the United States, indicating once more the presence of European initiative in establishing the institutions of European cooperation, rather than passive free riding.

THE PERSPECTIVES REVISITED

The hegemonic assurance perspective receives broad support from the history of European cooperation after the war. As the theory predicts, the United States and European states were conditional cooperators, but feared that others did not share this preference ordering. Hence, they constantly sought assurances that the others would be willing to cooperate. This is most clearly illustrated in the Marshall Plan, the Brussels Pact and NATO, and the ultimate decision to rearm Germany via the WEU and NATO in 1955. The United States sought assurances that the Europeans would work together so that U.S. aid would be effective, and the Europeans sought assurances that the United States would remain committed to Europe rather than retreat in a renewal of isolationism. The argument that France's relative nearness to Germany should reduce her willingness to cooperate is amply supported by the record. France was always the most reluctant to permit German revival and the most anxious to get guarantees from the United States in exchange. Also, U.S. cooperation did usually make it possible for France and the other European states to cooperate. The exceptions are the establishment of Bizonia, the initial proposal of the EDC and the eventual defeat of the EDC, when France rejected moves to revive Germany despite U.S. participation. However, these cases have extenuating circumstances. In the case of the Bizone, the U.S. guarantee was not very solid. In the case of the EDC, France worried that the United States might really see it as a ticket out of Europe, and, once it was defeated, quickly accepted measures that permitted German rearmament. Thus, the historical record of the early Cold War supports the hegemonic assurance perspective.

Benign hegemony fares much worse. In a host of cases, notably the Bizone, Treaty of Dunkirk, Brussels Pact, the birth of NATO and the NATO solution to German rearmament, we see genuine European cooperation that cannot plausibly be dismissed as free riding off a U.S. public good. International anarchy was only ameliorated, not eliminated by U.S. hegemony. Cooperation was not risk free, nor was it a foregone conclusion. Even U.S.-British relations went through a difficult period in the latter half of 1945 when the United States unceremoniously cut off lend-lease supplies and the two countries negotiated over a loan (Deighton 1990: 44). It was not clear that the United States would remain committed to Europe. European initiatives helped ensure that it did so and shaped the form in which that commitment took place. The best support for the benign hegemony position is the Marshall Plan, but even here it is clear that there was reciprocation in the form of a commitment to multilateral economic cooperation, not mere free riding.

Coercive hegemony receives only limited support. There are many cases of unforced European cooperation, notably the Dunkirk Treaty and the Brussels Pact. Even worse, there are cases where U.S. preferences were thwarted by much weaker powers. France proposed the Pleven Plan to delay German rearmament, in direct contravention of U.S. preferences; then when the United States switched to supporting the EDC, rejected it. Germany, weakest of all, rejected the Spofford Compromise provisions relating to raising German troops. In support of this perspective, France did often lose out to the United States and Britain in negotiations, notably in the London Accords on Germany and over the formation of NATO. Marshall Plan leverage was also used to pry concessions out of the recipients. In the grand scheme of things, however, if the United States had an empire in the Cold War, it was an "empire by invitation" rather than something imposed on the Europeans. At crucial stages in the path of Western cooperation, the Europeans invited the Americans to deepen their involvement in European affairs. Great Britain and France pushed for a continued American commitment to Europe, responded eagerly to Marshall's offer of aid, and pressed for the North Atlantic Treaty. France was reluctant to go along with German rearmament but ultimately did so in part because of the U.S. commitment to the continent.

Conclusion

In 1945, the Germans were defeated and distrusted by all. The threat from the Soviet Union provided an incentive for the Western states to cooperate, both on security issues and on economic ones. However, the deep distrust of Germany made it by no means clear that this cooperation would ultimately take place, especially as it was compounded by lesser distrust among the Western allies themselves. However, as the model of the previous chapter indicates, the presence of a hegemonic actor who is relatively trustworthy can make cooperation possible where it otherwise would not be. The United States played this role in the postwar era and enabled the European states to cooperate with each other and with Germany. American commitments to cooperate were relatively trustworthy, and American power made them significant inducements to the Europeans to cooperate in turn. The Americans were themselves able to cooperate in the face of very real uncertainty about the reliability of the other European states because the Europeans took steps to assure the Americans that they could be relied upon. French fears and German power were ultimately counterbalanced by American power and trustworthiness, enabling a virtuous spiral of increasing cooperation and trust-building in Europe that has continued in its broad outlines to the present day.

PART IV

Reassurance and the End of the Cold War

CHAPTER 7

Reassurance

WHEN MISUNDERSTANDINGS arise in everyday life we often smooth them out with some kind of reassurance. If you bump into someone on the street you say "excuse me," which tells them that you did not mean to jostle them and meant no disrespect. In general, cooperative behavior tends to reassure. In the Security Dilemma Game, cooperation has the effect of reassuring the other side and building trust. Given that only trustworthy types cooperate in the cooperative equilibrium, cooperation can be taken as a sure sign that the other side is trustworthy. Trust can be built up between trustworthy players, so long as their initial level of trust is high enough to make it worthwhile to take the risk of cooperating.

Unfortunately, if the players' initial level of trust is not high enough to justify taking that initial risk, defection ensues. In the noncooperative equilibrium of the Security Dilemma Game, no learning takes place about the other side's motivations because no one was willing to take a chance on establishing a cooperative relationship. In the spiral equilibrium of the Spiral Game, defection can even worsen mutual mistrust. Thus, states can be caught in a trap of mistrust, where their level of mistrust prevents them from cooperating, and their failure to cooperate prevents them from learning about each other's motivations and overcoming that mistrust.

As mentioned earlier, the noncooperative equilibrium accords well with the intuitions of offensive realism. States defect regardless of their motivations, because of a lack of trust. There is, therefore, no point worrying about state motivations. States have no friends, only interests. Instead, analysts should focus on state capabilities, and assume everyone is motivated by a desire for more power.

However, defensive realists, among others, argue that trust can be fostered through cooperative gestures that initiate chains of mutually rewarding behavior. These gestures often involve some vulnerability on the part of the side that makes them, confer some advantage to the recipient, and can be considered a type of costly signal (Spence 1973). In the Security Dilemma Game neither side has an opportunity to make such a gesture because the game has only one round. The parties have to cooperate or defect all at once, without any opportunity to learn about the other side. In this chapter I present a model of reassurance that does allow for such signals, and investigate how this changes the possibility for cooperation in the game.

The results provide grounds for optimism about the possibility of rational reassurance. In the Reassurance Game explored below, cooperation is possible for much lower levels of trust than in the Security Dilemma Game of chapter 2. Deeply distrustful players are able to send reassuring costly signals that build trust between them and lead to full cooperation. Indeed, this will be the case *regardless* of how mistrustful the players start out. This finding raises serious questions about offensive realism. If reassurance strategies exist that will build trust between initially distrustful states, international conflict is not an inevitable result of anarchy plus uncertainty about other state's motivations. Thus, this chapter, while fleshing out a Bayesian realist theory of reassurance via costly signals, also undermines the offensive realist analysis of how mistrust prevents cooperation.

REASSURANCE IN INTERNATIONAL RELATIONS

Reassurance can be defined as the process of building trust. It involves convincing the other side that you prefer to reciprocate cooperation, so that it is safe for them to cooperate. Mutual reassurance involves two parties, starting from a position of mistrust, simultaneously taking steps to reduce their mistrust. If trust can be increased then the two parties can eventually cooperate with each other, though they started out quite fearful of each other.

Reassurance has been accorded only sporadic attention in the field of international relations, but there has been a small literature related to the Cold War. In the early 1960s, two pioneering studies by Charles Osgood and Amitai Etzioni appeared with similar theses (Osgood 1962; Etzioni 1962).[1] Both authors identified the U.S.-Soviet arms race as a product of mistrust and suggested strategies for overcoming this fear through a program of gradual cooperative gestures. Osgood was especially critical of the conventional deterrence mindset, calling it the "Neanderthal Mentality" and characterizing it as a product of psychological bias. His recommended solution was dubbed GRIT (Graduated Reciprocation in Tension-reduction). The GRIT strategy involved making a series of unilateral cooperative gestures designed to increase the adversary's security without unduly weakening one's own, with an aim towards revising the other side's perceptions and increasing its level of trust. More recent advocates of reassurance have continued to critique deterrence theory as being excessively simplistic, rationalist, and belligerent while recommending cooperative gestures and less conflictual policies (Stein 1991).

---

[1] Schelling (1960: 45) also briefly discusses the idea.

GRIT has been the subject of several empirical studies, both historical and quantitative. Deborah Larson found GRIT in action in a case study of the 1955 Austrian State Treaty, while Joshua Goldstein and John Freeman analyzed GRIT and Tit for Tat in the context of U.S.-Soviet-Chinese relations (Larson 1987; Goldstein and Freeman 1990). Others have found support for GRIT in the experimental psychological literature and in case studies of Middle East peacemaking (Lindskold 1978; Kelman 1985). There has also been a lively debate about whether GRIT played an important role in the end of the Cold War, with Alan Collins arguing that it did and Richard Bitzinger arguing that it did not (Collins 1997, 1998; Bitzinger 1994; see also Ralph 1999 and Forsberg 1999). Reassurance is also central to the conflict resolution literature (Mitchell 2000), and studies of Japan's relations with China (Midford 2002).

While GRIT and related theories have contributed to our understanding of reassurance, there is still much to be learned. For one thing, we still lack a compelling theoretical explanation of when reassurance should work and when it should even be tried. Osgood, Stein, and other critics of deterrence theory leave the reader with the impression that leaders fail to reassure each other because they are cognitively or emotionally biased in favor of conflictual behavior. At the same time they acknowledge that sometimes reassurance will not work because the other side is biased in favor of conflictual behavior. If so, it would seem rational, not biased, to refrain from trying it. Similarly, we are left without a convincing rationale for why the gestures contemplated in GRIT should actually reassure. On the one hand, they are supposed to increase the security of the adversary, yet be nearly costless for one's own side. Critics of reassurance point out that there is little reason for an adversary to be reassured by a gesture that is not costly to the party that makes it.

In this chapter I present a rational choice approach to reassurance, based upon the concept of costly signals. The theory of costly signals was pioneered by Spence in the study of labor markets and higher education (Spence 1973).[2] The fact that college graduates make more money than high school graduates may seem puzzling if one considers that most college courses provide no skills of direct benefit to an employer. A knowledge of the works of Melville, or of the early Cold War for that matter, is of no real use to most firms. Why pay extra to hire someone with this knowledge? The answer provided by Spence is that it is not the knowledge per se that the employer values. Rather, the fact that the student was willing to invest in this useless knowledge serves as a signal that this potential employee finds learning and working to understand things relatively painless, at least in comparison to those who did not go to college. Employers who want

---

[2] See Riley 2001 for a review of economics applications.

employees who are capable of learning and making intelligent decisions, therefore, should pay extra for college students, who have demonstrated a tolerance for intellectual activity. At the heart of this story is uncertainty, in this case about the quality of the job candidates. If it were stamped on one's forehead how good an employee one would be, there would be no need for the costly signal. The costly signal on the part of the employees is a response to uncertainty on the part of employers about how productive the potential job candidates will be.

In recent years the concept of costly signaling has been applied to a number of international issues. Perhaps the most famous application is to crisis bargaining. James Fearon's work has shown how states involved in an international dispute send costly signals to each other in the form of actions that demonstrate a willingness to fight over the issue at stake (Fearon 1993). Crises arise because states are uncertain about what the other side is willing to fight for. For instance, in the Fashoda crisis of 1898, France staked a claim to the upper Nile at Fashoda by sending a token military force to occupy the town. Britain responded by threatening war if the troops remained. The crisis was eventually resolved when France gave in and removed the men. Presumably, the crisis would never have arisen to begin with if the French had known that the British would threaten war, and that France would back down in the face of this threat. As Kenneth Schultz argues, this uncertainty about how much the British would care about Fashoda led the French to gamble on initiating the crisis (Schultz 2001: 175–96).

If uncertainty is at the heart of crises, then communication is the key to resolving them. The problem is that ordinary communication does not work. If Britain were simply to say to France before the crisis started, if you go to Fashoda, we will fight, this communication might not be believable to the French. The problem is that Britain would have a great incentive to say this even if it were not true. Even if Britain planned to back down if pushed at Fashoda, if they could persuade the French not to even try just by saying they would fight, they would have every incentive to say so. For this reason, in contexts like this where two sides are bargaining, ordinary communication often fails to be credible, leading economists to call it "cheap talk" (Farrell and Rabin 1996). Instead, Britain must do things that would be costly if Britain did not intend to fight if pushed, such as mobilize troops, and publicly commit itself to fight so that domestic audiences, the press and eventually the electorate, would punish them if they backed down (Fearon 1994). These gestures carry conviction because if Britain did not intend to stand firm if pushed, it would find them very costly.

A similar logic applies in the issue area of trust and reassurance. Trust is also a matter of uncertainty, in this case over whether the other side prefers to reciprocate cooperation or exploit it. If it were obvious who would reciprocate cooperation and who would not, then trust would be automatic. Because it is not obvious, trust is a matter of beliefs as I argued in chapter 1. Given that uncertainty is the fundamental problem, it would seem that communication would solve it. If the trustworthy types could simply announce that they are trustworthy and would love to reciprocate cooperation, mistrust could be dispelled and cooperation would ensue. Unfortunately, such statements lack credibility in the trust context just as they do in the crisis bargaining context. Simple communication of this kind is cheap talk because, while trustworthy types have an incentive to say they are trustworthy, so do untrustworthy types. Untrustworthy types would love to persuade the other side that they are trustworthy because this would put them off their guard and persuade them to cooperate, making them easy to exploit. Hitler's statements that he had no further territorial demands in Europe were classic cheap talk, designed to lull the adversary into a false sense of security. For the same reason, one cannot trust an actor's statements about whether it is fearful of the other side. An expansionist state will have every incentive to claim that it is fearful, in hopes of eliciting some reassuring gesture from the other side that will leave it vulnerable. Trusting expansionists will earnestly claim to be fearful security seekers so long as there is any hope that the other side will believe them. In matters of trust, talk is cheap, and unpersuasive.[3]

To achieve reassurance therefore, it is necessary to go beyond simple assertions that you are trustworthy. The key mechanism that facilitates reassurance is costly signals. In the reassurance context, however, the nature of the costly signal is different than in the crisis bargaining context. In the crisis bargaining context, the signal is designed to show that one is resolute, tough, even belligerent, so that the other side should back down. In the reassurance context, the signal must achieve a different goal, demonstrating that one is moderate, not out to get the other side, willing to live and let live, preferring to reciprocate cooperation. Here, the costly signals must be small but at least somewhat costly gestures that benefit the other side and expose one to some risk of defection on their part. The key characteristic of the signal is that it be something that one would not do if one were the untrustworthy type, so that the other side can infer from it that one is trustworthy. Thus, in devising these signals, care must be taken that they are adequately costly, so that untrustworthy types would not send them too in an effort to trick the other side. At the same time they cannot be made too costly, or the trustworthy types may be unwilling to send them because they expose the trustworthy type to too great a level of risk in case the other side turns out to be untrustworthy and unwilling to reciprocate

---

[3] See Baliga and Sjöström 2001 for a partial exception to this logic.

cooperation. Achieving reassurance, therefore, is a careful balancing act. The signals cannot be too cheap, or untrustworthy types will send them too in an effort to lull the other side. They cannot be made too costly, or the trustworthy types will be afraid to send them lest the other side turn out to be untrustworthy. Balancing these two considerations is the key to achieving reassurance.

To better understand when these considerations can be balanced, we need to consider the strategic incentives formally in a model of reassurance that addresses these issues.[4]

The Reassurance Game

The Reassurance Game builds on the Security Dilemma Game of chapter 2, illustrated in Figure 2.1. However, instead of the one round structure of the Security Dilemma Game, the Reassurance Game has two rounds. This enables cooperative gestures to be made in the first round that may change the players' beliefs about each other, possibly building trust and enabling further cooperation in the second round.[5] In addition, whereas in the Security Dilemma Game cooperation was all or nothing, in the Reassurance Game the first round can be of lesser importance, so it can be used as a trial run. Thus, by allowing partial cooperative gestures in the first round of play that may build trust and foster cooperation in the second round, the Reassurance Game enables us to formalize the central intuitions behind reassurance.

The Reassurance Game is composed of two Security Dilemma Games back to back. In each round, the players choose to cooperate or defect, not knowing what the other side has chosen to do in that round. In the second round, though, they know what the other side did in the first round, so they can take that into account in deciding what to do next.

The initial moves by Nature that set up the information structure are the same as in the Security Dilemma Game. Player 1 has a t_1 likelihood of being security seeking, and a $1 - t_1$ likelihood of being expansionist, for player 2 the corresponding likelihoods are t_2 and $1 - t_2$.

The payoffs from each of the two rounds are not necessarily equal. To represent the idea of reassuring the other side with small initial costly signals, I multiply the payoffs from the first round by a fraction α_1 for player 1 and α_2 for player 2. The second round payoffs are multiplied by by the remainder, $1 - \alpha_1$ and $1 - \alpha_2$. The weight of the first round will typically

---

[4]For models of reassurance, see Ward 1989; Downs and Rocke 1990: 107; Watson 1999; and Kydd 2000a, b.

[5]See Swinth 1967 for an early experimental analysis along these lines.

TABLE 7.1
Notation in the Reassurance Game

g_i	Player i's value for gain.
l_i	Player i's potential loss from conflict.
π_i	The likelihood that player i wins if both defect.
ϕ_i	Player i's advantage of initiating a conflict.
c_i	Player i's cost of conflict.
t_i	The likelihood that player i is security seeking.
α_i	The importance of the first round for player i.
a_i	The minimum size threshold for the first round.
A_i	The maximum size threshold for the first round.

be less than that of the second round, $\alpha_i < 1 - \alpha_i$, so that the first round serves as a smaller warm up to the second round. Thus, the first round could be a trade treaty and the second round a security treaty. Cooperation over trade reassures the two players and enables them to then cooperate over a more important security matter. Notation for the Reassurance Game is summarized in Table 7.1.

The payoffs for the whole game are the simple sum of the payoffs in each of the two rounds, where the first round is weighted by α_i and the second round by $1 - \alpha_i$. Some examples will make the principle clear. For instance, if both players are security seeking and cooperate in both rounds, player 1 receives $\alpha_1(0)$ from the first round and $(1-\alpha_1)(0)$ from the second which sums to just 0. Player 2 likewise receives $\alpha_2(0) + (1 - \alpha_2)(0)$ or just 0. Consider the case in which player 1 is security seeking and player 2 is expansionist. Imagine that player 1 cooperates in the first round but defects in the second round, while player 2 defects in both rounds. In this case player 1 would receive $\alpha_1[(\pi_1 - \phi_2)g_1^s - (1 - \pi_1 + \phi_2)l_1 - c_1]$ from the first round because the other side exploited its cooperation, and $(1 - \alpha_1)[\pi_1 g_1^s - (1 - \pi_1)l_1 - c_1]$ from the second round because both sides defected. Player 1's total payoff is the sum, $\pi_1 g_1^s - (1 - \pi_1)l_1 - c_1 - \alpha_1\phi_2(g_1^s + l_1)$. Player 2 receives $\alpha_2[(\pi_2 + \phi_2)g_2^e - (1 - \pi_2 - \phi_2)l_2 - c_2]$ from the first round, the fruits of exploiting player 1's cooperation, and $(1 - \alpha_2)[\pi_2 g_2^e - (1 - \pi_2)l_2 - c_2]$ from the second where mutual defection ensues. The total payoff for the expansionist type of player 2 in this scenario is then $\pi_2 g_2^e - (1 - \pi_2)l_2 - c_2 + \alpha_2\phi_2(g_2^e + l_2)$.

Note that in modeling the idea of a costly reassuring gesture in this fashion I am assuming a certain degree of stationarity in the game, in the sense that the outcome in the first round does not alter the fundamental parameters of the game, such as the player's relative power, π_i, cost of conflict, c_i, etc. This assumption means that the signals envisioned in the game are limited in scope to issues that the parties care about, but which would not fundamentally alter the relationship depending on how they are resolved. The 1946 Iranian crisis is a good example or a reassuring signal that was not sent. When Stalin tried to make gains in Iran by reneging on the agreement to pull out troops, the stakes were real but limited. Having lost the resulting conflict, the Soviet Union was not materially weaker and went on to challenge U.S. influence in the region and elsewhere. Had the United States lost, the result would have been much the same. The 1987 Intermediate-range Nuclear Forces Treaty (INF) is a good example of a reassuring signal that was sent. Covering a very limited portion of the superpowers' nuclear arsenals, the treaty did not greatly affect the balance of power, nor would it have had one side or the other reneged. I adopt the stationarity assumption for simplicity and as a starting point, however it would obviously be interesting to modify it in future research to allow for gestures that weaken a state in subsequent disputes, for instance.

By repeating the Security Dilemma Game in this fashion, the Reassurance Game gives us a framework in which to investigate the possibility of reassurance. The players can now make preliminary cooperative gestures, the kind of trust-building moves envisioned in the costly signal theory of reassurance.

EQUILIBRIA IN THE REASSURANCE GAME

Shifting to a two-round structure necessitates that we consider more carefully what kind of equilibrium we are looking for, or what it means to play the game rationally. All of the games examined so far are one-round simultaneous move games, where the Nash equilibrium is a generally accepted solution concept. The Nash equilibrium just requires that players do what is optimal for them given their beliefs about what the other side is going to do, assuming that the other side is playing their role in the equilibrium. In the two-round game, however, we need to think about what the other side will believe after observing the first round of play, and how their behavior in the second round will be influenced by these beliefs.

For a game of incomplete information over time such as this one, an appropriate solution concept is the perfect Bayesian equilibrium (Morrow 1994b: 161). In a perfect Bayesian equilibrium, at each point in the game a player's strategy choice must be optimal given the player's beliefs and its beliefs must be updated in accordance with Bayes' rule where possible. In the two-round Reassurance Game, this implies the following three things. First, the strategies chosen in the first round must make sense given each side's initial beliefs about how likely the other side is to be security seeking or expansionist, and their expectations about what security seeking and expansionist types will do in equilibrium. Second, each side's beliefs about what type it faces after the first round must be updated in accordance with Bayes' rule given the strategies that each type was supposed to pursue in the first round. For example, if security seeking types were expected to cooperate and expansionist types were not, then if you see cooperation you should become convinced that the other side is security seeking. Finally, strategies in the second round must make sense given these updated beliefs. If the other side defects and only expansionist types defect in the first round, it makes sense to defect in the second round because expansionist types will defect there as well.

In thinking about what behavior to expect in the Reassurance Game, there is one thing that will be true in any equilibrium. Expansionist types have a dominant strategy to defect in the second round. There is no future retaliation to worry about and their immediate reward from defection is bigger than the payoff for cooperation. Everything else is contingent. The choices the players make are dependent on the prior levels of trust, the size of the first round, and the specific equilibrium.

There are several different types of equilibrium in the game. Details are given on each in the Appendix, here I focus on three equilibria that illustrate the range of possible behavior in the Reassurance Game. These equilibria are illustrated in Figure 7.1.[6]

The Noncooperative Equilibrium

As in the Security Dilemma Game, in the Reassurance Game an equilibrium is possible in which both types of both players defect, in this case, in both rounds. This follows again from the Assurance Game logic behind the security seeking type's payoffs in that if the other side is expected to defect for sure, the best response is to defect. This equilibrium is possible for any level of prior trust, hence throughout Figure 7.1. For higher levels of mutual trust, another equilibrium, the "time will tell" equilibrium discussed next, Pareto dominates the noncooperative equilibrium for the security seeking types. Because of this I would expect the security seeking types to coordinate on the more cooperative equilibrium, avoiding the noncooperative equilibrium. For lower levels of trust, the reassurance equilibria, discussed later, are possible.

---

[6]The parameter values used in the illustration are the same as in chapter 2: $g_i^s = 0$, $g_i^e = 0.5$, $l_i = 1$, $c_i = 0$, $\pi_i = 0.5$, and $\phi_i = 0.25$.

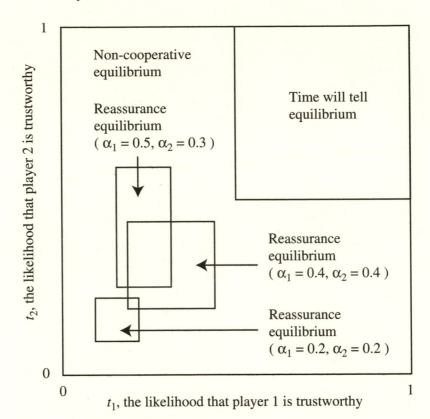

Figure 7.1 Equilibria in the Reassurance Game

The Time Will Tell Equilibrium

The time will tell equilibrium is possible for higher levels of mutual trust, in the upper right hand corner of Figure 7.1. In the first round, both types of player, security seeking and expansionist, cooperate. In the second round, if both players cooperated, security seeking types cooperate again, otherwise they defect. Expansionist types defect in the second round.[7] I call it the time will tell equilibrium because the uncertainty facing the players is preserved until the last move. Because the security seeking and the expansionist players do the same thing in the first round, there is no learning after observing the play. The players enter the final round with the same beliefs with which they started the game.

---

[7]There is a variant of this equilibrium in which after mutual defection the security seeking types cooperate; see the appendix for details. See Kreps et al. 1982; and Kreps and Wilson 1982 for similar equilibria.

When is this equilibrium possible? The time will tell equilibrium is the analog of the cooperative equilibrium of the Security Dilemma Game, and occupies the same territory, where mutual trust is high. The difference is that both types, security seeking and expansionist, must be sufficiently sure the other side is security seeking to be willing to cooperate.

For the security seeking types, the first round is easy. Since the other side is expected to cooperate for sure, the security seeking type wants to cooperate as well, since security seeking types prefer to reciprocate cooperation. Only the second round poses a genuine dilemma for them. Here, for the security seeking type of player i, cooperation nets $(1 - \alpha_i)\{t_j(0) + (1 - t_j)[(\pi_i - \phi_j)g_i^s - (1 - \pi_i + \phi_j)l_i - c_i]\}$, while defection would give $(1 - \alpha_i)\{t_j[(\pi_i + \phi_i)g_i^s - (1 - \pi_i - \phi_i)l_i - c_i] + (1 - t_j)[\pi_i g_i^s - (1 - \pi_i)l_i - c_i]\}$. Cooperation beats defection if the level of trust, t_j, exceeds a minimum trust threshold

$$t_j \geq \frac{\phi_j}{\frac{c_i + l_i}{g_i^s + l_i} - \pi_i - \phi_i + \phi_j}$$

which is the same minimum trust threshold as in the Security Dilemma Game. This makes sense since the trusting type is being asked to cooperate in the final round of the Reassurance Game having learned nothing about the other side, which is equivalent to being asked to cooperate in a one-round Security Dilemma Game.

Turning to the expansionist types, they must be given an incentive to cooperate in the first round, when defecting would raise their first-round payoff. The incentive is that if both sides cooperate in the first round, then the security seeking types will cooperate in the second, whereas if anyone defects, then the security seeking types will defect in the second round, giving the expansionist types no opportunity to exploit them. The conditions are specified in the appendix.

Since the conditions for the security seeking types are identical to those that are required for cooperation in the one-round Security Dilemma Game from chapter 2, it is apparent that the time will tell equilibrium is possible in the two-round game only when cooperation in the one-round Security Dilemma Game would be possible. This means that this equilibrium will not help with reassurance, the process of getting cooperation going when it would be impossible in the one-round Security Dilemma Game. The time will tell equilibrium may seem like a solution to a problem that does not exist, namely how to get cooperation going when the security seeking types are already trusting enough to cooperate. However, consider the welfare implications of this equilibrium. In the one-round Security Dilemma Game, the payoff for the security seeking type in the cooperative equilibrium is $t_j(0) + (1 - t_j)[(\pi_i - \phi_i)g_i^s - (1 - \pi_i + \phi_j)l_i - c_i]$. In the time will tell equilibrium, the security seeking type receives $\alpha_i(0) + (1 - \alpha_i)\{t_j(0) + (1 - t_j)[(\pi_i - \phi_i)g_i^s - (1 - \pi_i + \phi_j)l_i - c_i]\}$. The payoff from the time will tell equilibrium is unambiguously larger because of the guaranteed cooperation from expansionist types in the first round. Thus, if expansionist types are willing to fulfill their roles in the time will tell equilibrium, security seeking types are better off shifting from the one-round structure to the two-round structure, even if they are already trusting enough to cooperate. Of course, this assumes there are no costs in shifting to the two-round structure.

The Reassurance Equilibrium

The noncooperative equilibrium and the time will tell equilibrium both had clear analogies in the Security Dilemma Game. Neither one enabled cooperation to happen in the two-round game when it would not have been possible in the one-round game. Neither one made reassurance possible. The reassurance equilibrium fills this role. In this equilibrium, the security seeking types cooperate in the first round while expansionist types defect. In the second round, security seeking types cooperate if both players cooperated in the first round; otherwise they defect, while expansionist types defect under all conditions.[8] In Figure 7.1, I illustrate three versions of the reassurance equilibrium, two symmetric and one asymmetric. In one of the symmetric cases, the level of importance of the first round is 0.4, and in the other it is 0.2. The equilibrium for the less important first round, 0.2, is smaller in extent and closer to the origin, i.e., in a region of greater mutual distrust. In the asymmetric case, player 1 is more trusting than player 2 and the first round is consequently more important for player 1 ($\alpha_1 = 0.5$) than for player 2 ($\alpha_2 = 0.3$).

The reassurance equilibrium is a separating equilibrium. Since security seeking types and expansionist types pursue different strategies in the first-round, each player can tell from the other side's first round behavior whether they are security seeking or expansionist. If player 2 cooperated then player 1 knows that he is security seeking for sure; so that the posterior level of trust must equal 1. If player 2 did not cooperate, then he is identified as expansionist and the posterior level of trust goes to zero. Thus, after the first round the uncertainty that each side had about the other side's preferences has been resolved. Each side knows who they are dealing with and can act accordingly. Expansionist types will still prefer to defect because it is their dominant strategy. For the security seeking types, if both players cooperated they will believe each other to be trustworthy. It makes sense

---

[8]There is a Pareto inferior variant in which security seeking types defect after mutual cooperation in the first round; see the Appendix for details.

for security seeking types to cooperate in this case, because they can be assured of receiving their highest payoff for the second round, zero. If one of the players did not cooperate, it is believed to be expansionist, and will be expected not to cooperate in the second round. Security seeking types should then not cooperate either. Thus, the reassurance equilibrium separates the security seeking types from the expansionist types, allowing the security seeking types to recognize each other and cooperate subsequently, while avoiding being taken advantage of again by expansionist types.

When is the reassurance equilibrium possible? For the security seeking types, the payoff for playing the equilibrium strategy is $\alpha_i(t_j(0) + (1 - t_j)[(\pi_i - \phi_j)g_i^s - (1 - \pi_i + \phi_j)l_i - c_i]) + (1 - \alpha_i)(t_j(0) + (1 - t_j)[\pi_i g_i^s - (1 - \pi_i)l_i - c_i])$. If player i defects, she will persuade player j that she is expansionist, ensuring mutual defection for the second round. The payoff for defecting for the security seeking type is therefore $\alpha_i\{t_j[(\pi_i + \phi_i)g_i^s - (1 - \pi_i - \phi_i)l_i - c_i] + (1 - t_j)[\pi_i g_i^s - (1 - \pi_i)l_i - c_i]\} + (1 - \alpha_i)[\pi_i g_i - (1 - \pi_i)l_i - c_i]$. The equilibrium strategy beats the deviation if the level of trust exceeds a minimum trust threshold for the security seeking type,

$$t_j \geq \frac{\phi_j}{\frac{1}{\alpha_i}\left(\frac{c_i + l_i}{g_i^s + l_i} - \pi_i\right) - \phi_i + \phi_j}.$$

This condition indicates that the security seeking type requires a minimum level of trust to cooperate in the reassurance equilibrium, for a given level of α_i, the importance of the first round. The security seeking types are expected to cooperate in the first round. If they are too fearful, they will be unwilling to do so. This is much like the cooperative equilibrium in the Security Dilemma Game. The difference here is that the minimum trust threshold in the Reassurance Game can be much lower than in the Security Dilemma Game. As illustrated in Figure 7.1, the lower bound on the level of trust for the reassurance equilibrium when the size of the first round is 40 percent ($\alpha_i = 0.4$) is 0.2. That is, in the reassurance equilibrium, security seeking types are willing to cooperate even if there is only a 20-percent chance that they face another security seeking type on the other side, whereas in the Security Dilemma Game, they required at least a 50 percent chance. If the size of the first round is reduced to 0.2, security seeking types are willing to cooperate with only a 10 percent chance that the other side is also security seeking. Thus, cooperation is possible for much lower levels of trust in the Reassurance Game than in the Security Dilemma Game. Dividing the game into two rounds so that the parties can reassure each other enables cooperation to take place that otherwise would not have happened.

While the security seeking types demand a minimum level of trust to cooperate in the reassurance equilibrium, the expansionist types impose a maximum level. For the expansionist type, the equilibrium strategy involves not cooperating in the first round. If the other side is security seeking, it will cooperate in the first round, and the expansionist type will get $(\pi_i + \phi_i)g_i^e - (1 - \pi_i - \phi_i)l_i - c_i$. If the other side is expansionist, it will defect too so the payoff will be $\pi_i g_i^e - (1 - \pi_i)l_i - c_i$. In the second round, the other side will defect for sure, leading to a payoff of $\pi_i g_i^e - (1 - \pi_i)l_i - c_i$. The payoff for following this equilibrium strategy is therefore $\alpha_i\{t_j[(\pi_i + \phi_i)g_i^e - (1 - \pi_i - \phi_i)l_i - c_i] + (1 - t_j)[\pi_i g_i^e - (1 - \pi_i)l_i - c_i]\} + (1 - \alpha_i)[\pi_i g_i^e - (1 - \pi_i)l_i - c_i]$. If the expansionist type instead mimics the security seeking type by cooperating in the first round, this will fool the other side into thinking that it is security seeking, causing the other side to cooperate in the second round if it is security seeking. Player i, being, in reality, expansionist, will not reciprocate this second-round cooperation. The risk is that player j will be expansionist; in this case player i's first-round signal will bear no dividends because player j will not cooperate in either round. The payoff from deviating to the security seeking type's strategy is therefore $\alpha_i\{t_j(0) + (1 - t_j)[(\pi_i - \phi_j)g_i^e - (1 - \pi_i + \phi_j)l_i - c_i]\} + (1 - \alpha_i)\{t_j[(\pi_i + \phi_i)g_i^e - (1 - \pi_i - \phi_i)l_i - c_i] + (1 - t_j)[\pi_i g_i^e - (1 - \pi_i)l_i - c_i]\}$. For the expansionist type, the payoff for defecting must beat the payoff for cooperating, which implies that the level of trust must fall below a *maximum trust threshold*,

$$t_j \le \frac{\phi_j}{\frac{c_i + l_i}{g_i^e + l_i} - \pi_i - \phi_i + \phi_j + \left(\frac{1}{\alpha_i} - 1\right)\phi_i}.$$

The expansionist types are expected to defect in the first round. By deviating to cooperation they could fool the other side into believing that they are security seeking, getting the other side to cooperate in the next round, if the other side is security seeking. If the level of trust is too high, expansionist types will prefer to do just that, deviate to the security seeking type's strategy of cooperating. Thus, the preferences of the expansionist types impose an upper bound on the level of trust in a reassurance equilibrium.

While the prior levels of trust, t_i, are important, so is the size of the first round, α_i. What determines how important the first round should be if the goal is to achieve reassurance? To examine this question, the relations between the payoffs can be solved for α_i. The constraints imposed by the security seeking types payoffs provide a *maximum cost threshold*, A_i, for size of the first round

$$\alpha_i \le A_i \equiv \frac{\frac{c_i + l_i}{g_i^s + l_i} - \pi_i}{\phi_i + \left(\frac{1}{t_j} - 1\right)\phi_j}.$$

If the round is too important, then the security seeking type will be afraid to cooperate. That is, the larger the signal, the more risky it is for the security seeking types to send. They are destroying more missiles or demilitarizing more territory. There will be some upper limit on how large a signal the security seeking types are willing to send, on how costly the costly signal can become.

Consider now the expansionist types and the size of the first round. The constraints for the expansionist types place a *minimum cost threshold*, a_i, on the size of the first round:

$$\alpha_i \geq a_i \equiv \frac{\phi_i}{\pi_i + \phi_i - \frac{c_i + l_i}{g_i^e + l_i} + \phi_i + \left(\frac{1}{t_j} - 1\right)\phi_j}.$$

If the first round is too small, then the expansionist types will be tempted to cooperate in order to persuade the other side that they are security seeking, and thereby trick them into cooperating in the second round. If the signal is too trivial, therefore, it will be sent by the expansionist types as well. In this case, it will convey no information about the players' types and will not influence their beliefs. Since cheap talk has no impact on beliefs in this game, signals that are too small do not reassure.

A few words on the comparison between the time will tell equilibrium and the reassurance equilibrium are in order. A natural question that arises is, are they both possible at the same time for some set of parameter values? Any overlap would be confined to the area where t_j exceeds the minimum trust threshold for the Security Dilemma Game, that is, where the players are trusting enough to cooperate without reassurance. Where reassurance is needed, below these minimum trust thresholds, the time will tell equilibrium is impossible, leaving the field to the reassurance equilibrium and the noncooperative equilibrium. Above these thresholds, the time will tell equilibrium makes the security seeking types better off than the reassurance equilibrium would, so I would expect the time will tell equilibrium to be more likely there.

Costly Signals versus Cheap Talk

The implications of the Reassurance Game, as foreshadowed earlier, contrast sharply with that of offensive realism, and provide grounds for optimism about the possibility of overcoming mistrust under anarchy. First of all, the existence of the reassurance equilibrium in the zone where the cooperative equilibrium is not possible in the one-shot game means that by altering the structure of the interaction to allow costly signaling, cooperation is ultimately possible for much lower levels of trust than would otherwise be the case.

Implication 7.1   *The strategy of reassurance through costly signals makes cooperation possible for levels of mistrust that would otherwise prevent cooperation. Cheap talk has no effect on trust or cooperation.*

These signals must be not too large, nor too small, $a_i \leq \alpha_i \leq A_i$. The existence of the maximum cost threshold, A_i, provides a game theoretic foundation for perhaps the most widespread insight about reassurance, that it must start with small gestures. Advocates of reassurance such as Osgood and Etzioni constantly emphasize the small scale of the initial gestures, and the limitation on the level of risk for the initiator that this implied. The very names of their recommended strategies, "gradualism" for Etzioni and "Graduated Reciprocation in Tension-reduction" for Osgood emphasize this aspect of their thought. In part this was an effort to distinguish themselves from "naive" advocates of the more radical proposals for "general and complete" disarmament that prevailed in the 1950s (Osgood 1962: 87).[9] Advocates of more cooperative policies were vulnerable to the charge of disloyalty, and, hence, were under heavy pressure to demonstrate that their policies would not place the United States at risk. As a result, scholars like Osgood and Etzioni emphasized the lack of danger in trying cooperation on a small scale.

The necessity of a minimum cost threshold, a_i, has been less emphasized in the traditional reassurance literature, though Osgood suggests it when he posits that the gestures he advocates must risk some security if they are to "induce reciprocation from opponents" (Osgood 1962: 89). The danger is that they will be interpreted as a "Cold War trick," or a deception designed to win points in the propaganda war (Osgood 1962: 104). To overcome this, Osgood advocates a continued stream of modest conciliatory gestures, in the terms of the model, making the first round more important. The model demonstrates that the signal must be adequately costly, otherwise the expansionist type will mimic the security seeking type in an effort to dupe the other side. Thus, cheap talk does not work in reassurance, only costly signals.

THE SIZE OF THE SIGNAL

What determines how costly the signal has to be? Both the level of trust and the strategic situation affect the size of the signal. Increasing the level of trust will necessitate that the signals will have to be larger. The maximum cost threshold on the size of the signal, a product of the security

---

[9]The origins of modern arms control theory in the late 1950s as an "adjunct to strategic thought" rather than a moral crusade also reflected this environment, as well as the onset of strategic vulnerability on the part of the United States. See Schelling and Halperin 1961.

seeking type's concern about exploitation, increases as the level of trust rises, $\frac{\partial A_i}{\partial t_j} > 0$. This makes intuitive sense when one considers that larger signals imply greater risks. If suspicion is very deep, as between the United States and the Soviet Union in the 1950s, the size of the signals must be smaller, because the side sending them will be more afraid of the possibility of being taken advantage of. If suspicion diminishes, the states will be willing to send larger signals because, with a greater level of trust, the larger signal becomes less risky. This provides a game theoretic backing for the intuition that as trust increases, states can move on to more important cooperative efforts. The arms control treaties of the 1990s between the United States and Soviet Union, for instance, would have been impossible before the end of the Cold War substantially increased the level of trust.

If the level of trust increases, the minimum cost threshold on the size of the first round will shift up as well, $\frac{\partial a_i}{\partial t_j} > 0$. This means that signals which used to be large enough to prevent the expansionist type from sending them, are no longer sufficient. The increase in trust makes the expansionist types willing to risk the signal in the hopes of tricking the security seeking type into cooperating fully in the second round. Thus, the signal size will have to increase to keep the expansionist types from sending them as well. Increasing levels of trust not only enables the security seeking types to risk larger signals, it forces them to do so because the expansionist type is now also willing to risk larger signals in an effort to deceive the other side. In order to distinguish themselves from the expansionist types, therefore, security seeking types will have to send larger signals as the level of trust increases. Conversely, if the players become more fearful, this constraint will shift downwards. Signals that the expansionist type was once willing to send will become too risky, so that lower signals will begin to work in equilibrium. As the level of trust declines, then, the costliness of the signal will also decline. These considerations are summed up in the following implication.

Implication 7.2 *The lower the level of trust, the smaller the size of the costly signal, the higher the level of trust, the greater the size of the signal.*

For instance, the 1987 Intermediate-range Nuclear Forces Treaty mandated much larger cuts on the Soviet side than on the U.S. side, reflecting the greater degree of suspicion on the U.S. side. In the asymmetric example shown in Figure 7.1, player 1 is more trusting than player 2, and, hence, the signal for player 1, α_1, is 0.5, whereas the signal size for the more suspicious player 2, α_2, is 0.3. The size of the signals that the security seeking types must send in equilibrium to reassure each other, therefore, responds in a natural way to their level of trust. Greater trust mandates greater signals, lesser trust calls for smaller signals.

The player's power also affect the size of the signal. The more powerful the state is, the smaller the signal it will be willing to send; both the minimum and maximum cost threshold decline as power increases, $\frac{\partial A_i}{\partial \pi_i} < 0$ and $\frac{\partial a_i}{\partial \pi_i} < 0$. This follows from the fact that stronger states do better in conflict. Since they have a better chance of prevailing in conflict, they are less willing to take risks to avoid it. Conversely, weaker states, with a greater chance of doing badly if there is a conflict, will try harder to avoid one through reassurance.

Implication 7.3 *Stronger states will send smaller costly signals of reassurance; weaker states will make more costly gestures.*

The advantage of initiating the conflict has a similar effect; the worse it is to let the other side defect while you cooperate, the smaller the signal must be, $\frac{\partial A_i}{\partial \phi_j} < 0$ and $\frac{\partial a_i}{\partial \phi_j} < 0$. Preemptive defection prevents one from having to suffer the costs of the other side exploiting one's cooperation, so the higher these costs are, the greater the temptation to defect. To overcome this incentive, the signal must be smaller. Increasing one's own first strike advantage also lowers the size of the signal the security seekers will be willing to send, $\frac{\partial A_i}{\partial \phi_i} < 0$, while the effect on the minimum cost threshold, a_i, is contingent on a number of factors.

Implication 7.4 *The stronger the advantages to moving first, the smaller the signals of reassurance that will be sent.*

Finally, the greater the costs of conflict, c_i, the larger the signals each side will be willing to send, $\frac{\partial A_i}{\partial c_i} > 0$, and $\frac{\partial a_i}{\partial c_i} > 0$. As conflict grows worse, the parties will take greater risks to avoid it. For instance, U.S. interest in reassurance strategies rose sharply in the late 1950s and early 1960s, when Soviet nuclear capabilities reached a level where the U.S. homeland could be devastated in an all out war. Soviet interest in reassurance in the 1980s was sparked by the NATO deployment of missiles capable of hitting the Soviet Union in five minutes.

Implication 7.5 *The greater the costs of conflict, the stronger the reassuring signals states will be willing to send.*

When Reassurance Works

An important question raised by these implications, perhaps the most important question of all, is when are these constraints reconcilable? When can a signal be found that the security seeking type is willing to send and the expansionist type is unwilling to send? Mathematically, when is $a_i < A_i$? Knowing the answer to this question will tell us when reassurance is possible when actors are too fearful to cooperate all at once.

Some algebra (see the Appendix) shows that an appropriate level of importance for the first round can *always* be found. That is, $0 < a_i < A_i$ under all circumstances. In particular, cooperation is possible between security seekers in the reassurance equilibrium *no matter how mistrustful they are to begin with*. The two states can be nearly convinced that the other side is expansionist, but if they are genuine security seekers, they can find an appropriate set of costly signals that will enable them to reassure each other and cooperate completely over time.

Implication 7.6   *Costly signaling will permit reassurance and cooperation between rational security seekers no matter how mistrustful they are of each other to begin with.*

This is a strong result with broad ramifications. Essentially it says that states will be able to order the issues facing them over time such that their behavior on the earlier issues will be informative about how they will behave on the later ones. Security seeking states will be willing to cooperate on the earlier issues whereas expansionist types will not. Put another way, states will be able to design multiphased agreements in any particular issue area, such that states which are trustworthy with respect to that issue will be willing to cooperate in the early phases and those that are untrustworthy will not. The issues to tackle first, or the nature of the early phases of a multiphase agreement, will vary depending on the context in ways suggested by the previous results on how the parameters in the model affect the constraints on the size of the signal. In the end, however, the result says that an appropriate structure will always be available that will fulfill the requirement to separate the types.

This result establishes a strong prima facie case against offensive realism. The offensive realist argument was predicated on the inviolability of the noncooperative equilibrium in the low trust zones. In the Security Dilemma and Spiral Games, while cooperation was possible if the players' level of trust exceeded minimum trust thresholds, there was always a low trust zone in which the noncooperative equilibrium was unchallenged and no other equilibrium was possible. Hence, it was always open to offensive realists to claim that the prevailing level of international trust is low enough to put us in that region. This moves the argument into the difficult empirical terrain of measuring the level of international trust and comparing it to the minimum trust thresholds. In the Reassurance Game, however, this zone is now populated by reassurance equilibria, in which security seeking types reassure each other and end up cooperating fully. Now there is no portion of the parameter space in which security seeking types cannot cooperate with each other. This throws the burden on offensive realists who wish to interpret conflict as a rational product of mistrust to explain why the noncooperative equilibrium should be selected when the reassurance equilibrium is clearly better for the security seeking types. More broadly, it indicates that when we see rational actors confronted by mistrust, we should see them attempting reassurance strategies. These should succeed when the two sides are genuinely security seeking and interested in cooperation. Should they fail, the natural interpretation is that at least one of the parties was not security seeking, and was not interested in reciprocating cooperation, or that psychological factors prevented rational behavior or updating of beliefs in response to observed behavior. In either case, the offensive realist standpoint, that rational unitary security seeking states fail to cooperate through mistrust, is undermined.

While the Reassurance Game establishes a strong case for rational reassurance, it is only fair to acknowledge that it is a simple game and that further research is needed to fully identify the conditions under which reassurance is feasible in more complex or general settings. Possible generalizations include increasing the number of rounds, allowing a greater heterogeneity of payoffs across the various issues, and making various parameters such as bargaining power contingent on what happens in previous rounds. The existing literature on reassurance supports the implications of this model, however. In previous work based on a more general trust game, I have identified reassurance equilibria that are sometimes possible no matter what the initial level of trust (Kydd 2000b). Joel Watson examines a model of cooperation between firms in continuous time and identifies a reassurance equilibrium which uniquely meets a condition relating to renegotiation (Watson 1999). A variety of models in different contexts exhibit reassurance equilibria that have the same basic characteristics as the one identified here; all make cooperation possible for lower levels of trust than would otherwise be the case.

Perhaps the strongest counterargument on behalf of offensive realism is that a state's preferences can change over time, so that knowledge of a state's present motivations, while valuable, will not suffice to perfectly predict future behavior. This argument has long been a staple of realist thought and is sometimes taken to decisively refute the possibility of trust based cooperation under anarchy (Jervis 1976: 62; Mearsheimer 2001: 31). The argument is strongest in the context of a nonstationary model in which power varies as well. If cooperation in the present involves a substantial weakening in a state's relative power, and the future motivations of the other state are especially volatile, it might be difficult to establish a sufficient degree of reassurance to permit cooperation (Copeland 2000: 30). To fully examine this issue would require a multistage game in which there is a stochastic component to the preferences and future research should certainly explore such models. However, three considerations argue against an uncritical acceptance of the idea that uncertainty about future preferences inhibits present cooperation in general (Kydd 1997b: 147–52).

First, while each new day brings the possibility of preference change, it also brings a new opportunity for reassurance. Thus, a repeated version of the Reassurance Game, in which the preferences of the actors were subject to random shocks, might look quite similar to the one-round game. International institutions may play a role in fostering reassurance over time by embodying a system of standing costly signals: institutional constraints that would be irksome to an expansionist power (Ikenberry 2001; Weinberger 2003). If a state became expansionist, it would pull out of the institution, as Germany left the League of Nations after Hitler came to power. Its departure would ring an alarm bell, warning the other powers that it had become expansionist and putting them on their guard. The fact that institutional constraints can serve as costly signals and alarm bells helps explain why states with an interest in reassuring their neighbors, such as Germany at the end of the Cold War, advocate deepening institutional cooperation.

Second, sometimes the possibility of preference change facilitates cooperation rather than hindering it; indeed sometimes a state will cooperate with a currently expansionist state in the hope that its preferences will change for the better. The end of the Cold War can be seen as a case of radical preference change on the part of the Warsaw Pact states that greatly facilitated cooperation with their former adversaries. The goal of West German *ostpolitik*, and to some extent Kissingerian détente, was to gradually soften the communist expansionist impulse by building up ties across the iron curtain. Some argue that trade with China will empower potentially democratically minded citizens and help lead to democratization there as well. Both liberal and constructivist theory suggests that state preferences can be affected by international interactions. Constructivists point to the socializing impact of international institutions composed of democratic, security seeking states (Shimmelfennig 1998/99, 2001). Liberals argue that international trade strengthens economic interests that favor openness and international cooperation, leading to a virtuous circle of improved relations (Oneal and Russett 1997).

Finally, there are theoretical and empirical reasons for believing that preference change from security seeking to expansionist, the most troubling case, is rare. Security seeking states tend to be liberal democracies and nondemocracies with limited aims or capabilities. Mature liberal democracies are often quite stable in their foreign policy preferences. No one thinks that France might decide to launch a renewed bid for control of Southeast Asia after the next election, or that Britain will attempt to retake South Africa if the Conservatives defeat the Labor party. In part this is a result of the median voter theorem; democratic politics has a tendency to reflect the preferences of the swing voter, regardless of who wins.[10] Other states are more volatile, especially dictatorships run by mercurial leaders such as Libya. However, even in more volatile states, present preferences are often a good predictor of future preferences. Even authoritarian and oligarchic political institutions can impose a certain inertia on policy, along with other domestic constraints. Dramatic preference change is most often associated with great revolutions, such as the 1979 Iranian revolution, or the rise of antisystemic parties such as the Nazis in 1933. Such events are rare and do not play a great role in preventing cooperation between more stable moderate states such as the advanced democracies.

While the offensive realist thesis about preference volatility preventing cooperation in general may be overdrawn, the model does indicate one circumstance that will increase preference volatility in a dangerous way. When a state is growing in relative power, its preferences may become less stable. This is because as the Security Dilemma Game shows, increasing relative power π_i pushes a state closer to the border between security seeking and expansionist states. Small shifts in the gains from expansion, g_i, caused by an election, for instance, could then tip the balance between one set of preferences and another. This indicates that states that are growing in power, if they want to preserve a reputation as a security seeking state, will need to pay extra attention to reassurance, as West Germany did in 1990 when it moved towards reunification with East Germany. They need to demonstrate that their expansionist goals are so low that even with the anticipated accession of power, they will remain security seekers. As I will discuss in the last chapter, the United States is currently facing this problem, as a result of its unprecedented relative power advantages over other states.

CONCLUSION

This chapter examined how two players, who were too mistrustful to cooperate in the Security Dilemma Game, might get cooperation going by setting up an initial round to test the waters. If players start out too mistrustful to cooperate in the Security Dilemma Game, the Reassurance Game shows that they can nonetheless achieve cooperation through sending a reassuring signal. This signal must not be too large or the security seeking types will be afraid to send it, nor can it be too small, or the

---

[10] Partisan alternation does produce policy change in election models when there is uncertainty about the median voter's ideal point and the parties have different ideal points (Wittman 1990). However the swings in policy are dampened by the electoral mechanism, that is, the parties implement policies somewhere between their estimate of the median voter's ideal policy and their own.

expansionist types will send it in an effort to fool the security seeking types into cooperating in the next round. Such signals make cooperation possible even for players who start out with extremely low levels of mutual trust. As I will explore in the next chapter, this signaling process was an important part of the story of the end of the Cold War.

Appendix

I solve for perfect Bayesian equilibria. I make no general assumptions about off equilibrium path beliefs, but discuss the issue where appropriate when considering specific equilibria.

There are two players and two types for each player, making four actors total. There are five choices for each actor: what to do in the first round, what to do in the second round if both cooperated, if 1 cooperated and 2 defected, if 1 defected and 2 cooperated, and if both defected? With four actors and five choices there are 20 binary decisions that define an equilibrium. This implies that there are 2^{20} possible equilibrium patterns of behavior.

This can be whittled down to size as follows. First, in the second round, expansionist types of both player defect for sure. This eliminates eight choices, getting us down to 2^{12}. Also in the second round, security seeking types will either both cooperate or both defect. If one security seeking player were expected to defect in a certain circumstance, the other one would have to as well, because given that the expansionist types defect, the other side is certain to defect. Thus, in the second round, for each of the four possible sets of first round behavior, there are really only two possibilities, expansionist types defect and security seeking types cooperate, or both types of both players defect. Thus, with the four first round choices for the players (2^4 possible patterns) plus four binary possibilities for the second round (2^4 possible patterns), there are 2^8 possible equilibrium patterns of behavior.

Further reduction is possible by noting that in the first round, if the security seeking type of player i defects, the expansionist type of player i will as well. If the expansionist type were to cooperate in equilibrium while the security seeking type defected, the expansionist type could switch to defection, raise its first round payoff, and convince the other side that it is security seeking, which cannot harm its second-round payoff. In the second round player j will defect if it observes cooperation, which is a signal that the player is expansionist. It may or may not cooperate if it observes defection, a sign that the player is security seeking, but this chance of cooperation is greater than or equal to that on the equilibrium path, so the payoff must be as well. Combined with the strictly positive payoff increase from switching to defecting in the first round, the equilibrium is unsustainable. This eliminates seven patterns, leaving nine for the first round.

In combining the first- and second-round patterns, it should also be noted that if an expansionist type is to cooperate in the first round, it must be rewarded by having the security seeking types cooperate in the second round, and punished for switching to defection by having cooperation collapse in the second round. Also, if the types separate, defection in the first round will signal expansionist motivations and hence produce defection in the second round.

The remaining possibilities that survive are illustrated in Table 7.2. The first four entries in each row are the strategies for each player/type in the first round, the next four refer to whether the security seeking types cooperate in the second round or not after each possible pattern of first round behavior, CC, CD, DC and DD.

TABLE 7.2
Equilibrium Patterns of Behavior

#	Name	First Round				Second Round			
		1_s	1_e	2_s	2_e	CC	CD	DC	DD
1	Reassurance	C	D	C	D	C	D	D	D
						D	D	D	D
2	Player 1 Reassures	C	D	D	D	C	C	D	D
						D	C	D	D
3	Player 2 Reassures	D	D	C	D	C	D	C	D
						D	D	C	D
4	time will tell	C	C	C	C	C	D	D	D
						C	D	D	C
5	Reassurance/TWT	C	D	C	C	C	D	D	D
6	TWT/Reassurance	C	C	C	D	C	D	D	D
7	Player 1 Cooperates	C	C	D	D	D	C	C	D
						D	C	D	D
8	Player 2 Cooperates	D	D	C	C	D	C	C	D
						D	D	C	D
9	Non-cooperative	D	D	D	D	anything			

The Reassurance Equilibrium

In the reassurance equilibrium, there is no need to consider off equilibrium path beliefs because the game never goes off the equilibrium path.

There are two variants, one in which mutual cooperation leads to cooperation, discussed in the body, and one in which mutual cooperation leads to defection. In the latter version, defection takes place in the second round no matter what the players do in the first. The expansionist types are therefore happy to defect in the first round. The security seeking types will cooperate in the first round if it makes sense in the first round alone, that is, if the levels of trust exceed m_i. This equilibrium is therefore confined to the upper right quadrant, where cooperation would be possible in the one round game.

To prove the result from implication 7.6, we wish to show that

$$a_i \leq A_i$$

$$\frac{\phi_i}{\pi_i + \phi_i - \frac{c_i + l_i}{g_i^e + l_i} + \phi_i + \left(\frac{1}{t_j} - 1\right)\phi_j} \leq \frac{\frac{c_i + l_i}{g_i^s + l_i} - \pi_i}{\phi_i + \left(\frac{1}{t_j} - 1\right)\phi_j}$$

$$\phi_i\left(\phi_i + \left(\frac{1}{t_j} - 1\right)\phi_j\right) \leq \left(\frac{c_i + l_i}{g_i^s + l_i} - \pi_i\right)\left(\pi_i + \phi_i - \frac{c_i + l_i}{g_i^e + l_i} + \phi_i + \left(\frac{1}{t_j} - 1\right)\phi_j\right)$$

$$\left(\pi_i + \phi_i - \frac{c_i + l_i}{g_i^s + l_i}\right)\left(\phi_i + \left(\frac{1}{t_j} - 1\right)\phi_j\right) \leq \left(\frac{c_i + l_i}{g_i^s + l_i} - \pi_i\right) \times \left(\pi_i + \phi_i - \frac{c_i + l_i}{g_i^e + l_i}\right)$$

$$\pi_i + \phi_i - \frac{c_i + l_i}{g_i^s + l_i} \leq \frac{\left(\frac{c_i + l_i}{g_i^s + l_i} - \pi_i\right)\left(\pi_i + \phi_i - \frac{c_i + l_i}{g_i^e + l_i}\right)}{\phi_i + \left(\frac{1}{t_j} - 1\right)\phi_j}$$

which can be expressed as

$$(\pi_i + \phi_i)g_i^s - (1 - \pi_i - \phi_i)l_i - c_i$$
$$\leq \frac{(-1)\left(\pi_i g_i^s - (1 - \pi_i)l_i - c_i\right)\left((\pi_i + \phi_i)g_i^e - (1 - \pi_i - \phi_i)l_i - c_i\right)}{\left(\phi_i + \left(\frac{1}{t_j} - 1\right)\phi_j\right)(g_i^e + l_i)}.$$

The left-hand side is the security seeking type's payoff for defecting while the other side cooperates, which is negative by definition. The right hand side is positive. The first term in the numerator is the security seeking type's payoff for mutual defection, which is negative, times -1, making it positive. The second term is the expansionist type's payoff for defecting while the other side cooperates, which is positive by definition. The denominator is positive as well. Hence, the relation is always satisfied.

The final step is to show that a *positive* solution can be found; it would be no use if the appropriate signal size were negative. We can reexpress the lower bound a_i as follows.

$$a_i = \frac{\phi_i(g_i^e + l_i)}{(\pi_i + \phi_i)g_i^e - (1 - \pi_i - \phi_i)l_i - c_i + (g_i^e + l_i)\left(\phi_i + \left(\frac{1}{t_j} - 1\right)\phi_j\right)}.$$

The numerator is positive. The first three terms in the denominator are the expansionist type's payoff for attacking when the other side does not, which is positive by definition. The remaining term is also positive. Hence, the lower bound is positive, so a positive solution can be found that satisfies the two constraints.

The Player 1 Reassures and Player 2 Reassures Equilibria

In the player 1 reassures equilibrium, the security seeking type of player 1 cooperates and the expansionist player 1 does not, while both types of player 2 defect in the first round. In the second round, if player 1 cooperated and player 2 did not, security seeking types cooperate. If player 1 did not cooperate, then security seeking types defect. If both players cooperated, there are two versions: in version 1 security seeking types cooperate, in version 2, they defect.

I will solve the player 1 reassures equilibrium; the player 2 reassures equilibrium; is a mirror image.

The game goes off the equilibrium path if player 2 cooperates. If player 1 defected, this does not matter because player 2 will distrust player 1 leading security seeking types to defect. If player 1 cooperated, however, at CC, the question of off equilibrium path beliefs becomes important. If the posterior trust is high enough, version 1 will obtain in which security seeking types cooperate. If the belief is low enough, version 2 will hold. Given that the deviation is to cooperation, it may be natural to suppose that it will raise the level of trust, favoring version 1.

For the security seeking type of player 1, the payoff for cooperation is $\alpha_1((\pi_1 - \phi_2)g_1^s - (1 - \pi_1 + \phi_2)l_1 - c_1) + (1 - \alpha_1)(t_2(0) + (1 - t_2)[(\pi_1 - \phi_2)g_1^s - (1 - \pi_1 + \phi_2)l_1 - c_1])$ which must beat the payoff for defection, which is just $\pi_1 g_1^s - (1 - \pi_1)l_1 - c_1$ yielding

$$t_2 \geq \frac{\phi_2}{(1 - \alpha_1)\left(\frac{c_1 + l_1}{g_1^s + l_1} - \pi_1 + \phi_2\right)}.$$

For the expansionist type, the payoff for defection, $\pi_1 g_1^e - (1 - \pi_1) h_1 - c_1$, must beat that from cooperating, $\alpha_1 [(\pi_1 - \phi_2) g_1^e - (1 - \pi_1 + \phi_2) h_1 - c_1] + (1 - \alpha_1)(t_2 [(\pi_1 + \phi_1) g_1^e - (1 - \pi_1 - \phi_1) h_1 - c_1] + (1 - t_2)[\pi_1 g_1^e - (1 - \pi_1) h_1 - c_1])$ which gives

$$t_2 \leq \frac{\alpha_1}{1 - \alpha_1} \frac{\phi_2}{\phi_1}$$

For the security seeking type of player 2, in version 1 where switching to cooperate produces cooperation in the second round, the payoff from defection is $\alpha_2(t_1 [(\pi_2 + \phi_2) g_2^s - (1 - \pi_2 - \phi_2) h_2 - c_2] + (1 - t_1)[\pi_2 g_2^s - (1 - \pi_2) h_2 - c_2]) + (1 - \alpha_2)(t_1(0) + (1 - t_1)[\pi_2 g_2^s - (1 - \pi_2) h_2 - c_2])$ which must beat that from switching to cooperate, $\alpha_2(t_1(0) + (1 - t_1)[(\pi_2 - \phi_2) g_2^s - (1 - \pi_2 + \phi_1) h_2 - c_2]) + (1 - \alpha_2)(t_1(0) + (1 - t_1)[\pi_2 g_2^s - (1 - \pi_2) h_2 - c_2])$ which yields the minimum trust threshold for the Security Dilemma Game:

$$t_1 \leq \frac{\phi_1}{\frac{c_2 + h_2}{g_2^s + h_2} - \pi_2 - \phi_2 + \phi_1}.$$

Since the second rounds are the same, player 2 will defect if it pays to do so in the first round. In version 2, where mutual cooperation leads to defection, the equilibrium payoff must beat an alternative deviation payoff $\alpha_2(t_1(0) + (1 - t_1)[(\pi_2 - \phi_1) g_2^s - (1 - \pi_2 + \phi_1) h_2 - c_2]) + (1 - \alpha_2)[\pi_2 g_2^s - (1 - \pi_2) h_2 - c_2]$ which gives

$$t_1 \leq \frac{\phi_1}{\left(\frac{1}{\alpha_2} - 1\right)\left(\pi_2 - \frac{c_2 + h_2}{g_2^s + h_2}\right) + \phi_1 - \phi_2}.$$

The expansionist type of player 2 is always happy with this equilibrium. He gets to defect in the first round and the other side will still cooperate in the second round, if it is security seeking.

For the payoffs in the example used, this equilibrium is impossible. Hence, it is not illustrated in Figure 7.1.

The Time Will Tell Equilibrium

Here the game goes off the equilibrium path if anyone defects. This is not important if only one party defects, because unilateral defection must be punished by defection to keep the expansionist types cooperating in the first round. If both parties defect; however, there are two versions: in version 1, discussed in the text, security seeking types defect; in version 2, both types cooperate. Even this does not matter, however, because since DD is doubly off the equilibrium path (both players have to defect to get there) it need not be considered in calculating the incentives to deviate for each player. Thus, each version could take place anywhere in the range of the other version.

The conditions for the expansionist players are the following. The equilibrium strategy of cooperation nets an expansionist player i $\alpha_i(0) + (1 - \alpha_i)\{t_j[(\pi_i+\phi_i)g_i^e-(1-\pi_i-\phi_i)l_i-c_i]+(1-t_j)[\pi_i g_i^e-(1-\pi_i)l_i-c_i]\}$ because it produces mutual cooperation in the first round and an opportunity to exploit a security seeking opponent in the second. Switching to defecting would yield $\alpha_i[(\pi_i+\phi_i)g_i^e-(1-\pi_i-\phi_i)l_i-c_i]+(1-\alpha_i)[\pi_i g_i^e-(1-\pi_i)l_i-c_i]$ because it would take advantage of the other side's cooperation in the first round, at the price of producing mutual defection for sure in the second. Cooperation will beat defection if t_j exceeds a minimum trust threshold for the expansionist types

$$t_j \geq \frac{\pi_i + \phi_i - \frac{c_i+l_i}{g_i^e+l_i}}{\left(\frac{1}{\alpha_i}-1\right)\phi_i}.$$

The other side must be relatively likely to be security seeking, or the opportunity to exploit them in the second round will not be alluring enough to outweigh the temptation to defect in the first round.

The time will tell equilibrium also imposes a constraint on the size of the first round derived by solving the previous condition for α_i and is

$$\alpha_i \leq \frac{t_j\phi_i}{t_j\phi_i + \pi_i + \phi_i - \frac{c_i+l_i}{g_i^e+l_i}}.$$

The Time Will Tell/Reassurance Equilibria

The fifth and sixth types of equilibria are mixtures of the reassurance and time will tell equilibria, in which only one expansionist type defects. I will consider the fifth, the sixth is the mirror image.

In the first round the security seeking type player 1 cooperates and the expansionist type does not, while both types of player 2 cooperate. In the second round, the expansionist type of player 2 must be rewarded for cooperating at CC and punished with defection at CD. If player 1 defects, it is revealed as expansionist, so mutual defection will ensue at DC and DD. The game goes off the equilibrium path if player 2 defects, but this does not matter because mutual defection between security seeking types, the required response in this equilibrium, is possible regardless of beliefs.

When is this equilibrium possible? For the security seeking type of player 1, the first round poses no dilemma because player 2 is expected to cooperate regardless of type. On the equilibrium path, she must cooperate if player 2 cooperated, but without getting any new information, so the security seeking player 1 will be willing to fulfill this equilibrium if the level of trust exceeds the old minimum trust threshold from the Security Dilemma Game:

$$t_2 \geq \frac{\phi_2}{\frac{c_1 + h_1}{g_1^e + h_1} - \pi_1 - \phi_1 + \phi_2}.$$

For the expansionist type of player 1, it is defecting, when shifting to cooperate would raise the possibility of cooperation in the second round. The condition is slightly different from the pure reassurance equilibrium, however, because the other side is expected to cooperate for sure in the first round. The equilibrium strategy of defecting yields $\alpha_1[(\pi_1 + \phi_1)g_1^e - (1 - \pi_1 - \phi_1)h_1 - c_1] + (1 - \alpha_1)[\pi_1 g_1^e - (1 - \pi_1)h_1 - c_1]$. Deviating to cooperation would yield $\alpha_1(0) + (1 - \alpha_1)(t_2[(\pi_1 + \phi_1)g_1^e - (1 - \pi_1 - \phi_1)h_1 - c_1] + (1 - t_2)[\pi_1 g_1^e - (1 - \pi_1)h_1 - c_1])$ so we have

$$t_2 \leq \frac{\pi_1 + \phi_1 - \frac{c_1 + h_1}{g_1^e + h_1}}{(\frac{1}{\alpha_1} - 1)\phi_1}.$$

For the security seeking type of player 2, the situation is as in the reassurance equilibrium; it must cooperate knowing only the security seeking type on the other side will also cooperate,

$$t_1 \geq \frac{\phi_1}{\frac{1}{\alpha_2}\left(\frac{c_2 + h_2}{g_2^e + h_2} - \pi_2\right) + \phi_1 - \phi_2}.$$

For the expansionist type of player 2, it must cooperate even though cooperation from the other side is not assured, so the condition is the reverse of the reassurance equilibrium. Its payoff for cooperation is $\alpha_2(t_1(0) + (1 - t_1)[(\pi_2 - \phi_1)g_2^e - (1 - \pi_2 + \phi_1)h_2 - c_2]) + (1 - \alpha_2)(t_1[(\pi_2 + \phi_2)g_2^e - (1 - \pi_2 - \phi_2)h_2 - c_2] + (1 - t_1)[\pi_2 g_2^e - (1 - \pi_2)h_2 - c_2])$. The payoff for defecting is $\alpha_2(t_1[(\pi_2 + \phi_2)g_2^e - (1 - \pi_2 - \phi_2)h_2 - c_2] + (1 - t_1)[\pi_2 g_2^e - (1 - \pi_2)h_2 - c_2]) + (1 - \alpha_2)[\pi_2 g_2^e - (1 - \pi_2)h_2 - c_2]$ which yields

$$t_1 \geq \frac{\phi_1}{\frac{c_2 + h_2}{g_2^e + h_2} - \pi_2 - \phi_2 + \phi_1 + \left(\frac{1}{\alpha_2} - 1\right)\phi_2}.$$

For the payoffs underlying the example in Figure 7.1, this equilibrium is impossible. The problem, once again, is that if the security seeking type of player 1 were willing to cooperate, the expansionist type would be as well.

The One Side Cooperates Equilibria

In the seventh and eighth equilibria one side cooperates while the other defects. I will focus on the first equilibrium, where player 1 cooperates and player 2 defects.

Since the expansionist player 1 cooperates in the first round, in the second round the security seeking types must cooperate at CD and defect at DD to establish the proper incentives. At CC, defection must also result or the security seeking player 2 would prefer to switch to cooperation in the first round since player 1 is cooperating for sure. If both players deviate in the first round, at DC, there are two versions: in the first mutual cooperation ensues; in the second, mutual defection. In either case the equilibrium conditions are the same because it would take two simultaneous deviations to reach that point.

Here the game goes off the equilibrium path if 1 defects or if 2 cooperates, i.e.. at three of the four possible second round circumstances. At CC and DD, security seeking types defect, which is possible for any beliefs. At DC, in one version the security seeking types cooperate and at the other they defect; off equilibrium path beliefs will determine which takes place. Given that player 1 defected unexpectedly, this might be a sign of untrustworthiness, favoring the second version. In either case, it has no impact on when the equilibrium is possible, because the node is not reached without two simultaneous deviations.

In the version where player 1 cooperates and player 2 defects, for the security seeking type of player 1, the payoff for cooperating is $\alpha_1[(\pi_1 - \phi_2)g_1^s - (1 - \pi_1 + \phi_2)l_1 - c_1] + (1 - \alpha_1)(t_2(0) + (1 - t_2)[(\pi_1 - \phi_2)g_1^s - (1 - \pi_1 + \phi_2)l_1 - c_1])$ which must beat the payoff for defection, $\pi_1 g_1^s - (1 - \pi_1)l_1 - c_1$ which gives

$$t_2 \geq \frac{\phi_2}{(1 - \alpha_1)\left(\frac{c_1 + l_1}{g_1^s + l_1} - \pi_1 + \phi_2\right)}.$$

For the expansionist type of player 1, the payoff for cooperation is $\alpha_1[(\pi_1 - \phi_2)g_1^e - (1 - \pi_1 + \phi_2)l_1 - c_1] + (1 - \alpha_1)(t_2[(\pi_1 + \phi_1)g_1^e - (1 - \pi_1 - \phi_1)l_1 - c_1] + (1 - t_2)[\pi_1 g_1^e - (1 - \pi_1)l_1 - c_1])$ which must beat the payoff for defection which is $\pi_1 g_1^e - (1 - \pi_1)l_1 - c_1$ which gives

$$t_2 \geq \frac{\alpha_1}{1 - \alpha_1}\frac{\phi_2}{\phi_1}.$$

For the security seeking type of player 2, the payoff for defection is $\alpha_2[(\pi_2 + \phi_2)g_2^s - (1 - \pi_2 - \phi_2)l_2 - c_2] + (1 - \alpha_2)(t_1(0) + (1 - t_1)[(\pi_2 - \phi_1)g_2^s - (1 - \pi_2 + \phi_1)l_2 - c_2])$ which must beat the incentive to switch to cooperation $\alpha_2(0) + (1 - \alpha_2)[\pi_2 g_2^s - (1 - \pi_2)l_2 - c_2]$ so

$$t_1 \geq \frac{\left(\frac{\alpha_2}{1 - \alpha_2}\right)\left(\frac{c_2 + l_2}{g_2^s + l_2} - \pi_2 - \phi_2\right) + \phi_1}{\frac{c_2 + l_2}{g_2^s + l_2} - \pi_2 + \phi_1}.$$

For the expansionist type of player 2, the incentive to defect $\alpha_2[(\pi_2 + \phi_2)g_2^e - (1 - \pi_2 - \phi_2)l_2 - c_2] + (1 - \alpha_2)(t_1[(\pi_2 + \phi_2)g_2^e - (1 - \pi_2 - \phi_2)l_2 - c_2] + (1 - t_1)[\pi_2 g_2^e - (1 - \pi_2)l_2 - c_2])$ must beat the payoff for cooperation $\alpha_2(0) + (1 - \alpha_2)[\pi_2 g_2^e - (1 - \pi_2)l_2 - c_2]$ which it always does.

For the payoffs in the example in Figure 7.1, this equilibrium is possible in part of the zone in which the time will tell equilibrium is possible, but it is very suboptimal and counterintuitive. Essentially, the equilibrium is being maintained by threatening the security seeking type of player 2 with mutual defection if it cooperates in the first round. This threat makes no sense for the security seeking type on the opposing side, so it is difficult to see why it would be made. In its absence, the equilibrium shifts to the time will tell equilibrium, in which both types of player 2 cooperate. Because of the peculiarity of this suboptimal threat I do not illustrate this equilibrium in the figure.

The Noncooperative Equilibrium

Finally, the ninth pattern is the noncooperative equilibrium in which everyone defects in the first round. All sixteen second-round patterns are possible.

In eight of them, after mutual defection, DD, the players cooperate. These eight are therefore restricted to the upper-right quadrant, where $t_j > m_i$ so that the security seeking types are willing to cooperate without any new information. All eight are possible in this zone, provided that cooperation off the equilibrium path does not diminish trust too much. If cooperation off the equilibrium path has no effect on trust or increases it, they will be possible throughout this zone. These equilibria are all Pareto inferior to the time will tell equilibrium.

In the other eight, the players defect at DD on the equilibrium path. The one in which defection occurs in the second round no matter what happened in the first is possible for any off equilibrium path beliefs, and any level of trust. Other ones in which the security seeking types sometimes cooperate off the equilibrium path must be sustained by off equilibrium path beliefs that raise trust after observing a defection, and may not work for some levels of trust.

CHAPTER 8

The End of the Cold War: 1985–91

> Stalin was saying he was for peace, against war. But nobody
> believed him. Khrushchev almost got people to believe him.
> Brezhnev was droning on about peaceful coexistence for twenty
> years.... And nobody believed him. But they believe Gorbachev.
> Because he's begun to make our deeds match our words.
>
> —Anatoly Chernyaev

IN 1984 THE COLD WAR was alive and kicking. In the late 1970s the Russians
had deployed a new generation of intermediate range missiles (the SS-20s)
targeting Western Europe. NATO responded in 1979 with a decision to
deploy similar weapons, while leaving the door open to negotiation. After
a fierce political struggle and inconclusive arms negotiations, the NATO
forces began to be deployed in 1983. The Russians broke off arms control
negotiations and, for the first time since the early 1970s, there were no
ongoing talks. The Soviets were embroiled in a war in Afghanistan, and the
United States was supporting the Afghan resistance. At the same time, the
United States supported a rebel force in Sandinista-controlled Nicaragua
and supported the government forces in El Salvador and Guatemala against
Marxist rebels.

In 1990, the Cold War was over. The Eastern bloc regimes had abandoned communism and the Warsaw Pact, Germany was reunified on
voluntary and, hence, Western, terms. Arms control was bursting out
all over, with intermediate range missiles banned, conventional forces
limited, and a deal on strategic forces within sight. The failure of the
August 1991 coup against Gorbachev and the subsequent dissolution of
the Soviet Union merely confirmed that the Cold War would stay dead.
This development was surely the most revolutionary change in international relations since the end of World War II. Explaining it is an essential
task for international relations theory.

In this chapter, I will trace the evolution of U.S.-Soviet relations in the
late 1980s with special attention to Soviet gestures designed to reassure
the United States and their impact on U.S. perceptions of Soviet motivations. I will argue that the decisive events that ended the Cold War
can be interpreted as costly signals in the framework of the Reassurance
Game. As Anatoly Chernyaev, one of Gorbachev's closest aids said soon

after Gorbachev took office, Russia had begun to match words with deeds (Chernyaev 2000: 44). Several events stand out in the period 1985–90 as particularly clear examples of signals by the Soviets that their motivations had changed. These include the 1987 Intermediate-range Nuclear Forces (INF) Treaty, the 1988 withdrawal from Afghanistan and announcement of conventional force reductions, and the 1989 revolutions in Eastern Europe. Another critical indication that Soviet motivations had changed was the process of democratization beginning with the 19th Party Conference in 1988, and continuing on with elections to the Congress of People's Deputies in 1989 and the progressive transfer of power from the communist party to the state institutions. All of these events provided conclusive evidence that Soviet motivations had changed for the better and they played a central role in ending the Cold War. Before considering them in detail, however, I will consider the broader debate on the end of the Cold War.

Explaining the End of the Cold War

The end of the Cold War has not been ignored by international relations experts (Suri 2002). There are chronological overviews (Oberdorfer 1991; Garthoff 1994; Beschloss and Talbott 1993), oral histories (Wohlforth 1996a, 2003), studies of Gorbachev (Kaiser 1992; Brown 1997), studies of particular issues such as Afghanistan (Mendelson 1998), the Helsinki Accords and human rights movements (Thomas 2001), German unification (Zelikow and Rice 1995; Stent 1999), the fall of Eastern Europe (Gati 1990; Levesque 1997) as well as collections of essays (Alan and Goldman 1992; Hogan 1992; Lebow and Risse-Kappen 1995; Summy and Salla 1995), a raft of memoirs (Reagan 1990; Shultz 1993; Baker and Defrank 1995; Matlock 1995; Chernyaev 2000) and analyses of the end of the Soviet Union itself (Suny 1994; Beissinger 2002).

The debate over the end of the Cold War has taken on a somewhat different contour than the debate over its origins. Some prominent post-revisionists have shifted in a traditional direction.[1] The question of U.S. motivations has faded into the background. Revisionists and Orwellians, having explained the Cold War as a product of U.S. expansionism, had a hard time explaining its end given that the United States remained unchanged. Hence, the modal response of revisionists and Orwellians to the end of the Cold War was to point to continuing U.S. wrong

---

[1] Leffler (1999) notes, and criticizes, this evolution in Gaddis 1997. Compare also Jervis 1993: 659 with Jervis 2001: 58. See Jones and Woods 1993 for a review of postrevisionism in the wake of the Cold War's end.

doing in the third world and to deny that anything important had happened.[2]

The new debate is often represented as being between explanations emphasizing material constraints and those emphasizing the role of ideas or identity. The material factors' side is compatible with offensive realism. The ideas' side contains a diverse range of arguments compatible with defensive realism, liberalism, and constructivist theory. I briefly describe each perspective below.

Material Constraints

The material constraints account, advanced by Stephen Brooks and William Wohlforth (2000/01), is perhaps the simplest explanation of the end of the Cold War.[3] It focuses on two key realist variables identified in chapter 2, power, π_i, and the costs of conflict, c_i, and how they are affected by Soviet economic decline and nuclear weapons.

The Cold War is portrayed as a power transition that never quite happened. The reigning hegemon, the United States, kept growing throughout the Cold War. For a while the rising challenger, the Soviet Union, seemed to be catching up economically, and did catch up in quantitative military terms. In the 1970s, however, Soviet economic growth began to slow down. The West, meanwhile, despite oil shocks and recessions, remained on an upward trajectory. The capitalist world, knit ever closer by trade, was taking ever greater advantages of the possibilities of specialization and division of labor (Brooks and Wohlforth 2000/01). The free flow of information and the development of information technology further increased productivity. For the Russians, the burdens of empire in Eastern Europe, Afghanistan, and in terms of military spending, grew ever greater, while the economy continued to underperform. Ultimately the decline in π_i meant that retrenchment was necessary. Hence, the Soviets struck arms control deals, pulled out of Afghanistan, and ultimately cut the Eastern European regimes loose.

Of course, retrenchment is not the only possible response to decline; preventive war is also an option (Copeland 2000: 39). Why did the Russians chose to accommodate rather than fight? Here the costs of war, c_i, are key. In 1989 the Russians had a stockpile of over ten thousand nuclear warheads. Several scholars have argued that the presence of nuclear weapons created a more benign security environment for the Soviets, eliminating the need to respond violently to decline (Deudney and Ikenberry 1991/92;

---

[2] See Cox 1993; LaFeber 1992; Cumings 1992; Chomsky 1991: 28–29; Kaldor 1990: 252.

[3] See also Wohlforth 1993, 1994/95, 1998; Schweller and Wohlforth 2000; Brooks and Wohlforth 2002, 2003.

Oye 1995). Nuclear weapons make war much more costly, which reduces the incentives to launch a preventive war in two ways. First, it has a direct effect, making the preventive war more costly and, hence, less appealing. Second, it reduces the likelihood that the other side, the United States in this case, will take advantage of one's decline by launching a war of aggression in the future. This indirect effect further reduces the appeal of a preventive war. Russian economic strength and conventional military forces could be allowed to run down dramatically; the threat of nuclear annihilation would keep potential invaders at bay.[4]

The material constraints' argument is compatible with the offensive realist position that state behavior is determined primarily by material factors, expansionist and security seeking states behave the same, and hence that trust was not important at the end of the Cold War.[5] The underlying model is a complete information bargaining game where the distribution of power is shifting over time, as analyzed by Robert Powell (1999: 115–32). The allocation of the pie is determined by relative power and cost tolerance. When power shifts, the side growing weaker makes concessions so the side growing stronger gets more. Accordingly, Brooks and Wohlforth minimize the role of trust at the end of the Cold War. While acknowledging that "personal relationships of trust" developed very late in the process, they claim that it is "difficult to disentangle the importance of interpersonal synergy from the dictates of dire necessity, in the case of Gorbachev, and the delights of getting exactly what one wants, in the case of Bush and Kohl" (Brooks and Wohlforth 2003: 307–08).

Transnational Networks and the Security Dilemma

The alternatives to the material constraints argument emphasize the distinction between "old thinkers" and "new thinkers" in the Soviet political context. Old thinkers represent the Stalinist past, and are held accountable for the Cold War.[6] New thinkers broke with the old orthodoxies to make key innovations that brought the Cold War to an end. The specific nature of the new thinking that was important for ending the Cold War varies across analysts.

Some analysts argue that the new thinkers learned new concepts from the Western scientific community and dovish politicians that changed

---

[4]Wohlforth argues that the fact that the Russians were a declining challenger rather than a declining hegemon accounts for the peaceful outcome, but the high costs of war due to nuclear weapons seems to me a simpler and more compelling explanation (Wohlforth 1994/95: 98–99).

[5]It is also compatible with a classical realist argument that all states want to expand as much as possible so that state interests rise and fall with state power (Zakaria 1998: 38).

[6]On old thinkers, see Wohlforth 1993: 32–58 and English 2000: 17–48.

their way of thinking about international relations. Effectively, the new thinkers discovered that the Cold War was a tragic spiral, realized that the appropriate policy was to reassure the West, implemented this policy, and thereby ended the Cold War. This viewpoint is, therefore, compatible with defensive realism, though it does highlight the role of nonstate actors in facilitating state learning.

Thomas Risse argues that a set of concepts based on the security dilemma, "common security," "defensive defense," and "reasonable sufficiency," originated in Western liberal circles and were communicated to Soviet academic elites through transnational links (Risse-Kappen 1994; see also Risse-Kappen 1995a and 1995b for other examples of transnational influence). Risse identifies a "liberal internationalist community" composed of U.S. arms controllers, Western European peace researchers, social democratic politicians, and Russian physicists and think tankers. The Western European component of this community originated ideas like common security, the claim that security must be mutual in the nuclear age, and nonoffensive defense, the argument that, if defensive forces were incapable of offensive action, it would eliminate the security dilemma (Jervis 1978). These concepts were disseminated through transnational networks. For instance, in 1982 the Palme Commission brought together Eastern and Western dignitaries who issued a report endorsing common security. The Soviet representative, Georgy Arbatov, was in close contact with Gorbachev, who endorsed the ideas at the twenty-seventh Party Congress in 1986. The concept of nonoffensive defense later reappeared when the Soviets began reducing their conventional forces, under the slogans of defensive defense and reasonable sufficiency.

Matthew Evangelista makes a parallel argument that the Soviet decision to implement a testing moratorium in 1985, and to avoid any attempt to match the U.S. strategic defense program, were strongly influenced by the international scientific and arms control community (Evangelista 1995, 1999). Evangelista traces the influence of two groups, the Pugwash Conferences of scientists interested in world affairs, and the International Physicians for the Prevention of Nuclear War (IPPNW) on Soviet policy from Khrushchev to Gorbachev and argues that transnational networks had substantial impact. Transnational groups pressed for and supported Gorbachev's nuclear testing moratorium and implemented the first on-site inspection system in the Soviet Union to verify the halt. They also helped persuade the Russians to not respond in kind to the Strategic Defense Initiative (SDI), or even to make arms reductions conditional on U.S. abandonment of the program, but to press forward for nuclear reductions anyway. Thus, in both its overall conceptual underpinnings, and in terms of specific moves, Gorbachev's policy was influenced by the liberal Western community of activists and intellectuals.

While these scholars are keen to establish the existence and importance of transnational influence, they are sometimes a bit vague on why the new thinkers were persuaded by the transnational advice they were receiving. One answer is that "life itself," as Gorbachev liked to say, was driving these lessons home. Andrew Bennett argues that Soviet failure in Afghanistan, and U.S. support for the mujaheddin, helped convince Soviet leaders of the futility of intervention and the mutuality of security (Bennett 1999: 249). The same thing can be said for the Soviet SS-20 missile deployments and the failure of their subsequent campaign to convince the West not to respond in kind (Risse-Kappen 1991: 173). Alan Collins makes explicit an answer that is implicit in the work of others, when he argues that the new ideas were correct and the old ones wrong. Collins argues that the Cold War was the product of the security dilemma, but previous Soviet leaders failed to realize this. This failure, as Jervis points out, leads to inappropriate policies because decisionmakers fail to realize the provocative nature of their military buildups and regional involvements. As Collins puts it, "The first step towards mitigating the security dilemma is the realization by at least one state that it is a victim of a security dilemma. . . . Gorbachev was aware of the security dilemma and . . . this awareness played a role in changing Soviet policies" (Collins 1997: 157).

Liberalization

As discussed in chapter 1, liberal international relations theory argues that domestic interests and state structures determine national preferences that the state then attempts to secure in the international arena (Moravcsik 1997; Legro and Moravcsik 1999). The democratic peace thesis holds that democratic states are unlikely to fight each other, in part because their domestic institutional structure empowers ordinary citizens who have little to gain from conflict and suffer high costs (low g_i, high c_i) (Russett 1993; Bueno De Mesquita et al. 1999). Democratic openness also permits outside observers to gather information about state preferences that would otherwise be difficult to come by, which will lessen the likelihood of unjustified mistrust (low ε_i). Democracies are therefore security seeking states who know this about each other, and, hence, can cooperate.

The Soviet Union underwent a remarkable process of liberalization between the nineteenth Party Conference in 1988 and the ultimate breakup in 1991. It is clear that this process was intimately related to the end of the Cold War and the end of the Soviet Union itself.[7] The role of liberalization at the end of the Cold War is not quite as envisioned in standard

---

[7] In particular it opened the way to a "tidal wave" of nationalist mobilization that ultimately doomed the Union (Beissinger 2002).

accounts of the democratic peace, however. Despite drastic institutional reform, multiparty elections to the Congress of People's Deputies and the transfer of power from the communist party to the state institutions, the Soviet Union was ruled to the end by leaders who had not been directly elected and were not subject to the institutional constraints envisioned by the theory. The mechanisms that keep the peace between consolidated democracies were therefore not in place. Rather, the move towards democratization served as a powerful signal that Soviet preferences had changed, and would continue to evolve in a benign direction. Democratization may not have been primarily motivated by its signaling value in the West. However, it had a dramatically positive effect on Western perceptions, as attested by leaders such as Margaret Thatcher and U.S. ambassador Jack Matlock. It was the move towards democratization that provided the most decisive evidence that the Soviet Union was not merely retrenching in the face of material constraints (low π_i, high c_i) but had experienced a change in preferences that would lead to a reduction in its expansionist impulse, (lower g_i).

Identity Change

Another important factor influencing state preferences is national identity, conceived of as "a distinct sense of mission or purpose" or membership in a "political or economic grouping of states" (English 2000: 6; Wendt 1994, 1999). Some constructivists argue that Russia experienced a change in national identity during the Cold War, ultimately deciding that it wanted to be part of the West, not in opposition to it. This argument comes in two versions—one couched at the elite level and another at the mass level. Robert English and Robert G. Herman focus on identity change at the elite level (English 2000; Herman 1996). They argue that the end of the Cold War was one more episode in an age-old Russian struggle between westernizers and slavophiles over the identity of Russia. Westernizers since Peter the Great have attempted to bring Russia into the modern age, adopting European dress, language, manners, customs, ideas, and policies. Slavophiles have resisted change and championed the sacredness of traditional Russia (English 2000: 19–25; Herman 1996: 313; Levesque 1997: 37–39; Neumann 1996). The communists, initially westernizers, eventually filled the slavophile role by isolating Russia from the rest of Europe and adopting a hostile stance to it. The generation of Soviet intellectuals that came of age in the 1950s rejected this identity, and became the most enthusiastic and successful westernizers ever. This new thinking, "did not just posit an end to conflict with the West or the desirability of cooperation with the liberal international community. It argued that the USSR was, or should be, a *member* of that community" (English 2002: 5, emphasis in the original).

Complementary to this elite driven story, other authors point to Western cultural influences on Soviet identity at the mass level. Some argue that the Cold War is not so much a battle of ideas as a cultural revolution in which the yellow submarine of Western popular culture torpedoes the grey battleship of socialist realism. In this view, while NATO was necessary to hold the Red Army at bay, the Cold War was really won by the hamburger eating, blue jeans wearing, rock'n'roll shock troops of Western cultural decadence.[8] In an alternate version, Daniel Thomas argues that the provisions on human rights in the 1975 Helsinki Accords, signed for instrumental reasons by the Soviets, led to the creation of movements for human rights which resulted in genuine normative change (Thomas 2001).[9]

Evaluating the Perspectives

In the narrative that follows, I will show that a signaling process took place at the end of the Cold War that reassured the West about Soviet motivations. The West went from being persuaded that the Soviets were expansionists to being convinced that they were security seekers. Furthermore, there is evidence that this shift in beliefs substantially mirrored reality, that is, that the Soviets did undergo a shift in preferences at the end of the Cold War. This process supports the model of reassurance developed in the last chapter in several ways. As implication 7.1 indicates, cheap talk had little reassuring affect; costly signals were required to shift western opinion. Gorbachev's early arms control initiatives were ineffective; only with more substantial concessions starting with the INF Treaty did beliefs begin to change in a major way. Implication 7.2 says that less trusting states make smaller signals, and this is evident in that the United States, the less trusting party, made smaller gestures throughout the period than the more trusting Soviets did. Implication 7.3 argues that weaker states make bigger reassuring gestures, and this is also borne out; the Soviets were weaker than the United States.[10] Thus, the narrative will establish that the Soviets underwent a change in preferences, and that this was revealed to the West via costly signals.

How does this affect our evaluation of the various perspectives on the end of the Cold War? In the end, each perspective receives some support, and a full explanation of the end of the Cold War must include elements

[8] See Timothy Ryback's (1990: 4, 5) wonderful history of rock music in the East bloc, and for other analyses of culture in the Cold War see Shaw 2001; Hixon 1997; Poiger 1996.

[9] See Hopf 2002 for a comparison of Cold War Soviet identity with post–Cold War Russian identity as reflected in literature.

[10] Technically these hypotheses cannot be independently verified in this case since the Soviet side was both weaker and more trusting, so they make the same prediction.

of each. This reflects the fact that these explanations are complementary, rather than logically exclusive like the explanations for the onset of the Cold War discussed in chapter 4.

Brooks and Wohlforth are correct that Soviet economic decline weakened their bargaining leverage and led them to make concessions, but they go too far when they claim that reassurance was not an important part of the end of the Cold War. The evidence for belief change is abundant, and makes it more likely that the parties were in the separating reassurance equilibrium than in the pooling noncooperative equilibrium. In fact, the two forces highlighted by the material constraints perspective, economic decline and nuclear weapons, helped convert the Soviets into security seekers. As I discussed in chapter 2, the lower the relative power, π_i, the higher the costs for conflict, c_i, and the lower the intrinsic desire for expansion, g_i, the more likely a state is to be a security seeker. The growing number of nuclear weapons dramatically raised the costs of all-out conflict, while economic decline raised the cost of lesser conflicts and lowered Soviet relative power. This helps account for why the old thinkers failed to resist, and even subsequently endorsed, many of Gorbachev's concessions on the grounds that economic constraints mandated retrenchment (Brooks and Wohlforth 2000/01, 2002, 2003). Even old thinkers who retained a high intrinsic desire for expansion were becoming more trustworthy as they became more aware of their economic predicament.

However, the record shows that the level of rapprochement was deeper than could have been achieved with old thinkers, and that the Soviet intrinsic desire for expansion, g_i, declined as well. In part this is due to the same key variable, that is, economic decline also affected g_i. After all, the principal rationale for expansion in the Soviet Union was found in communist ideology, which was based in turn on a set of claims about the superiority of communism that were undermined by the collapse of the communist economic model. Communism was a "God that failed" (Crossman 2001 [1950]) and once it failed, it could no longer inspire expansionist zeal, or more cynically, justify expansionist policies designed to keep the regime in power (Brzezinsky 1989; Fukuyama 1992).

Yet the failure of communism cannot by itself account for the direction that the Soviet Union took at the end of the Cold War. Communism could have been replaced by some other anti-Western ideology. Gorbachev could have pursued the Chinese course and violently suppressed domestic movements for reform and autonomy while adopting an authoritarian capitalist system. Even worse, he could have exacerbated nationalist strife and led the Soviet Union down the path towards civil war as happened in Yugoslavia. Instead, Gorbachev and his followers attempted to democratize the Soviet Union, all the while maintaining a fundamental commitment against using violence, even to preserve the Union (Zubok 2003;

English 2003).[11] The explanation for this aspect of the end of the Cold War seems to lie in the preference and identity changes embodied in the new thinking, and in the transnational networks in which the new thinkers participated. The existence of a thriving community of states in which democracy and prosperity went hand in hand had a powerful appeal to the new thinkers. Had the Western European states been authoritarian throughout the Cold War, it is unlikely that the Soviets would have opted for democracy in the late 1980s. Thus, the fact that the old rationale for expansion was not replaced by another is, in part, due to the identity changes in the Soviet Union studied by constructivist scholars.

New Thinking before 1985

Studies of the origins of new thinking have traced the development of a counter-elite of intellectuals in the Soviet Union with views radically diverging from the prevailing orthodoxy (English 2000; Checkel 1997). One of the key personal experiences that united many new thinkers was exposure to the West. Gorbachev himself had a Czechoslovakian friend in college, travelled to Eastern Europe, and visited Holland, Belgium, France, Italy, and Germany in the 1970s. As Brown argues, "It was during such trips ... that the discrepancy between Soviet propaganda concerning capitalist countries and the reality first came home to him" (Brown 1996: 43,115; Evangelista 1999: 260–61). Anatoly Chernyaev, a Gorbachev foreign policy advisor, got first hand experience in the West as a soldier in the second World War, along with thousands of other Soviet citizens (English in Chernyaev 2000: xix). Younger generations were able to travel to the West in the thaw period, and as Robert English argues, "It is difficult to overstate the devastating impact that firsthand exposure to the West had on old beliefs and stereotypes" (English 2000: 75). As Georgy Arbatov put it, "Dogmas about capitalist stagnation, total impoverishment of the Western working class and others were rejected while new concepts came into political circulation [such as] European integration ... multiple paths of third-world development ... and so on. There emerged new research methods and an objective look at [the West]" (quoted in English 2000: 76). A diplomat with Western experience said, "Sooner or later, those who worked in the West for any length of time all came to the conclusion that our system was just no good" (English 2000: 105).

---

[11] The Soviet Union did use limited force in Lithuania and Georgia in an effort to suppress nationalist mobilization, but not on a large enough scale nor with the conviction required to succeed.

As a result, new thinkers began to criticize the Soviet system, and their critiques were "uniformly pro-market" (English 2000: 97). Driven by the failure of the West to succumb to the predicted contradictions, and the failure of socialism to catch up, Soviet economists as early as the 1960s began to consider reforms of the central planning mechanism.[12] Soviet autarchy came in for criticism, and the benefits of international trade and specialization in comparative advantage were emphasized. New thinkers also identified with the Prague spring, and "socialism with a human face," and were deeply disturbed by the Soviet role in crushing that experiment (English 2000: 111). By the end of the 1960s, then, new thinkers were questioning both the Soviet economic system and the legitimacy of Soviet foreign policy in Eastern Europe.

The Soviet leadership, however, failed to see things in quite the same way. For who could deny that the 1960s was an era in which the Soviets began to catch up to the West, in military terms, and that in the 1970s Soviet missiles even began to outnumber their American counterparts? At the same time, revolutionary successes in Cuba and Vietnam seemed to confirm that socialism had broad appeal in the Third World, that the "correlation of forces" was shifting in socialism's favor, and that bandwagoning was prevalent (Bennett 1999: 127–36). So it is perhaps not surprising that Soviet political/military elites, with tremendous vested interests in the status quo, little exposure to the West, and little concern for the welfare of average Soviet citizens, should require more evidence of the failings of their system before they would be willing to countenance change. As a result, the Brezhnev era became known as the era of stagnation.

Further evidence began to pour in in the first half of the 1980s. The invasion of Afghanistan became a Soviet Vietnam War, protracted, difficult to fight, generating opposition abroad and dissent at home. Soviet economic performance continued to skid, while the West, after dealing with the 1979 oil shock and a subsequent bout of economic turbulence, took off. NATO governments decided to build intermediate range nuclear missiles in Europe to match the new Soviet SS-20s, and an intense and popular nuclear freeze campaign failed to stop their deployment. The United States was led by an aggressively anticommunist president whose cognitive limitations and verbal gaffes seemed to do little to diminish the popularity of his message. President Reagan also initiated a program of research in antiballistic missile technology, the Strategic Defense Initiative (SDI), which promised to be intensive in precisely the kinds of technology in which the Soviets lagged, especially computing and information technology. All this new information came into the Soviet Union at a time in which the leadership of the country for some time to come was up for grabs. After Leonid

---

[12] For the Liberman debate and Kosygin reforms of the 1960s, see Mau 1996: 17–24.

Brezhnev's death in 1982, Yuri Andropov began a mild reform campaign focusing on greater discipline. His sudden demise was followed by an even shorter period of reaction under the terminal Konstantin Chernenko. His death in 1985 opened the door for Andropov's chosen successor, Mikhail Gorbachev.

THE ADVENT OF GORBACHEV

In March 1985, Gorbachev assumed power having told his wife, he later claimed, that "we could not go on living like that" (Oberdorfer 1991: 111).[13] Even before attaining the highest office, he had introduced the terms with which he will be forever associated, *glasnost* (openness) and *perestroika* (restructuring) (Brown 1996: 121–29). In the early months of his tenure, however, emphasis was given to *uskorenie* (acceleration), a quickening of economic growth without fundamental change in the system (Chernyaev 2000: 54). A campaign was undertaken to strengthen discipline and cut back on drunkenness by reducing the sale of alcohol. In the international sphere, Gorbachev made two arms control gestures: a moratorium on nuclear testing and one on SS-20 intermediate range ballistic missile (IRBM) deployments. These moves were largely ineffective in changing opinions in the West.[14] In light of the Reassurance Game of the previous chapter, the moratorium on SS-20 deployment can be said to fall short of the crucial threshold, α_i, making it cheap talk. The Soviets were believed to have deployed most of their IRBM's, while NATO had just begun, so an IRBM freeze would have locked in a huge Soviet numerical advantage and was viewed as an attempt to manipulate the political process of deployment in the West. Thus, the signal failed, largely because it was regarded as a move which did not really hurt the Soviets (Garthoff 1994: 213–14).

The test moratorium is a more interesting case. The U.S. administration argued that this signal too was "without real costs to Soviet programs" because the Soviets had accelerated testing before the moratorium and could do so afterwards (Evangelista 1999: 265). U.S. officials also raised doubts about the verifiability of the halt. However, some evidence exists of genuine opposition to the halt in testing in the Soviet military. As Gorbachev continued to extend the moratorium, military leaders began

---

[13] Similarly, Eduard Shevardnadze had told Gorbachev in 1984 that "everything is rotten" and had to be changed (Brown 1996: 81).

[14] Bitzinger (1994: 75) argues that this was a failure for GRIT because the United States did not reciprocate. Collins (1998: 205) and Goldstein and Freeman (1990: 116) counter that though there was no direct response, these gestures did "change the climate" in a more subtle way and set the stage for later, more important gestures.

to criticize it (Evangelista 1999: 265–67). The Soviets also took care of the verification issue in a highly unorthodox way, by allowing a private U.S. group to establish seismic monitoring stations on Soviet territory near the testing range. This may have had a greater impact on beliefs than the moratorium itself, given that it was a radical innovation, whereas testing pauses had been tried before. It would also appear that the moratorium did effect more liberal public opinion in the West, e.g., in Germany and among Democrats in the U.S. Congress. Efforts to cut off funding for U.S. testing, however, ultimately failed. The test moratorium is perhaps best seen as a signal that is not quite cheap, but not quite costly enough; an inexpensive signal that persuaded some but not the crucial decisionmakers.

The first U.S.-Soviet summit of the Reagan administration was held in 1985 in Geneva. President Reagan's attitudes towards the Soviet Union had already evolved somewhat since his first inauguration. By late 1983 he had come to the conclusion that Soviet leaders were genuinely afraid of the United States and that, therefore, a personal meeting in which he could reassure them would be desirable (Reagan 1990: 588; Oberdorfer 1991: 15; Shultz 1993: 164). As the summit approached he began to speak of "misunderstandings" that could be cleared up, rather than of the irrevocably evil nature of the Soviets (Garthoff 1994: 235). The summit appears to have improved Reagan's image of Gorbachev somewhat but Gorbachev's image of Reagan was unchanged, according to Chernyaev, but not uniformly hostile, according to Pavel Palazchenko (Wohlforth 1996a: 14–23; and see Brown 1996: 233). Agreement was reached "in principle" on 50 percent reductions in strategic nuclear weapons, and to limit intermediate range nuclear forces. The Soviets also seemed to soften their position on Afghanistan. But in the end, fundamental attitudes appeared to remain unchanged, though surface tensions were lessened. At this time, 37 percent of U.S. public opinion held that the Soviets sought limited objectives while 55 percent thought the Soviets sought global domination (Richman 1991).

In 1986 there were two major developments, the nuclear accident at Chernobyl in April and the Reykjavik summit in October. The Chernobyl disaster highlighted the limited progress of glasnost. Most Soviet citizens learned about the accident from Western media because the Soviet system was in damage control mode, attempting to cover up and minimize the significance of the catastrophe (Brown 1996: 163). It also contributed to a stronger antinuclear sentiment on the part of Gorbachev and the country at large, which strengthened support for arms control measures (Brown 1996: 231). Meanwhile, Gorbachev was learning more about his foreign counterparts. In the summer, Gorbachev met with Francois Mitterand, the President of France. Mitterand told him that Reagan should not be identified with the American military industrial complex, that he was "not an automaton," but a "human being," which impressed Gorbachev (Chernyaev 2000: 76).

The October U.S.-Soviet summit in Reykjavik was far more dramatic than Geneva, but no more successful in the short term. Gorbachev made dramatic concessions in the negotiations on strategic and intermediate range nuclear forces. In a process of one-upmanship the two leaders moved from agreements to eliminate INF missiles in Europe and cut strategic forces by 50 percent to a rather visionary program to eliminate all nuclear weapons in ten years. For Gorbachev, however, the linchpin was adherence to the ABM Treaty and limiting SDI to the laboratory. Reagan balked at this final element of the deal and the summit broke up without agreement and with considerable anger on Reagan's part (Reagan 1990: 667, Oberdorfer 1991: chap. 5; Shultz 1993: 757). However, Gorbachev was apparently moved by Reagan's initial agreement to his radical denuclearization proposals, and never spoke ill of him again (Chernyaev 2000: 85). Though Reykjavik was an intense encounter, it would appear to have had little impact on U.S. evaluations of Soviet intentions (Garthoff 1994: 289). There was a further interesting signal in December 1986, however: the release of the famous physicist and dissident, Andrei Sakharov. According to Brown, Gorbachev was "aware that neither the democratization of the country nor normal relations with the outside world would be possible so long as Sakharov remained in exile" (Brown 1996: 165). His return to Moscow impressed foreign and domestic audiences as an implicit attack on old thinking (Kaiser 1992: 146–49). However, in January 1987, a White House policy paper still postulated that, "Moscow seeks to alter the existing international system and establish Soviet global hegemony" (Garthoff 1994: 308). In May 1987, those in the United States who thought the Soviets sought limited aims, 40 percent, were still outnumbered by those who thought they sought global domination, at 54 percent (Richman 1991).

THE INF TREATY

In 1987 the Soviets made their first important costly signal in the form of the Intermediate-range Nuclear Forces (INF) Treaty. On February 28, Gorbachev picked out the INF portion of the Reykjavik deal and announced that he was willing to go ahead with it by itself, with no reference to SDI. This essentially represented acceptance of the "zero option" proposed by Reagan in 1981, and, hence, was a substantial victory for the United States. Negotiations continued through the year on the details of the agreement and concluded in November. The Soviets agreed to destroy far more missiles than the United States, a total of 1,846 as opposed to the

848 for the United States (Garthoff 1994: 327). Even more of a departure from Soviet practice were the intrusive verification procedures agreed upon. Past Soviet objections to verification by any means other than "national technical" (spy satellites) were abandoned and on-site inspections were allowed.

Advocates of the material constraints perspective argue that the INF Treaty was a product of simple tough bargaining by the West and economic weakness on the part of the Soviets, rather than a reassurance strategy by Gorbachev (Wohlforth 1994/95: 113; Bitzinger 1994: 77). However, as Thomas Risse argues, it is extremely unlikely that the INF Treaty would have emerged in anything like its eventual form without the change in leadership in the Soviet Union and the consequent shift to new thinking (Risse-Kappen 1991). Although the Soviets had clearly failed to prevent NATO from deploying its own intermediate-range forces, there was nothing preventing it from living with the new status quo. The defect-defect outcome was perfectly viable; indeed, destroying the missiles would lead to short-term costs. Instead, Gorbachev seized on the INF issue as a vehicle for reassurance. Particularly noticeable is that the signal was of an intermediate range of importance, much like the missile themselves. Getting rid of an entire class of missiles served as an undeniably costly signal, without yet addressing the entire range of issues concerning the East-West relationship, including the peak arms control issue of the day: strategic nuclear weapons. Thus, the signal size, α_i, was positive but less than 1 as indicated by implication 7.1 of the previous chapter.

Another important aspect of the agreement is the aforementioned asymmetry—the Soviets gave up more than NATO. As implications 7.2 and 7.3 from the last chapter indicate, in situations of mutual mistrust, the side with a higher level of trust and the side that is weaker will make the greater signal. The Soviet Union was certainly weaker, and the new thinking leaders also trusted the West more than the West trusted them at this point; hence, their signal had to be stronger. However, the United States did destroy some missiles, so the INF Treaty cannot be coded as a purely unilateral concession on the part of the Russians. Though the zero option was the U.S. bargaining position, the United States could have changed its mind and decided to keep its missiles and let the Russians destroy theirs if they felt it was necessary financially. Thus, the treaty is one with asymmetric, but mutual concessions.[15]

The INF Treaty and the Washington summit that followed began to shift Western opinion towards the Soviets. Some evidence suggests that Reagan

---

[15]When proposed, the zero option was a demand for a unilateral Soviet concession, because NATO had not deployed any weapons. Once the NATO buildup was in progress, however, the zero option was a compromise, thought an asymmetric one.

still viewed Gorbachev as simply making the best of a bad situation, that is, not fundamentally less aggressive in motivation but just more realistic about Soviet limitations and the failures of communism (Reagan 1990: 703; Garthoff 1994: 332). On the other hand, Secretary of State George Shultz claims that Reagan realized that Gorbachev, "represented a powerful drive for a different Soviet Union in its foreign policy" (Shultz 1993: 1015). Shultz's own attitude seems to have been decisively affected by late 1987. On November 6, in a meeting with CIA analysts on the Soviet Union, Robert Gates described Gorbachev as a Leninist who was merely trying to secure a breathing space for a future round of conflict. Shultz disagreed, and later wrote, "I felt that a profound, historic shift was underway; the Soviet Union was, willingly or unwillingly, consciously or not, turning a corner; they were not just resting for round two of the Cold War" (Shultz 1993: 1003). He pointed to the Soviets desire to leave Afghanistan, and their diminishing role in other regional trouble spots as well as the INF agreement. Thus, by late 1987, Shultz would seem to have come to the conclusion that Soviet motivations were changing.

The INF Treaty was signed at the Washington summit in December of 1987, an event with considerable public relations impact of its own. With the public at large, "Gorbymania" had taken hold; Gorbachev had a 65 percent approval rating from the American people, and was more popular in some European countries than Reagan.[16] In January 1988, the number of people thinking the Soviets had limited aims exceeded for the first time those who thought the Russians sought global domination, 46 percent to 44 percent (Richman 1991). Gorbachev's personal style, his ability to mingle with crowds, and his fresh approach to international security issues won him popular approval and began to change attitudes towards the Soviet Union. A debate also began in the media in which some began to consider the possibility of serious Soviet change. Some commentators, even Richard Pipes, pointed to the intrusive verification measures as indicating a fundamental change of Soviet policy for the better.[17] However, other voices in the press were more skeptical. On December 2 the *Washington Post* carried an editorial acknowledging some concessions on Gorbachev's part but expressing skepticism about his motives. David Broder in the same issue warned that Gorbachev was good at public relations but not to be trusted. Charles Krauthammer the next day equated Gorbachev's values with those of Brezhnev. The *New York Times* was similarly circumspect,

---

[16] The "Gorbachev Effect," *The Economist*, February 27, 1988, 38. For an analysis of public opinion in reaction to these events, see Peffley and Hurwitz 1992 and also Hurwitz and Peffley 1990.

[17] Gary Lee, "INF Treaty Shows Impact of Gorbachev," *Washington Post*, November 29, 1987, A1.

generally positive towards the treaty yet skeptical of Gorbachev.[18] Critics of the treaty, including former president Richard Nixon and many conservative senators, worried about the large Soviet conventional advantage that would remain after the missiles were gone (Shultz 1993: 1007). Reagan himself began to be the object of vitriolic assault from the right, and he struck back by accusing his attackers of believing that war with the Soviets was inevitable (Shultz 1993: 1007).[19]

AFGHANISTAN, LIBERALIZATION, AND THE UN SPEECH

U.S. suspicions about Soviet motivations were further undermined in 1988. Four events are of special importance: the beginning of the Soviet withdrawal from Afghanistan, the nineteenth Party Conference, the Moscow summit, and Gorbachev's announcement of conventional force reductions in December in a speech to the United Nations.

In February, Gorbachev announced that the Soviet Union would withdraw from Afghanistan upon the conclusion of international negotiations that were duly completed in April 1988. This development, like the INF Treaty, can be interpreted as a costly signal in accordance with the Reassurance Game. To the extent that Afghanistan was a pawn in the superpower struggle, letting it go served both to reduce Soviet threat to the West and to demonstrate a lack of territorial ambitions. As Sarah Mendelson argues, "After the summit at Reykjavik, Gorbachev and his advisors came to the conclusion that the United States would not entertain seriously the idea of new political thinking until a Soviet withdrawal from Afghanistan was complete" (Mendelson 1993: 356). Coming on the heels of the INF Treaty, it supported the notion that the Soviet new thinking on security represented a genuine change. On February 19, Robert Manning argued in an op-ed piece in the *New York Times* that the withdrawal from Afghanistan will "begin to render credible Moscow's "new thinking" about the Soviet role in the world."[20] Robert Kaiser underlined the importance of the move, "Nothing he could have done made a stronger statement than that decision—it proved that he meant what he said about 'new thinking'."[21] Even the conservative former ambassador to the United Nations Jeanne Kirkpatrick, argued that it constituted "dramatic

[18] "Gorbachev, the Movie and the Reality," *New York Times,* December 2, 1987, A34.

[19] Reagan's endorsement of the treaty did defang much of the conservative opposition however (Sigelman 1990).

[20] Robert A. Manning, "Exorcising Brezhnev's Foreign Policy," *New York Times,* February 19, 1988, A35.

[21] Robert G. Kaiser, "Finally the New Soviet Man Appears," *Washington Post,* May 24, 1988, A23; see also Kaiser 1992: 259–60.

evidence of Gorbachev's determination to de-emphasize military action and also to change the Soviet image" while explicitly denying that it was economically motivated (Kirkpatrick 1990: 188).[22] Others remained skeptical. The *Economist* claimed that, "His whole programme—the economic reforms, the diplomatic boldness—is intended to make his country a more formidable adversary for the West, not a partner with it."[23] The *Washington Post* weighed in with a skeptical editorial on February 9 that contained no praise for Gorbachev.

The second major international event was the Moscow summit in May and June. For the first time Reagan had a broad and direct exposure to the Soviet Union. He met with a wide swath of Soviet society, among whom were Soviet officials, dissidents, Orthodox clergy, and university students. While attempting to project a benign image of the United States, he appears to have developed a more benign image of the Soviets. In a famous interchange, Reagan was asked if he still held to the idea that the Soviet Union was an "evil empire," and he responded "No, I was talking about another time, another era" (Garthoff 1994: 352). This marked increasing movement towards the view that Soviet intentions had fundamentally altered. In his memoirs, Reagan notes how he realized that "the world was changing" (Reagan 1990: 711).

Soviet domestic politics were also in flux in 1988. Conservative opposition to Gorbachev began to crystallize around Yegor Ligachev. The continuing power of the old thinkers was demonstrated in the Nina Andreeva affair. An anti-perestroika manifesto, nominally written by a Leningrad school teacher, was published on March 13. The letter was widely thought to have been orchestrated by conservatives at the top, led by Ligachev. Many believed a new line was being articulated, and pro-glasnost forces faltered. Finally, on April 5, a critique of the article was published, and anti-Stalinists once more took heart and joined the assault (Brown 1996: 172–75).

Shortly after the Moscow summit, at the nineteenth Party Conference, Gorbachev went on the offensive and launched the process of liberalization that would ultimately transform the Soviet Union.[24] The Conference approved Gorbachev's plan for a new Congress of People's Deputies that would be selected through competitive elections, and which, in turn,

[22] In a column from November 1989, Kirkpatrick described the withdrawal as very much in the costly signal vein, and though she was somewhat moved by it, she still inferred a Soviet desire for a defenseless Western Europe. She closed by calling for more signals. Jeanne Kirkpatrick, "Change and Chutzpah," *Washington Post*, November 1, 1989, A 25.

[23] "As Russia Retreats," *Economist*, April 16, 1988, 13.

[24] Party Conferences were unusual interim events between regularly scheduled Congresses, held to consider important matters that could not be postponed. The last one had been held in 1941.

would select a new Supreme Soviet to act as a standing legislature. While obviously flawed by modern democratic standards, this system represented a radical break with the past. Equally important was the emphasis given to freedom of speech and the press, as well as the separation of powers and the rule of law. When Ambassador Matlock first saw the "theses" proposed for the Conference in May he believed that if they were carried out it would mean the "liberation of the country" (Matlock 1995: 122).

The third major international event of 1988 was Gorbachev's December speech at the United Nations in which he promised substantial force reductions in Eastern Europe. Traditional Soviet strategy mandated that should war break out for whatever reason, the Red Army would launch an overwhelming offensive with the object of pushing NATO forces off the continent. Throughout much of the Cold War the Soviets had a strong numerical advantage in several categories of conventional weaponry and posed a severe threat to NATO.[25] Gorbachev decided, relatively early on in his administration, to abandon this long-standing pillar of Soviet strategy and adopt a policy of "defensive defense" (Garthoff 1990). This approach mandated attempting to hold the line in Central Europe if attacked while mobilizing additional forces and attempting to negotiate a speedy conclusion to the war. Such a strategy had two advantages: it was significantly less costly, as it required far fewer conventional forces, and it was much less threatening to one's potential adversaries. However, the strategy change cut against vested military interests in the traditional offensive doctrine. As several scholars have argued, military bureaucracies have an affinity for offensive doctrine in part because of the larger resources needed to carry them out (Posen 1984b; Snyder 1984; Sagan 1994). Thus, for a long time this policy could not be fully implemented because of opposition from the military. Only in the spring of 1987, in the wake of Matthias Rust's embarrassing landing in Red Square, did Gorbachev begin to consolidate his hold on the military through large scale personnel changes.

In December of 1988 Gorbachev felt able to move ahead. In a speech to the United Nations he announced a unilateral troop reduction of 500,000 men, including six tank divisions, in Eastern Europe. The significance of the reduction lay in four aspects. First, it was sizable and could not readily be dismissed as a propaganda device. The conventional force reduction could not be easily explained as a feint or ploy, as the 1985 nuclear testing moratorium was. Second, it provided evidence that the Soviets were indeed shifting to a strategy of "defensive defense" and, thus, posed much less of a threat to NATO. Third, by removing troops from

---

[25] Some academics disputed this conventional wisdom, arguing that NATO would be able to hold the line or even prevail in a conventional war: see Cohen 1988; Mearsheimer 1982; and Posen 1984a.

Eastern Europe, it began to cut away the props from under the fragile Eastern European communist regimes and signaled a Soviet disengagement from the region. Finally, it answered the Western critics of the INF Treaty who were concerned about Soviet conventional superiority in a less nuclear Europe.

Gorbachev himself was quite consciously aware of the costly signaling logic behind his proposals. In a Politburo meeting he said,

> We can state that our initiatives have pulled the rug out from under the feet of those who have been prattling, and not without success, that new political thinking is just about words. The Soviet Union, they said, should still provide evidence. There was plenty of talk, many nice words, but not a single tank is withdrawn, not a single cannon. Therefore the unilateral reduction left a huge impression, and, one should admit, created an entirely different background for perceptions of our policies and the Soviet Union as a whole.
>
> (Cold War International History Project Bulletin 12/13: 24)

Gorbachev was also aware that there was a danger that the troop reductions would be interpreted once again as a result of economic constraints. As he acknowledged ruefully, "If we say today how much we are removing for defense from the national revenue, this may reduce to naught [the effect] of the speech at the United Nations...[they] will tell us: your proposal is rubbish, you should cut your military expenditures by three fourths" (Cold War International History Project Bulletin 12/13: 28).[26]

While there was some remaining negative press reaction, opinion was definitely shifting in a positive direction. On the one hand, the *Washington Post* opined that Gorbachev was still motivated by economic factors, and had not shown himself a "reliable partner." Conservatives blasted the move in op-ed pieces; for example George Will railed against an "epidemic of complacency" while the *Economist* asserted once again that economic factors were the prime motivator and that if the Soviet Union were to recover under Gorbachev it would be a greater threat than ever.[27] However, these voices were becoming atypical. Admiral William T. Crowe, Chairman of the Joint Chiefs of Staff, asserted that the move "lent credence" to Soviet moves towards a defensive strategy. Other military experts declared that the move would make a surprise attack impossible, and the *New York Times* called it an "invitation the West can't ignore."[28] As Bill Keller reported in the *New York Times*, "As the Soviet leader prepares for his second trip to

[26] For more in the same vein on Gorbachev's thoughts before the speech, see Chernyaev 2000: 194–95.

[27] "Unfortunately 1917 did Happen," *Economist*, December 17, 1988, 12–13; George Will, "Epidemic of Complacency," *Washington Post*, December 8, 1988, A27.

[28] Jonathan Dean, "On Arms: We Need the Details," *Washington Post*, December 11, 1988, C7; and "An Invitation We Can't Ignore," *New York Times*, December 11, 1988, E24.

America, Western curiosity and skepticism seem to have shifted from his intentions to his prospects: not 'Does he mean it?' but 'Can he pull it off?'."[29] Margaret Thatcher, who had presciently asserted that Gorbachev was a "man with whom we can do business" before he even took office, had declared that the Cold War over on the eve of the UN speech (Garthoff 1994: 193–94). In July 1988, 50 percent of U.S. respondents thought the Soviets had limited aims, only 38 percent thought they wanted global domination (Richman 1991).

THE SINATRA DOCTRINE

The process of reassurance was essentially completed in 1989. After George H.W. Bush took office in January, however, his administration initiated a "pause" while it reviewed its policy towards the Soviet Union (Chollet and Goldgeier 2003). The new National Security Advisor, Brent Scowcroft was especially skeptical of the recent arms control treaties, however, the new Secretary of State, James Baker, favored a more active policy (Wohlforth 2003: 26, 32–33). A new policy document, NSD-23, drafted in March 1989, coined the phrase "beyond containment" to summarize the new U.S. policy. The document suggested that it might be possible to shift to a strategy which "actively promotes the integration of the Soviet Union into the international system" (Beschloss and Talbott 1993: 69).

Evidence of trust and mistrust was mingled in this period. The United States proposed cutting U.S. troops stationed in Europe by 20 percent, and limiting troops by each side to 275,000 (Beschloss and Talbott 1993: 77). In part this was motivated by the desire to make a bold initiative to recipro-cate Soviet arms reductions, but the goal of weakening the Soviet hold on Eastern Europe was also in mind (Wohlforth 2003: 26). Gorbachev, in a meeting with Baker announced a reduction of 500 short-range missiles, but the timing, in the middle of a contentious intra-NATO debate on modern-izing its own short-range missiles, struck Western observers as an attempt to sow discord in the alliance (Wohlforth 2003: 32–33). However, in a very significant indicator of the new level of trust, the Bush administration also began to press for an accord on chemical weapons without the usual empha-sis on verification. When Scowcroft objected, Bush responded, "[M]y gut just tells me that the danger of proliferation is more important than the risk of Soviet cheating." The Soviets themselves realized the importance of the development. Sergei Tarasenko, an aid to Shevardnadze, told his boss, "This is really something new and important. The Americans are no

---

[29] Bill Keller, "Gorbachev's Grand Plan: Is it Real or a Pipe Dream?," *New York Times,* December 5, 1988, A1.

longer quite so obsessed with our cheating" (Beschloss and Talbott 1993: 120). This shift is crucial because the concern for verification is a relatively good indicator of the level of trust between two states. The less each side trusts the other, the more extensive will verification procedures have to be to enable cooperation to take place. The more trust exists, the more relaxed verification standards can be because the other side is assumed to have less desire to cheat, and, hence, less willingness to expend resources to deceive the verification regime.

The spring of 1989 saw real steps towards democratization with elections for the Congress of People's Deputies, the convening of the Congress, and the selection of the Supreme Soviet. Boris Yeltsin's election, despite obvious opposition from the communist hierarchy, served to confirm that the elections were free, though not all the seats were contested. The meetings were televised to an interested nation, and the beginnings of an organized political opposition emerged among the reformers in the Supreme Soviet. All of this was eagerly followed by the U.S. ambassador, who wrote in June that the movement towards representative government was a turning point that would probably endure (Matlock 1995: 201–24).

The change in Western beliefs accelerated tremendously in the summer and autumn as the Eastern European regimes crumbled one by one and the Soviets permitted them to fall. The Soviet nonuse of force represented the "height of credibility of the USSR's new foreign policy" (Levesque 1997: 3). Gorbachev had begun to reformulate policy towards Eastern Europe in a speech celebrating the seventieth anniversary of the Bolshevik revolution in November 1987 (Chafetz 1993: 73). He spoke of the need to reexamine the Soviet invasion of Czechoslovakia in 1968, and asserted that the Soviet Union no longer viewed itself as a model that had to be followed by all socialist states. By the nineteenth Party Conference in 1988 he had effectively repudiated the Brezhnev doctrine by endorsing each country's "freedom to choose," in a move that was targeted at reassuring Western audiences along with the withdrawal from Afghanistan (Levesque 1997: 80). Gorbachev exercised considerable restraint, however, in not pressing the Eastern European regimes to pursue glasnost and perestroika, though he remained convinced through the end that reformed socialism could work in the East bloc.

The ball began to roll when Solidarity returned to an active role in Poland in late 1988 and early 1989. In January 1989, the Soviet press commented favorably on the beginning of multiparty politics in Poland. In April Gorbachev explicitly rejected the use of force in Eastern Europe. In the summer after Solidarity's triumph in the Polish elections, Gorbachev once again publicly ruled out interference in the affairs of allies (Levesque 1997: 118). This set the stage for the cataclysm of the fall of 1989.

At various stages, East Europeans consulted with the Soviets, fearing a negative reaction. Before Hungary opened their border with Austria, precipitating the outflow of East Germans that would ultimately doom the German Democratic Republic (GDR), they consulted Shevardnadze, who replied that the decision concerned Hungary and the two German states. Czechoslovakian leaders were warned against using force to hold on to power (Levesque 1997: 153, 186). As regime after regime fell to peaceful protest, Western observers were stunned. When the Berlin wall fell on November 9, Bush acknowledged, with legendary understatement, that the Soviets were, "more serious than I realized" (Beschloss and Talbott 1993: 132). The fall of the wall also affected press attitudes. As late as October 1989, conservative columnists were asserting that "The Russians are Still Coming" and that Gorbachev would most likely become a hardline dictator.[30] Yet few now questioned Gorbachev's desire to end the Cold War, and some explicitly acknowledged that he had abandoned the old Soviet goal of hegemony.[31] Bush was openly chided for his mild response to the breach of the wall, however justified it might have been by a desire to avoid undermining Gorbachev by gloating over the collapse of communism (Beschloss and Talbott 1993: 135). In February 1990, those believing the Soviets had limited aims numbered 60 percent, while those saying they sought global domination had dwindled to 25 percent (Richman 1991).

The material constraints view explains the nonuse of force in Eastern Europe as a product of Soviet economic difficulties and the increasing burden of subsidizing the bloc. Brooks and Wohlforth point out that old thinkers did not advocate the use of force to retain control. The East bloc countries had become an increasingly heavy burden on the Soviet economy in the 1980s (Brooks and Wohlforth 2000/01: 23; Stone 1996). While this was the case, old thinkers were certainly not advocating ending subsidies to the bloc, much less abandoning it altogether. In fact no one envisioned a near-term collapse of the bloc; reformers hoped that a process of controlled evolution could keep socialist parties in power (Levesque 1997: 88).[32] And it is clear that the regimes did not slip out of control until after repeated signals from Gorbachev that he would not interfere with force.

---

[30] Richard Pipes, "The Russians are Still Coming," *New York Times,* October 9, 1989, A17; and William Safire, "Goodbye to Glasnost," *New York Times,* October 19, 1989, A17. For a French conservative attack on perestroika of this era, see Thom 1989.

[31] David Broder, "Our Great Mission in Europe," *Washington Post,* November 16, 1989, A36; and Hobart Rowen, "Transitions East and West," *Washington Post,* November 16, 1989, A27.

[32] See Levesque 2001 for three Soviet documents on East European policy in early 1989.

LESS SOCIALISM, MORE UNITY

At the beginning of 1990 the Cold War was over, but there were some important loose ends to be tied up and the question remained as to whether it would stay over.[33] The most important loose end was the German Democratic Republic, and its ruling Socialist Unity party (SED). Events in East Germany, as in the rest of the Soviet bloc, were driven by popular forces once the fear of Soviet intervention was dispelled. In the fall of 1989, after Hungary opened its border to Austria, East Germans began using this indirect route to get to the West. Mass street protests led to a struggle within the ruling elite over whether to use force to restore order, and Erich Honecker, long-time SED leader, perestroika foe and advocate of the "Chinese solution" was ejected and replaced by Egon Krenz. Because of the outflow problem, the government decided to permit free movement, in the hopes that if people were assured they could leave at any time, they would feel less need to leave right away. In a bureaucratic mixup, the wall was opened before the new laws could even be implemented (Zelikow and Rice 1995: 85–101; Stent 1999: 74–97).

The opening of the wall precipitated the demise of the GDR. The wall had been built for a reason, after all, because given a choice many Germans preferred West to East. The fact that this was still the case thirty years later greatly weakened the position of the East German regime in negotiating with Bonn. German unity was driven by three actors. Helmut Kohl, the West German leader, believed that he faced a unique opportunity to achieve a forty-year-old dream and reunite Germany. The East German population, initially hesitant, came to embrace unity as the quickest road to democracy and prosperity. Finally, the United States embraced the goal of unity as well. It was a long-standing goal of U.S. policy, and it was inevitable in the long run, so one might as well go on record as a supporter rather than an opponent, and the Germans could now be trusted with the increased power that would come with unity.

As a result, the "two plus four" talks that were convened in March 1990, comprising the two Germanies and the four occupying powers, were highly likely to end in near-term unity on West German terms. However, there was a great deal of reassurance involved in the process of getting there (Risse 1997). With respect to perceptions of the Soviets, German unification provided yet more evidence of Gorbachev's commitment to nonviolence and self-determination. Russia still had troops in East Germany with which it could intervene to prevent political outcomes it did not favor. However, Gorbachev had given up the option of using these forces, which was

---

[33] In a Chicago Council on Foreign Relations poll in the fall of 1990, 73 percent of respondents believed the Cold War to be over (Murray 1996: 39).

reassuring, but it greatly reduced his leverage (Wohlforth 2003: 51, 54). Perhaps the most sensitive issue was whether the new Germany would be free to remain in NATO if it so chose. This condition, it will be recalled, was the condition raised by the West in the early negotiations over German unity in the 1950s in the hope, soon confirmed, that it would be rejected by the Russians. At the summit meeting in Washington in May 1990, the United States insisted on this condition again and Gorbachev granted it, to the great dismay of his advisors (Baker 1995: 253). But, having embraced the principle of self-determination, nonintervention, and sovereignty for Germany, Gorbachev had little choice (Zelikow and Rice 1995: 277–79; Beschloss and Talbott 1993: 220). The concession underlined, however, the extent to which these principles were accepted, at the expense of traditionally defined Soviet security interests. It was also important in causing the Bush administration to agree to a trade deal that would normalize U.S.-Soviet trade, a goal long sought by Gorbachev (Copeland 1999/2000: 53).

In addition, the West, through NATO, tried to reassure the Soviets that withdrawing from East Germany would not harm their security. The two key steps were agreeing to limit NATO troops on the territory of the former GDR, and a NATO summit in London in July 1990 that declared that the Cold War was over, nuclear arms should be weapons of last resort, and that conventional and nuclear forces should be reduced and restructured. Nuclear artillery would also be eliminated. These steps were important in enabling Gorbachev to defend his policy from conservatives (Baker and Defrank 1995: 258; Stent 1999: 133; Risse 1997: 174).

Germany, too, had some reassuring to do if it was to get to unity in the near term. Germany's neighbors were concerned about the potential increase in power that Germany would enjoy upon reunification, just as they were forty years earlier when the first steps to revive Germany were undertaken.[34] The Poles feared that German revanchists would reopen the question of the Oder-Niesse border. British and French leaders expressed fears about future German leaders. For instance, a memorandum documenting a meeting held by British Prime Minister Margaret Thatcher with academic experts on Germany contained some undiplomatic reflections on the German national character but claimed that, "No one had serious misgivings about the present leaders or political elite of Germany. What, however, about ten, fifteen or twenty years from now? Could some of the unhappy characteristics of the past reemerge with just as destructive consequences?" (Powell 1992). Mitterand was also deeply worried about the prospect of a reunified Germany, as were Gorbachev and Shevardnadze (Zelikow and Rice 1995: 137–38, 345).

---

[34]Bush had admitted at Malta that the Soviet Union was "in the same boat" as the European NATO allies on German unification (Chernyaev 2000: 240).

Two factors permitted these fears to be overcome. First, the United States made it plain that it would maintain the institutionalized security commitment it had made in the early Cold War for just this purpose. As discussed in chapters 5 and 6, trusted hegemons foster cooperation in the face of mistrust problems. Second, also as a continuation of early Cold War strategies of reassurance, Germany sought to further engage itself in international institutions. This was seen in both the push for the 1992 Maastricht Treaty on European Union, in the formation of the Euro-corps with France (shades of the European Defense Community), and in the strong support for the maintenance of NATO and a continued presence of NATO troops on German territory. Germany also committed to a package of military limitations and financial aid for Russia (Stent 1999: 146). These moves were essentially costly signals of reassurance. As Zelikow and Rice put it,

> There is no evidence that the Germans had made any serious analysis of how the $15–20 billion in credit would help perestroika. That, for Kohl, was not the point–any more than he had made a serious analysis of the form or effect of a European political union before he had become a cosponsor of that enterprise. After all, his primary motive in both cases was political–the need to make powerful symbolic gestures. Kohl supported a move to political union because he believed in the European ideal and believed that the Germans now had to show themselves to be placing Europe ahead of German nationalism.
>
> (Zelikow and Rice 1995: 326)

These steps were important not because institutions directly prevent Germany from engaging in aggressive behavior; Germany could at any time withdraw from NATO, evict foreign troops and withdraw from the European Union. Instead, Germany's involvement in international institutions serves as a costly signal in two ways. First, the infringement of autonomy and presence of foreign troops inherent in such institutions would be more costly to a nationalistic leadership, and, hence, membership in the institutions serves as a costly signal of lack of xenophobic attitudes. Indeed the vehemence of nationalist opposition to the Maastricht Treaty in Denmark and France lent special significance to its relatively smooth acceptance in Germany, just as Germany's acceptance of the EDC treaty spoke volumes in light of its rejection by nationalist forces in France. Second, institutional membership forms a series of "alarm bells" that would have to be rung by any regime that wanted to take Germany back down the course of unilateral aggression. To regain full military and economic autonomy, a new regime would have to take a series of very public and disturbing steps, which would serve as signals that the regime was returning to a militarist stance. While nothing would physically prevent the regime from taking these steps, the institutions ensure that they would not go unnoticed. Indeed, the willingness of the present regime to deploy such alarm bells in the path of possible future more aggressive regimes serves as an additional signal of their present lack of aggressive intentions. Only a regime that was not contemplating taking such steps under any circumstances would be willing to make it so politically costly for itself to do so.

Thus, German reunification generated a multilateral process of reassurance. The Soviets decision not to use their trump card, troops on the ground, reinforced the perception that they took noninterference and self-determination seriously. Germany engaged in reassurance strategies to reconcile its neighbors to the prospect of an increase in German power. Thus the settlement of the most divisive issue at the beginning of the Cold War further increased mutual trust in Europe at the end of the Cold War.

THE END OF THE SOVIET UNION AND THE RUSSIAN EMPIRE

The other events of 1990 and 1991 offer further evidence of reassurance at work. Two important arms control agreements were negotiated, the Conventional Forces in Europe (CFE) Treaty and the first Strategic Arms Reduction Treaty (START I). The CFE negotiations were a successor to the deadlocked Mutual and Balanced Force Reduction talks, which had haggled over conventional forces in Europe for many years. The new talks produced a treaty within a year, which was signed in November 1990. Once again the Russians made the lion's share of the reductions, essentially coming down to NATO levels. This further supported mutual trust by eliminating, with verification, the conventional weapons advantage that had seemed to give the Soviets a capacity to invade Western Europe. Hardline elements in the military were not enthusiastic about the treaty, however, and attempted to save military equipment from destruction by withdrawing it beyond the Urals and relabeling it as belonging to the navy (Dean and Forsberg 1992; Falkenrath 1995). The START I Treaty was the long-delayed culmination of strategic arms control negotiations since the Geneva summit. Signed in July 1991, it reduced strategic warheads on both sides to roughly six thousand and reduced the number of Russian heavy ICBM's.

However, the relationship between the Soviet Union and the West had progressed so far that arms control was really a second tier issue in this period. The Iraqi invasion of Kuwait in August of 1990 posed a serious test as a former Soviet client threatened the West's oil supply. Once again Gorbachev and Shevardnadze broke the Soviet mold by supporting U.S. efforts to contain Iraq, and ultimately eject Iraq from Kuwait (Beschloss and Talbott 1993: 280–87). As Chernyaev put it, "This was probably going to be the most difficult test of [Gorbachev's] loyalty to the 'new thinking.' ... We were sustaining heavy material losses (oil, weapons exports worth $1.2 billion.) We showed that ideological considerations had finally given way to principles of morality and law" (Chernyaev 2000: 283). The American side also saw this as a confirmation of the importance of the new found trust in the relationship (Wohlforth 2003: 85–86).

Even more important was Soviet domestic politics. The process of democratization begun in 1988 continued to gather steam. In March 1990 the Soviet constitution was amended to remove the reference to the leading role of the communist party. The post of President was created to further transfer power from the party to the state institutions. Open political debate was now a fact of life in the Soviet Union, but the effects were not as anticipated by the reformers. Insistent demands for national liberation were raised in the Baltic states and in the other republics. There followed a tense political struggle between the center and the republics. Force was used on occasion to suppress nationalist demonstrations, but never enough to have a decisive impact, and never with explicit authorization from the top.[35] *The Economist*, as late as May 1990, entertained the possibility that Gorbachev was still responding to constraints, but by October had decided that he was aiming for a free market economy and multiparty democracy.[36]

In the fall and winter, Gorbachev made a "turn to the right" in which he attempted to diffuse conservative criticism built up over the loss of Eastern Europe and democratization by backing off somewhat on economic reform and liberalization (Brown 1996: 269). With the fate of the Union at stake, Gorbachev drafted a new Union treaty that would replace the Soviet Union with a looser federal structure. In the spring of 1991, he tacked back towards the reformers in an effort to get the Union treaty approved.

When Gorbachev was on vacation in August 1991, a conspiracy of hardliners attempted a putsch. Gorbachev was placed under house arrest, but Muscovites rallied outside the Russian parliament building led by Boris Yeltsin, the Russian President. Yeltsin's role in thwarting the coup increased his prestige dramatically and Gorbachev was fatally weakened. In December, Yeltsin negotiated an agreement with Ukraine and Belarus to set up the Commonwealth of Independent States (CIS) to replace the Soviet Union. This "second coup" spelled the end not just of the Soviet Union but of the Russian empire, built up over centuries of expansion. On Christmas day Gorbachev resigned and the Soviet Union ceased to exist (Beschloss and Talbott 1993: 458–64).

---

[35] Chernyaev almost resigned over the use of force in Lithuania in January 1991, and wrote in a draft resignation letter that Gorbachev had lost "the most important thing that we've gained from new thinking–trust" (Chernyaev 2000: 321).

[36] "A Friend in Need," *The Economist*, May 12, 1990, 13; "Massed Against the Past," *The Economist*, October 20, 1990, 3.

The Depth of Trust

While trust was certainly built, an interesting question is how deep this trust ran. It was clear that the Soviets had learned the lessons that nuclear weapons and economic decline raised the costs and lowered the likelihood of success of expansionist behavior. Old thinkers had, by and large, learned these lessons as well as new thinkers. However, many argue that Gorbachev's values changed as well, that is, his desire for expansion, g_i, evaporated and that this differentiated new thinkers from old. For instance, some argue that Gorbachev's final goal for the Soviet Union was a social-democratic multinational state participating fully in the global economic system, and that the level of trust the West developed for him was correspondingly deeper.[37]

What evidence is there that the rapprochement was deeper, based on the abandonment of expansionist goals? I have already mentioned some direct evidence of Western beliefs. Shultz believed that the Soviets were "not just resting for round two of the Cold War," which would have been the case if their goals were unchanged. Ambassador Matlock, writing of an early 1989 effort to prod the new Bush team into action notes:

> Another argument I rejected was that perestroika was a trick to lull the West while the Soviet Union revamped its economy and surpassed us in arms. Of course, the goal of perestroika was to improve the Soviet economy, but the methods Gorbachev had chosen were undermining the power of the Communist Party and the military industrial complex to control the country. Perestroika would succeed only if it transformed the country into an open society with a government controlled by is citizens. There was no chance that such a society would devote a quarter or more of its gross national product to armaments.... I was convinced that Gorbachev's goals were consistent with ours.
>
> (Matlock 1995: 188)

He also recommended economic steps to support perestroika, especially trade. Bush believed that the risk of the Soviets cheating was low enough to justify going ahead with a chemical weapons treaty, though cheating on such a treaty would be fairly costless, in fact abiding by the treaty involved substantial costs.[38] Even the skeptical *Economist* was ultimately persuaded of Gorbachev's bonafides.

---

[37] Shaknazarov testifies that Gorbachev by 1989 had embraced social democracy, quoting him as saying, "And if we speak about the final goal, insofar as it is possible today to be definite, that is integration into the world community by peaceful means. By conviction I am close to social democracy." Ligachev also thought he was a social democrat (Brown 1996: 102).

[38] Russia has as of this writing only begun to comply with its Chemical Weapons Convention mandated destruction of materials, and that after several extensions.

In addition, of course, there is direct evidence of the abandonment of communist ideology, which was intimately related to the expansionist goals of the Soviet state. Gorbachev's relation to Leninism went through an interesting evolution. At the beginning he stressed that his program would perfect the existing system, correcting defects and producing greater growth. As this failed, he began urging more radical steps, while justifying them as a return to a correct understanding of Lenin, even when the ideas, such as the subordination of class struggle to universal human values and the importance of freedom and human rights, were antithetical to Leninism (Kull 1992: 45–50). By 1989 Gorbachev was employing the flexible term "socialist idea," which could as easily refer to Sweden as Lenin, and in the December 1989 New Year's message he avoided all mention of Lenin or communism (Matlock 1995: 289, 296). Lenin and the October revolution came back in during the turn to the right, and even after the coup, he declared allegiance to these symbols, though without any of the content that they once had.

Besides considering direct evidence, one can engage in a counterfactual analysis of what might have happened if the old preferences remained in place. For instance, what would have happened if Gorbachev had suffered a stroke in 1987 or 1988 and Ligachev had taken over? Even if General Secretary Ligachev would have eventually wound down the arms race and evacuated Eastern Europe, building a certain degree of trust with the West, there seem to be at least two crucial steps old thinkers would not have taken.

The first is the decision to democratize the Soviet Union by shifting power to the state institutions, holding increasingly free elections, and eventually, in 1990, eliminating the leading role of the communist party from the constitution and allowing the free formation of parties. These steps were opposed by old thinkers whenever an opportunity arose, beginning with the Nina Andreyeva letter in 1988. Many observers, including Ambassador Matlock, stressed the importance of democratization, as was discussed above. Margaret Thatcher also impressed on Gorbachev how reassuring democratization would be and how hard it would be to trust a nondemocratic Soviet Union (English 2003: 265–66).

The second is the decision to not use force to preserve the Soviet Union. Almost any leader could be expected to use force to preserve the unity of the state; a democratically elected Abraham Lincoln certainly did in 1861.[39] As early as February 1988 Ligachev advocated using force to keep the Baltics in line (Chernyaev 2000: 188). In the winter of 1990/91, during Gorbachev's turn to the right, it would have still been possible to use the

---

[39] The Lincoln analogy was much discussed at the time; for instance, William Safire, "Let Lithuania Go," *New York Times,* March 23, 1990, A35.

military to suppress secessionists, even in the Baltics where the desire to leave was strongest. It would have meant serious loss of life and a strengthening of authoritarian forces, to be sure, but most leaders would have paid such a price. The West would have also reacted negatively, but its reaction to Tiananmen in 1989 was short lived. The fact that Gorbachev did not use force, and that his main rival by that point, Yeltsin, also would not, meant that several centuries of Russian imperialism had come to an end.[40]

An old thinking Soviet Union could have struggled on, with the communists clinging to power. A type of authoritarian capitalist reform could have been attempted, much as China has implemented, which promised economic growth and political stability (Kramer 1999: 570). China's relations with its East Asian neighbors and the United States are a reminder that a transition path from communism exists that does not involve as deep a level of reassurance of the outside world as Gorbachev achieved. While few old thinkers explicitly advocated such a path, it seems quite likely that economic constraints combined with their unwillingness to relinquish power would have forced them in this direction eventually. The fact that the post-Cold War world looked decidedly different helps account for the greater degree of trust that was established.

Conclusion

In looking at the end of the Cold War, then, one can observe a series of costly signals leading to mutual trust between former adversaries. The attitudes of Western leaders, press, and the public towards the Soviet Union all underwent a substantial transformation. Soviet military and geopolitical concessions, particularly the INF Treaty, the withdrawal from Afghanistan, the December 1988 conventional arms initiative, and the withdrawal from Eastern Europe were decisive in changing overall Western opinion about the Soviet Union. By 1990, most observers viewed the Soviet Union as a state that had abandoned its hegemonic ambitions and could be trusted to abide by arms control agreements and play a constructive role in world politics. Gorbachev's failure to use force, even to preserve the union, ratified this image and Yeltsin's role in defeating the 1991 putsch helped in transferring this image to the Russian successor state to the Soviet Union.

---

[40]For the most part. Yeltsin did decide to use force rather than allow secession from the Russian Federation and in 1994 this led to civil war in Chechnya (Bennett 1999: chap. 8).

PART V

Trust and Mistrust
in the Post–Cold War Era

CHAPTER 9

Conclusion

IN THE FIFTH CENTURY BCE, the Greek city-states, led by Athens and Sparta, united to defeat the Persian empire. In the aftermath of victory, however, Athens continued to build up its empire and Sparta became fearful and contemplated war. At the Spartan council, which was called to decide on a course of action, Thucydides had an Athenian representative defend his country's conduct in the following speech.

> We did not gain our empire by force. It came to us at a time when you were unwilling to fight on to the end against the Persians. At this time our allies came to us of their own accord and begged us to lead them. It was the actual course of events which first compelled us to increase our power to its present extent: fear of Persia was our chief motive, though afterwards we thought, too, of our own honor and our own interest. Finally there came a time when we were surrounded by enemies, when we had already crushed some revolts, when you had lost the friendly feelings that you used to have for us and had turned against us and begun to arouse our suspicion: at this point it was clearly no longer safe for us to risk letting our empire go...We have done nothing extraordinary, nothing contrary to human nature in accepting an empire when it was offered to us and then in refusing to give it up.
>
> (Thucydides 1972: 79–80).

In the end, Sparta and Athens fought a long and disastrous war which ended in defeat for Athens.

The Peloponnesian War was often used as a metaphor for the Cold War, with Germany cast as defeated Persia, the United States as democratic Athens and the Soviet Union as authoritarian Sparta (Kagan 1989). With the end of the Cold War, however, it is perhaps more fruitful to cast the Soviets as Persia and imagine ourselves in the period before the Peloponnesian war has begun. The American Cold War "empire," like the Athenian, was an empire by invitation. Many states flocked to the U.S. side when they were threatened by the Soviet Union, including a number of Spartan dictatorships. The U.S.-led alliance won a great victory in 1991 by prevailing peacefully over the longest lived totalitarian ideology of the twentieth century. Yet some argue that the United States, like Athens, is beginning to lose the good will built up in this struggle, and that a heavy-handed approach in a changed political environment may alienate states whose cooperation is essential for U.S. security in the new world. Of course, in the post–Cold War era there is no direct counterpart of Sparta; no great power capable of challenging the United States in open war. However, the terrorists the United States now identifies as the most important threat to its national security were once U.S. allies in the struggle against the Soviets in Afghanistan. If Al Qaeda and its offshoots wish to be the new Sparta, modern technology, the openness of Western societies, tactical innovation, and a willingness to die may enable them to pose a serious threat.[1]

The Cold War now belongs to history, albeit a recent history that still casts a long shadow over the present. It therefore seems worthwhile to consider how the analysis of this book can be brought to bear on more current issues. The role of trust in international relations is just as important today as it was in the Cold War, and it plays a central role in the policy dilemmas confronted by the United States and other countries in the twenty-first century.

THE SOLITARY SUPERPOWER

After the end of the Cold War, the United States became the sole remaining superpower and the world system could be characterized as unipolar (Krauthammer 1990/91; Wohlforth 1999; Posen 2003). In quantitative terms, the United States has a bigger economy, spends more on the military, and, hence, has greater military capabilities than any other state. In qualitative terms the gap is even more stark, the U.S. ability to wage warfare with precision, speed, and minimum casualties is unmatched. But perhaps even more important than the way the system as a whole is characterized is the power relationships between the United States and the remaining states in the world with whom it has serious political differences. Here the new reality is clear, the United States is massively more powerful than most states with which it might come into conflict.

This fact, in conjunction with the models of this book, has several implications for the post–Cold War world. First, as the Security Dilemma Game in chapter 2 shows, the greater a state's likelihood of success in a conflict and the lower the costs it faces, the more likely its gains from expansion, g_i, will exceed the threshold required to make it an expansionist state, g_i^*.

---

[1] For a sample of the debate on the United States as an empire today, see Snyder 2003 and Rosen 2003. Rosen, arguing that America should learn the military lessons of past empires, echoes the Athenian representative at Sparta and notes that, "The Athenians could not afford to wage war against every island state that might defy them. The Melians had to be crushed, therefore, so that no other island state would even think about rebelling against Athens" (Rosen 2003: 59).

States which have great power and low costs for conflict must have very little to gain from conflict to remain status quo powers. Any significant interests in expansion and they will become untrustworthy. Thus, the United States today, in some of its conflicts with weak states, may be near the threshold between security seeking and expansionism, even though, in the Cold War context, with its much greater costs and much lower likelihood of success, the United States was firmly on the security seeking side of the line.

Second, also following from the Security Dilemma Game, in conflicts with weak adversaries the United States will have a very high minimum trust threshold, m_i. Greater power and lower costs for fighting raise the minimum trust threshold, so that even small doubts that another country is untrustworthy may be enough to tip the United States over the edge into conflict. When a country is extremely good at fighting, the incentive to trust the other side to keep their word diminishes, and the incentive to take matters into one's own hands grows. By contrast, other countries with lesser capabilities will have lower minimum trust thresholds. They will be willing to try cooperation in cases where the United States prefers to defect. This difference will set up conflicts over strategy between the United States and its allies, even when there is agreement on basic goals.

Third, a low threshold for expansionism, g_i^*, and a high minimum trust threshold, m_i, could lead to increasingly conflictual behavior initiated by the United States against weak adversaries. States that are nearly expansionist themselves and require a great deal of trust to cooperate with others are likely to defect preemptively. In accordance with this implication, the U.S. National Security Strategy, released in 2002, endorsed preventive war as a replacement for the Cold War strategy of containment. Employing classic preventive war logic, it argued that "Given the goals of rogue states and terrorists, the United States can no longer rely solely on a reactive posture as we have in the past.... We cannot let our enemies strike first."[2] This policy was most clearly exemplified in the invasion of Iraq in 2003. As President Bush put it at the opening of the war, "The people of the United States and our friends and allies will not live at the mercy of an outlaw regime that threatens the peace with weapons of mass murder. We will meet that threat now, with our Army, Air Force, Navy, Coast Guard and Marines, so that we do not have to meet it later with armies of fire fighters and police and doctors on the streets of our cities."

A fourth implication is that, as a result of its increasingly bellicose behavior, international distrust for the United States is likely to grow. As the Spiral Game in chapter 3 indicates, external observers become more

[2] *The National Security Strategy of the United States of America*, p. 15, available on the White House Web site.

suspicious of a state's motivations the more noncooperative behavior it initiates. The Soviets experienced this as a result of their oppression of Eastern Europe and their bullying behavior in Turkey and Iran at the beginning of the Cold War. Increasing U.S. unilateralism will have a similar impact on public opinion abroad in the post–Cold War era. The extent of this decline in trust may be attenuated by two factors highlighted in the Spiral Game. First, the United States remains relatively transparent (low ε_i), and, hence, there will be a certain amount of publicly available information about motivations. If the United States can establish high prior beliefs about its trustworthiness, this may overcome the message sent by its defection. Second, the states the United States tends to get into conflict with are conflict prone themselves, supporting the inference that U.S. defections are caused by defensive considerations, rather than expansionist motivations (implication 3.6). Nonetheless, from implication 3.4, aggressive behavior will rationally increase suspicion of the United States, at least to some extent.[3]

Fifth, because U.S. power puts it on the edge of expansionism, U.S. policy will be more volatile than during the Cold War. It is often observed that the international system constrains small powers more than stronger ones. In the U.S. case, this reaches its logical limit, in that the United States is perhaps less constrained by the international system than any state in modern history. This means that the specific goals and beliefs of elected leaders matter more than ever. Broad agreement could be secured on many Cold War policies because leaders with preferences within a certain range could all agree on their wisdom. In the post–Cold War era, small differences in policy preferences may lead some to advocate preventive war while others advocate deterrence or sanctions. Thus, U.S. policy may experience wide swings as parties and personnel alternate in power.

These structural implications of the unprecedented post–Cold War power of the United States, however, are not immutable. As the

---

[3] In the Multilateral Trust Game of chapter 5, increasing the power of the hegemon makes it more trustworthy, which can foster international cooperation. This result seems in conflict with the previous results based on the Security Dilemma Game, in which making a state more powerful makes it more likely to be expansionist, which will reduce the likelihood of cooperation. The contrast arises because in the Multilateral Trust Game, trustworthiness is a function of willingness to provide public goods, and increasing size makes one more willing to do so, while in the Security Dilemma Game, increasing size makes one more likely to attack one's potential adversaries. Even in the Multilateral Trust Game, however, increasing the hegemon's power does not necessarily promote cooperation, as we saw in chapter 5. The politics surrounding the war in Iraq suggests that it would be interesting to combine the two models, so that the public good in question is the prevention of a threat from a third party. Increasing the hegemon's power could reduce the support offered by other states if it made the hegemon seem expansionist, particularly in the presence of uncertainty over the level of threat posed by the third party.

Reassurance Game in chapter 7 shows, reassurance between genuinely trustworthy actors is possible even for very low initial levels of trust. Thus, it should be possible for the United States to build trust through conscious policies of reassurance as it did after World War II, and as the Soviet Union did in the late 1980s. These policies could take the form of accepting institutional constraints or engaging in costly signaling of some other kind. The volatility of U.S. policy just discussed, however, will make the task of reassurance all the more difficult.

These trends will have effects across the spectrum of U.S. foreign policy. Their effects were seen in the early post Cold War years, and are growing stronger over time.

THE POST–COLD WAR DECADE

During the 1990s there was a strong element of continuity in policy from the end of the Cold War. Some realists predicted that the institutional structures built up during the Cold War to link the United States to Europe and the European states to each other would collapse after the threat that led to their creation evaporated (Mearsheimer 1990: 5; Walt 1997: 171). Instead, these structures flourished. Germany continued to pursue a strategy of institutional reassurance, binding itself to the other European states. The United States continued to play the role of a trusted hegemon, maintaining a reduced level of forces in Europe to ensure stability.

U.S. policy in this period oscillated between multilateral engagement and multilateral neglect. In the immediate post–Cold War period, the United States worked within international institutions to achieve its ends.[4] To legitimize and fight the Gulf War, the United States built a wide coalition and held it together through the conflict (Lake 1999). Early in the Clinton administration, however, the United States encouraged the Europeans to take the lead on the horrendous civil war in Bosnia and the United States and Europe stood by while hundreds of thousands were massacred in Rwanda. While this policy was, in essence, one of free riding, the hope, with respect to Bosnia, was that Europeans would pick up the slack and fulfill Eisenhower's dream of a European Union able to take care of itself (Daalder 2000: 7). Hence, it can be termed a form of multilateral neglect,

---

[4] Secretary of State James A. Baker III wrote in his memoirs, "Without institutions, it's hard to get work done because all your consultations have to be done bilaterally; with an institution, you create a forum for consultation and can greatly expand cooperation. Thus, much of our time at State was spent creating new institutions (APEC), adapting old ones (NATO), or creating interim quasi-institutional arrangements (for example, the "Two-plus-Four" process for German unification) (Baker and Defrank 1995: 45)."

that is, neglect motivated by the hope that multilateral actions by others would succeed. Chastened by these failures, the United States took the lead once more, negotiating the Dayton accords to settle the Bosnian conflict, and spearheading a NATO bombing campaign to coerce Serbia into ending its ethnic cleansing campaign in Kosovo. European and Atlantic institutions were strengthened by these cases of joint action to enforce peace in Europe. The United Nations, however, was bypassed in the Kosovo campaign because of fears of Russian and Chinese vetos (Daalder and O'Hanlon 2000: 44).

Strengthening European institutions sometimes had an unfortunate side effect, however. U.S.-Russian relations were harmed by the decision to expand the NATO alliance to include former Warsaw Pact members Poland, the Czech Republic, and Hungary, and by the campaign against Serbia to secure autonomy for the Kosovo Albanians. NATO enlargement can be seen as a tragic dilemma of trust building and trust breaking (Kydd 2001). The chief purpose of expanding NATO was to enlarge the zone of peace and mutual trust to Eastern Europe in hopes of preventing future wars there. The chief drawback was that it violated implicit pledges to Russia that NATO would not move closer to its borders, and, hence, fostered distrust on the part of a Russia that was left out in the cold. This distrust was exacerbated by U.S. intervention against a traditional Russian ally, Serbia. Americans and Europeans, convinced that Milosevic instigated the prior conflicts in Croatia and Bosnia culminating in the massacre at Srebrenica, felt that a line needed to be drawn if he was not to orchestrate another round of ethnic cleansing. Russia, fighting separatists in Chechnya, sympathized with Serbia's desire to retain control of the province. The result was a further decline in Russian trust for the United States, as the West ignored Russian protests and pursued its policy in Kosovo. Chinese suspicions of U.S. motives also grew, not least because of the bombing of the Chinese Embassy in Belgrade.

In the 1990s then, the United States maintained a primarily multilateral policy that strengthened Atlantic institutions and continued the cooperative patterns of the Cold War. U.S. relations with Russia and China worsened, however, and the United Nations was bypassed in crucial cases.

The Twenty-first Century

In the twenty-first century, U.S. policy has shifted dramatically from this post–Cold War pattern, highlighting its volatility and dependence on electoral outcomes and domestic politics. The administration of George W. Bush began by pursuing a policy of unilateral neglect and shifted to a policy of unilateral engagement. From its inception, it was averse to treaty-based cooperation and refused to enter new treaties, such as the Kyoto Accords on greenhouse gasses, while moving towards withdrawal from old ones, such as the Anti-Ballistic Missile Treaty. The administration's major security policy initiative was to move towards near-term deployment of a national missile defense, indicating again a preference for unilateral solutions to security problems over cooperative ones.[5]

After the terrorist attacks of September 11, 2001, the United States shifted to a policy of unilateral engagement. As I just discussed, the administration formally abandoned containment in favor of preventive war in the 2002 National Security Strategy. The United States would now attack potential threats before they could strike the United States, particularly states that were suspected of developing weapons of mass destruction or of having ties to terrorist groups. The invasions of Afghanistan and especially Iraq most clearly highlight the new trends in U.S. foreign policy. In the case of Afghanistan, the Taliban's harboring of Al Qaeda provided a rationale for war that was credible to other nations. The execution of the policy was basically unilateral, but the damage to international cooperation was limited and the United Nations and NATO were quickly brought in to lend support to the nation building effort.

The case of Iraq was much more controversial. The United States, with its high minimum trust threshold, favored preventive war while the Europeans and the rest of the world, with much lower minimum trust thresholds, favored a continuation of the inspections regime and deterrence (Gordon and Shapiro 2004). The United States made it clear that it would go it alone, but this failed to generate support and in the end the United States and Britain invaded Iraq without broader institutional backing. The result has been a serious weakening in international trust for the United States. This decline in trust has been exacerbated by the failure to discover any weapons of mass destruction or installations for their production, the hypothesized existence of which provided the rationale for attacking immediately rather than waiting.

The extent of the decline is revealed in international public opinion data. In a survey of global attitudes a year after the invasion of Iraq, the Pew Research Center for the People and the Press asked respondents, "As a consequence of the war, do you have more confidence or less confidence that the U.S. is trustworthy?"[6] The results are reported in Table 9.1. Overwhelming majorities in every country surveyed (aside from the United

---

[5] Steven Lee Myers and James Dao, "The President's Budget: Military Spending; Bush's Plans for the Pentagon Include Base Closings and Money for Missile Defenses," *New York Times*, February 27, 2001, A14.

[6] The Pew Research Center for the People and the Press, Pew Global Attitudes Project: Nine Nation Survey (March 2004).

TABLE 9.1
Is the U.S. More or Less Trustworthy after Iraq?

	More	Less	Same	Don't Know
United States	58%	29%	6%	7%
Great Britain	24%	58%	12%	6%
France	14%	78%	6%	2%
Germany	10%	82%	5%	3%
Russia	8%	63%	21%	8%
Turkey	8%	74%	11%	7%
Pakistan	5%	64%	7%	24%
Jordan	4%	50%	38%	8%
Morocco	12%	72%	7%	9%

Source: The Pew Research Center for the People and the Press, Pew Global Attitudes Project: Nine Nation Survey (March 2004).

States) have less confidence that the United States is trustworthy in the wake of the Iraq invasion. Even in Great Britain 58 percent have less confidence in U.S. trustworthiness, in Russia the figure is 63 percent, in Pakistan 64 percent, and in Germany, a country with some experience in matters of trust and reassurance, 82 percent have less confidence that the United States is trustworthy as a result of the war.

Other results from the survey are equally indicative of negative attitudes towards the United States. Great Britain is the only country surveyed in which a majority (58 percent) have a favorable opinion of the United States. In France only 37 percent are favorable, in Germany 38 percent, in Turkey 30 percent, in Pakistan 21 percent and in Jordan a mere 5 percent. Large majorities in every country are convinced that the United States takes little account of their interests in making decisions; even for the three NATO allies, the figures are 61 percent in Britain, 84 percent in France, and 69 percent in Germany. Majorities in every country but Britain and the United States believe that reducing terrorism is not the real goal behind the U.S. war against terrorism. Instead, majorities believe that the United States wishes to control Middle East oil and large percentages think the United States wishes to harm unfriendly Muslim governments and protect Israel. Most striking, in light of the Soviet experience in the Cold War, the percentage thinking that the United States wishes to "dominate the world" is 24 percent in Great Britain, 53 percent in France, 47 percent in Germany, 44 percent in Russia, 61 percent in Turkey, 55 percent in Pakistan, 61 percent in Jordan, and 60 percent in Morocco. This is approximately where U.S. public opinion about Russian motivations was in early to mid-1946, after the imposition of the iron curtain in Eastern Europe and around the time of the Iranian crisis.[7]

This decline in trust is one of the most serious problems the United States faces in its efforts to protect itself against terrorism. Those believing suicide bombings against Westerners in Iraq were justified ranged from 31 percent in Turkey, to 46 percent in Pakistan, 70 percent in Jordan, and 66 percent in Morocco. Even more chilling, 65 percent percent of Pakistanis expressed a favorable opinion of Osama bin Laden, along with 55 percent of Jordanians and 45% of Moroccans. This climate of opinion gives terrorists an ocean in which to swim, an ocean that cannot be entirely drained through force directed at easily vanquished states. The fate of the Taliban will naturally make most governments reluctant to openly embrace Al Qaeda and provide large scale training facilities and safe havens. But in the many grey areas of the world, where state sovereignty is limited, committed, well-funded and armed groups can thrive. An anti-American stance can give such groups a populist appeal that will attract money and recruits, and secure protection from sympathetic officials.

The United States therefore needs to understand and address the roots of this mistrust. The models of this book provide a starting point, but the topic requires much additional research on both theoretical and empirical problems. On the theoretical side, three avenues of advance seem especially important. First, the models presented here assume that state actions are automatically recognizable. Observers are not uncertain about who does what and what it means. This assumption is a simplification even in the Cold War case, and in the new world uncertainty about basic facts such as these is rampant. The proliferation of conspiracy theories about the causes of the 9/11 attacks are but one example. Models, therefore, need to incorporate uncertainty about who has done what as well as what motivations each player has.[8] Second, I have focused on games with limited numbers of actors, where the actors represent states. However, mistrust of the United States is a mass-level phenomenon and it needs to be studied using models featuring mass publics. The role of the media in transmitting and distorting information needs to be incorporated, as well as the role of governments and nongovernmental actors attempting to sway popular opinion for various purposes. Finally, the challenge of more fully integrating Bayesian

[7] Gallup 1972: 591.

[8] A starting point is the literature on the repeated Prisoner's Dilemma that incorporates uncertainty about whether the parties have cooperated or defected, e.g., Downs and Rocke 1990; Bendor et al. 1991.

theories of belief change with nonrationalist theories of preference, belief, and identity formation needs to be squarely faced. The common priors assumption behind most game theoretic models is extremely unrealistic in the context of global public opinion. Individuals interact with others who have radically different worldviews. Beliefs are influenced by many factors besides a rational assessment of observed facts. These factors need to be more carefully integrated with formal models, so that we lose as little rigor as possible while increasing the versimilitude and scope of application of the theory.

The structural features of the post-Cold War era indicate that U.S. foreign policy may become increasingly volatile and prone to interventions that raise world suspicions about U.S. motivations. If the United States is to counteract these suspicions, it will need to implement a policy of reassurance by taking actions that a more expansionist United States would reject. The Reassurance Game of chapter 7 suggests that reassurance is possible even between actors that deeply distrust each other. Further research will be needed to determine if the optimistic conclusions of that model hold in more complicated settings that better represent the post-Cold War period.

Bibliography

Abdelal, Rawi, Yoshiko Herrera, Alistair I. Johnston, and Rose McDermott. 2004. Identity as a Variable. Unpublished manuscript, Harvard University.

Acheson, Dean. 1969. *Present at the Creation: My Years in the State Department*. New York: Norton.

Adler, Emanuel, and Michael Barnett. 1998. *Security Communities*. Cambridge: Cambridge University Press.

Alan, Pierre, and Kjell Goldmann, eds. 1992. *The End of the Cold War*. Dordrecht: Martinus Nijhoff Publishers.

Allison, Graham T. 1988. Testing Gorbachev. *Foreign Affairs* 67 (1): 18–32.

Axelrod, Robert. 1984. *The Evolution of Cooperation*. New York: Basic Books.

Baker, James A., III, and Thomas M. Defrank. 1995. *The Politics of Diplomacy*. New York: G. P. Putnam's Sons.

Baliga, Sandeep, and Tomas Sjöström. 2001. Arms Races and Negotiations. *Review of Economic Studies* 71 (2): 351–69.

Bates, Robert H., Avner Grief, Margaret Levi, Jean-Laurent Rosenthal, and Barry R. Weingast. 1998. *Analytic Narratives*. Princeton: Princeton University Press.

Bayes, Thomas. 1958 [1763]. An essay towards solving a problem in the doctrine of chances. *Biometrika* 45: 293–315.

Baylis, John. 1984. Britain, the Brussels Pact and the Continental Committment. *International Affairs* 60 (4): 615–29.

———. 1993. *The Diplomacy of Pragmatism: Britain and the Formation of NATO, 1942–1949*. London: Macmillan.

Beissinger, Mark R. 2002. *Nationalist Mobilization and the Collapse of the Soviet State*. Cambridge: Cambridge University Press.

Békés, Csaba. 1988. Soviet Plans to Establish the COMINFORM in Early 1946: New Evidence from the Hungarian Archives. *Cold War International History Project Bulletin* 10: 135–36.

Bendor, Jonathan, Roderick M. Kramer, and Suzanne Stout. 1991. When in Doubt...: Cooperation in a Noisy Prisoner's Dilemma. *Journal of Conflict Resolution* 35 (4): 691–719.

Bennett, Andrew. 1999. *Condemned to Repetition? the Rise, Fall, and Reprise of Soviet-Russian Military Interventionism, 1973–1996*. Cambridge, Mass.: MIT Press.

Bennett, P. G., and M. R. Dando. 1982. The Arms Race as a Hypergame: A Study of Routes Towards a Safer World. *Futures* 14 (4): 293–306.

Bennett, P. G., and M. R. Dando. 1983. The Arms Race: Is It Just a Mistake? *New Scientist* February 17, 432–35.

Berle, Adolph A. 1973. *Navigating the Rapids 1918–1971*. New York: Harcourt Brace Jovanovich.

Bernstein, Barton J. 1974. The Quest for Security: American Foreign Policy and International Control of Atomic Energy, 1942–1946. *Journal of American History* 60 (4): 1003–44.

Beschloss, Michael R. and Strobe Talbott. 1993. *At the Highest Levels: The Inside Story of the End of the Cold War.* Boston: Little, Brown and Company.

Best, Richard A. 1986. *"Cooperation with Like-Minded Peoples": British Influences on American Security Policy, 1945–1949.* New York: Greenwood Press.

Bigley, Gregory A., and Jone L. Pearce. 1998. Straining for Shared Meaning in Organization Science: Problems of Trust and Mistrust. *Academy of Management Review* 23 (3): 405–21.

Birmingham, Robert L. 1969. The Prisoner's Dilemma and Mutual Trust: Comment. *Ethics* 79 (2): 156–58.

Bitzinger, Richard A. 1994. Gorbachev and GRIT, 1985–1989: Did Arms Control Succeed Because of Unilateral Actions or In Spite of Them? *Contemporary Security Policy* 15 (1): 68–79.

Blacker, Coit D. 1993. *Hostage to Revolution: Gorbachev and Soviet Security Policy, 1985–1991.* New York: Council on Foreign Relations Press.

Borhi, Laszlo G. 2000. The Merchants of the Kremlin: The Economic Roots of Soviet Expansion in Hungary. Cold War International History Project Working Paper No. 28, Washington, D.C.

Boyle, Peter G. 2000. The Cold War Revisited. *Journal of Contemporary History* 35 (3): 479–89.

Braithwaite, Valerie, and Margaret Levi, eds. 1998. *Trust and Governance.* New York: Russell Sage Foundation.

Braumoeller, Bear F. 2003. Perspectives on Pluralism. *PS: Political Science and Politics* 36 (3): 387–89.

Breslauer, George W., and Phillip E. Tetlock, eds. 1991. *Learning in U.S. and Soviet Foreign Policy.* Boulder: Westview Press.

Brooks, Stephen G. 1997. Dueling Realisms. *International Organization* 51 (3): 445–77.

Brooks, Stephen G., and William C. Wohlforth. 2000/01. Power, Globalization, and the End of the Cold War: Reevaluating a Landmark Case for Ideas. *International Security* 25 (3): 5–52.

———. 2002. From Old Thinking to New Thinking in Qualitative Research. *International Security* 26 (4): 93–111.

———. 2003. Economic Constraints and the End of the Cold War. In *Cold War Endgame: Oral History, Analysis, Debates,* edited by W. C. Wohlforth. University Park: Pennsylvania State University Press.

Brown, Archie. 1996. *The Gorbachev Factor.* Oxford: Oxford University Press.

Brown, Michael E., Owen R. Cote Jr., Steven E. Miller, and Sean M. Lynn-Jones, eds. 2000. *Rational Choice and Security Studies.* Cambridge, Mass.: MIT Press.

Brzezinski, Zbigniew. 1989. *The Grand Failure: The Birth and Death of Communism in the Twentieth Century.* New York: Charles Scribner's Sons.

Bueno de Mesquita, Bruce, and David Lalman. 1992. *War and Reason.* New Haven: Yale University Press.

Bueno de Mesquita, Bruce, James D. Morrow, Randolph M. Siverson, and Alastair Smith. 1999. An Institutional Explanation of the Democratic Peace. *American Political Science Review* 93 (4): 791–807.

Butterfield, Herbert. 1951. *History and Human Relations.* London: Collins.

Buzzanco, Robert. 1999. What Happend to the New Left? Toward a Radical Reading of American Foreign Relations. *Diplomatic History* 23 (4): 575–607.

Camerer, Colin F. 2003. *Behavioral Game Theory.* Princeton: Princeton University Press.

Cantril, Hadley. 1948. Opinion Trends in World War II: Some Guides to Interpretation. *Public Opinion Quarterly* 12 (1): 30–44.

Chafetz, Glenn R. 1993. *Gorbachev, Reform and the Breshnev Doctrine: Soviet Policy towards Eastern Europe, 1985–1990.* Westport, Conn.: Praeger.

Chan, Steve. 1997. In Search of the Democratic Peace: Problems and Promise. *Mershon International Studies Review* 41 (1): 59–91.

Checkel, Jeff. 1993. Ideas, Institutions, and the Gorbachev Foreign Policy Revolution. *World Politics* 45 (2): 271–300.

———. 1997. *Ideas and International Political Change.* New Haven: Yale University Press.

Chernyaev, Anatoly. 2000. *My Six Years with Gorbachev.* State College: Pennsylvania State University Press.

Chollet, Derek H., and James M. Goldgeier. 2003. Once Burned, Twice Shy? The Pause of 1989. In *Cold War Endgame: Oral History, Analysis, Debates,* edited by W. C. Wohlforth. University Park: Pennsylvania State University Press.

Chomsky, Noam. 1982. *Towards a New Cold War: Essays on the Current Crisis and How We Got There.* New York: Pantheon Books.

———. 1991. *Deterring Democracy.* New York: Hill and Wang.

Chuev, Felix. 1991. *Molotov Remembers: Inside Kremlin Politics.* Chicago: Ivan R. Dee.

Cohen, Eliot A. 1988. Toward Better Net Assessment: Rethinking the European Conventional Balance. *International Security* 13 (1): 50–89.

Coleman, James S. 1990. *Foundations of Social Theory.* Cambridge, Mass.: Belknap Press.

Collins, Alan. 1997. *The Security Dilemma and the End of the Cold War.* New York: St. Martin's Press.

———. 1998. GRIT, Gorbachev, and the End of the Cold War. *Review of International Studies* 24 (2): 201–20.

Conquest, Robert. 1987. *Harvest of Sorrow: Soviet Collectivization and the Terror Famine.* Oxford: Oxford University Press.

———. 1990. *The Great Terror: A Reassessment.* Oxford: Oxford University Press.

Conybeare, John A. C. 1984. Public Goods, Prisoners' Dilemmas and the International Political Economy. *Intenational Studies Quarterly* 28 (1): 5–22.

Copeland, Dale C. 1999–2000. Trade Expectations and the Outbreak of Peace: Detente 1970–74 and the End of the Cold War 1985–1991. *Security Studies* 9 (1/2): 15–58.

———. 2000. *The Origins of Major War.* Ithaca: Cornell University Press.

Cornes, Richard, and Todd Sandler. 1996. *The Theory of Externalities: Public Goods and Club Goods.* Cambridge: Cambridge University Press.

Cox, Michael. 1993. Radical Theory and the New Cold War. In *From Cold War to Collapse: Theory and World Politics in the 1980's,* edited by M. Bowker and R. Brown. Cambridge: Cambridge University Press.

Creswell, Michael. 2002. Between the Bear and the Phoenix: The United States and the European Defence Community. *Security Studies* 11 (4): 89–124.

Creswell, Michael, and Mark Trachtenberg. 2003. France and the German Question, 1945–1955. *Journal of Cold War Studies* 5 (3): 5–28.

Crossman, R.H.S., ed. 2001 [1950]. *The God That Failed.* New York: Columbia University Press.

Cumings, Bruce. 1981. *The Origins of the Korean War: Liberation and the Emergence of Seperate Regimes, 1945–1947.* 2 vols. Vol. 1. Princeton: Princeton University Press.

———. 1990. *The Origins of the Korean War: The Roaring of the Cataract, 1947–1950.* 2 vols. Vol. 2. Princeton: Princeton University Press.

———. 1992. The Wicked Witch of the West is Dead. Long Live the Wicked Witch of the East. In *The End of the Cold War: Its Meanings and Implications,* edited by M. J. Hogan. Cambridge: Cambridge University Press.

———. 1995. "Revising Postrevisionism," Or the Poverty of Theory in Diplomatic History. In *America in the World: The Historiography of American Foreign Relations Since 1941,* edited by M. J. Hogan. Cambridge: Cambridge University Press.

Daalder, Ivo H. 2000. *Getting to Dayton: The Making of America's Bosnia Policy.* Washington, D.C.: Brookings Institution Press.

Daalder, Ivo H., and Michael E. O'Hanlon. 2000. *Winning Ugly: NATO's War to Save Kosovo.* Washington, D.C.: Brookings Institution Press..

Dasgupta, Partha. 1988. Trust as a Commodity. In *Trust: Making and Breaking Cooperative Relations,* edited by Diego Gambetta. New York: Basil Blackwell.

de Figueiredo Jr., Rui J. P., and Barry R. Weingast. 1999. The Rationality of Fear: Political Opportunism and Ethnic Conflict. In *Civil Wars, Insecurity and Intervention,* edited by Barbara F. Walter and Jack Snyder. New York: Columbia University Press.

Dean, Jonathan, and Randall Watson Forsberg. 1992. CFE and Beyond: The Future of Conventional Arms Control. *International Security* 17 (1): 76–121.

Deighton, Anne. 1990. *The Impossible Peace.* Oxford: Clarendon Press.

DeLong, J. Bradford, and Barry Eichengreen. 1993. The Marshall Plan: History's Most Successful Structural Adjustment Program. In *Postwar Economic Reconstruction and Lessons for the East Today,* edited by R. Dornbusch, W. Nolling and R. Layard. Cambridge, Mass.: MIT Press.

Delzell, Charles F. 1956. Russian Power in Central-Eastern Europe. In *The Meaning of Yalta: Big Three Diplomacy and the New Balance of Power,* edited by J. L. Snell. Baton Rouge: Louisiana State University Press.

Deudney, Daniel, and G. John Ikenberry. 1991/92. The International Sources of Soviet Change. *International Security* 16 (3): 74–118.

———. 1999. Realism, Structural Liberalism, and the Western Order. In *Unipolar Politics: Realism and State Strategies After the Cold War,* edited by E. B. Kapstein and M. Mastanduno. New York: Columbia University Press.

Deutsch, Karl W., Sidney A. Burrell, Robert A. Kahn, Maruice Lee, Martin Lichterman, Raymond E. Lindgren, Francis L. Loewenheim, and Richard W. Van Wagenen. 1957. *Political Community in the North Atlantic Area: International Organization in the Light of Historical Experience*. Princeton: Princeton University Press.

Deutsch, Morton. 1958. Trust and Suspicion. *Journal of Conflict Resolution* 2 (4): 265–79.

Djilas, Milovan. 1962. *Conversations with Stalin*. New York, Harcourt Brace and World.

Dockrill, Saki. 1991. *Britain's Policy for West German Rearmament 1950–1955*. Cambridge: Cambridge University Press.

Downs, George W., and David M. Rocke. 1990. *Tacit Bargaining, Arms Races, and Arms Control*. Ann Arbor: University of Michigan Press.

Doyle, Michael. 1983a. Kant, Liberal Legacies and Foreign Affairs, part 1. *Philosophy and Public Affairs* 12 (3): 205–35.

———. 1983b. Kant, Liberal Legacies, and Foreign Affairs, part 2. *Philosophy and Public Affairs* 12 (4): 323–53.

Edelstein, David. 2000. Choosing Friends and Enemies: Perceptions of Intentions in International Politics. Ph.D. diss., University of Chicago.

———. 2002. Managing Uncertainty: Beliefs about Intentions and the Rise of Great Powers. *Security Studies* 12 (1): 1–40.

Eichengreen, Barry, ed. 1995. *Europe's Post War Recovery*. Cambridge: Cambridge University Press.

Eisenberg, Carolyn Woods. 1996. *Drawing the Line: The American Decision to Divide Germany, 1944-1949*. Cambridge: Cambridge University Press.

Elman, Colin, and Miriam Fendius Elman, eds. 2001. *Bridges and Boundaries: Historians, Political Scientists and the Study of International Relations*. Cambridge, Mass.: MIT Press.

English, Robert D. 2000. *Russia and the Idea of the West*. New York, Columbia University Press.

———. 2002. Power, Ideas, and New Evidence on the Cold War's End: A Reply to Brooks and Wohlforth. *International Security* 26 (4): 70–92.

———. 2003. The Road(s) Not Taken: Causality and Contingency in Analysis of the Cold War's End. In *Coldwar Endgame: Oral History, Analysis, Debates*, edited by W. C. Wohlforth. University Park: Pennsylvania State University Press.

Etzioni, Amitai. 1962. *The Hard Way to Peace: A New Strategy*. New York: Crowell-Collier Press.

Evangelista, Matthew. 1995. The Paradox of State Strength: Transnational Relations, Domestic Structures, and Security Policy in Russia and the Soviet Union. *International Organization* 49 (1): 1–38.

———. 1999. *Unarmed Forces: The Transnational Movement to End the Cold War*. Ithaca: Cornell University Press.

Falkenrath, Richard A. 1995. *Shaping Europe's Military Order: The Origins and Consequences of the CFE Treaty*. Cambridge, Mass.: MIT Press.

Farrell, Joseph, and Matthew Rabin. 1996. Cheap Talk. *Journal of Economic Perspectives* 10 (3): 103–18.

Fearon, James D. 1993. Threats to Use Force: Costly Signals and Bargaining in International Crises. Ph.D. diss., University of California, Berkeley.

———. 1994. Domestic Political Audiences and the Escalation of International Disputes. *American Political Science Review* 88 (3): 577–92.

———. 1995. Rationalist Explanations for War. *International Organization* 49 (3): 379–414.

———. 1998. Bargaining, Enforcement and International Cooperation. *International Organization* 52 (2): 269–305.

Feis, Herbert. 1957. *Churchill, Roosevelt, Stalin: The War they Waged and the Peace they Sought*. Princeton: Princeton University Press.

———. 1970. *From Trust to Terror: The Onset of the Cold War, 1945–1950*. New York: Norton.

Filitov, Aleksei M. 1996. Problems of Post-War Construction in Soviet Foreign Policy Conceptions during World War II. In *The Soviet Union and Europe in the Cold War 1943–53*, edited by F. Gori and S. Pons. New York: St. Martin's Press.

Folly, Martin H. 1988. Breaking the European Vicious Circle: Britain, The United States and The Genesis of The North Atlantic Treaty. *Diplomatic History* 12 (1): 59–77.

Forsberg, Tuomas. 1999. Power, Interests and Trust: Explaining Gorbachev's Choices at the End of the Cold War. *Review of International Studies* 25 (4): 605–21.

Frieden, Jeffry A. 1999. Actors and Preferences in International Relations. In *Strategic Choice and International Relations*, edited by D. A. Lake and R. Powell. Princeton: Princeton University Press.

Friedman, Jeffrey, ed. 1996. *The Rational Choice Controversy: Economic Models of Politics Reconsidered*. New Haven: Yale University Press.

Fukuyama, Francis. 1992. *The End of History and the Last Man*. New York: Avon.

———. 1995. *Trust: The Social Virtues and the Creation of Prosperity*. New York: Free Press.

———. 1999. *The Great Disruption: Human Nature and the Reconstitution of Social Order*. New York: Free Press.

Fursdon, Edward. 1980. *The European Defense Community: A History*. London: Macmillan Press Ltd.

Gaddis, John L. 1972. *The United States and the Origins of the Cold War: 1941–1947*. New York: Columbia University Press.

———. 1974. Was the Truman Doctrine A Real Turning Point? *Foreign Affairs* 52 (2): 386–402.

———. 1982. *Strategies of Containment: A Critical Appraisal of Postwar American National Security Policy*. Oxford: Oxford University Press.

———. 1983. The Emerging Post-Revisionist Synthesis on the Origins of the Cold War. *Diplomatic History* 7 (3): 171–204.

———. 1997. *We Now Know: Rethinking Cold War History*. Oxford: Clarendon Press.

Gallagher, John, and Ronald Robinson. 1953. The Imperialism of Free Trade. *Economic History Review* 6 (1): 1–15.

Gallup, George H. 1972. *The Gallup Poll: Public Opinion 1935–1971.* New York: Random House.

Gambetta, Diego, ed. 1988. *Trust: Making and Breaking Cooperative Relations.* New York: Basil Blackwell.

Gamson, William A., and Andre Modigliani. 1971. *Untangling the Cold War: A Strategy for Testing Rival Theories.* Boston: Little, Brown and Company.

Garthoff, Raymond L. 1994. *The Great Transition: American-Soviet Relations and the End of the Cold War.* Washington, D.C.: Brookings Institution.

Gati, Charles. 1986. *Hungary and the Soviet Bloc.* Durham, N.C.: Duke University Press.

———. 1990. *The Bloc that Failed: Soviet-East European Relations in Transition.* Bloomington: Indiana University Press.

Gibbons, Robert. 2001. Trust in Social Structures: Hobbes and Coase Meet Repeated Games. In *Trust in Society,* edited by K. S. Cook. New York: Russell Sage Foundation.

Gillingham, John. 1991. *Coal, Steel and the Rebirth of Europe, 1945–1955: The Germans and French from Ruhr Conflict to Economic Community.* Cambridge: Cambridge University Press.

Gilpin, Robert. 1981. *War and Change in World Politics.* Cambridge: Cambridge University Press.

Glaser, Charles L. 1992. Political Consequences of Military Strategy: Expanding and Refining the Spiral and Deterrence Models. *World Politics* 44 (4): 497–538.

———. 1994/95. Realists as Optimists: Cooperation as Self Help. *International Security* 19 (3): 50–90.

———. 1997. The Security Dilemma Revisited. *World Politics* 50 (1): 171–202.

———. 2002. Anarchy and Information. Manuscript, Irving B. Harris Graduate School of Public Policy Studies, University of Chicago.

Glaser, Charles L., and Chaim Kaufmann. 1998. What Is the Offense-Defense Balance and Can We Measure It? *International Security* 22 (4): 44–92.

Goldstein, Joshua S., and John R. Freeman. 1990. *Three-Way Street: Strategic Reciprocity in World Politics.* Chicago: University of Chicago Press.

Gordon, Philip, and Jeremy Shapiro. 2004. *Allies at War: America, Europe and the Crisis over Iraq.* Washington D.C: Brooking Institution Press.

Gowa, Joanne. 1989. Rational Hegemons, Excludable Goods, and Small Groups: An Epitaph for Hegemonic Stability Theory? *World Politics* 41: 307–24.

Green, Donald P., and Ian Shapiro. 1994. *Pathologies of Rational Choice Theory: A Critique of Applications in Political Science.* New Haven: Yale University Press.

Grey, Edward. 1925. *Twenty-Five Years, 1892–1916.* New York: Frederick A. Stokes.

Haas, Peter. 1992. Banning Chloroflourocarbons: Epistemic Community Efforts to Protect the Stratospheric Ozone. *International Organization* 46 (1): 187–224.

Harbutt, Fraser. 1981–82. American Challenge, Soviet Response: The Beginning of the Cold War, February-May 1946. *Political Science Quarterly* 96 (4): 623–39.

Hardin, Russell. 2002. *Trust and Trustworthiness.* New York: Russell Sage Foundation.

Held, Virginia. 1968. On the Meaning of Trust. *Ethics* 78 (2): 156–59.

Hempel, Carl G. 1966. *Philosophy of Natural Science.* Englewood Cliffs, N.J.: Prentice-Hall.

Herman, Robert G. 1996. Identity, Norms and National Security: The Soviet Foreign Policy Revolution and the End of the Cold War. In *The Culture of National Security: Norms Identity and World Politics,* edited by P. J. Katzenstein. New York: Columbia University Press.

Herz, John H. 1950. Idealist Internationalism and the Security Dilemma. *World Politics* 2 (2): 157–80.

Hess, Gary R. 1974. The Iranian Crisis of 1945-46 and the Cold War. *Political Science Quarterly* 89 (1): 117–46.

Hitchcock, William I. 1998. *France Restored: Cold War Diplomacy and the Quest for Leadership in Europe.* Chapel Hill: University of North Carolina Press.

Hixon, Walter L. 1997. *Parting the Curtain: Propaganda, Culture, and the Cold War, 1945–1961.* New York: St. Martin's Press.

Hobson, John Atkinson. 1988 [1902]. *Imperialism: A Study.* London: Unwin and Hyman.

Hobbes, Thomas. 1968 [1651]. *Leviathan.* London: Penguin.

Hoffman, Aaron M. 2002. A Conceptualization of Trust in International Relations. *European Journal of International Relations* 8 (3): 375–401.

Hogan, Michael J. 1987. *The Marshall Plan: America, Britain, and the Reconstruction of Western Europe, 1947–1952.* Cambridge: Cambridge University Press.

Hogan, Michael J., ed. 1992. *The End of the Cold War: Its Meaning and Implications.* Cambridge: Cambridge University Press.

Holloway, David. 1994. *Stalin and the Bomb.* New Haven: Yale University Press.

Hopf, Ted. 2002. *Social Construction of International Politics: Identities and Foreign Policies, Moscow, 1955 and 1999.* Ithaca: Cornell University Press.

Hurwitz, Jon, and Mark Peffley. 1990. Public Images of the Soviet Union: The Impact of Foreign Policy Attitudes. *Journal of Politics* 52 (1): 3–28.

Hwang, Peter, and Willem P. Burgers. 1999. Apprehension and Temptation: The Forces Against Cooperation. *Journal of Conflict Resolution* 43 (1): 117–30.

Ikenberry, G. John. 2001. *After Victory: Institutions, Strategic Restraint, and the Rebuilding of Order after Major Wars.* Princeton: Princeton University Press.

Ireland, Timothy. P. 1981. *Creating the Entangling Alliance: The Origins of the North Atlantic Treaty Organization.* Westport, Conn.: Greenwood Press.

Jervis, Robert. 1970. *The Logic of Images in International Relations.* New York: Columbia University Press.

———. 1976. *Perception and Misperception in International Politics.* Princeton: Princeton University Press.

———. 1978. Cooperation under the Security Dilemma. *World Politics* 30 (2): 167–214.

———. 1980. *The Impact of the Korean War on the Cold War. Journal of Conflict Resolution* 24 (4): 563–92.

———. 1993. The End of the Cold War on the Cold War? *Diplomatic History* 17 (4): 651–60.

————. 2001. Was the Cold War a Security Dilemma? *Journal of Cold War Studies* 3 (1): 36–60.

Jones, Howard, and Randall B. Woods. 1993. The Origins of the Cold War in Europe and the Near East: Recent Historiography and the National Security Imperative. *Diplomatic History* 17 (2): 251–76.

Kagan, Donald. 1989. *The Outbreak of the Peloponnesian War.* Ithaca: Cornell University Press.

Kaiser, Robert G. 1992. *Why Gorbachev Happened: His Triumphs, His Failure and His Fall.* New York: Simon and Schuster.

Kaldor, Mary. 1990. *The Imaginary War: Understanding the East-West Conflict.* Oxford: Basil Blackwell.

Kant, Immanuel. 1991. *Political Writings.* Cambridge: Cambridge University Press.

Karber, Phillip A., and Jerald A. Combs. 1998. The United States, NATO and the Soviet Threat to Western Europe: Military Estimates and Policy Options, 1945–1963. *Diplomatic History* 22 (3): 399–429.

Karklins, Rasma, and Roger Peterson. 1993. Decision Calculus of Protesters and Regimes: Eastern Europe 1989. *Journal of Politics* 55 (3): 588–614.

Kavka, Gregory S. 1986. *Hobbesian Moral and Political Theory.* Princeton: Princeton University Press.

Kelman, Herbert C. 1985. Overcoming the Psychological Barrier: An Analysis of the Egyptian-Israeli Peace Process. *Negotiation Journal* 1 (3): 213–35.

Kennan, George F. 1947. The Sources of Soviet Conduct. *Foreign Affairs* 25 (4): 566–82.

Keohane, Robert. 1984. *After Hegemony.* Princeton: Princeton University Press.

————. 1986. Reciprocity in International Relations. *International Organization* 40 (1): 1–27.

Keohane, Robert O., and Lisa L. Martin. 1995. The Promise of Institutionalist Theory. *International Security* 20 (1): 39–51.

Kindleberger, Charles. 1973. *The World in Depression, 1929–1939.* Berkeley: University of California Press.

King, Gary. 1989. *Unifying Political Methodology: the Likelihood Theory of Statistical Inference.* Cambridge: Cambridge University Press.

King, Gary, Robert O. Keohane, and Sidney Verba. 1994. *Designing Social Inquiry: Scientific Inference in Qualitative Research.* Princeton: Princeton University Press.

Kirkpatrick, Jeanne J. 1990. *The Withering Away of the Totalitarian State . . . and Other Surprises.* Washington, D.C.: AEI Press.

Kolko, Joyce, and Gabriel Kolko. 1972. *The Limits of Power: The World and United States Foreign Policy, 1945–1954.* New York: Harper and Row.

Kollock, Peter. 1994. The Emergence of Exchange Structures: An Experimental Study of Uncertainty, Committment and Trust. *American Journal of Sociology* 100 (2): 313–45.

Kort, Michael. 1998. *The Columbia Guide to the Cold War.* New York: Columbia University Press.

Koslowski, Rey, and Friedrich V. Kratochwil. 1994. Understandinng Change in International Politics: The Soviet Empire's Demise and the International System. *International Organization* 48 (2): 215–47.

Kramer, Mark. 1999. Ideology and the Cold War. *Review of International Studies* 25: 539–76.

Krasner, Stephen D. 1976. State Power and the Structure of International Trade. *World Politics* 28 (3): 317–47.

———., ed. 1983. *International Regimes*. Ithaca: Cornell University Press.

Krauthammer, Charles. 1990/91. The Unipolar Moment. *Foreign Affairs* 70 (1): 23–33.

Kreps, David M., Paul Milgrom, John Roberts, and Robert Wilson. 1982. Rational Cooperation in the Finitely Repeated Prisoner's Dilemma. *Journal of Economic Theory* 27 (2): 245–52.

Kreps, David M., and Robert Wilson. 1982. Reputation and Imperfect Information. *Journal of Economic Theory* 27 (2): 253–79.

Kreps, David M. 1990. *Game Theory and Economic Modelling*. Oxford: Clarendon Press.

Krock, Arthur. 1968. *Memoirs: Sixty Years on the Firing Line*. New York: Funk and Wagnalls.

Kuhns, Woodrow J., ed. 1997. *Assessing the Soviet Threat: The Early Cold War Years*. Washington, D.C.: CIA,: Center for the Study of Intelligence.

Kull, Steven. 1992. *Burying Lenin: The Revolution in Soviet Ideology and Foreign Policy*. Boulder, Colo.: Westview Press.

Kuniholm, Bruce R. 1980. *The Origins of the Cold War in the Near East: Great Power Conflict and Diplomacy in Iran, Turkey and Greece*. Princeton: Princeton University Press.

Kuran, Timur. 1991. Now out of Never: The Element of Surprise in Eastern European Revolution of 1989. *World Politics* 44 (1): 7–48.

Kydd, Andrew. 1997a. Game Theory and the Spiral Model. *World Politics* 49 (3): 371–400.

———. 1997b. Sheep in Sheep's Clothing: Why Security Seekers Do Not Fight Each Other. *Security Studies* 7 (1): 114–55.

———. 2000a. Arms Races and Arms Control: Modeling the Hawk Perspective. *American Journal of Political Science* 44 (2): 222–38.

———. 2000b. Trust, Reasurance and Cooperation. *International Organization* 54 (2): 325–57.

———. 2000c. Overcoming Mistrust. *Rationality and Society* 12 (4): 397–424.

———. 2001. Trust Building, Trust Breaking: The Dilemma of NATO Enlargement. *International Organization* 55 (4): 801–28.

Labs, Eric J. 1997. Beyond Victory: Offensive Realism and the Expansion of War Aims. *Security Studies* 6 (4): 1–49.

LaFeber, Walter. 1992. An End to Which Cold War? In *The End of the Cold War: Its Meanings and Implications,* edited by M. J. Hogan. Cambridge: Cambridge University Press.

LaFeber, Walter. 1997. *America, Russia and the Cold War*. New York: McGraw-Hill.

Laitin, David D. 1993. The Game Theory of Language Regimes. *International Political Science Review* 14 (3): 227–39.

———. 1994. The Tower of Babel as a Coordination Game: Political Linguistics in Ghana. *American Political Science Review* 88 (3): 622–34.

Lake, David A. 1993. Leadership, Hegemony and the International Economy: Naked Emperor or Tatterd Monarch with Potential? *International Studies Quarterly* 37 (4): 459–89.

———. 1999. Ulysses's Triumph: American Power and the New World Order. *Security Studies* 8 (4): 44–78.

———. 2001. Beyond Anarchy: The Importance of Security Institutions. *Intenational Security* 26 (1): 129–60.

Lake, David A., and Robert Powell, eds. 1999. *Strategic Choice and International Relations.* Princeton: Princeton University Press.

Large, David Clay. 1996. *Germans to the Front: West German Rearmament in the Adenauer Era.* Chapel Hill: University of North Carolina Press.

Larson, Deborah Welch. 1985. *Origins of Containment A Psychological Explanation.* Princeton: Princeton University Press.

———. 1987. Crisis Prevention and the Austrian State Treaty. *International Organization* 41(1): 27–60.

———. 1991. Bandwagon Images in American Foreign Policy: Myth or Reality? In *Dominoes and Bandwagons: Strategic Beliefs and Great Power Competition in the Eurasian Rimland,* edited by R. Jervis and J. Snyder. Oxford: Oxford University Press.

———. 1997. *Anatomy of Mistrust: U.S.-Soviet Relations During the Cold War.* Ithaca: Cornell University Press.

Lawson, Fred H. 1989. The Iranian Crisis of 1945-1946 and the Spiral Model of International Conflict. *International Journal of Middle East Studies* 21: 307–26.

Layne, Christopher. 1993. The Unipolar Illusion: Why New Great Powers Will Rise. *International Security* 17 (4): 5–51.

Lebow, Richard Ned, and Janice Gross Stein. 1994. *We All Lost the Cold War.* Princeton: Princeton University Press.

Lebow, Richard Ned, and Thomas Risse-Kappen, eds. 1995. *International Relations Theory and the End of the Cold War.* New York: Columbia University Press.

Leffler, Melvyn P. 1985. Strategy, Diplomacy, and the Cold War: The United States, Turkey, and NATO, 1945–1950. *Journal of American History* 71 (4): 807–25.

Leffler, Melvyn P. 1986. Adherence to Agreements: Yalta and the Experiences of the Early Cold War. *International Security* 11 (1): 88–123.

———. 1992. *A Preponderance of Power: National Security, the Truman Administration and the Cold War.* Stanford, Calif.: Stanford University Press.

———. 1999. The Cold War: What Do "We Now Know"? *American Historical Review* 104 (2): 501–24.

Legro, Jeffrey W. 1996. Culture and Preferences in the International Cooperation Two Step. *American Political Science Review* 90 (1): 118–37.

Legro, Jeffrey W., and Andrew Moravcsik. 1999. Is Anybody Still a Realist? *International Security* 24 (2): 5–55.

Lemke, Douglas, and William Reed. 2001. The Relevance of Politically Relevant Dyads. *Journal of Conflict Resolution* 45 (1): 126–44.

Lenin, Vladimir Il'ich. 1996 [1916]. *Imperialism: the Highest Stage of Capitalism.* London: Pluto Press.

Levesque, Jacques. 1997. *The Enigma of 1989: The USSR and the Liberation of Eastern Europe.* Berkeley: University of California Press.

———. 2001. Soviet Approaches to Eastern Europe at the Beginning of 1989. *Cold War International History Project Bulletin* (12/13): 49–72.

Levy, Jack S. 1984. The Offensive/Defensive Balance of Military Technology: A Theoretical and Historical Analysis. *International Studies Quarterly* 28 (2): 219–38.

———. 1988. Declining Power and the Preventive Motivation for War. *World Politics* 40(1): 82–107.

———. 1994. Learning and Foreign Policy: Sweeping a Conceptual Minefield. *International Organization* 48 (2): 279–312.

———. 2001. Explaining Events and Developing Theories: History, Political Science, and the Analysis of International Relations. In *Bridges and Boundaries: Historians, Political Scientists, and the Study of International Relations,* edited by C. Elman and M. F. Elman. Cambridge, Mass.: MIT Press.

Lewis, Jeffrey B., and Kenneth A. Schultz. 2003. Revealing Preferenecs: Empirical Estimation of a Crisis Bargaining Game with Incomplete Information. *Political Analysis* 11 (4): 345–67.

Lindskold, Sven. 1978. Trust Development, the GRIT Proposal, and the Effects of Conciliatory Acts on Conflict and Cooperation. *Psychological Bulletin* 85 (4): 772–93.

Lipson, Charles. 1984. International Cooperation in Economic and Security Affairs. *World Politics* 37 (1): 1–23.

Lovett, A. W. 1996. The United States and the Schuman Plan. A Study in French Diplomacy 1950–1952. *The Historical Journal* 39 (2): 425–55.

Luard, Evan. 1982. *A History of the United Nations.* Vol. 1, *The Years of Western Domination, 1945–1955.* New York: St. Martin's Press.

Luhmann, Niklas. 1979. *Trust and Power.* New York: John Wiley and Sons.

Lundestad, Geir. 1990. *The American "Empire" and Other Studies of US Foreign Policy in a Comparative Perspective.* Oxford: Oxford University Press.

Lynn-Jones, Sean M. 1995. Offense Defense Theory and Its Critics. *Security Studies* 4 (4): 660–91.

Macdonald, Douglas J. 1995/96. Communist Bloc Expansion in the Early Cold War: Challenging Realism, Refuting Revisionism. *International Security* 20 (3): 152–88.

Mark, Eduard. 1979. Charles E. Bohlen and the Acceptable Limits of Soviet Hegemony in Eastern Europe: A Memorandum of 18 October 1945. *Diplomatic History* 3 (2): 201–13.

———. 1981. American Policy Toward Eastern Europe and the Origins of the Cold War, 1941–1946: An Alternative Explanation. *Journal of American History* 68 (2): 313–36.

────. 1989. October or Thermidor? Interpretations of Stalinism and the Perception of Soviet Foreign Policy in the United States, 1927-1947. *American Historical Review* 94 (4): 937–62.

────. 1997. The War Scare of 1946 and its Consequences. *Diplomatic History* 21 (3): 383–415.

────. 2001. Revolution by Degrees: Stalin's National-Front Strategy for Europe, 1941–1947. Cold War International History Project Working Paper Series No. 31.

Martin, Andrew D., and Kevin M. Quinn. 2001. Bayesian Learning about Ideal Points of Supreme Court Justices, 1953–1999. University of Washington. Unpublished manuscript.

Mastny, Vojtech. 1979. *Russia's Road to the Cold War.* New York: Columbia University Press.

────. 1996. *The Cold War and Soviet Insecurity: The Stalin Years.* Oxford: Oxford University Press.

Matlock, Jr., Jack F. 1995. *Autopsy on an Empire.* New York: Random House.

Mau, Vladimir. 1996. *The Political History of Economic Reform in Russia, 1985–1994.* London: Center for Research into Communist Economies.

Mawby, Spencer. 1999. *Containing Germany: Britain and the Arming of the Federal Republic.* New York: St. Martin's Press.

McAllister, James. 2002. *No Exit: America and the German Problem, 1943–1954.* Ithaca: Cornell University Press.

Mearsheimer, John J. 1982. Why the Soviets Can't Win Quickly in Central Europe. *International Security* 7(1): 3–39.

────. 1990. Back to the Future: Instability in Europe after the Cold War. *International Security* 15 (1): 5–56.

────. 1994/5. The False Promise of International Institutions. *International Security* 19 (3): 5–49.

────. 2001. *The Tragedy of Great Power Politics.* New York: Norton.

Mendelson, Sarah E. 1993. Internal Battles and External Wars: Politics, Learning, and the Soviet Withdrawal from Afghanistan. *World Politics* 45 (3): 327–60.

────. 1998. *Changing Course: Ideas, Politics, and the Soviet Withdrawal from Afghanistan.* Princeton: Princeton University Press.

Mercer, Jonathan. 1995. Anarchy and Identity. *International Organization* 49 (2): 229–52.

Messer, Robert L. 1982. *The End of an Alliance: James F. Byrnes, Roosevelt, Truman, and the Origins of the Cold War.* Chapel Hill: University of North Carolina Press.

Midford, Paul. 2002. The Logic of Reassurance in Japan's Grand Strategy. *Security Studies* 11 (3): 1–43.

Milgrom, Paul, and John Roberts. 1994. Comparing Equilibria. *American Economic Review* 84 (3): 441–59.

Mills, C. Wright. 1958. *The Causes of World War Three.* New York: Simon and Schuster.

Milner, Helen. 1991. The Assumption of Anarchy in International Relations Theory: A Critique. *Review of International Studies* 17: 67–85.

Milward, Alan S. 1984. *The Reconstruction of Western Europe: 1945–1951*. Berkeley: University of California Press.

Mitchell, Christopher. 2000. *Gestures of Conciliation: Factors Contributing to Successful Olive Branches*. New York: St. Martin's Press.

Moravcsik, Andrew. 1997. Taking Preferences Seriously: A Liberal Theory of International Politics. *International Organization* 4 (7): 513–53.

Morris, Stephen, and Hyun Song Shin. 1998. Unique Equilibrium in a Model of Self-Fulfilling Currency Attacks. *American Economic Review* 88 (3): 587–97.

———. 2003. Global Games: Theory and Applications. In *Advances in Economics and Econometrics (Proceedings of the Eighth World Congress of the Econometric Society)*, edited by M. Dewatripont L. Hansen and S. Turnovsky. Cambridge: Cambridge University Press.

Morrow, James D. 1994a. Modeling the Forms of International Cooperation: Distribution vs. Information. *International Organization* 48 (3): 387–423.

———. 1994b. *Game Theory for Political Scientists*. Princeton: Princeton University Press.

Murray, Shoon Kathleen. 1996. *Anchors Against Change: American Opinion Leaders' Beliefs after the Cold War*. Ann Arbor: University of Michigan Press.

Naimark, Norman, and Leonid Gibianskii. 1997. Introduction to *The Establishment of Communist Regimes in Eastern Europe, 1944–1949*, edited by N. Naimark and L. Gibianskii. Boulder, Colo.: Westview Press.

Nation, R. Craig. 1992. *Black Earth, Red Star: A History of Soviet Security Policy, 1917–1991*. Ithaca: Cornell University Press.

Neumann, Iver B. 1996. *Russia and the Idea of Europe*. London: Routledge.

Niou, Emerson M. S., Peter C. Ordeshook and Gregory F. Rose. 1989. *The Balance of Power: Stability in International Systems*. Cambridge: Cambridge University Press.

Oberdorfer, Don. 1991. *The Turn: From the Cold War to a New Era 1983–1990*. New York: Poseidon Press.

Olson, Mancur. 1965. *The Logic of Collective Action*. Cambridge, Mass.: Harvard University Press.

Olson, Mancur, and Richard Zeckhauser. 1966. An Economic Theory of Alliances. *Review of Economics and Statistics* 48 (3): 266–79.

Oneal, John R., and Bruce M. Russett. 1997. The Classical Liberals Were Right: Democracy, Interdependence and Conflict: 1950–1985. *International Studies Quarterly* 41 (2): 267–93.

Osborne, Martin J. 2004. *An Introduction to Game Theory*. Oxford: Oxford University Press.

Osgood, Charles. 1962. *An Alternative to War or Surrender*. Urbana: University of Illinois Press.

Ostermann, Christian F. 1998. "This is not a Politburo, but a Madhouse" The Post-Stalin Succession Struggle, Soviet *Deutschlandpolitik* and the SED: New Evidence from Russian, German and Hungarian Archives. *Cold War International History Project Bulletin* 10: 61–110.

Ostrom, Elinor, and James Walker, eds. 2003. *Trust and Reciprocity: Interdisciplinary lessons from Experimental Research*, New York: Russell Sage Foundation.

Oye, Kenneth A. 1986. Explaining Cooperation Under Anarchy: Hypotheses and Strategies. In *Cooperation Under Anarchy*, edited by Kenneth A. Oye. Princeton: Princeton University Press.

―――. 1995. Explaining the End of the Cold War: Morphological and Behavioral Adaptations to the Nuclear Peace? In *International Relations Theory and the End of the Cold War*, edited by R. N. Lebow and T. Risse-Kappen. New York: Columbia University Press.

Pahre, Robert. 1999. *Leading Questions: How Hegemony Affects the International Political Economy*. Ann Arbor: University of Michigan Press.

Parks, Craig D., Robert F. Henager, and Shawn D. Scamahorn. 1996. Trust and Reactions to Messages of Intent in Social Dilemmas. *Journal of Conflict Resolution* 40 (1): 134–51.

Parrish, Scott D., and Mikhail M. Narinsky. 1994. New Evidence on the Soviet Rejection of the Marshall Plan, 1947: Two Reports. Cold War International History Project Working Paper 9. Washington, D.C.

Pechatnov, Vladimir O. 1995. The Big Three After World War II: New Documents on Soviet Thinking about Post War Relations with the United States and Great Britain. Cold War International History Project Working Paper No. 13. Washington, D.C.

―――. 1999. "The Allies are Pressing on you to Break your Will . . . " Foreign Policy Correspondance between Stalin and Molotov And Other Politburo Members, September 1945–December 1946. Cold War International History Project Working Paper No. 26. Washington, D.C.

Peffley, Mark, and Jon Hurwitz. 1992. International Events and Foreign Policy Beliefs: Public Response to Changing Soviet-U.S. Relations. *American Journal of Political Science* 36 (2): 431–61.

Plous, S. 1985. Perceptual Illusions and Military Realities. *Journal of Conflict Resolution* 29(3): 363–89.

―――. 1987. Perceptual Illusions and Military Realities: Results from a Computer-Simulated Arms Race. *Journal of Conflict Resolution* 31(1): 5–33.

―――. 1988. Modeling the Nuclear Arms Race as a Perceptual Dilemma. *Philosophy and Public Affairs* 17(1): 44–53.

―――. 1993. The Nuclear Arms Race: Prisoner's Dilemma or Perceptual Dilemma? *Journal of Peace Research* 30(2): 163–79.

Poiger, Uta G. 1996. Rock 'n' Roll, Female Sexuality and the Cold War Battle over German Identities. *Journal of Modern History* 68 (3): 577–616.

Pollard, Robert A. 1985. *Economic Security and the Origins of the Cold War, 1945–1950*. New York: Columbia University Press.

Poole, Keith T., and Howard Rosenthal. 1997. *Congress: A Political-Economic History of Roll Call Voting*. Oxford: Oxford University Press.

Posen, Barry R. 1984a. Measuring the European Conventional Balance: Coping with Complexity in Threat Assessment. *International Security* 9(3): 47–88.

―――. 1984b. *The Sources of Military Doctrine: France, Britain and Germany between the Wars*. Ithaca: Cornell University Press.

―――. 2003. Command of the Commons: The Military Foundation of U.S. Hegemony. *Intenational Security* 28 (1): 5–46.

Powell, Charles. 1992. What the PM Learnt About the Germans. In *When the Wall Came Down: Reactions to German Unification,* edited by H. James and M. Stone. New York: Routledge.

Powell, Robert. 1990. *Nuclear Deterrence Theory: The Problem of Credibility.* Cambridge: Cambridge University Press.

———. 1993. Guns, Butter, Anarchy. *American Political Science Review* 87(1): 115–32.

———. 1999. *In the Shadow of Power.* Princeton: Princeton University Press.

———. 2002. Game Theory, International Relations Theory, and the Hobbesian Stylization. In *Political Science: The State of the Discipline,* edited by I. Katznelson and H. Milner. New York: W. W. Norton.

Quester, George H. 1977. *Offense and Defense in the International System.* New York: John Wiley and Sons.

Raack, R. C. 1995. *Stalin's Drive to the West 1938–1945.* Stanford: Stanford University Press.

Ralph, Jason. 1999. Security Dilemmas and the End of the Cold War. *Review of International Studies* 25 (4): 721–25.

Ray, James Lee, Donald J. Puchala, and Charles W. Kegley Jr., eds. 1998. *Democracy and International Conflict: An Evaluation of the Democratic Peace Proposition.* Columbia: University of South Carolina Press.

Reagan, Ronald. 1990. *An American Life.* New York: Simon and Schuster.

Reiter, Dan. 1995. Exploding the Powder Keg Myth: Preemptive Wars Almost Never Happen. *International Security* 20(2): 5–34.

Richman, Alvin. 1991. Changing American Attitudes Towards the Soviet Union. *Public Opinion Quarterly* 55 (1): 135–48.

Richter, James. 1993. Re-examining Soviet Policy Towards Germany in 1953. *Europe-Asia Studies* 45 (4): 671–91.

Riley, John G. 2001. Silver Signals: Twenty-Five Years of Screening and Signaling. *Journal of Economic Literature* 39: 432–78.

Ripsman, Norrin M. 2000/2001. The Curious Case of German Rearmament: Democracy, Structural Autonomy, and Foreign Security Policy. *Security Studies* 10 (2): 1–48.

Risse-Kappen, Thomas. 1991. Did "Peace Through Strength" End the Cold War? Lessons From INF. *International Security* 16 (1): 162–88.

———. 1994. Ideas do Not Float Freely: Transnational Coalitions, Domestic Structures and the End of the Cold War. *International Organization* 48 (2): 185–214.

———. ed. 1995a. *Bringing Transnational Relations Back In: Non-State Actors, Domestic Structures and International Institutions.* Cambridge: Cambridge University Press.

———. 1995b. *Cooperation Among Democracies.* Princeton: Princeton University Press.

Risse, Thomas. 1997. The Cold War's Endgame and German Unification. *International Security* 21 (4): 159–85.

Roberts, Geoffrey. 2002. Litvinov's Lost Peace, 1941–1946. *Journal of Cold War Studies* 4 (2): 23–54.

Rose, Gideon. 1998. Neoclassical Realism and Theories of Foreign Policy. *World Politics* 51 (1): 144–72.

Rosen, Stephen Peter. 2003. An Empire, If You Can Keep It. *The National Interest* 71 (1): 51–61.

Ruane, Kevin. 2000. *The Rise and Fall of the European Defence Community: Anglo-American Relations and the Crisis of European Defence, 1950–55.* New York: St. Martin's Press.

Ruggie, John Gerard. 1998. What Makes the World Hang Together? Neo-Utilitarianism and the Social Constructivist Challenge. *International Organization* 52 (4): 855–85.

Rummel, Rudolph J. 1983. Libertarianism and International Violence. *Journal of Conflict Resolution* 27 (1): 27–71.

Russett, Bruce. 1993. *Grasping the Democratic Peace.* Princeton: Princeton University Press.

Ryback, Timothy W. 1990. *Rock Around the Bloc: A History of Rock Music in Eastern Europe and the Soviet Union.* Oxford: Oxford University Press.

Sagan, Scott D. 1994. The Perils of Proliferation: Organization Theory, Deterrence Theory and the Spread of Nuclear Weapons. *International Security* 18(4): 66–107.

Sandler, Todd, and Keith Hartley. 2001. Economics of Alliances: The Lessons for Collective Action. *Journal of Economic Literature* 39 (3): 869–96.

Sartori, Ann E. 2002. The Might of the Pen: A Reputational Theory of Communication in International Disputes. *International Organization* 56 (1): 121–49.

Schelling, Thomas C. 1960. *The Strategy of Conflict.* Cambridge: Harvard University Press.

———. 1978. *Micromotives and Macrobehavior.* New York: W. W. Norton.

Schelling, Thomas C., and Morton H. Halperin. 1961. *Strategy and Arms Control.* New York: Twentieth Century Fund.

Schimmelfennig, Frank. 1998/99. NATO Enlargement: A Constructivist Explanation. *Security Studies* 8 (2/3): 198–234.

———. 2001. The Community Trap: Liberal Norms, Rhetorical Action, and the Eastern Enlargement of the European Union. *International Organization* 55 (1): 47–80.

Schultz, Kenneth A. 2001. *Democracy and Coercive Diplomacy.* Cambridge: Cambridge University Press.

———. 2004. A Learning Model of Cooperation and Conflict. Stanford University. Unpublished manuscript.

Schwartz, Thomas. 1991. *America's Germany: John J. McCloy and the Federal Republic of Germany.* Cambridge, Mass.: Harvard University Press.

Schweller, Randall L. 1992. Domestic Structure and Preventive War: Are Democracies More Pacific? *World Politics* 44 (2): 235–69.

———. 1994. Bandwagoning for Profit: Bringing the Revisionist State Back In. *International Security* 19 (1): 72–107.

———. 1996. Neorealism's Status Quo Bias: What Security Dilemma? *Security Studies* 5 (3): 90–121.

————. 1998. *Deadly Imbalances: Tripolarity and Hitler's Strategy of World Conquest.* New York: Columbia University Press.

Schweller, Randall L., and William C. Wohlforth. 2000. Power Test: Evaluating Realism in Response to the End of the Cold War. *Security Studies* 9 (3): 60–107.

Shaw, Tony. 2001. The Politics of Cold War Culture. *Journal of Cold War Studies* 3 (3): 59–76.

Sheetz, Mark S. 1999. Exit Strategies: American Grand Designs for Postwar European Security. *Security Studies* 8 (4): 1–43.

Shultz, George. 1993. *Turmoil and Triumph: My Years as Secretary of State.* New York: Charles Scribner's Sons.

Seligman, Adam B. 1997. *The Problem of Trust.* Princeton: Princeton University Press.

Sigelman, Lee. 1990. Disarming the Opposition: The President, the Public, and the INF Treaty. *Public Opinion Quarterly* 54 (1): 37–47.

Signorino, Curtis S. 1999. Strategic Interaction and the Statistical Analysis of International Conflict. *American Political Science Review* 93 (2): 279–97.

————. 2003. Structure and Uncertainty in Discrete Choice Models. *Political Analysis* 11: 316–44.

Silberberg, Eugene. 1990. *The Structure of Economics: A Mathematical Analysis.* 2nd ed. New York: McGraw-Hill.

Snell, John L., ed. 1956. *The Meaning of Yalta: Big Three Diplomacy and the New Balance of Power.* Baton Rouge: Louisiana State University Press.

Snidal, Duncan. 1985. The Limits of Hegemonic Stability Theory. *International Organization* 39 (4): 579–614.

————. 1986. The Game Theory of International Politics. In *Cooperation Under Anarchy.* edited by K. A. Oye. Princeton: Princeton University Press.

————. 1991. Relative Gains and the Pattern of International Cooperation. *American Political Science Review* 85 (3): 701–26.

Snyder, Glen H. 1971. "Prisoner's Dilemma" and "Chicken" Models in International Politics. *International Studies Quarterly* 15 (1): 66–103.

————. 1984. The Security Dilemma in Alliance Politics. *World Politics* 36 (4): 461–95.

Snyder, Jack. 1984. *The Ideology of the Offensive: Military Decisionmaking and the Disasters of 1914.* Ithaca: Cornell University Press.

————. 1991. *Myths of Empire.* Ithaca: Cornell University Press.

————. 2003. Imperial Temptations. *The National Interest* 71 (1): 29–40.

Spence, A. M. 1973. Job Market Signaling. *Quarterly Journal of Economics* 87(3): 355–74.

Spirtas, Michael. 1996. A House Divided: Tragedy and Evil in Realist Theory. *Security Studies* 5 (3): 385–423.

Sprinz, Detlef, and Yael Wolinsky, eds. 2004. *Models, Numbers, and Cases: Methods for Studying International Relations.* Ann Arbor: University of Michigan Press.

Stein, Janice G. 1991. Reassurance in International Conflict Management. *Political Science Quarterly* 106 (3): 431–51.

Steininger, Rolf. 1990. *The German Question: The Stalin Note of 1952 and the Problem of Reunification.* New York: Columbia University Press.

Stent, Angela E. 1999. *Russia and Germany Reborn: Unification, the Soviet Collapse, and the New Europe*. Princeton: Princeton University Press.

Stone, Randall W. 1996. *Satellites and Commissars: Strategy and Conflict in the Politics of Soviet-Bloc Trade*. Princeton: Princeton University Press.

Summy, Ralph, and Michael E. Salla, eds. 1995. *Why the Cold War Ended: A Range of Interpretations*. Westport, Conn.: Greenwood Press.

Suny, Ronald Grigor. 1994. *The Revenge of the Past: Nationalism, Revolution and the Collapse of the Soviet Union*. Stanford: Stanford University Press.

Suri, Jeremi. 2002. Explaining the End of the Cold War: A New Historical Consensus? *Journal of Cold War Studies* 4 (4): 60–92.

Swinth, Robert L. 1967. The Establishment of the Trust Relationship. *Journal of Conflict Resolution* 11 (3): 335–44.

Taliaferro, Jeffrey W. 2000/01. Seeking Security Under Anarchy: Defensive Realism Revisited. *International Security* 25 (3): 128–61.

Tannenwald, Nina. 2001. The Role of Ideas and the End of the Cold War: Advancing the Theoretical Agenda on Ideas. Brown University. Unpublished manuscript.

Taubman, W. 1982. *Stalin's American Policy: From Entente to Detente to Cold War*. New York: W. W. Norton.

Thom, Françoise. 1989. *The Gorbachev Phenomenon*. London: Pinter Publishers.

Thomas, Daniel C. 2001. *The Helsinki Effect: International Norms, Human Rights, and the Demise of Communism*. Princeton: Princeton University Press.

Thompson, E. P. 1957. Socialist Humanism: An Epistle to the Philistines *The New Reasoner* 1 (1): 105–43.

———. 1985. *The Heavy Dancers*. New York: Pantheon Books.

Thucydides. 1972. *History of the Peloponnesian War*. London: Penguin Classics.

Topkis, Donald M. 1998. *Supermodularity and Complementarity*. Princeton: Princeton University Press.

Trachtenberg, Marc. 1995. "Melvyn Leffler and the Origins of the Cold War." *Orbis* 39 (3): 439–55.

———. 1999. *A Constructed Peace: the Making of the European Settlement, 1945–1963*. Princeton: Princeton University Press.

Tullock, Gordon. 1967. The Prisoner's Dilemma and Mutual Trust. *Ethics* 77 (3): 229–30.

Ulam, Adam B. 1974. *Expansion and Coexistence: Soviet Foreign Policy, 1917–73*. 2nd ed. New York: Praeger Publishers.

United States Department of State. *Foreign Relations of the United States* [FRUS]. *The Conferences at Malta and Yalta, 1945*. Washington, D.C.: GPO, 1955.

———. *The Conference of Berlin (The Potsdam Conference), 1945*. 2 vols. Washington, D.C.: GPO, 1960.

———. *1945*. Vol. 2, *General: Political and Economic Matters*. Washington, D.C.: GPO, 1967.

———. *1945*. Vol. 5, *Europe*. Washington, D.C.: GPO, 1967.

———. *1946*. Vol. 5, *The British Commonwealth; Western and Central Europe*. Washington, D.C.: GPO, 1969.

———. 1946. Vol. 6, *Eastern Europe; The Soviet Union*. Washington, D.C.: GPO, 1969.

———. 1946. Vol. 7, *The Near East and Africa*. Washington, D.C.: GPO, 1969.

Uslaner, Eric M. 2002. *The Moral Foundations of Trust*. Cambridge: Cambridge University Press.

Van Dijk, Ruud. 1996. The 1952 Stalin Note Debate: Myth or Missed Opportunity for German Unification? Cold War International History Project Working Paper 14. Washington, D.C.

Van Evera, Stephen. 1999. *Causes of War*. Ithaca: Cornell University Press.

Voeten, Erik. 2000. Clashes in the Assembly. *International Organization* 54 (2): 185–215.

Wagner, R. Harrison. 1980. The Decision to Divide Germany and the Origins of the Cold War. *Intenational Studies Quarterly* 24 (2): 155–90.

———. 1983. The Theory of Games and the Problem of International Cooperation. *American Political Science Review* 77 (2): 330–46.

———. 1986. The Theory of Games and the Balance of Power. *World Politics* 38 (4): 546–76.

Wall, Irwin M. 1991. *The United States and the Making of Postwar France, 1945–1954*. Cambridge: Cambridge University Press.

Walt, Stephen M. 1987. *Origins of Alliances*. Ithaca: Cornell University Press.

———. 1997. Why Alliances Endure or Collapse. *Survival* 39 (1): 156–79.

———. 1999. Rigor or Rigor Mortis? Rational Choice and Security Studies. *International Security* 23 (4): 5–48.

Waltz, Kenneth. 1979. *Theory of International Politics*. New York: Random House.

———. 1988. The Origins of War in Neo-Realist Theory. In *The Origin and Prevention of Major Wars*, edited by Robert I, Rotberg and Theodore K. Rabb. Cambridge: Cambridge University Press.

Ward, Hugh. 1989. Testing the Waters: Taking Risks to Gain Reassurance in Public Goods Games. *Journal of Conflict Resolution* 33 (2): 274–308.

Warren, Mark E., ed. 1999. *Democracy and Trust*. Cambridge: Cambridge University Press.

Watson, Joel. 1999. Starting Small and Renegotiation. *Journal of Economic Theory* 85 (1): 52–90.

Weathersby, Kathryn. 1993. Soviet Aims in Korea and the Origins of the Korean War, 1945–1950: New Evidence from Russian Archives. Cold War International History Project, Working Paper No. 8. Washington, D.C.

———. 1995. To Attack or Not Attack? Stalin, Kim Il Sung, and the Prelude to War. *Cold War International History Project Bulletin* 5: 1–9.

———. 1995/96. New Russian Documents on the Korean War. *Cold War International History Project Bulletin* 6–7: 30–84.

———. 2002. "Should We Fear This?" Stalin and the Danger of War with America. Cold War International History Project Working Paper No. 39. Washington, D.C.

Weinberger, Seth. 2003. Institutional Signaling and the Origins of the Cold War. *Security Studies* 12 (4): 80–115.

Wendt, Alexander. 1994. Collective Identity Formation and the International State. *American Political Science Review* 88 (2): 384–96.

————. 1999. *Social Theory of International Politics*. Cambridge: Cambridge University Press.

Williams, William Appleman. 1959. *The Tragedy of American Diplomacy*. New York: World Publishing Company.

Wittman, Donald. 1990. Spatial Strategies When Candidates Have Policy Preferences. In *Advances in the Spatial Theory of Voting*, edited by J. M. Enelow and M. J. Hinich. Cambridge: Cambridge University Press.

Wohlforth, William. C. 1993. *The Elusive Balance: Power and Perceptions During the Cold War*. Ithaca: Cornell University Press.

————. 1994/95. Realism and the End of the Cold War. *International Security* 19 (3): 91–129.

————., ed. 1996a. *Witnesses to the End of the Cold War*. Baltimore: Johns Hopkins University Press.

————. 1996b. Scholars, Policy Makers, and the End of the Cold War. In *Witnesses to the End of the Cold War*, edited by W. C. Wohlforth. Baltimore: Johns Hopkins University Press.

————. 1998. Reality Check: Revising Theories of International Politics in Response to the End of the Cold War. *World Politics* 50 (4): 650–80.

————. 1999. The Stability of a Unipolar World. *International Security* 24 (1): 5–41.

————., ed. 2003. *Cold War Endgame: Oral History, Analysis, Debates*. University Park: Pennsylvania State University Press.

Wolfers, Arnold. 1962. *Discord and Collaboration: Essays on International Politics*. Baltimore: Johns Hopkins University Press.

Woods, Randall B., and Howard Jones. 1991. *Dawning of the Cold War: The United States' Quest for Order*. Athens: University of Georgia Press.

Yegorova, Natalia I. 1996. The "Iran Crisis" of 1945–46: A View from the Russian Archives. Cold War International History Project Working Paper No. 15. Washington, D.C.

Yergin, Daniel. 1977. *Shattered Peace: The Origins of the Cold War and the National Security State*. Boston: Houghton Mifflin Company.

Young, John W. 1984. *Britain, France and the Unity of Europe 1945–1951*. Leicester: Leicester University Press.

————. 1990. *France, the Cold War and the Western Alliance 1944–49: French Foreign Policy and Post-War Europe*. Leicester: Leicester University Press.

Zakaria, Fareed. 1998. *From Wealth To Power: The Unusual Origins of America's World Role*. Princeton: Princeton University Press.

Zelikow, Philip, and Condoleezza Rice. 1995. *Germany Unified and Europe Transformed*. Cambridge, Mass.: Harvard University Press.

Zubok, Vladislav, and Constantine Pleshakov 1996. *Inside the Kremlin's Cold War*. Cambridge, Mass.: Harvard University Press.

Zubok, Vladislav M. 2003. Gorbachev and the End of the Cold War: Different Perspectives on the Historical Personality. In *Coldwar Engame: Oral History, Analyses, Debates*, edited by W. C. Wohlforth. University Park: Pennsylvania State University Press.

Index